Toward a Universal Theology
of Religion

FAITH MEETS FAITH

An Orbis Series in Interreligious Dialogue

Paul F. Knitter, General Editor

In our contemporary world, the many religions and spiritualities stand in need of greater intercommunication and cooperation. More than ever before, they must speak to, learn from, and work with each other, if they are to maintain their own vitality and contribute to a better world.

FAITH MEETS FAITH seeks to promote interreligious dialogue and cooperation by providing a forum for exchange between followers of different religious paths, making available to both the scholarly community and the general public works that will focus and give direction to this emerging encounter among the religions of the world.

FAITH MEETS FAITH SERIES

Toward a Universal Theology of Religion

Leonard Swidler, Editor

ORBIS BOOKS

Maryknoll, New York 10545

Second Printing, March 1988

The Catholic Foreign Mission Society of America (Maryknoll) recruits and trains people for overseas missionary service. Through Orbis Books Maryknoll aims to foster the international dialogue that is essential to mission. The books published, however, reflect the opinions of their authors and are not meant to represent the official position of the society.

Published by Orbis Books, Maryknoll, NY 10545
Manufactured in the United States of America

Manuscript Editor: William E. Jerman

Library of Congress Cataloging-in-Publication Data

Toward a universal theology of religion.

    Includes bibliographies.
    1. Christianity and other religions. 2. Religions.
3. Religion.   I. Swidler, Leonard J.
BR127.T58   1987   291.2   87-9213
ISBN 0-88344-580-8
ISBN 0-88344-555-7 (pbk.)

Contents

Proem

Toward a Universal Theology of Religion?

LEONARD SWIDLER

Interreligious, interideological dialogue is something quite new under the sun. For a variety of reasons it has largely been precipitated by Christians, although of course many adherents of other religious traditions have collaborated. Because of this, the reflexive level of theological reflection on the implications of the various dialogues on a global level has been reached by certain outstanding Christian thinkers. Raimundo Panikkar, Wilfred Cantwell Smith, John Cobb, and Hans Küng have clearly been among the most comprehensive, penetrating, influential, and creative in their thought on a global theology of religion. They have begun to raise the question: How can Christians reflect on their faith in ways that will be understandable for Jews, Muslims, Hindus, Buddhists, humanists, and others, that will make room for them as they understand themselves, and still keep faith with Christianity?

Further, it is being requested that the same interreligious reflection be done for their own communities by Jewish, Muslim, Hindu, Buddhist, and other thinkers. Then, in the total global enterprise of reflection on religious faith or "ideology" (including thinkers who are a-theistic, such as Theravada Buddhists, some humanists, Marxists, and others), a way of thinking, of speaking—in fact, a whole new receptive consciousness—must be forged, which at the same time will be faithful to the universal realities of religious faith or "ideology" and also to its particularities. Just to itemize the task almost stops us in our tracks! But above all it should serve us as a challenge.

Might such an enterprise be best called "a universal theology of religion"? What would such a name mean? Literally the word "theology" means the study of God, and of the relationship of everything else to God. Though it was

invented by the ancient Greeks, it has subsequently been used mostly by
Christians and has come to mean the systematic reflection on the faith or
religion one holds (religion meaning generally "an explanation of the meaning
of life, and how to live accordingly"—an "ideology" being such a creed and
code *without* the transcendent). Universal here would first of all be understood
materially—that is, the matter to be reflected on should in some significant
way include *all* the religions (and ideologies). But it also has a formal sense in
that the intended audience of the reflection is not just a particular religious
community, but *all* religious (and ideological) communities. That would mean
that "theologians" would have to reflect and speak in a way that would be
understandable by all, in a language shared by all—without, of course, thereby
replacing particular religious languages.

Simply proposing the project of a universal theology of religion (not to be
confused with a universal religion!) precipitates a series of fundamental questions that must be clarified, analyzed, and judged. Can one even meaningfully
think about a *universal* theology of religion, or is pluralism so radical in reality
that it would be absurd even to attempt it? Or, should it nevertheless be
attempted, even though, like the horizon, it would always exceed our grasp?
Or, is the "perspectivism" in all statements about the meaning of reality so
thoroughgoing that the only meaningful way to proceed is by way of reflections *ex professo* from particular religious perspectives—for example, Christian? Or, should one attempt to move from a particular perspective through
dialogue with other perspectives toward a never complete, but ever more
complete, universal perspective? Or . . . ?

All these and other profound, fundamental—and ultimately highly
practical—questions were generated by the papers, responses, and discussions
in a conference, "Toward a Universal Theology of Religion," held at Temple
University, Philadelphia, October 17–19, 1984. I wrote a preconference paper
spelling out the idea of a universal theology of religion and arguing in its favor.
A copy of it was sent to all the conference speakers and respondents. The four
thinkers mentioned above—Smith, Cobb, Panikkar, and Küng—were asked to
write papers on the topic and make them available early enough for respondents to be able to write serious, lengthy responses. As indicated before, the
main speakers were all Christians—two Catholics and two Protestants—
hence, twelve respondents from the major world religions were invited:
Zalman Schachter (Jewish), Antony Fernando (Catholic), Kenneth Inada
(Buddhist), Kana Mitra (Hindu), Stanley Harakas (Orthodox Christian), Hos-
sein Nasr (Shiite Muslim), Bibhuti Yadav (Hindu), Thomas Dean (Protestant),
Charles Fu ("Taoist-Buddhist"), Paul Knitter (Catholic), Ellen Charry (Jewish), Khalid Duran (Sunni Muslim).

This volume contains the lectures and all but one of the responses of the
above, in somewhat revised form. It also contains an additional lecture by
Hans Küng. Subsequent to the conference, Küng and I jointly conducted a
seminar at the University of Tübingen during the summer semester of 1985.
The seminar focused on the papers from the Universal Theology of Religion

Conference. Toward the end of that semester Küng wrote a lecture, "What Is the True Religion?," summarizing his subsequent reflections on interreligious dialogue, and addressing directly the issues of the conference. That lecture has been translated and is published here for the first time.

The cosponsors of the conference were the *Journal of Ecumenical Studies* and the Religion Department of Temple University, both of which were founded approximately twenty years earlier. Both also have been dealing with interreligious dialogue in an extraordinarily creative way. The *Journal of Ecumenical Studies*, whose structure, from authors through editors, is thoroughly interreligious, has been judged by the directors of ecumenical and interreligious institutes around the globe to be the world's foremost journal in the field of interreligious dialogue. The Religion Department of Temple University is similarly interreligious and interdisciplinary in its faculty, graduate students, courses, and orientation. Its faculty consists of twenty scholars from Jewish, Catholic, Lutheran, Methodist, Baptist, Reformed, Evangelical, Episcopal, Muslim, Hindu, and Buddhist traditions; its two hundred graduate students come from an even wider spread of religious traditions and cultures. It was therefore most fitting that these two institutions should celebrate their twentieth anniversaries by sponsoring a conference that strove to provide a breakthrough into the next stage of interreligious dialogue on a world basis.

It was likewise a happy coincidence that 1984 was the hundredth anniversary of the founding of Temple University by a Baptist preacher, Russel Conwell, for poor men and women. Since then it has grown to be a great university with over thirty thousand students, and in 1966 became a state-related university, opening the way for the extraordinary flowering of the interreligious dialogue that has been stimulated by its *Journal of Ecumenical Studies* and Religion Department.

A special word of thanks must also be said to the Friars of the Atonement, who helped make the conference possible through a generous grant.

Preconference Paper

Interreligious and Interideological Dialogue: The Matrix for All Systematic Reflection Today

LEONARD SWIDLER

I want to argue in these reflections that interreligious and interideological dialogue is the most appropriate matrix within which all thinkers ought to carry out their systematic reflections on their explanations of the meaning of life and how to live accordingly—called theology by Christians. (Most explanations of the meaning of life and how to live accordingly have in the past entailed a belief in a divinity—Theravada Buddhism is a clear exception—and in recent centuries have been called religions by the West. More recent explanations of the meaning of life and how to live accordingly, which do not include a belief in a divinity—for example, Marxism—have at times been called ideologies. I am here adopting that terminology.)

After a description of what is meant by dialogue, I shall describe briefly the recent process of deabsolutizing our understanding of truth and how this has led to the possibility and necessity of dialogue; applying this fact to theology and other systematic reflections leads to the need for interreligious, interideological dialogue, for which I shall outline some necessary ground rules. But how to carry out interreligious, interideological dialogue? This will be the heart of this essay: an attempt to show the way forward, not in the "practical" and "spiritual" areas (each of them warrants separate, full treatment), but in the "cognitive" area by way of "ecumenical Esperanto." A Christian experiment in "ecumenical Esperanto" will then be essayed. The conclusion will be that no systematic reflection, including Christian theology, can appropriately be done today outside this matrix of interreligious, interideological dialogue.

DIALOGUE

Dialogue of course is conversation between two or more persons with differing views, the primary purpose of which is for each participant to learn from the other so that both can change and grow. Minimally, the very fact that I learn that my dialogue partner believes "this" rather than "that" changes my attitude toward that person; and a change in my attitude is a significant change, and growth, in me. We enter into dialogue, therefore, so that *we* can learn, change, and grow, not so that we can force change on the *other.* In the past, when we encountered those who differed with us in the religious and ideological sphere, we did so usually either to defeat them as an opponent, or to learn about them so as to deal with them more effectively. In other words, we usually faced them as in confrontation—whether more openly polemically, or more subtly, with the ultimate goal of overcoming them because we were convinced that we alone had the truth.

But that is not what dialogue is. Dialogue is *not* debate. In dialogue each partner must listen to the other as openly and sympathetically as possible, in an attempt to understand the other's position as precisely and, as it were, as much from within, as possible. Such an attitude automatically includes the assumption that if at any point we might find the partner's position persuasive, we—our integrity being at stake—would have to change.

Until quite recently in almost all religious traditions, and certainly within Christianity, the idea of seeking religious, ideological wisdom, insight, truth, by way of dialogue, other than in a very initial, rudimentary fashion, occurred to very few persons, and certainly had no influence in the major religious or ideological communities. The further idea of pursuing religious or ideological truth through dialogue between differing religions and ideologies was even more unheard of (if one can speak thus!). For example, it was merely a century and a half ago that Pope Gregory XVI penned those fateful lines:

> We come now to a source which is, alas! all too productive of the deplorable evils afflicting the Church today. We have in mind indifferent-ism, that is, the fatal opinion everywhere spread abroad by the deceit of wicked men, that the eternal salvation of the soul can be won by the profession of any faith at all, provided that conduct conforms to the norms of justice and probity. . . . From this poisonous spring of indif-ferentism flows the false and absurd, or rather the mad principle (*delira-mentum*) that we must secure and guarantee to each one liberty of conscience.[1]

Not only was dialogue with the other disallowed, so was even *being* other!

Today the situation is dramatically reversed. No less a person than Pope Paul VI in 1964 in his very first encyclical focused on dialogue, stating that "dia-logue is *demanded* nowadays . . . is *demanded* by the dynamic course of action which is changing the face of modern society. It is *demanded* by the pluralism of society and by the maturity man has reached in this day and age. Be he religious or not, his secular education has enabled him to think and speak, and to conduct dialogue with dignity."[2] We hear many more official words of encouragement from the Vatican Secretariat for Non-believers: "All Christians should do their best to promote dialogue . . . as a duty of fraternal charity suited to our progressive and adult age." Further, "the willingness to engage in dialogue is the measure and strength of that general renewal which must be carried out in the Church." Moreover, this dialogue is not thought of solely in terms of "practical" matters, but in a central way is to focus on theology and doctrine, and to do so without hesitation or trepidation:

> Doctrinal dialogue should be initiated with courage and sincerity, with the greatest of freedom and with reverence. It focuses on doctrinal questions which are of concern to the parties in dialogue. They have different opinions but by common effort they strive to improve mutual understanding, to clarify matters on which they agree, and if possible to enlarge the areas of agreement. In this way the parties to dialogue can enrich each other.[3]

DEABSOLUTIZING TRUTH

Why this dramatic change? Why, indeed, should one pursue the truth in the area of religion and ideology by way of dialogue? A fundamental answer to these questions lies in the even more dramatic shift in the understanding of truth that has taken place first in Western civilization, and now beyond it, throughout the nineteenth and twentieth centuries, making dialogue not only possible but necessary.

Whereas the notion of truth was largely absolute, static, and exclusive up to the last century, it has subsequently become deabsolutized, dynamic, and dialogic—in a word, "relational." This new view of truth came about in at least four different, but closely related, ways:

1. Historicization of truth: truth is deabsolutized and dynamized in terms of time, both past and future, with intentionality and action playing a major role in the latter.
2. Sociology of knowledge: truth is deabsolutized in terms of geography, culture, and social standing.
3. Limits of language: truth as the meaning of something, and especially as talk about the transcendent, is deabsolutized by the nature of human language.
4. Hermeneutics: all truth, all knowledge, is seen as interpreted truth and knowledge, and hence is deabsolutized by the observer, who always is also interpreter.

1. *The historicization of truth.* Before the nineteenth century, truth—that is, a correct statement about reality—was conceived in Europe in quite an absolute, static, exclusivistically either-or manner. It was thought that if something was true at some time or other, it was always true, and not only with regard to empirical facts but also with regard to the meaning of things or the oughtness that was said to flow from them. For example, if it was true for the Pauline writer to say in the first century that women should keep silence in the church, then it was always true that women should keep silence in the church. If it was true for Pope Boniface VIII in 1302 to state in definitive terms that "we declare, state, and define that it is absolutely necessary for the salvation of all human beings that they submit to the Roman Pontiff," then it was always true that they need do so. At bottom the notion of truth was based on the Aristotelian principle of contradiction: a thing could not be true and not true in the same way at the same time. Truth was defined by way of exclusion; A was A because it could be shown not to be not-A. Truth was thus understood to be absolute, static, exclusively either-or. This is a *classicist* or *absolutist* view of truth.

In the nineteenth century many scholars came to perceive all statements about the truth of the meaning of something as being partially products of their historical circumstances. Those concrete circumstances helped determine the fact that the statement under study was even called forth, that it was couched in particular intellectual categories (for example, abstract Platonic, or concrete legal language), particular literary forms (for example, mythic or metaphysical language), and particular psychological settings (for example, a polemical response to a specific attack). It was argued by these scholars that only by placing truth statements in their historical situation, their historical *Sitz im Leben,* could they be properly understood (understanding of a text could be found only in its context), and that to express the same original meaning in a later *Sitz im Leben* one would require a proportionately different statement. Thus, all statements about the meaning of things were seen to be deabsolutized in terms of time. This is a *historical* view of truth. Clearly at its heart is a notion of *relationality:* a statement about the truth of the meaning of something has to be understood in relationship to its historical context.

Later, especially with the work of thinkers like Max Scheler and Karl Mannheim, a corollary was added to this historicizing of knowledge; it concerned not the past but the future. They and other scholars also conceived of the knowledge of truth as having an element of intentionality at the base of it, as being oriented ultimately toward action, praxis. They argued that we perceive certain things as questions to be answered and set goals to pursue certain knowledge because we wish to do something about those matters; we intend to live according to the truth, the meaning of things, that we hope to discern in the answering of the questions we pose, in gaining the knowledge we decide to seek. Thus, the truth of the meaning of things as stated by anyone was seen as deabsolutized by the action-oriented intentionality of the thinker-speaker. This is a *praxis* view of truth, and it too is basically *relational*—that is, a statement has to be understood in relationship to the action-oriented intention of the speaker.

2. *The sociology of knowledge.* As the statements of the truth about the meaning of things were seen by some thinkers to be historically deabsolutized in time, so also starting in this century such statements were seen to be deabsolutized by the cultural, class (and so forth) standpoint of the thinker-speaker, regardless of time. Thus, a statement about the true meaning of things will be partially determined by worldview of the thinker-speaker. All reality was said to be perceived from the cultural, class, sexual (and so forth) perspective of the perceiver. Therefore, any statement of the truth of the meaning of something was seen to be perspectival—"standpoint-bound," *standortgebunden* as Karl Mannheim put it—and thus deabsolutized. This *perspectival* view of truth is likewise *relational,* for all statements are fundamentally related to the standpoint of the speaker.

3. *The limitations of language.* Many thinkers (following Ludwig Wittgenstein and others) have come to understand that all statements about the truth of things necessarily can at most be only partial descriptions of the reality they are trying to describe. This is said to be the case because, although reality can be seen from an almost limitless number of perspectives, human language can express things from only one, or perhaps a very few, perspectives at once. This is now also seen to be true of our so-called scientific truths. A fortiori it is the case concerning statements about the truth of the meaning of things. The very fact of dealing with the truth of the "meaning" of something indicates that the knower is essentially involved and hence reflects the perspectival character of all such statements. A statement may be true, of course—that is, it may accurately describe the extramental reality it refers to—but it will always be cast in the particular categories, language, concerns, and so forth, of a particular "standpoint," and in that sense always will be limited, deabsolutized. This also is a *perspectival* view of truth, and therefore also *relational.*

Moreover, the limited and limiting, as well as liberating, quality of language is especially seen when there is talk of the transcendent. By definition the transcendent is that which goes beyond our experience. Hence, all statements about the transcendent are seen to be extremely deabsolutized and limited even beyond the limiting factor of the perspectival character of statements.

4. *Hermeneutics.* Hans-Georg Gadamer and Paul Ricoeur led the way in the development of the science of hermeneutics, which argues that all knowledge of a text is also an *interpretation* of it, thereby still further deabsolutizing claims about the "true" meaning of a text. But this basic insight goes beyond the knowledge of a text and applies to all knowledge.

Some of the key notions here can be compressed in the following mantra (a seven-syllable phrase that capsulizes an insight): "Subject, object, two is one." The whole of hermeneutics is here *in nuce:* all knowledge is interpreted knowledge; the perceiver is part of the perceived, especially, but not only, in the humane disciplines; the subject is part of the object. When the object of study is some aspect of humanity, it is obvious that the observer is also the observed, which "deobjectivizes," deabsolutizes the resultant knowledge, truth. The same, however, is also fundamentally true, though in a different way, of all knowledge, truth, of the natural sciences, for various aspects of nature are observed only through the categories we provide, within the horizon we establish, under the paradigm we utilize, in response to the questions we raise, and in relationship to the connections we make—a further deabsolutizing of truth, even of the "hard" sciences.

To move on to the second half of the mantra, "two is one," we see that knowledge comes from a subject perceiving an object, but inasmuch as the subject is also part of the object, the two therefore are one in that sense. Also, in knowing, the object as such is taken up into the subject, and thus again the two are one. And yet there is also a radical twoness there, for it is the very *process* of the two *becoming* one (or, alternatively, the two being perceived as one, or even better, the becoming aware that the two, which are very really two, are also in fact very really one) that is what we call knowing. This is an *interpretive* view of truth. It is clear that *relationality* pervades this hermeneutical, interpretive, view of truth.

A further development of this basic insight is that I learn by dialogue—that is, not only by being open to, receptive of, in a passive sense, extramental reality, but by having a dialogue with extramental reality. I not only "hear," receive, reality, but I also—and I think, first of all—"speak" to reality. That is, I ask it questions, I stimulate it to speak back to me, to answer my questions. Furthermore, I give reality the specific categories, language, with which, in which, to speak, to respond to me. It can "speak" to me—really communicate to my mind—only in a language, in categories, that I understand. When the speaking, the responding, becomes more and more *un*understandable to me, I slowly begin to become aware that there is a new language being developed here and that I must learn it if I am to make sense out of what reality is saying to me. This is a *dialogic* view of truth, whose very name reflects its *relationality*.

With this new, and irreversible, understanding of the meaning of truth, the critical thinker has undergone a radical Copernican turn. Just as the greatly resisted shift in astronomy from geocentrism to heliocentrism revolutionized that science, and much else (!), so too the paradigm or model shift in the understanding of truth statements has revolutionized all the humanities, including theology-ideology. The macroparadigm or macromodel with which critical thinkers operate today (or the "horizon" within which they operate, to use Bernard Lonergan's term) is characterized by historical, social, linguistic, hermeneutical, praxis, relational, and dialogic consciousness. This paradigm or model shift is far advanced among thinkers and doers; but as with Copernicus, and even more dramatically with Galileo, there are still many resisters in positions of great institutional power.

In the understanding of reality and how to live accordingly it is difficult to overestimate the importance of the role played by the conceptual paradigm or model one has of reality. The paradigm or model within which we perceive reality not only profoundly affects our intellectual understanding of reality, but also has immense practical consequences. For example (as pointed out by Henry Rosemont, Fulbright Professor of Philosophy at Fudan University, Shanghai, 1982–84), in Western medicine the body is usually conceived of under the model of a highly nuanced, living machine, and therefore, if one part wears out, the obvious thing to do is to replace the worn part—hence, organ transplants originated in Western medicine. However, in Oriental medicine, the body is conceived of under the model of a finely balanced harmony. If "pressure" is exerted on one part of the body, it is assumed that it has an effect on some other part of the body—hence, acupuncture originated in Oriental medicine.

Furthermore, obviously some attempts at perceiving reality through a particular paradigm or model will fit the data better than others, and they will then be preferred—consider the shift from the geocentric to the heliocentric model in astronomy. But sometimes different models will both in their own ways "fit" the data more or less well—as in the example of Western and Oriental medicine. The differing models would then be viewed as complementary. Clearly it would be foolish to limit one's perception of reality to only one of two or more complementary paradigms or models. Perhaps at times a more comprehensive model, a megamodel, can be conceived to subsume the two or more complementary models, but surely it will never be possible to perceive reality except through paradigms or models. Hence *meta*model thinking is not possible, except in the more limited sense of meta-*mono*model thinking—that is, perceiving reality through multiple, differing models that cannot be subsumed under one megamodel, but must stand in creative, polar tension in relationship to each other. Such might be called multimodel thinking.[4]

With the deabsolutized view of the truth of the meaning of things, we come face to face with the specter of relativism, which is the opposite pole of absolutism. Unlike *relationality*, which is a neutral term, merely denoting the quality of being in relationship, *relativism* is a basically negative term (as are most "isms"). If one can no longer claim that any statement of the truth of the meaning of things is absolute, totally objective, because the claim does not square with our experience of reality, it is equally impossible to claim that every statement of the truth of the meaning of things is completely relative, totally subjective, for that also does not square with our experience of reality, and furthermore would logically lead to an atomizing solipsism (self-alone-ism) that would stop all discourse, all statements to others.

Our perception, and hence description, of reality is like viewing an object in the center of a circle of viewers. My view and description of the object (reality) will be true, but it will not include what someone on the other side of the circle perceives and describes, which will also be true. So neither of the perceptions/ descriptions of the object (reality) is total, complete—"absolute" in that sense—or "objective" in the sense of not in any way being dependent on a "subject." At the same time, however, it is also obvious that there is an "objective," doubtless "true," aspect to each perception/description, even though each is relational to the perceiver-"subject."

At the same time that the always partial, perspectival, deabsolutized view of all truth statements is recognized, the common human basis for perceptions/descriptions of reality and values must also be kept in mind. All human beings experience certain things in common. We all experience our bodies, pain, pleasure, hunger, satiation, and the like. Our cognitive faculties perceive certain structures in reality—for example, variation and symmetries in pitch, color, form, etc. All humans experience affection, dislike, and so forth. Here, and in other commonalities, are the bases for building a universal, fundamental epistemology, esthetics, value system. Of course it will be vital to distinguish carefully between those human experiences/perceptions that come from nature and those that come from nurture. However, because nurture can sometimes override nature, it will at times be difficult to discern precisely where the distinction is. In fact, all our "natural" experiences will be more or less shaped by our "nurturing"—that is, all our experience, knowledge, will be interpreted through the lens of our "nurturing" structures.

But if we can no longer hold to an absolutist view of the truth of the meaning of things, we must take certain steps so as not to be logically forced into the silence of total relativism, including at least the following two. First, besides striving to be as accurate and fair as possible in our gathering and assessing of information, submitting it to the critiques of our peers and other thinkers and scholars, we need also to dredge out, state clearly, and analyze our own presuppositions—but this is a constant, ongoing task. However, even in doing this we will be operating from a particular "standpoint." Therefore, we need, secondly, to complement our constantly critiqued statements with statements from different "standpoints." That is, we need to engage in dialogue with those who have differing cultural, philosophical, social, religious viewpoints so as to strive toward an ever fuller—but never ending—perception of the truth of the meaning of things. If we do not engage in such dialogue, we will not only be trapped within the perspective of our own "standpoint," we will now also know it. Hence, we will no longer with integrity deliberately be able to remain turned in on ourselves. Our search for the truth of the meaning of things makes it a necessity for us as human beings to engage in dialogue. Knowingly to refuse dialogue today could be an act of fundamental human irresponsibility—in Judeo-Christian terms, a sin.

Paul Knitter has noted much the same thing particularly in the shift in the model of truth from the exclusively either-or model to the dialogic or relational model:

> In the new model, truth will no longer be identified by its ability to exclude or absorb others. Rather, what is true will reveal itself mainly by its ability to *relate* to other expressions of truth and to *grow* through these relationships: truth defined not by exclusion but by relation. The new model reflects what our pluralistic world is discovering: no truth can stand alone; no truth can be totally unchangeable. Truth, by its very

nature, needs other truth. If it cannot relate, its quality of truth must be open to question.[5]   *ko other Name.*

If this is true for all human beings in the search for the truth of the meaning of things, it is most intensely so for religious persons and those committed to ideologies, such as Marxism. Religions and ideologies describe and prescribe for the whole of life, they are holistic, all-encompassing, and therefore tend to blot out—that is, either convert or condemn—outsiders even more than other institutions that are not holistic. Thus the need for due modesty in truth claims and complementarity for particular views of the truth, as described above, is most intense in the field of religion.

But the need for dialogue in religion and ideology is also intensified in the modern world because slowly, through the impact of mass communications and the high level of mobility of contemporary society in the West, and elsewhere, we more and more experience "others" as living holistic, "holy" lives—not in spite of, but because of their religion or ideology. To be concrete: when I as a Christian come to know Jews as religious persons who are leading whole, holy human lives out of the fullness of their Judaism, I am immediately confronted with the question: What is the source of this holiness, this wholeness? It obviously is not Christianity. Unless I really work at duping myself, I cannot say that it is unconscious or anonymous Christianity, for if there is any religion that has for two thousand years consciously rejected Christianity, that religion is Judaism. Clearly, the only possible answer is that the source of the holiness, the wholeness, of the Jew is the Jewish religion, and the God who stands behind it, the God of Abraham, Isaac, Jacob—and Jesus. Using traditional theological language "from above," it should be noted that Christianity, like Judaism, is a religion that believes that God enters into self-revelation to us through events and persons; to learn God's message, God's Torah, good news, gospel, we Christians must seek to listen to God wherever and through whomever God speaks—that is, we must be in dialogue with *Barus* persons of other religions to learn what God is saying to us through them.

GROUND RULES FOR INTERRELIGIOUS, INTERIDEOLOGICAL DIALOGUE

We are here, then, speaking of a specific kind of dialogue, an interreligious, interideological dialogue. To have such, it is not sufficient that the dialogue partners discuss a religio-ideological subject—that is, the meaning of life and how to live accordingly. Rather, they must come to the dialogue as persons somehow significantly identified with a religious or ideological community. If I were neither a Christian nor a Marxist, for example, I could not participate as a "partner" in a Christian-Marxist dialogue, though I might listen in, ask some questions for information, and make some helpful comments.

The following are some basic ground rules of interreligious, interideological dialogue that must be observed if dialogue is actually to take place. These are not theoretical rules given from "on high," but ones that have been learned from hard experience.

First Rule: *The primary purpose of dialogue is to learn—that is, to change and grow in the perception and understanding of reality, and then to act accordingly.* We come to dialogue that *we* might learn, change, and grow, not that we might induce change in the *other,* as one hopes to do in debate—a hope realized in inverse proportion to the frequency and ferocity with which debate is entered into. On the other hand, because in dialogue *all* partners come with the intention of learning and changing themselves, one's partner in fact will also change. Thus the intended goal of debate, and much more, is accomplished far more effectively by dialogue.

Second Rule: *Interreligious, ideological dialogue must be a two-sided project—within each religious or ideological community, and between religious or ideological communities.* Because of the "corporate" nature of interreligious, interideological dialogue, and because the primary goal of dialogue is that each partner learn and change, it is also necessary that each participant enter into dialogue not only with partners across a faith line—Catholics with Protestants, for example—but also with coreligionists, with fellow Catholics or fellow Protestants, to share with them the fruits of interreligious dialogue. Only thus can the whole community eventually learn and change, moving toward an ever more perceptive insight into reality.

Third Rule: *Each participant must come to the dialogue with complete honesty and sincerity.* It should be made clear in what direction the major and minor thrusts of the tradition move, what the future shifts might be, and, if necessary, where the participants have difficulties with their own traditions. No false fronts have any place in dialogue.

Conversely, *each participant must assume complete honesty and sincerity in the other partners.* Not only will the absence of sincerity prevent dialogue from happening, the absence of the assumption of one's partners' sincerity will do so as well. In brief: no trust, no dialogue.

Fourth Rule: *In interreligious, interideological dialogue we must not compare our ideals with our partner's practice,* but rather our ideals with our partner's ideals, our practice with our partner's practice.

Fifth Rule: *All participants must define themselves.* Only the Jew, for example, can define from the inside what it means to be a Jew. The rest can only describe what it looks like from the outside. Moreover, because dialogue is a dynamic medium, as Jewish participants learn, they will change and hence continually deepen, expand, and modify their self-definition as Jews—being careful to remain in continual dialogue with fellow Jews. Thus it is mandatory that all dialogue partners define what it means to be an authentic member of their own tradition.

Conversely, *the interpreted must be able to recognize themselves in the interpretation.* This is the golden rule of interreligious, interideological hermeneutics, as has been often reiterated by the "apostle of interreligious dialogue,"

Raimundo Panikkar.[6] For the sake of understanding, dialogue participants will naturally attempt to express for themselves what they think is the meaning of the partners' statements; the partners must be able to recognize themselves in that expression. The advocate of a "world theology," Wilfred Cantwell Smith, would add that the expression must also be verifiable by critical observers not involved.[7]

Sixth Rule: *Each participant must come to the dialogue with no hard-and-fast assumptions as to points of disagreement.* Rather, each partner should not only listen to the other partner with openness and sympathy, but also attempt to agree with the dialogue partner as far as possible, while still maintaining integrity with one's own tradition. Where one absolutely can agree no further without violating personal integrity, precisely there is the real point of disagreement—which most often turns out to be different from the point of disagreement assumed ahead of time.

Seventh Rule: *Dialogue can take place only between equals*—as Vatican II put it, *par cum pari.* Both must come to learn from each other. Therefore, if, for example, the Muslim views Hinduism as inferior, or if the Hindu views Islam as inferior, there will be no dialogue. If authentic interreligious, inter-ideological dialogue between Muslims and Hindus is to take place, then both the Muslim and the Hindu must come mainly to learn from each other; only then will it be "equal with equal," *par cum pari.*

Eighth Rule: *Dialogue can take place only on the basis of mutual trust.* Although interreligious, interideological dialogue must occur with some kind of "corporate" dimension—that is, the participants must be involved as members of a religious or ideological community—for instance, as Marxists or Taoists—it is also fundamentally true that it is only *persons* who can enter into dialogue. But a dialogue among persons can be built only on personal trust. Hence it is wise not to tackle the most difficult problems in the beginning, but rather to approach first those issues most likely to provide some common ground, thereby establishing the basis of human trust. Then, gradually, as this personal trust deepens and expands, the more thorny matters can be undertaken. Thus, just as in learning we move from the known to the unknown, so in dialogue we proceed from commonly held matters—which, given our mutual ignorance resulting from centuries of hostility, will take us quite some time to discover fully—to discuss matters of disagreement.

Ninth Rule: *Persons entering into interreligious, interideological dialogue must be at least minimally self-critical of both themselves and their own religious or ideological tradition.* A lack of such self-criticism implies that one's own tradition already has all the correct answers. Such an attitude makes dialogue not only unnecessary, but even impossible, because we enter into dialogue primarily so that *we* can learn—which obviously is impossible if our tradition has never made a misstep, if it has all the right answers. To be sure, in interreligious, interideological dialogue one must stand within a religious or ideological tradition with integrity and conviction, but such integrity and conviction must include, not exclude, healthy self-criticism.

Without it there can be no dialogue—and, indeed, no integrity.

Tenth Rule: *Each participant eventually must attempt to experience the partner's religion or ideology "from within."* A religion or ideology is not merely something of the head, but also of the spirit, heart, and "whole being," individual and communal. John Dunne here speaks of "passing over" into another's religious or ideological experience and then coming back enlightened, broadened, and deepened.

DIALOGUE AREAS AND PHASES

Interreligious, interideological dialogue operates in three areas: the practical, where we collaborate to help humanity; the "spiritual," where we attempt to experience the partner's religion or ideology "from within"; and the cognitive, where we seek understanding and truth. Interreligious, interideological dialogue also has three phases. In the first phase (which we never completely outgrow) we unlearn misinformation about each other and begin to know each other as we truly are. In phase two we begin to discern values in the partner's tradition and wish to appropriate them into our own tradition. For example, in the Buddhist-Christian dialogue, Christians might learn a greater appreciation of the meditative tradition, and Buddhists might learn a greater appreciation of the prophetic, social justice tradition—both values strongly, though not exclusively, associated with the other's community. If we are serious, persistent, and sensitive enough in dialogue, we may at times enter into phase three. Here we together begin to explore new areas of reality, of meaning, of truth, of which neither of us had even been aware before. We are brought face to face with previously unknown dimensions of reality only because of questions, insights, probings brought to light in dialogue. We may thus dare to say that patiently pursued dialogue can become an instrument of new "re-velation," a further "un-veiling" of reality—on which we must then act.

Dialogue in Practice

Religions and ideologies are not only explanations of the meaning of life, but also ways (e.g., *Hodos,* Christianity; *Halakah*, Judaism; *Sharī'ah,* Islam; *Tao,* Chinese religion) to live according to that explanation. For example, the Buddhist is not only to seek liberation interiorly, but also to practice the virtues of justice, honesty, compassion. In Judaism the prophetic tradition of social justice is even encoded into specific laws in the Talmud. At the beginning of Christianity Jesus said that those are saved who feed the hungry, clothe the naked, house the homeless, instruct the ignorant. St. John said that those who say they love God but hate their brother are liars. St. James said that faith without works is dead. Marxism also offers not just a social theory, but also a social program and practice.

Many human problems elicit social action on the part of many different religions and ideologies: peace, hunger, discrimination, social justice, defense of human rights. In many instances joint action on these concrete problems will be more effective than any number of individual, parallel, or even duplicative actions. This cooperation for the good of humanity will also break down barriers between the religions and ideologies, and lead to dialogue about the respective self-understandings and motivations that underlay commitment to the action undertaken by the different religions and ideologies involved. For example, the Christians and the atheistic humanists who ended up in the Selma, Alabama, jail together because of their marching with Martin Luther King, Jr., for equal rights for blacks in America entered into dialogue to learn how their differing faiths and ideologies led to the same radical action.

Interreligious, interideological action that does not eventually lead to dialogue will end up mindless, and hence ineffective. Interreligious, interideological dialogue that does not eventually lead to action will end up hypocritical, and hence ineffective.

"Spiritual" Dialogue

In the area of "spiritual" or in-depth dialogue we experience the partner's religion or ideology "from within." Raimundo Panikkar speaks of this when he says that "religious dialogue must be genuinely *religious,* not merely an exchange of doctrines or intellectual opinions. . . . Dialogue must proceed from the depths of my religious attitude to these same depths in my partner."[8] He even goes so far as to state: "I 'left' as a Christian; I 'found' myself a Hindu; and I 'returned' as a Buddhist, without having ceased to be a Christian."[9] Perhaps such double or multiple "belonging" is not possible for most religious persons, most religious thinkers, or those ideologically committed, but experiencing another's religion or ideology "from within" at least to some extent is possible for all. John Dunne's "passing over" is one very effective means for doing so. He describes it thus: "Passing over is a shifting of standpoint, a going over to the standpoint of another culture, another way of life, another religion. It is followed by an equal and opposite process we might call 'coming back,' coming back with new insight to one's own culture, one's own way of life, one's own religion."[10]

Here imagination plays a key role. After entering into the feelings of one's partner and permitting that person's symbols and stories to stimulate images in one's own mind, these images are to be allowed to move, leading one where they will, so that eventually one will return to one's own tradition—greatly enriched. Dunne writes:

> The technique of passing over is based on *the process of eliciting images* from one's feelings, attaining insights into the images, and then turning insight into a guide of life. What one does in passing over is to try to enter sympathetically into the feelings of another person, become receptive to the *images* which give expression to his feelings, attain insight into those images, and then come back enriched by this insight to an understanding of one's own life which can guide one into the future.[11]

Moreover, as Paul Knitter notes:

> Passing over, while it is mainly the work of the imagination, also requires some hard intellectual homework . . . and proves that although one never attains a final answer, one can come to more answers, real answers. The imagination is persistently excited; new insights are born; the horizon of knowledge expands. Interreligious dialogue, like all life, is seen not as a nervous pursuit of certainty but a freeing, exciting pursuit of understanding.[12]

Knitter also points out that David Tracy's *The Analogical Imagination* "might be read as a handbook of guidelines on the nature of dialogue with other traditions and the pivotal role of the imagination in such dialogue."[13] Tracy confirms "the possibilities of approaching the conversation among the religious traditions through the use of an analogical imagination. . . . If I have already lived by an analogical imagination within my own religious and cultural heritages, I am much more likely to welcome the demand for further conversation."[14]

A Universal Systematic Reflection (Theology) of Religion-Ideology

But what of the cognitive area (which of course must not be isolated from the practical and "spiritual" areas), where perhaps the greatest challenge to interreligious, interideological dialogue lies? How can one proceed beyond mutually informative lectures? I believe the question can be helpfully phrased as follows: in reflecting upon my own religious or ideological belief—that is, in Christian terminology, in "theologizing"—how can I speak so that I on the one hand maintain integrity with my own religious, ideological convictions and tradition, and on the other allow my dialogue partners to understand and recognize themselves in my language? To be concrete, how can I as a Christian speak about the central insights of my faith in such a way that the Jew, or the Marxist, or indeed both, would be able to say, "Yes, that sounds like familiar territory. I feel somehow included in those concepts, terms, images, although I might not use precisely the same ones in my own faith or ideological reflections—that is, 'theologizing' "?

To put the problem in a positive way, we who are convinced of not only the advantage but also the necessity of interreligious, interideological dialogue (not only for the *bene esse,* but even the *esse* of creative religious, ideological reflection today) need to work together to forge a "universal systematic reflection (theology) of religion-ideology." I am aware that there are difficulties already in this naming of the project. However, any naming of a project with such a comprehensive scope will necessarily entail difficulties. There is no way that we can speak of things except within a particular cultural framework, no matter how broad the cultural framework might be. Even an extremely broad cultural framework is particular and would automatically be other than a whole range of other particular cultural frameworks, and one would then have to justify the choice of that cultural framework rather than another. In fact, the choice of this particular cultural framework is not essential. What is essential is simply the choice of *a* particular cultural framework. I have chosen the one that I personally am most familiar with so that I might better explain precisely what is meant, and thereby, I hope, eliminate possible confusions through unclarity.

By *theology* here is meant simply a systematic, reasoned reflection upon the convictions—"religious" or "ideological"—that are held by one or more human beings. (The term "philosophy" would seem inadequate here, for it often means a reasoned reflection that does not include sources of wisdom in a tradition outside ratiocination. Though "theology" is largely a Christian term—the pre-Christian Greeks invented it, however—it has the advantage of including both reasoning and other wisdom sources in a tradition—for example, "sacred" books—whether the Bible, the Qur'ān, the Vedas, or *Das Kapital.* Hence despite its theistic and Christian particularity, until a better term is found or forged, I shall utilize the shorthand "theology" to refer to the systematic reasoned reflections upon the "religious" or "ideological" convictions held by human communities.) In speaking of a universal theology of *religion-ideology,* I mean to indicate all the insights of a faith or ideology that attempts to explain the meaning of life and how to live accordingly—whether that includes the notion of *Theos* or not. What makes it *universal* is that the categories of reflection are such that they can be understood and embraced by persons of all religions or ideologies, not just a particular one, or particular set—for instance, Christianity, the Abrahamic religions, the theistic religions.

If that is the task, the way forward, I believe, is for the thinkers in each religious and ideological tradition to attempt to express their reflections, their "theologizing," in categories, terms, images, that others will be able to understand, and in which they will feel included. Does this seem an impossible task? How can Christians, for example, speak of the insights into the meaning of human life given them by the Christian tradition in categories, terms, images other than Christian? In fact, it seems to me that Christians do already something of that sort, at least in some instances. Christians very often speak a language that is extremely familiar to Jews. When it is recollected that Jesus was not born a Christian but a Jew, and all his first followers were Jews, and that many of our prayers come from the Hebrew Bible, this idea is not surprising. The fact that Muhammad also looked upon the Hebrew Bible and the New Testament as sacred books means that much of our Christian language will likewise be familiar to Muslims. So Christians might try to do some of their reflection using only a vocabulary that would in fact be familiar to the other two Abrahamic religions. Indeed, this is precisely the sort of thing that can reasonably be attempted within the framework of a trialogue.

However, some modern critical thinkers immediately have a difficulty even in this relatively limited step toward "a universal theology of religion-ideology." Much of the language of the Jewish and Christian traditions no longer finds a clear resonance among many Jews and Christians who have been bred in the atmosphere of modern critical thought. (Of course this does not mean that modern critical thinkers are automatically somehow less religious or committed than precritical thinkers. Indeed, a moment's recollection will recall that Moses, Jesus, and Muhammad were extremely "critical" thinkers in the religious sphere vis-à-vis what existed up until their time. In fact, it was the very radicalness of their "critical" thinking that made them the fountain-heads of new religious streams.) For such critical thinkers language needs to be found that will effectively communicate the authentic insights of religious tradition in ways that will find true resonance in understanding and life.

"ECUMENICAL ESPERANTO"

It is precisely this challenge from within the Jewish and Christian traditions, this demand for a language, a way of understanding the ancient religious insights in terms of critical thought, that, I believe, points out the way forward in trying to forge a "universal theology of religion-ideology." We must build our "theological" language, terms, categories, and images on our common humanity. This is what the traditional Jew, Christian, Muslim, the modern critical thinker, the Hindu, Buddhist, Marxist have in common. To the extent that we can speak of a religious, ideological insight in such "humanity-based" language, we shall be building a "universal theology of religion-ideology." Put in other words, we must attempt to cast our religious and ideological insights in language "from below"—that is, from our humanity, and not "from above," not from the perspective of the transcendent, the divine. From a slightly different perspective, we must attempt to develop a "theological" language that is "from within," not "from without." We must try to speak a language of immanence, not of transcendence. This does not mean that religious persons should no longer speak of, let alone believe in, the transcendent. No, I mean that in this particular task of forging a "universal theology of religion-ideology" we must learn to speak of the transcendent in immanent terms, imagery, categories, and the like.

This new "theological" language "from below," "from within," immanent rather than transcendent, might be called a theologico-ideological "Esperanto," for, like Esperanto is supposed to be, it would be an intercultural language that takes something from various living languages, but is so simplified, so "rational," so "generally human," that anyone with a native tongue and a little knowledge of other tongues will easily be able to master it. (This analogy of a "theologico-ideological Esperanto," like all analogies, is appropriate up to a point—*omnia analogia claudet.* For example, the analogy used by Jesus of the incompetent steward who, upon being dismissed, reduced his master's debtors' obligations by half was not meant to be pushed to the point of concluding that Jesus was condoning "white-collar crime"; his analogy was making a quite different point. Likewise, the analogy here with Esperanto can be helpful in several ways, and hence should be used to that extent—*but it should not be pushed to the point where it no longer fits, where it is no longer helpful.*)

Until fairly recently it was largely thought that all talk about the transcendent was necessarily "religious" in the sense of being "super-natural"—other than and outside our day-to-day and scientific experience and language. It is now recognized more and more that the transcendent is imbedded in our everyday and scientific experience and language. We "simply" need to become aware of it and develop thought categories and a language to reflect on and speak of it more penetratingly, precisely, and purposefully. Fundamentally the transcendent, the "religious," dimension appears when we come up against "limit" situations (e.g., the death of a loved one, or something as simple as the appearance of our first gray hairs, leading to an existential awareness of our own personal finitude or "limit") and we are led to recognize our own "limit" or "grounding" awareness, such as the meaningfulness of existence, the trustworthiness of our senses and intellect. In everyday life and in modern science human beings are continually engaged in acts of—or at least attempts at—self-transcendence, of going beyond their present status, whether in learning more, acting more efficiently, more morally, and so forth.[15] Ultimately, every human being and every scientist is ineluctably led to ask what are the conditions, the grounds that make possible the unending process of self-transcendence. They are led to "reflect upon each level of self-transcending inquiry to understand what horizon or dimension it presupposes. . . . [The scientist] can also ask such limit-questions as . . . Can these answers work if the world is not intelligible? Can the world be intelligible if it does not have an intelligent ground? . . . The question can be described as a religious-as-limit question."[16] Here we encounter that which goes beyond, transcends, or—to use another metaphor—undergirds, grounds our everyday and scientific experience. And it is this "limit," "horizon," "ground," "transcendent" dimension that is characteristic of the "religious," the "divine," as noted at the beginning of these reflections.

What is especially important to note here is that this "transcendent" dimension is not something alien to our everyday, "from below," "from within," "immanent," "human" experience and language, but is imbedded in it or, conversely, is the bed within which all else lies and is spoken of. It is this fact that we must become increasingly conscious of and articulate about, not only to understand ourselves ever more profoundly, but also to understand others ever more fully. The basis of this self-knowledge and knowledge of others is our common humanity, imbedded in transcendence. Hence the pressing need for developing a humanity-based "language" that will articulate the transcendent in the immanent, an "ecumenical Esperanto."

There is of course much of the past heritage of the various great traditions of thought both East and West that contribute to the development of an "ecumenical (universal) Esperanto." A further step forward toward its development was taken in the eighteenth/nineteenth-century European Enlightenment with its stress on our common human reason and the cosmopolitan citizen. Its universal quality was fed by European contact with the rest of the world both in receiving and in imparting information and impulses. The Enlightenment was then chastened and deepened by the subsequent critiques of historicism, hermeneutics of suspicion (Feuerbach, Nietzsche, Freud, Mannheim), crosscultural analysis, and so forth. It is this ever widening, penetrating, worldwide, dialogic Enlightenment that makes possible today the development of an "ecumenical Esperanto." Further, the founding and growth in the last hundred years of the social sciences—psychology, sociology, anthropology—is increasingly helping to provide the thought categories and vocabulary of a language that is "humanity-based," "from below," "from within," "immanent." Before their development it would have been almost impossible even to conceive the possibility of such an "ecumenical Esperanto." But it is now.

Moreover, an "ecumenical (universal) Esperanto" cannot be developed solely by means of a rational verbal vocabulary. Rather, it must include symbols, esthetic expressions, actions. Of course, a completely culture-free vocabulary can never be devised, but if the structuralists among the anthropologists, the Jungians among the psychologists, and other similarly oriented scholars are not completely mistaken, there are certain elements in humanity that are pervasive and perennial, as is sketchily indicated above,[17] and it is upon these that an "ecumenical Esperanto symbolics" will have to be built. Likewise, the point of Esperanto is to facilitate communication on a broad international, intercultural level. Esperanto was never intended to take the place of all or even of any of the world's living languages. Rather, it was merely to be an international supplementary language, but as such it could be of immense value.

Now here, I believe, the analogy breaks down, or at least I hope it will, for in fact Esperanto has not been a success in terms of its goal. Perhaps only twenty million persons throughout the whole world know Esperanto; hence it can hardly fulfill its stated function. (Further, it is based on an Indo-European language culture.) The "ecumenical (universal) Esperanto" of the "universal theology of religion-ideology" must go beyond gaining the adherence of a relatively small coterie of theologico-ideological thinkers in various religio-ideological traditions. If it does not do so, it will in fact suffer the fate, to a large extent at least, that Esperanto has in the linguistic world. We ought, therefore, not be like the fools who learn from their own mistakes, but rather like the wise who learn from the mistakes of others, and effectively work to make "ecumenical Esperanto" a vitalizing means of developing a "universal theology of religion-ideology."

Of course, no illusory goal such as an ultimately all-comprehensive, and therefore unchanging, single humanity-based "language" is envisioned. As stressed earlier, all knowledge is interpreted knowledge, is perceived from a particular perspective. Consequently every knower will know reality somewhat differently from every other knower. At the same time, however, even to know that we come to know reality differently from others, there must also be a certain commonness from which we realize we all somewhat deviate. It is precisely that commonness of human experience that provides the bases for our various cultural languages—English, German, Catalan. Because of a variety of particular historical, geographical and other reasons, our sharing of the commonness of human experience is limited in such ways that the various cultural languages result. However, despite the unending variety of human languages (reflecting of course the variety of human knowledge of reality), there is at the same time the commonness of their all being precisely human languages (a tautology, of course). Thus there will always be variety in the human perception and expression of reality, but there will also be the commonness of the (varying, perspectival) *human perception* and *expression* of reality. Just as there is no one, all-comprehensive, undifferentiated, unchanging English language, there is also a sufficient commonness that allows us to speak intelligently of the variations of the *English* language—and what is more important, *commun*icate through it.

Thus it will also be with a generic, humanity-based "ecumenical Esperanto" and the "universal theology of religion-ideology," to which it will increasingly give expression and at the same time help to formulate. It follows that epistemologically, and hence linguistically also, there will always be an ultimate pluralism, but simultaneously a sufficient commonness for humans to be able to know that they perceive reality in a pluralistic variety. Hence, an "ecumenical Esperanto," and the "ecumenical consciousness" and the "universal theology of religion-ideology" that it expresses and helps to form, are all never-ending, never end*able,* projects that ineluctably draw human beings on—for human beings unendingly seek reality, even if it be in unendingly differing ways.

In developing a "universal theology of religion-ideology," we probably can find some help in the analogy of learning a foreign language. One of the fundamental things that must be done in learning a new language is to learn to "hear," to "discern" the new sounds. This is usually more difficult the older the person is—that is, the more that we are used to and steeped in our own particular linguistic sounds—or, to speak of our primary subject here, used to and steeped in our own particular religious, theological, ideological, language: categories, terms, images, stories. Moreover, all our religious traditions have grown up and developed in an era when the tendency was to speak "from above," "from without," from the perspective of the transcendent, of God. Hence it is going to be especially difficult for us to "attune" our theological, our religious, ears to hearing the same "meaning" in those different sounds of that other language so strange to our traditions—namely, that "ecumenical Esperanto," "from below," "from within," of immanence rather than transcendence, or perhaps better said, *transcendence within immanence.* Ideologies, like Marxism, for example, on the other hand, may have greater difficulty discovering the "spiritual" dimension.

We all in fact have before us not only the gigantic task of developing a new language, an "ecumenical Esperanto," but also the even more challenging task of forging a "new consciousness" that will be capable of "hearing" and "understanding" this new "ecumenical Esperanto." Clearly this task is not one that can be performed in two sequential steps, one after the other. Rather, it must be carried out in dialectical, dialogical fashion, with a continual back-and-forth interplay, mutuality, between the forming of the new ecumenical language and the new consciousness, the "ecumenical consciousness." However, what could be more fitting as a method for carrying out the task of providing a "theology" for worldwide interreligious, interideological dialogue?[18]

Because interreligious, interideological dialogue is always necessarily a two-sided project—within each religious or ideological community as well as between religious and ideological communities—at least one further step in this process is necessary. I have noted above that it is also necessary that interreligious, interideological dialogue participants enter into dialogue not only with their partners across the faith-ideology line, but also with their coreligionists, coideologists, to share with them the fruits of the interreligious, interideological dialogue. Only thus can the whole community eventually learn, change, and grow toward an even more perceptive insight into reality. In order to fulfill this intrareligious, intraideological dialogue as the other half of the interreligious, interideological dialogue, which is making use of the "ecumenical Esperanto" and forging a new "ecumenical consciousness" to hear and understand that new "universal theology of religion-ideology," it is necessary all along the way to make the connections between the newly formed "ecumenical Esperanto" and each of the traditional religious languages: when we say X in "ecumenical Esperanto," it corresponds to A in Christianity, B in Judaism, C in Marxism. Thus we would really be able to talk to and understand each other to a large extent by means of the "translation" of our traditional languages into "ecumenical Esperanto."

However, we must at the same time note that, just as in all translations, a translated definition may not be precisely the same as the original. Therefore, although X will be perhaps essentially, fundamentally, the same as A, B, and C, none of them will be precisely the same as each other. This, of course, is not something to be deplored but, on the contrary, something to be deeply appreciated. All life is complex, and human life is the most complex. Someone who could understand and express all the complexities of human life would have to comprehend all the human persons who have ever lived, who ever will live, and who ever could live. When one adds to this the further, indeed, infinite complexity (so to speak) of the transcendent related to all humanity, actual and possible, it is clear that one would have to be fully divine in order to have such all-comprehending knowledge. Obviously this goes beyond us. Hence, the absolute necessity of our attempting to gain an ever fuller insight into the meaning of human life by a dialogue with an ever fuller set of expressions of that meaning. In other words: variety, yes, even to infinity; but with an access to that variety by way of an adequate simplicity that will facilitate, not obfuscate, understanding.

It must also be borne in mind that when speaking of "ecumenical Esperanto" I am not recommending some sort of pale, reductionist, least-common-denominator kind of "theological" expression. I am not speaking of a "theology" that will be more superficial than what we have at present, but rather one that is more profound, that goes even more deeply into our psyches, individual and communal. "Ecumenical Esperanto" must not be simply a superficial Enlightenment rationality warmed up again. No, it must go far beyond that and also include all the advances made in our understanding of knowledge referred to earlier, in history, sociology of knowledge, limitations of language, hermeneutics, plus ideology critique, praxis dialectics, paradigm shift, and so forth. All these new insights from Western culture must be utilized, but by these very principles it must be seen that they too are necessarily culture-bound. Hence, to be truly humanity-based, the religious, ideological thinker must also strive to incorporate all insights into what it means to be human, including insights from outside Western culture. The "we" implicit in the terms "from below" and "from within" must be as broad a "we" as possible, in fact an *ever increasingly* broad "we." And this can be done only by moving beyond—without abandoning—Western culture, beyond Judaism, Christianity, Western humanism, and Marxism, to absorb the insights of Islam, Hinduism, Buddhism. This can be done only by hard study of, "passing over" into the inner heart of, patient and profound dialogue with, other religions, ideologies, and cultures.

If anything like this is to be realized, all educated religious and ideologically committed persons, besides studying their own tradition deeply, must also study other religious and ideological traditions, and preferably in association with persons who not only are trained in but also stand in those religious or ideological traditions, so they might have an enhanced chance of learning to know that tradition "from within." If one expands the term "ecumenism" to include dialogue with all religions and ideologies, one finds strong support for this recommendation in both the documents of Vatican II and subsequent Vatican documents:

> We *must* become familiar with the outlook of our separated brethren. Study is *absolutely* required for this, and it should be pursued in fidelity to the truth and with a spirit of good will. Catholics . . . need to acquire a more adequate understanding of the respective doctrines of our separated brethren, their history, their spiritual and liturgical life, their religious psychology and cultural background. Most valuable for this purpose are meetings of the two sides—especially for discussion of theological problems—where each can treat with the other on an equal footing (*par cum pari*).[19]   *Decree on Ecumenism.*

The "Directory Concerning Ecumenical Matters," issued by the Vatican Secretariat for Christian Unity in 1970, made the point more concrete:

> All Christians should be of an ecumenical mind . . . hence, the princi-
> ples of ecumenism sanctioned by the Second Vatican Council should be
> appropriately introduced in all institutions of advanced learning. . . .
> Bishops . . . religious superiors and those in authority in seminaries,
> universities and similar institutions should take pains to promote the
> ecumenical movement and *spare no effort* to see that their teachers keep
> in touch with advances in ecumenical thought and action.[20]

Surely these reflections are valid for all religious and ideological communities.
In the area of Christian missiology a similar point is made by Paul Knitter:

> In order to promote the kingdom, Christians must witness to Christ. All
> peoples, all religions, must know of him in order to grasp the full content
> of God's presence in history. Here is part of the purpose and the motiva-
> tion for going forth to the ends of the earth. But in the new ecclesiology
> and in the new model for truth, one admits also that all peoples should
> know of Buddha, of Muhammad, of Krishna. This, too, is part of the
> goal and inspiration for missionary work: to be witnessed to, in order
> that Christians might deepen and expand their own grasp of God's
> presence and purpose in the world. Through this mutual witnessing, this
> mutual growth, the work of realizing the kingdom moves on.[21]

GOALS OF INTERRELIGIOUS, INTERIDEOLOGICAL DIALOGUE

A number of things have already been said about the goals of interreligious,
interideological dialogue: participants are to learn so as to grow, to know the
other, to discern and appropriate values, to encounter new dimensions of
reality, to witness and be witnessed to. Nevertheless, it would be helpful at this
point to try to summarize systematically what the goals of interreligious,
interideological dialogue are, and are not.

First, a distinction must be made between intra-Christian (and perhaps intra-
Jewish, intra-Muslim etc.?) dialogue on the one hand, and Christian-Buddhist,
Hindu-Muslim, Jewish-Hindu dialogues on the other. The goal of the former is
some kind of overarching, "organic," yet pluralistic, unity (*not* uniformity). A
simple, overarching, organic, world religion-ideology is not the goal of interreligious, interideological dialogue. Rather, the goals could be said to be three:
(1) to know oneself ever more profoundly; (2) to know the other ever more
authentically; (3) to live ever more fully accordingly.

We come to know ourselves largely by contrast, by encountering the other. I
discovered dimensions of my American cultural heritage only as a result of
living for several years in Europe—and my common Western cultural heritage
by living in the Orient. Through interreligious, interideological dialogue we
will come to know better our own religious, ideological selves with all their
consistencies and contradictions, their admirable and abhorrent aspects. Our
dialogue partners will serve as mirrors for us, showing us our true selves. Such a

prize alone is worth the price of frustration in dialogue.

We do not come to know our partners in dialogue simply as objects over against ourselves. Rather, we learn to know our partners in dialogic fashion— that is, in relationship to us. (Because we are here talking about interreligious, interideological dialogue, we must also keep its corporate nature in mind.) Hence, we come to know what we have in common ever more fully—which, as we already know from experience, will be almost immeasurably more than, and deeper than, we had previously even imagined was possible. But at the same time we shall learn to know our true differences. These authentic differences will be of two kinds: contradictory and complementary—and we also know from experience that the latter will probably outnumber the former.

As indicated before, we must be extremely cautious about "placing" our differences, lest in acting precipitously we mis-place them. So too, we must not too easily and quickly place our true differences in the contradictory category. For example, it might be that the Hindu *mokṣa,* the Zen Buddhist *satori,* the Christian "freedom of the children of God," and the Marxist "communist state" could be understood as different, but complementary, descriptions of true human liberation. Further, inasmuch as we here are speaking of true, though complementary, differences, we are not talking about discerning values in our partner's tradition, which we will then wish to appropriate for our own tradition, which was said to occur in phase two of interreligious, interideological dialogue. That indeed does, and should happen, but then we are speaking of something that the two traditions ultimately hold in common, either actually or potentially. But, again, here we are speaking of authentic differences. However, if they are perceived as complementary rather than contradictory, they will be seen to operate within the total organic structure of the other religion-ideology and to fulfill their function properly only within it. They could not have the same function—the same relationship to the other parts—in *our* total organic structure, and hence would not be understood to be in direct opposition, in contradiction to the "differing" element within our structure.

Nevertheless, we can at times find contradictory truth claims, value claims, between different religio-ideological traditions. That happens only when they cannot be seen as somehow ultimately different expressions of the same thing (a commonality) or as complementary. But when it happens, even though it be relatively rare, a profound, unavoidable problem faces the two communities: What should be their attitude and behavior toward each other? Should they remain in dialogue, tolerate each other, ignore each other, or oppose each other? The problem is especially pressing in matters of value judgments. For example, how does the Christian (or Jew, Muslim, Marxist, or other) react to the (fortunately now suppressed) Hindu tradition of *suttee*—widows "voluntarily" cremating themselves on their husband's funeral pyre? Try to learn its value, tolerate it, ignore it, oppose it (in what manner?). Or the Nazi policy of exterminating Jews? These are clear-cut issues, but what of a religion-ideology that approves of slavery (as Christianity, Judaism, and Islam did until a century ago)? Perhaps that is clear enough today, but what of sexism? The capitalism-socialism conflict? The proper course of action becomes less and less clear-cut. It was eventually clear to most non-Hindus in the nineteenth century that the proper attitude toward Hinduism on *suttee* was not dialogue, but opposition; but apparently it was not so clear to all non-Nazis that opposition to Jewish genocide was the right stance to take. Further, it took Christians eighteen hundred years to come to a negative conclusion concerning slavery—but they did come to it. Many religions and ideologies today stand in the midst of a battle over sexism, many of them even refusing to admit that there even is such an issue. Finally, the controversial nature of the capitalism-socialism issue speaks for itself.

Thus, it is apparent that there are important contradictory differences between religions-ideologies, and at times these differences warrant not dialogue, but even opposition. We in fact also make such judgments of "better or worse," of acceptable or not, within religio-ideological traditions—and even do so rather frequently within our individual lives. But surely this exercise of our critical faculties is not to be limited to ourselves and our own tradition; this perhaps most human of faculties should be made available to all—with all the proper constraints and concerns for dialogue detailed at length above.

We must then ask, on what grounds can we judge whether a religio-ideological difference is in fact contradictory and of such importance and nature as to warrant active opposition? Inasmuch as all religions and ideologies are attempts to explain the meaning of human life and how to live accordingly, it would seem that doctrines and customs hostile to human life are to be perceived not as complementary but as contradictory, and that opposition should be proportional to their life-threatening quality. What all is included in an authentically full human life will then have to be the measure against which all elements of all religions-ideologies will have to be tested in making judgments about their being in harmony, complementarity, or contradiction, and then acted upon accordingly.

It is vital to recall, however, that the human being is by nature a historical being. Hence, what it means to be fully human will evolve, both in terms of basic capabilities and in terms of a growing recognition of what in fact human nature entails. At basis everything distinctively human flows from the essential human structure—the ability to think and to make free decisions. By these abilities humanity has gradually, through history, come to the contemporary situation where claims are made in favor of "human rights": conditions that are due to all humans specifically because they are human. This position was for the most part hardly conceived until recently. As noted, it was only a little over a century ago that slavery was still widely accepted—even vigorously defended and practiced by Christian churchmen (not to speak of Christian, Jewish, Muslim, and other slave traders). This radical violation of "human rights" has today been largely eliminated, not only de facto but also de jure. No thinker or public leader would today contemplate justifying slavery (see the Universal Declaration of Human Rights by the United Nations in 1948, article 4). Here is a glaringly obvious example of the historical evolution of the understanding of what it means to be fully human in terms of *recognition* of what was always the case: that human beings are by nature radically free.

However, the human right to private property (Universal Declaration, art. 17), which was first publicly acknowledged in eighteenth-century Europe, would have been unthinkable without previous developments in control over matter. The same is true of the twentieth-century claim to the right to work (Universal Declaration, art. 23): "The development of this new control over nature—first over external nature and increasingly also over human nature . . . has made possible entirely new dimensions of human self-development, and its apparently illimitable expansion leads to the expectation, at least in the developed countries, that it can release a sufficient potential so that everyone can participate in them—and consequently has a right to participate therein."[22] Here are clear examples of the historical evolution of the understanding of what it means to be fully human in terms of the expansion of the basic *capabilities* of humanity. (Of course, the general acknowledgment of a human right unfortunately, as humanity painfully knows, does not automatically guarantee its realization—but it is the indispensable first step thereto.)

What fundamentally has been acknowledged in this century as the foundation of being human is that human beings ought to be autonomous in their decisions—such decisions being directed by their own reason and limited only by the same rights of others: "All human beings are born free and equal in dignity and rights. They are endowed with reason and conscience and should act toward one another in a spirit of brotherhood" (Universal Declaration, art. 1). This autonomy in the ethical sphere, which Thomas Aquinas had recognized in the thirteenth century,[23] expanded into the social and political spheres in the eighteenth century—well enshrined in the slogan of the French revolution: Liberty, Equality, Fraternity! In the term "liberty" is understood all the personal and civil rights; in the term "equality" is understood the political rights of participation in public decision-making; in the term "fraternity" is understood (in an expanded twentieth-century sense) the social rights.

The great religious communities of the world, though frequently resistant in the past and too often still in the present, have likewise in many ways expressed a growing awareness of and commitment to many of the same notions of what it means to be fully human. One such joint, global-level expression reflecting the thought and *engagement* of leaders of all the major world religions (221 delegates) was issued at Kyoto, Japan, in October 1970:

> As we gathered together in concern for the overriding subject of peace, we discovered that the things which unite us are more important than the things which divide us. We found that in common we possessed:
>
> a conviction of the fundamental unity of the human family, of the equality and dignity of all human beings;
> a feeling for the inviolability of the individual and his conscience;
> a feeling for the value of the human community;

a recognition that might does not make right, that human power is not sufficient unto itself and is not absolute;

the belief that love, compassion, selflessness and the power of the spirit and of inner sincerity ultimately have greater strength than hate, enmity and self-interest;

a feeling of obligation to stand on the side of the poor and oppressed against the rich and the oppressor;

deep hope that ultimately good will will be victorious.[24]

Thus through dialogue humanity is slowly, painfully, creeping toward a consensus on what is involved in an authentically full human life. The 1948 United Nations Declaration of Human Rights was an important step in that direction. But, of course, much more consensus needs to be attained if inter-religious, interideological dialogue is to reach its full potential.

FULL HUMAN LIFE

If the language of a "universal theology of religion-ideology" is to be "from below," humanity-based, there need to be articulations not only of what a minimally acceptable human life, "by right," is, but also what a *full* human life is. Only as we become increasingly more explicit about what it means to be fully human will we be able in fact to live that ever-fuller human life (a never-ending task both for the individual and for humanity as a whole), and only thus will a humanity-based theologico-ideological language become available to us. Let me try, then, to articulate an understanding of full human life in terms that should be understandable to all sensitive humans, theists and nontheists, religious and nonreligious.

I believe it can be helpful to view full human life in terms of three relatively distinct but closely connected areas: the practical, the cognitive, and the "spiritual." In the cognitive area we seek to understand and articulate in various conscious, intellectual ways our perceptions of the world and experiences of life. In the practical area we act and make things; we seek not to understand the world, but to *affect* and *effect* it. In the "spiritual" or in-depth area we discern the deeper meanings of our experiences and of the world. This in-depth dimension of human life is where our imagination and feelings, and the more synthetic aspect of the intellect, come more into play. It is characteristic of this area that it brings the images, emotions, and interconnections of our inner life to the conscious level. Each of these areas needs to be ever more fully developed as life progresses. Furthermore, it is also absolutely necessary that they be interconnected, integrated, so that they might mutually energize each other and evoke a holistic life.

In nineteenth- and twentieth-century Western civilization there has been a decided tendency to downplay the "spiritual" dimension, to the point where it had very seriously atrophied. Moreover, as mentioned before, the traditional Judeo-Christian images and structures—the four Cs: creed, code, cult, community—have been increasingly incapable of effectively illuminating the life experiences of modern critical-thinking "Westerners," in whatever part of the globe they reside. Consequently, it is often precisely the "Western" intellectual who needs first to be awakened to even the existence of the "spiritual" dimension of full human life, and then assisted in its cultivation. As contact is made with the inner process of one's life, as its images and feelings are acknowledged and allowed their proper effect, as meanings beyond rational expressions are discerned and connections between portions of life are made and larger integrations formed, this "spiritual" dimension of life will affect the other two areas of life. It is especially important that the various in-depth experiences of modern persons be brought to the conscious level, so that their power can be fully developed and also be made available to the other two areas of life.

As these in-depth experiences are raised to the conscious level, they will not only provide a deeper meaning to the rational expressions of the cognitive area of life, they will also make demands for a rearticulation of those newly discerned meanings in intellectual categories and expressions that more adequately reflect the contemporary intellectual world. This step, too, is vital, lest the "spiritual" dimension come to be perceived as something out of a fairy tale and eventually again be rejected—to the disastrous loss of the full human person. In turn, of course, as the conundrums of life, on all levels, are more fully and richly analyzed and articulated, the cognitive area of life will also in turn spill its newly released energies over into the "spiritual" area, providing it with more adequate means to raise in-depth experience to the conscious level and synthesize integrative connections in terms that "make sense" in contemporary critical language.

One of the strengths of modern Western civilization has been its stress on effective human action, both individual and corporate. The West has been nothing if not "practical," efficient, and this dimension has often been closely linked with the cognitive dimension. However, if the in-depth dimension is seriously atrophied, the practico-cognitive dimensions will be more limited, shallower than they could or should be. But as our action becomes more effective, our cognitive life will be stimulated to understand the new circumstances, new realities, that are created by our action—which will also generate the need to discern still further insights and integrations in our "spiritual" dimension.

A special danger in the intensification of the "spiritual" life that must be guarded against is what can be called privatizing. An extremely important insight into human reality that the West has generated in the last two centuries is the recognition of the pervasive power of social structures. All humans are massively formed by the structures of the society in which they live. Even when some few "rise above" societal structures, they are immensely influenced by them—in this case rather negatively, by being forced to "overcome" them, though of course they are never *completely* "overcome." The West then went on to understand—and partially to act on its understanding—that if the lot of humans is to change significantly, social structures must be changed (and they can be). Most persons will not alter their lives profoundly all by themselves. Put somewhat colloquially: the world cannot be "saved" simply by trying to "save" individual persons; the social structures within which individual persons live must also be "saved." It is absolutely vital to a full human life that this precious insight be preserved, magnified, and acted on as the "spiritual" dimension of life is reactivated and intensified. That "insight" from the "practical" dimension must pour its energies into not only the cognitive dimension of life but also the "spiritual," and in turn be energized by the other two.

A key, if not *the* key, of a full human life is the maximizing of awareness in all dimensions. "Being awareness" is not being human. But acting, making, reasoning, feeling—all increasingly suffused with awareness in expanding depth, breadth, and interconnectedness—is, I believe, a good description of a full human life. For example, acting with spontaneity is a human good. But, without eliminating the spontaneity, also becoming aware that I am acting with spontaneity, of what that feels like, of what significance it has for other aspects of my life, for other persons and things I am related to, and so forth—all that is clearly an enrichment of my life, making it a fuller human life. The fact that when life is reduced to unreflective action we describe it as unhuman, or even inhuman, or robotlike (and if life is further reduced, as in a coma, the person is said to merely be vegetating) clearly indicates negatively that awareness is of the essence of human life. As awareness approaches zero, life ceases, death is approached. Conversely, as awareness expands toward infinity, human life intensifies, moving toward the bursting of all bounds—for which all religions and other worldviews have specific terms: *mokṣa* or liberation (Hindu), *nirvana* or "reality" (Buddhist), *basileia theou* or reign of God (Christian). It is that Omega point of total awareness toward which all human life tends.

In sum: the greatest dangers to a full human life are the severe atrophication of any of the three essential dimensions of life, and their existing in unconnected, unaware, fashion—a disintegrated life. Stated positively, in a full human life all three dimensions continue to grow maximally, become ever more fully conscious, and are closely integrated so that they mutually enrich each other, producing an always increasing unity, a *holos*.

A CHRISTIAN EXPERIMENT IN "ECUMENICAL ESPERANTO"

Perhaps the goal and the suggested means to the goal are now about as clear as they can be made in a purely theoretical way. The next step is to try to put the theory into action. I as a Christian theologian need to attempt to reflect on my Christian faith in an "ecumenical Esperanto," "from below" and "from within," that can claim to be recognizably Christian, and yet make room for non-Christians to recognize their own faith or ideology therein, to somehow feel included in that language. This will be a difficult undertaking for both sides: both the new language and the new consciousness to hear and understand the new language need to be forged by us together. We need from both sides to stretch ourselves as far as we can to meet and understand our dialogue partner *in optimam partem,* while staying in integral touch with our own sources. To my non-Christian sisters and brothers I must say: Let us help each other. Let us try together.

Jesus, the Primary Standard for Christianity

It is important at this point to say something about how Christian theology is arrived at. I am in fundamental agreement with those who speak of the two poles, or sources, or horizons, of Christian belief—namely, the Christian tradition and contemporary experience.[25] Schillebeeckx would more recently want to speak of two poles within one source of Christian belief, so as to emphasize the overarching mutuality and unity of how Christians arrive at their beliefs.[26] Fair enough. The dialogic character of how not only Christians but all persons arrive at their beliefs is an extremely important lesson to be learned, one that can hardly be overstressed.

I wish to make four extended—and related—remarks, three pertaining to all persons and one specifically to Christians. First for the specifically Christian remark.

Although I will later on nuance the standard Christian claim of the universal significance for salvation of Jesus Christ, I want to argue here that the historical person Jesus of Nazareth must be the primary standard for what is Christian. The historical Jesus naturally includes the Hebraic and Judaic traditions as they had developed up to his time, with the particular interpretation he gave them, but equally naturally does not include later "Christian" reflections about him unless they agree with this primary measure, this *Urstandard.* I am aware of the grave difficulties of arriving at an authoritative, clear image of the historical Jesus. But to the extent that we can, there is the standard.

Of course all the subtle difficulties involved in the "history of effects," the *Wirkungsgeschichte,* of two thousand years of the Christian tradition will prevent our ever arriving at a completely "objective" image of Jesus. But that is true of everything. Every fact is relativized by the perceiver, as I argued at length above. It is also true that we can come to a fuller grasp of a fact if we have perceptions of it from several different standpoints—the whole argument in favor of dialogue. But it is the original datum, the *Urtatsache,* that one is trying to grasp so that one can somehow relate it to oneself. This purpose of course again relativizes the original fact—that is, puts it in relation to me (and this relationship is further complexified and relativized by the whole history of effects between the original fact and my perception of it), but it is the *Urtatsache* that I am trying to grasp and relate to me. I now know that I can never fully grasp it as it "objectively" originally existed (analogously to modern physics where we now realize that to pass light or electrons, or whatever, through an object so as to "observe" it already changes it). Still, with that now chastened knowledge that we can never attain a completely "objective" image of something, like the Parmenidian continuum, we can always strive to come closer. It is this, I believe, that we should do in regard to the historical figure of Jesus.

Then, with due modesty and openness, it seems to me that the best image of the historical Jesus that we are able to attain at a given moment has priority over all explanations as to his meaning. *What Jesus thought, taught, and wrought is the "Jesuanic," if not the "Christian," gospel*, even though we learn it only through what others have told us he thought, taught, and wrought. (If communicating what Jesus had thought, taught, and wrought had been the primary purpose of the gospel writers, finding it out would be much easier; but of course they primarily wanted to tell what they and their sources believed were the most important "meanings" of what he thought, taught, and wrought—and that makes this task more difficult, but not impossible.)

In a way we Christians are in somewhat of a difficult position as far as our name "Christian" is concerned. If our name had derived from the name "Jesus," my argument that the historical person Jesus of Nazareth ought to be the primary standard for what is Christian would have at least a prima facie, etymological, plausibility. Unfortunately the one common word, in English at least, that is derived from the name Jesus has come to mean quite the opposite of what the historical Jesus supposedly stood for: Jesuitical. Nevertheless, I still believe that all who call themselves Christians claim to center their religion on Jesus, and that therefore anything that is said about the meaning of Jesus (christology) must in fact not run counter to what Jesus thought, taught, and wrought. (To be concrete, but magnificently overbrief, it has long puzzled me how Jesus could be God and yet not know it—and this was obviously the case, as seen in numerous New Testament sayings.) Of course, many things developed in the Christian tradition that are called Christian and which did not come from Jesus—for example, veneration of martyrs, religious orders, and so forth. Thus, even though they cannot be attributed to Jesus, yet because they do not run counter to what he thought, taught, and wrought, and because they have been incorporated in the Christian tradition, it is perfectly proper to call them Christian in that extended or secondary sense.

What does a contemporary Christian do with the historical fact that in the development of Christianity the "teaching Jesus" quickly became the "taught *Christos*," even within the time of the writing of the New Testament? Clearly the resurrection experience was a transforming one for the followers of Jesus. However one understands the New Testament reports of the empty tomb, the resurrection experiences had a profound impact on them. As mentioned above, they doubtless began to perceive things about Jesus that they had not been conscious of when they were with him. Clearly, the Jesus they knew was not transformed into some kind of magic figure or totem for them, so that merely by their waving this magic wand or figure, salvation would be accomplished (though later and too often this "magical" use, or rather misuse, of Jesus did take place in the history of Christianity). Rather, in the resurrection experience the followers of Jesus were first of all inwardly confirmed in their precrucifix-ion experience of the encounter with the divine through Jesus, through what he had thought, taught, and wrought.

Thus, in teaching Jesus, his followers attempted to teach what they had learned from him. However, what they had learned from him could not be limited to what he had put into words (what he "taught"); they obviously were deeply struck by his inner self, which appeared to be so full of wisdom and effective love (what he "thought"), and how this exuded into his every action (what he "wrought"), as is evident in the synoptic reportage. Jesus' whole person was the source of this utterly transformative "learning" experience for his followers, and this transformation was so profound, so pervasive, that, rather than being shattered by the shattering of Jesus on the cross (its agony both for him and for his followers proved to be the crucible in which their "enlightenment" and love were purified, strengthened, transformed), they were enabled, as it were, to go down into the tomb with him and rise with the reconfirmation of their precrucifixion experience of Jesus. Their experience of him was true, authentic, after all; he really was—is!—the source of true life; he lived on! Thus the "taught Jesus" (i.e., the taught or proclaimed *Christos*) was first of all the fullest way to hand on the "teaching Jesus"—that is, what he thought, taught, and wrought in his *whole* person.

Hence, any move to understand the proclaimed *Christos* as someone, something, other than the "teaching Jesus" can easily become problematic; any move to understand the "proclaimed *Christos*" in contrast to the "teaching Jesus," to what he thought, taught, and wrought in his whole person, would be to play false with not only Jesus but also his first disciples.

The theology of the Gospel of Luke is even clearer in its insistence that it is primarily what Jesus *preached,* rather than the person of Jesus, that should be preached by Christians. The Catholic scripture scholar Joseph G. Kelly notes:

[According to Luke] Jesus always points not to himself but to God. As a result, the preacher cannot become the preached. . . . The disciples are not called upon to preach the person of Jesus. What they must do is preach the message of Jesus. . . . Jesus shows Christians the Way and Christians see themselves on the Way. Therefore, what Christians must now preach is the Way which Jesus preached: repentance and the forgive-ness of sin—release [*aphesin,* liberation, Luke 4:18]. This Way is preached in the name of Jesus and is followed by Jesus' disciples because Jesus is the one who has accomplished this Way. But, for Luke, Jesus is not the "Way." The Way is what Jesus taught must be done. The message is not Jesus, but release [liberation]. Jesus did not glorify himself, but lived in such a way as to give glory to God. This resulted in God's glorifying Jesus. Jesus did not proclaim himself, but said that his person and life made God known. Every time that the reign breaks in at a moment of release, one can glimpse God. God is the end and the goal. One of the ways to find God is to follow the Way of Jesus, but Jesus' Way is not the only way.[27]

At the same time it should be remembered that not everything true, good, and beautiful comes from Jesus or Christianity. So, claiming that Jesus is the primary standard for what is Christian does not mean that Christians cannot appropriate true, good, and beautiful things from elsewhere, but that they should not be called Christian in a primary sense unless they are found in what Jesus thought, taught, or wrought, or Christian in a secondary sense if they have not been assimilated into the Christian tradition. It is conceivable that a Christian would find it necessary to espouse a position that runs counter to Jesus—persons claiming to be Christians, including priests, bishops, and popes, have been doing so for centuries—they simply should not say that such a position is Christian.

The "I" and Radical Openness

This brings me to my first remark pertaining to all persons. Granted the dialogic character of the contemporary Christian's affirming, appropriating, and acting on Christian belief, moving dialectically between the Christian tradition (with Jesus as its primary standard) and contemporary experience, in the last analysis it is I (right now—and "I" includes looking to the past and the future, includes "me" in context and community, and therefore really an "I-we," deciding within the horizon of the Ultimate Meaning of life) who am the final decider on what is proper to affirm intellectually, trust emotionally-spiritually, and act on. To paraphrase Newman, when all the agonizing is over, it is conscience first and pope second. That is eminently true even when we decide that pope—or tradition, or whatever—is first, for in reality it is precisely that which our conscience tells us is proper in that case. Put in other words: all talk in religion, indeed, all talk about God, is ultimately really talk about ourselves. For all religion is about the ultimate meaning of *our* lives; we know God only insofar as God is related to *us*. That is why many persons, religious and would-be religious, become impatient over theological speculation that does not rather clearly have a soteriological aim, whether it is called redemption, the reign of God, *moksa,* nirvana, or whatever.

My second remark pertaining to all persons concerns the search for religious meaning and truth more generally. All those searching for religious meaning and truth, no matter how convinced by and committed to a particular tradition or position, if they would act with integrity, must have a "radical" openness, an openness "in principle." That is, for example, they must be willing to say with total seriousness that for the sake of integrity it is possible in the future that they might have to cease being a Christian, at least as they now understand it—or cease being a theist, at least as they now understand it. It may not seem at all likely, but they must be open to the possibility.[28]

If I may add a personal note: when I was younger I suffered great anxieties, at times agonies, whenever my well-learned beliefs were seriously challenged by doubts. I very slowly learned to find ever deeper, ever more complex, yet simpler, explanations. The deeper the challenge, the more profound the resultant clarification when it finally came. Then I eventually realized that if I was like Faust, *immer strebend (—aber sanft,* I would add), they always did come. So that now maintaining a radical openness not only fills me with no anxiety, rather it fills me with an inner calm, trust, even joy of anticipation.

Stages of Faith Development and Interreligious, Interideological Dialogue

And now my third general remark. Earlier it was pointed out that authentic dialogue occurs only when each partner comes primarily to learn from the other, when both therefore assume that they do not have the fullness of truth; consequently they meet each other fundamentally as equals, *par cum pari.* Obviously this cannot happen if the partners do not share in some significant ways a deabsolutized understanding of truth statements. When partners do not hold some sort of relational understanding of truth statements, but an absolute one, then interreligious, interideological encounters with them can only be prolegomena to authentic dialogue. Of course, it is absolutely vital that these prolegomena be traversed so as to arrive at authentic dialogue one day.

However, it is extremely helpful to note that there is a relationship between an individual's cognitional, moral judgment, and faith-ideology development. These relationships have been worked out by pioneer scholars such as Erik Erikson, Jean Piaget, Lawrence Kohlberg, and James Fowler.[29] The relationship might be summed up in the two words "prerequisites" and "stages." Cognitional capacities and psycho-social experiences must reach certain minimums before the individual can advance to the next level of moral judgment or faith-ideology. The advance does not necessarily occur, but without the presence of the prerequisite capacities and experiences, it cannot occur. Moreover, a more advanced level of moral judgment or faith-ideology cannot be attained without passing through the lower stages.

Kohlberg and his colleagues have developed a schema of three pairs of stages of moral judgment development; he calls them preconventional, where the standard for moral judgment tends to be the self, conventional, where the standards come from the outside society, and postconventional, where the standards tend to go beyond societal patterns to general principles.[30] (It should be noted also that in all these various advancements, the attainments of the previous stages are not rejected, but are taken up into the next higher stage and transformed.) James Fowler, building on the work of Piaget and Kohlberg and adding to it that of Erikson with his emphasis on the psycho-social dimension of human development, has built an impressive body of field research and analysis, on the basis of which he formulated his theory of six stages of faith-ideology development.

What has special bearing on the matter of interreligious, interideological dialogue are the characteristics Kohlberg and his colleagues have found in what they call the postconventional stages, stages five and six, and what Fowler and his colleagues have found in his stages five and six of faith-ideology development (faith, as used by Fowler, clearly is not restricted to "religious" faith, but includes all grounding explanations of life—i.e., ideologies). Kohlberg comments on the move from conventional to postconventional moral reasoning: "The rejection of conventional moral reasoning begins with the perception of relativism, the awareness that any given society's definition of right and wrong, however legitimate, is only one among many, both in fact and theory."[31] Thus it would seem necessary for a person to have moved to Kohlberg's stage five in moral reasoning in order to engage in authentic interreligious, interideological dialogue.

In writing about his stage five in faith-ideology development, Fowler has some startlingly pertinent things to say:

> Stage 5 accepts as axiomatic that truth is more multidimensional and organically interdependent than most theories or accounts of truth can grasp. Religiously, it knows that the symbols, stories, doctrines, and liturgies offered by its own or other traditions are inevitably partial, limited to a particular people's experience of God, and incomplete. Stage 5 also sees, however, that in the relativity of religious traditions what matters is not their relativity to each other, but their relativity—*relate-ivity*—to the reality to which they mediate relation. Conjunctive faith [stage 5], therefore, is ready for significant encounters with other traditions than its own, expecting that truth has disclosed and will disclose itself in those traditions in ways that may complement or correct its own. Krister Stendahl is fond of saying that no interfaith conversation is genuinely ecumenical unless the quality of mutual sharing and receptivity is such that each party makes him- or herself vulnerable to conversion to the other's truth. This would be Stage 5 ecumenism.
>
> This position implies no lack of commitment to one's own truth tradition. Nor does it mean a wishy-washy neutrality or mere fascination with the exotic features of alien cultures. Rather, conjunctive faith's radical openness to the truth of the other stems precisely from its confidence in the reality mediated by its own tradition and in the awareness that that reality overspills its mediation. The person of Stage 5 makes her or his own experience of truth the principle by which other claims to truth are tested. But he or she assumes that each genuine perspective will augment and correct aspects of the other, in a mutual movement toward the real and the true.[32]

Again, it would seem clear that Stage 5 faith-ideology is a prerequisite of authentic interreligious, interideological dialogue. Before that, interreligious, interideological encounters would be prolegomena to authentic interreligious, interideological dialogue.

The age pattern of the appearance of Stage 5 faith-ideology also has a bearing on this issue. According to Fowler, transitional stage 4–5 does not appear until the twenties, and then only in relatively small numbers when covering the whole spectrum of U.S. society. However, of those adults over thirty whom his team interviewed in depth (359 persons over eight years), a third of them attained transitional stage 4–5 or higher, meaning that a third of the population (if the sample is truly representative) over thirty is capable of authentic dialogue. It should also be noted that with higher levels of education, the percentage of more advanced faith-ideology stages proportionally increases. Inasmuch as, by the very nature of the enterprise, those persons most likely to be interested in interreligious, interideological dialogue will also tend to have higher than average education levels, the percentage of persons participating in interreligious, interideological dialogue who are at Stage 5 faith-ideology development and hence capable of authentic dialogue should be considerably higher than 33 percent—but statistics are not available.

Thus, it is important to know at what stage potential participants in interreligious, interideological dialogue are, so as to avoid unwarranted expectations—and subsequent disillusionments. Being forewarned about what stage potential dialogue participants are at, a sensitive person should be able to help all concerned to work their way through the necessary prolegomena more successfully, and perhaps even more rapidly. Obviously much work needs to be done in correlating faith-ideology development and the practice of interreligious, interideological dialogue.

What also needs even more research and thought is the correlation between stages of faith-ideology development and interreligious, interideological dialogue on the level of the group and culture. Bernard Lonergan raises the issue when speaking about the educational process "in the difference between the child beginning kindergarten and the doctoral candidate writing his dissertation. But the difference produced by the education of individuals is only a recapitulation of the longer process of the education of mankind, of the evolution of social institutions and of the development of cultures. Religions . . . all had their rude beginnings, slowly developed, reached their peak."[33]

One need only think of the official stance of the Catholic Church toward dialogue with non-Catholic Christians, let alone non-Christians, before Vatican II and after. The former was vigorously negative, and the latter just as vigorously positive. Vatican II was clearly a conversion experience on the level of a whole religious institution, and it clearly was based on the attainment, officially, of a new level of cognitive capacity, which allowed the institution to also advance to Stage 5 in faith development. Again, one need only do a comparative study of Vatican documents in regard to the limitations on absolute claims resulting from an awareness of history, or in regard to the possibility of learning from other religions, both before Vatican II (e.g., *Mortalium Animos,* 1928, *Humanae Generis,* 1950) and during and after. The transition from Stage 3 and 4, ideology-centered, to Stage 5, dialogue-oriented, is very apparent. Of course the implementation of the official transition has been anything but smooth and painless; resistance on the part of those Catholic officials in positions of power who personally have not yet themselves made the transition has been vigorous.

I am in agreement with Fowler when he writes:

Careful theological work is required in a faith tradition to determine the normative images of adulthood which that tradition envisions. By normative images of adulthood I mean to ask, what developmental trajectory into mature faith is envisioned and called for by a particular faith tradition, at its best? While unable to speak for others, I am convinced that the normative image of adulthood envisioned in Christian faith leads out toward Universalizing faith [Stage 6].

I also agree when he writes:

> The modal developmental level is the average expectable level of development for adults in a given community. . . . The operation of the modal level in a community sets an effective limit on the ongoing process of growth in faith. My observations lead me to judge that the modal developmental level in most middle-class American churches and synagogues is best described in terms of Synthetic-Conventional faith [Stage 3, ideology-centered] or perhaps just beyond it.[34]

What of the 33 percent of the over-thirty population that are at transitional stage 4–5 or higher? Have they left the churches? Are they often frustrated and underutilized by them? If they were mostly present and active and not restricted, it would seem there would be a great deal more creative interreligious, interideological dialogue occurring on the grassroots level and above than seems to be. What of those church members at Stages 2 and 3 who are held back rather than encouraged to advance to their full capabilities? The potential for good within the churches is immense; the actuality is much less so. Might the situations in other Western religions and ideologies—for example, Marxism—be similar?

Learning how things stand in non-Western cultures, non-Western religious and ideological traditions, requires careful work, the importance of which for interreligious, interideological dialogue, for theology, for ideology, for religions in general, and human life on this globe can hardly be overemphasized.

"Reconciling the World to God through Christ"

After these prolegomena, let me finally try to theologize as a Christian in "ecumenical Esperanto." Although I have argued that the historical Jesus ought to be the primary standard for what is considered Christian, at the same time I do not want to give the impression that I wish to dismiss everything that was said "about" Jesus by the New Testament writers. Their words have often been precious and insightful to me. Hence, I should like to reflect on a very key notion found in the New Testament that has been formative of much of subsequent Christian history and at the same time the source of tremendous difficulties for non-Christians, including critical Western thinkers.

Let me begin by posing the problem this way: Does the Pauline statement that the world is reconciled to God through Christ (Rom. 5:10f.; 2 Cor. 5:19f.) have to be understood in a way that is unacceptable, even ununderstandable, to the modern critical mind, and also antithetic to the possibility that other world religions are valid, authentic ways for humanity to be "reconciled to God"? I believe it does not.

Paul here is obviously talking about something that far transcends the everyday life experience that we have of reality. Clearly, then, he is not going to be able to use language in its normal, everyday sense. Still, like all human beings, he will nevertheless have to use the one language that we have—human language—with all its limitations, formed by the everyday experience we have—and then, perhaps at most, extend it out from that everyday experience to lend it additional variations of meaning.[35]

Although Paul necessarily used everyday language, he sometimes used it in a way that was quite common in his time in order to convey meanings that went far beyond our everyday experience of things. Such use of language very often is called *mythic*—that is, using a connected set of images that points to a meaning beyond the surface meaning—like a metaphor. And that is what Paul is doing here. That means that his language will *sound* as if he were describing in a very empirical, perhaps even physical, ontological, manner what he understood *really* to have happened on a different level in the relationship between the world and God in the Christ event.

The image projected by Paul is as if somehow the world, meaning mainly humanity, was in a way pointed in the wrong direction, away from God—who existed in some transcendent fashion, outside the world. Then, through the Christ event, as it were, Christ reached his huge hand up and grasped the world by the scruff of its neck and turned it around so that it was facing God once again. Thus, there was a sort of ontological, cosmic "reconciling of the world with God through Christ."

But of course this is a transphysical, mythic, metaphorical image. Paul was not so naive as to think that he was in fact empirically describing the way things really are physically with this language, in the same way as he might describe the various parts of a tent, how they are related to each other, what materials they are made of, and so forth. Rather, he was attempting to communicate some insight that would contribute to an explanation of the meaning of life. This is what mythic stories are supposed to do. Just what was this insight contributing to the explanation of the meaning of life that Paul was trying to communicate with this mythic image? It seems to me that it can be explained as follows.

Paul obviously had a profound experience of Jesus Christ, even though he never met him personally when Jesus was alive on earth. This experience of Jesus Christ was for Paul quite obviously a breakthrough-kind of experience, or, said in other words, a "turn-around," a *metanoia,* a conversion, experience. Through it he felt that he now had a profoundly positive kind of relationship with the ultimate meaning of life for him, which he called God, and this for him new, profoundly positive, relationship came through his encounter with Jesus Christ. For Paul, Jesus Christ provided the opportunity, the occasion, the means, to have this positive relationship with the ultimate meaning of life, God. Put in other words, Paul was much more interested in soteriology than christology; Paul was much more concerned about "Christ's incarnation in Christians" than in "God's incarnation in Christ."[36]

In similar fashion, for other Christians Jesus Christ has also been this means of attaining a profoundly positive relationship with the ultimate meaning of life, God. From Jesus Christ, Christians learn that the ultimate meaning of life is to stand in the center of one's being and turn and reach outward; it is to love, to reach out beyond oneself to the good, to being, to all that exists. Primarily for human beings this means other persons, but it also includes all beings, and ultimately the Source, Sustainer, and Goal of all being, whom Christians and many others call God. (Nontheists, like Theravada Buddhists, may prefer to use terms such as "universe" or "nature"—perhaps not unlike that school of Western thought that spoke of *Deus sive Natura*.) This is not in any way self-destructive, for as was pointed out by Jesus when he cited from the Hebrew Bible, we are to love our neighbor as our self. We can love our neighbor, then, only to the extent that we truly love ourselves. Authentic self-love and authentic love of the other are not only not mutually exclusive, they are necessarily mutually inclusive.

There is of course much, much more to the further understanding of the living out of this central insight that Christians claim to find in the life of Jesus. Christians believe, they are convinced, that in this man Jesus of Nazareth this central insight into the meaning of human life, and the attendant insights and implications, were so fully exemplified and lived out that they feel compelled to use language that speaks of the meeting of the human and the divine in him. At any rate, by looking at Jesus, by encountering him, Christians claim that they are thereby enabled to have a profound positive relationship with God. In other words, they are "reconciled to God."

Christians, further, are convinced that the inflow of insights as to the meaning of life was so overwhelming in Jesus that to express this perception they had to turn to hyperbolic language, language that was metaphorical, poetic, for this kind of language normally is what human beings must use when trying to express something that transcends everyday language. (This is the same point made earlier when speaking of Paul's use of what I called mythic language.) Hence, Christians eventually began to speak of Jesus of Nazareth as the meeting point of the divine and the human, so that later, in the fourth and fifth centuries, when Christianity had become the state religion of the Roman empire and had largely embraced the Hellenistic thought world and means of conceptualization, orthodox Christians began to speak of the God-man. Unfortunately for subsequent Christians, and for the rest of the world, the profound insight that the first Christians had in their liberating encounter with Jesus of Nazareth was now translated out of its poetic, metaphorical language into Hellenistic empirical, ontological language in a manner that took the original language to also be empirical, ontological. Not to perceive that almost all the original language of the first Christians as expressed in the New Testament was in fact poetic, metaphorical, when speaking in its most ecstatic terms about the significance and meaning of Jesus of Nazareth,[37] was a profound misjudgment.

However, given the difference between the Semitic and Hellenistic thought worlds, perhaps such a misperception was unavoidable. Hellenistic Christians had to try to understand the meaning of Jesus in their own thought categories. Inasmuch as the Hellenistic world did not have a historical, relational view of truth, but rather an absolutist one, it was almost impossible for it to conceive of authentically valid statements about the meaning of life in categories other than its own absolutist, ontological ones, assuming that all true statements about the meaning of life could be properly expressed only in such categories. Of course, in today's mental world, with its historical, relational understanding of truth, we need not, *may not,* remain thus limited. We must attempt to recapture the original "historical" significance of what Jesus thought, taught, and wrought, and express it in contemporary historical, deabsolutized, critical-thought categories.[38]

Even in the New Testament, however, the early Christians spoke of Jesus as if he were not only *a* possible way to learn the meaning of human life, and thereby to become reconciled with God, but they felt that in comparison with all other possibilities, he was so vastly far in advance, so radically better than the others, that they spoke of him in absolute language. Or at least they did so at times. Again, it becomes apparent that they were speaking in hyperbolic terms—just as when Jesus spoke of plucking out an eye that was a source of scandal. No one understood him to mean a physical destruction of one's eye. It was a metaphorical way of communicating a profoundly important religious message. The central notions and insights that Jesus was communicating—those of love of God and love of neighbor as being the two greatest commandments—were not exclusively his, but rather were the central pillars not only of the ancient Israelite religion, but also quite specifically those of Pharisaic Judaism. Then one might ask, What about other great religious leaders in the history of humankind? For example, are not many of the insights found in the core teachings of the fathers of rabbinic Judaism very helpful to all persons in leading them to understand more fully the meaning of human life—that is, to "be reconciled to God"? Cannot similar things be said of the incredibly beautiful teachings of Moses, Muhammad, Gautama the Buddha, and others? One would have to say, yes.

Nevertheless, Christians are those who are persuaded that in Jesus of Nazareth one finds the full explanation, the living out of the meaning of life—a reconciliation with God. They claim that all human beings in fact *could* find the meaning of life through Jesus of Nazareth. Therefore they make a universal claim that Jesus of Nazareth provides salvation for all human beings—that is, he provides a way to "be reconciled with God" for all human beings. However, at the same time, one must also recognize that not all human beings *in fact* have been, are, or will be in a position to receive this insight, to be "reconciled with God through Christ." They may, in fact, have other paths by which they come to this insight, this "reconciliation."

But what, then, of the claim of the early Christians about the universal salvific significance of Jesus Christ? Could it not be understood to be a *potentially* universal salvific significance? The insights and exemplification of how to live an authentic human life in a proper relationship to God given by Jesus are believed by Christians in fact to be the true way to be fully human, to be in a right relationship to God, the ultimate meaning of life. But is it not possible that there could be other ways in which to express these insights, not only in terms of ideas, teachings, and stories, but also in various practices, patterns of social relationship, and the like? That would mean there would be all sorts of ways of teaching and passing on these profound insights into the meaning of life. These would then coalesce around certain outstanding teachers, and form various social patterns or structures, which we call religions or ideologies. This is not to say, of course, that everything taught and practiced in every religion or ideology is necessarily authentically human, authentically a "reconciliation of the world with God," as Christians believe they find in Jesus. This is not any more likely than that everything Christians have taught and practiced in the past two thousand years has been authentic in its expression of the meaning of life, has been in fact true to the insights and example given by Jesus.

There are a number of other considerations that lead to the same conclusions. For example, it should be noted that "christological statements should be regarded as belonging not to the language of philosophy, science or dogmatics, but rather to the language of confession and testimony."[39] Or to use the terminology of Krister Stendahl, they are in "religious language . . . love language, caressing language."[40] One can attempt to translate love language into philosophical language, poetry into prose (though there will be an inevitable loss), but it would be a gross error and distortion to treat love language or poetry as if it were actually philosophical prose. That has happened too often in Christianity (and other religions as well?), with the all too frequent result that the message is distorted, and even destroyed; that has been especially true of the statements of the first followers of Rabbi Jesus.[41]

Furthermore, as noted, the ancient world lived with the mentality of classicist culture where the view of truth was static, absolute, exclusively either-or, as was outlined above. Hence, if they believed something about Jesus was true, it therefore *had* to be unchangeable, absolute, exclusive, for that was the nature of truth, as they understood it. But with the paradigm or model shift in the modern critical worldview to the historical, praxis, perspectival, interpretive views of truth, critical Christians are now able to, *must,* affirm the salvific, "reconciling," truth about Jesus—what he thought, taught, and wrought—without being absolutistic and exclusivistic. Paul Knitter writes:

Certainly the early Christians were aware that there were many truth claims in the world around them. For the most part, however, they felt that if any one of these claims really were true, it had to either conquer or absorb the others. That is what truth did. Unavoidably, then, when they encountered the overwhelming truth of Jesus, they would *have* to describe it as the only or the final truth. In today's world of historical consciousness, however, coupled with a new experience of pluralism it seems possible for Christians to feel and announce the saving truth about Jesus and his message without the requirements of classicist culture— that is, without having to insist that Jesus' truth is either exclusive or inclusive of all other truth.[42]

It must be remembered that the world of the Way (*hodos,* which was how the first Christians named themselves, according to the Acts of the Apostles) of Rabbi Jesus was a world of Jewish eschatological apocalypticism: the end of the world was imminent, as was also the "second coming." The reign of God that Jesus preached was about to be fulfilled through him. As a result, one of the earliest community reflections on the meaning of Jesus was a "Maranatha christology."[43] Hence, there could have been no thought at all about the possibility of other saviors; there was no time for them: "Quick, get ready now!" But when the final end of this world by its transformation into the reign of God through the second coming of Jesus did not happen, the finality of the *end-time* was shifted to the *center* of history, as has been analyzed by Rosemary Ruether.[44] Jesus as the *final,* eschatological prophet was simply moved to be the *center* of history: a shift from an apocalyptic to a classicist worldview. Again, with the passing of both of these worldviews, the saving significance of Jesus can, must, be expressed without its absolutistic and exclusivistic "protective coloring."

CONCLUSIONS

If there is any validity in the remarks I have been making, it should be apparent that Christians need not, should not, take a condemnatory attitude toward non-Christians, particularly those who are adherents of other religions or ideologies, for fear that they would be disloyal to their Christian commitment. Rather, they would be disloyal to their Christian commitment (that is, *effectively* to preach the good news to today's, critical, world—that is, in a language that is dynamic and dialogic) if they did not seek to recognize the same truths, the same insights, wherever they find them. This immediately implies that Christians ought to take a stance not of debate, but rather of dialogue with non-Christians. In this dialogue they will doubtless learn that there are many valuable insights in their own Christian tradition that they had overlooked, or suppressed, or distorted, and they can be brought to this rediscovery of their own treasures through finding those very same insights held forth in another religion or ideology in exemplary fashion.

Moreover, is it not also possible that they will discover in another religious, ideological tradition insights that in fact do not seem to have been expressed in their own Christian tradition? If they can resist the temptation to be doctrinaire and triumphalistic, they will have to say yes, it is possible; we can hope to gain truly new insights into the meaning of life.

What does this do to the Christian notion that Jesus Christ is somehow the fullness of what it means to be human? For one thing, it would be said that presumably none of the new insights gathered would in fact run contrary to what had already been exemplified ("revealed," to use theological language, "from above") in Jesus Christ. Further, one can speak of a development, an unfolding, an evolution. One can take the language of a Teilhard de Chardin and speak of moving from the Alpha to the Omega point. Is it not the case that even the early Christians spoke of *another* coming of the Christ? Surely another coming is not going to be identical with the first coming. If it were, it would not be another coming; it would be the first coming. There will of course be profound similarities, but if it is to be another, then there must also be some differences. Might not these "new insights" constitute part of these differences? If in fact Christians come to be persuaded that Muhammad and Marx, for example, provided some "new insights," might they not be seen as part of the "other coming"? Does the second coming of Christ have to be seen and understood only in terms of being at a specific time at the end of history? Obviously that is not necessary, for here clearly we are again dealing with metaphorical, hyperbolic, poetic, mythic language. The *eschaton* is clearly beyond our everyday experience. However, cannot events within history be taken to be stages toward, even constitutive elements leading to, that *eschaton,* that Omega point, to again use Teilhardian language? If so, then there need be no opposition ultimately between the Christian understanding of how the world is "reconciled to God through Christ" and how many persons will in fact experience this reconciliation to God, this learning of the ultimate meaning of human life, through means other than Jesus Christ.

This is my initial statement in the dialogue. I am persuaded that my theological reflection here is in integral touch with the source of my Christian faith on this matter—in fact, I believe that it is in much closer touch than many other attempted interpretations have been for a very long time. I of course need to be in dialogue with my fellow Christians on this contention—the intrareligious dialogue dimension. I also hope that in this reflection I have moved toward the shaping of an "ecumenical Esperanto" in which modern critical thinkers— Jews, Muslims, Hindus, Buddhists, humanists, Marxists, and others—will be able to say that they can "understand" the insights I am struggling to express and that they somehow feel included in those concepts, terms, and images. If I have succeeded at all, regardless of the modifications that may be necessary as a result of subsequent dialogue, we will have taken one step toward the forging of a "universal theology of religion-ideology."

It is within this matrix of interreligious, interideological dialogue that future creative "theologizing" will have to take place.[45] Come, let us dialogue.

NOTES

1. *Mirari Vos,* 1832, quoted in Leonard Swidler, *Freedom in the Church* (Dayton: Pflaum, 1969), p. 47.

2. *Ecclesiam Suam,* no. 9; italics added.

3. Secretariat for Unbelievers, *Humanae Personae Dignitatem,* printed in full in Austin Flannery, *Vatican Council II* (Collegeville, Minn.: Liturgical Press, 1975), pp. 1003, 1007.

4. For a fuller analysis of the notion of the paradigm shift as it applies to theology, see Hans Küng's paper "Paradigm Change in Theology," prepared for the international ecumenical symposium "Ein neues Paradigma von Theologie?" held in Tübingen, May 23–26, 1983.

5. Paul Knitter, *No Other Name?* (Maryknoll, N.Y.: Orbis, 1985), p. 219.

6. See Raimundo Panikkar, *The Intrareligious Dialogue* (New York: Paulist Press, 1978), p. 30.

7. Wilfred Cantwell Smith, *Toward a World Theology* (Philadelphia: Westminster, 1981), p. 60.

8. Panikkar, *Intrareligious Dialogue,* p. 50.

9. Raimundo Panikkar, "Faith and Belief: A Multireligious Experience," *Anglican Theological Review,* 53 (1971) 220.

10. John S. Dunne, *The Way of All the Earth* (New York: Macmillan, 1972), p. ix. Another creative approach might be by way of Ira Progoff's "process mediation."

11. Ibid., p. 53. For further use of the technique of "passing over" by John Dunne, see his *A Search for God in Time and Memory* (University of Notre Dame Press, 1977); *The City of the Gods* (University of Notre Dame Press, 1978).

12. Knitter, *No Other Name?* p. 215.

13. Ibid.

14. David Tracy, *The Analogical Imagination* (New York: Crossroad, 1981), p. 451.

15. Cf. Walter E. Conn, *Conscience: Development and Transcendence* (Birmingham, Ala.: Religious Education Press, 1981), pp. 79ff.

16. David Tracy, *Blessed Rage for Order* (New York: Seabury, 1979), p. 98.

17. See above, p. 12.

18. The same notion of the contemporary need of a new consciousness in both intra- and inter-religious, interideological dialogue was expressed by Ewert Cousins when speaking of Raimundo Panikkar as a pioneer in its formation: "When Christian consciousness opens to global consciousness, a new type of systematic theology can be born. This new theology calls for a new kind of theologian with a new type of consciousness—a multi-dimensional, cross-cultural consciousness characteristic of mutational man. I believe that Raimundo Panikkar is such a new theologian and that he has already begun to develop such a Christian systematic theology" (Ewert Cousins, "Raimundo Panikkar and the Christian Systematic Theology of the Future," *Cross Currents* [Summer 1979] 146).

19. Vatican II, *Decree on Ecumenism,* no. 9; italics added.

20. *Spiritus Domini,* 1970, nos. 64 and 79, in Flannery, *Vatican II,* pp. 515, 526.

21. Knitter, *No Other Name?* p. 222.

22. Johannes Schwartländer, ed., *Modernes Freiheitsethos und christlicher Glaube* (Munich/Mainz: Kaiser/Grünewald, 1981), p. 11.

23. See Franz Böckle, "Theonome Autonomie in der Begründung der Menschenrechte," ibid., p. 306.

24. Homer A. Jack, ed., *Religion for Peace* (New Delhi: Gandhi Peace Foundation, 1973), p. ix.

25. This is true of Küng, Schillebeeckx and many other prominent Catholic and Protestant theologians; see Leonard Swidler, ed., *Consensus In Theology?* (Philadelphia: Westminster, 1980). Hans Küng: "And for the Catholic Christian too this criterion can be nothing but the Christian message, the *Gospel* in its ultimate concrete form, *Jesus Christ himself,* who for the Church and—despite all assertions to the contrary—also for me is the Son and Word of God. He is and remains the norm in the light of which every ecclesiastical authority—which is not disputed—must be judged: the norm by which the theologian must be tested and in the light of which s/he must continually justify her/himself in the spirit of self-criticism and true humility" (p. 163).

26. Edward Schillebeeckx, in a lecture upon his formal retirement from the University of Nijmegen, Feb. 19, 1983.

27. Joseph G. Kelly, "Lucan Christology and the Jewish-Christian Dialogue," *Journal of Ecumenical Studies,* 21/4 (Fall 1984) 693, 704, 708.

28. Quite some time after writing the first draft of this section I came across very strong corroboration in the writings of two Catholic theologians, Bernard Lonergan and Walter E. Conn. In speaking about conversion, first of all in the intellectual sphere, Conn—here following Lonergan—writes that "its really crucial significance is found in the kind of personal, existential self-appropriation that we have been discussing, the appropriation of oneself as a free, responsible, and self-constituting originator of value, who in one's own self-transcending judgments and choices is the criterion, of the real and the truly good" (Walter E. Conn, *Conscience: Development and Self-Transcendence* [Birmingham, Ala.: Religious Education Press, 1981], p. 192). Elsewhere, Conn—also picking up on the paradigm shift in the radical involvement of the thinker in truth statements discussed above—writes of "the possibility of cognitive conversion: the critical recognition of the constitutive and normative role of one's own judgment in knowing reality and therefore value. A person who experiences such critical understanding of self as knower ceases to look beyond the self somewhere 'out there' for a criterion of the real or the valuable. For cognitive conversion consists precisely in discovering that criterion in one's own realistic judgment" (Walter E. Conn, "Conversion: A Developmental Perspective," *Cross Currents* [Fall 1982], pp. 325f.). Lonergan, speaking of the move from intellectual to moral conversion, wrote: "Moral conversion goes beyond the value, truth, to values generally. It promotes the subject from cognitional to moral self-transcendence. It sets him on a new, existential level of consciousness and establishes him as an originating value" (Bernard Lonergan, *Method in Theology* [New York: Herder and Herder, 1972], p. 241). The notion of "radical openness" is also confirmed by Conn: "It is right that each person should be able to take a stand on his or her own conscience, uncoerced by external force. But everyone who does so should also recognize that appeals to conscience do not automatically or necessarily make one right, that some consciences are more authentic than others, and that one's commitment to his or her 'conscience' must always remain critical. Sincerity to what one feels deeply about, or spontaneously 'thinks best,' in other words, is not enough. Sincerity must be fully and continually self-critical if it is to be authentic. For such self-criticism, of course, a radical openness to other viewpoints is a prerequisite; and such openness seems to have its necessary condition in a deep sense of humility" (*Conscience,* p. 207).

29. The work of the first three men is admirably summed up in James Fowler, *Stages of Faith* (New York: Harper & Row, 1981).

30. The work of Kohlberg is to some extent challenged by his co-worker Carol Gilligan with her argument that he did not take women into account in his surveys. See Carol Gilligan, *In a Different Voice* (Cambridge: Harvard University Press, 1982). However, that problem does not arise in the work of Fowler, for he interviewed fifty-fifty women and men.

31. Lawrence Kohlberg and Carol Gilligan, "The Adolescent as a Philosopher: The Discovery of the Self in a Postconventional World," *Daedalus,* 100 (Fall 1971) 1072.

32. Fowler, *Stages of Faith,* pp. 186f.

33. Bernard Lonergan, *Collection,* F. E. Crowe, ed. (New York: Herder and Herder, 1967), p. 254.

34. Fowler, *Stages of Faith,* p. 107.

35. The careful word studies by Friedrich Büchsel in Gerhard Kittel, ed., *Theological Dictionary of the New Testament* (Grand Rapids: Eerdmans, 1964), I, pp. 254ff., and by other scholars in various reference works, really do not resolve the problem as I have posed it. It is clear from these studies that the word used by Paul (and he is only one who uses it in the New Testament), *katallassein,* and its variant *katallagēnai,* fundamentally means to change, and in this case to change the relationship between God and humanity in a positive direction—that is, to reconcile. *Theòs ēn en Christō kósmon katallássōn heautō* is how Paul put it in 2 Cor. 5:19, and Jerome translated it: *Deus erat in Christo mundum reconcilians sibi.* Of course the very notion of reconciliation in whatever language is perforce on the transphysical, "metaphorical" plane; it is not used to describe material, physical things, but rather the relationship between beings on the mental or psychological level. The word studies tend not to point out that obvious fact—perhaps because it is such an obvious given. But when the theologians go to work on the meaning of Paul's statements, they often seem to be oblivious of this fact.

36. See Joseph A. Fitzmyer, "Jesus the Lord," *Chicago Studies,* 17 (1978) 91.

37. It is ironic that two Christian scholars, one a moderate Protestant and the other a moderate Catholic, should both use modern critical analysis—here mainly audience criticism (i.e., learning how the original audience would have understood words and phrases used so as to determine their meanings as intended by the New Testament authors)—to arrive at slightly differing conclusions, which when taken together document solidly that all the New Testament writers were using language metaphorically when speaking of Jesus in divinizing terms. The first, James D. G. Dunn, argues that this was the case everywhere, except in some Johannine texts—specifically excluding the Pauline texts (*Christology in the Making* [Philadelphia: Westminster, 1980], pp. 210ff.). The second, Edward Schillebeeckx, argued that this was the same everywhere, except in some Pauline texts—specifically excluding the Johannine texts (*Jesus* [New York: Seabury, 1979], pp. 556ff.).

38. There are of course many issues that will need to be aired and resolved at this point; Christian scholars need to get on with this vital task. One of the objections likely to be raised by traditionalists is that this description of the meaning of Jesus Christ—christology—is simply that of nineteenth-century liberal Protestantism. First of all, it is precisely the traditionalists who should know that merely pointing out that something has been said before does not thereby make it false. Moreover, given the huge advances in the scriptural sciences in the past hundred years, despite surface similarities, the differences between the two positions will also be significant. As to the problem of immutably fixing the interpretation of the scriptural gospel message in ontological language in the fourth and fifth centuries in Hellenistic Christianity, it should be remembered that—assuming that my argument, and that of many other scholars, is

correct—the radical shift between metaphorical and metaphysical language was made once between the first and the fourth centuries, between the Semitic and Hellenistic milieux. *Ab esse ad posse*—if it happened, it is possible. Put otherwise: if it happened once, why not twice, or more times?

A solemn decree from an ecumenical council can never be changed? Compare the following statements from two councils recognized to be fully ecumenical by the Roman Catholic Church: The sixteenth ecumenical council, Constance (1414–1418): "This synod declares first that, being legitimately convoked in the Holy Spirit, forming a general council, and representing the universal Church, it has immediate power from Christ, which every state and dignity, even if it be the papal dignity, must obey in what concerns faith, the eradication of the mentioned schism [there were three popes at that time, the so-called Western Schism], and the reformation of the said Church in head and members. Likewise, it declares that whoever of whatever condition, state, dignity, even the papal one, refuses persistently to obey the mandate, statutes, and orders of pre-scripts of this sacred synod and of any other general council legitimately convened, above set out, or what pertains to them as done or to be done, will be penalized and duly punished with recourse if necessary to other means of law." Vatican Council I (1870) on the other hand stated: "All the faithful of Christ are bound to believe that the holy apostolic See and the Roman pontiffs have primacy over the whole world . . . that the judgment of the apostolic See, whose authority has no superior, can be reviewed by none; and that no one is allowed to judge its judgments. Those, therefore, stray from the straight way of truth who affirm that it is lawful to appeal from the judgments of the Roman pontiffs to an ecumenical council—as to an authority superior to the Roman pontiff" (quoted in Leonard Swidler, *Freedom in the Church* [Dayton: Pflaum, 1969], pp. 92f.). Again, if it happened once, it can happen again.

39. Frances Young, "A Cloud of Witnesses," in: John Hick, ed., *The Myth of God Incarnate* (Philadelphia: Westminster, 1977), p. 13.

40. Krister Stendahl, "Notes for Three Bible Studies," in: Gerald Anderson and Thomas Stransky, eds., *Christ's Lordship and Religious Pluralism* (Maryknoll, N.Y.: Orbis, 1981), pp. 14f.

41. Paul Knitter has a helpful comment on the issue of the kind of language used and the understanding of its truth content: "This is not to imply that there was no metaphysical truth in what the early Christians said or that they were conscious of this distinction between metaphysical and confessional language. If they could have made such a distinction, they most likely would have said that the cognitive or metaphysical content of their confessional language was that there was no one else like Jesus. I am suggesting that given the nature of their language, such metaphysical claims are not intrinsic to that language. Today, Christians can hear and use the same language with different metaphysical content" (*No Other Name?* p. 261).

42. Ibid.

43. See Schillebeeckx, *Jesus,* pp. 405ff.

44. Rosemary Ruether, *To Change the World* (New York: Crossroad, 1981).

45. Paul Knitter writes: "If Christians, trusting God and respecting the faith of others, engage in this new encounter with other traditions, they can expect to witness a growth or evolution such as Christianity has not experienced since its first centuries. This growth will paradoxically both preserve the identity of Christianity and at the same time transform it. Such paradox is no mystery; we are acquainted with it in our own personal lives as well as in nature" (*No Other Name?* p. 230).

I.

Theology and the World's Religious History

WILFRED CANTWELL SMITH

"A UNIVERSAL THEOLOGY OF RELIGION"

Professor Swidler, implicitly by organizing this conference, explicitly in its title and in his preconference paper, has set forth a vision of a new day dawning for the theological world. That vision is being seen by a minority of Christians; we are perhaps a small minority but a growing one. Some see it only dimly, or simply feel that it is, or ought to be, coming.

The important task is that the vision be articulated, and then refined and even corrected, by that even smaller minority who can clarify the vision and thereby facilitate the coming of that new day. My own sense is that this may prove more difficult, and meet more resistance, than Professor Swidler acknowledges. The arguments in favor, several of which he forcefully enunciates, are in danger of being opposed with vigor by those who think and feel in inherited and established ways, seemingly threatened by radical displacement. Whether a new style of Christian theology will prevail, I do not know. Our task at this conference is to delineate it and to proffer reasons for it. My own contribution to this corporate endeavor is to propose here a new basis for theological thinking, on the grounds that it promises to lead to truer, and as well to a more reverential, awareness. I am not unaware, however, that to suggest a different foundation for the theological task is indeed radical. "A Universal Theology of Religion," toward which this conference explicitly

---

Some editorial conventions used throughout the rest of this volume are not used by Professor Smith, for his own good reasons.—ED.

invites us to move, *is* a radical new idea. It can be attained, I am suggesting, by adopting a rather new starting point.

Nonetheless, what I proffer turns out to be more in line with earlier Christian outlooks than are more recent and now accepted ones. It is in some ways more continuous with the Church's past tradition than with—or than are some—current modes.

THEOLOGY: SPEAKING THE TRUTH ABOUT GOD

Theology, several voices these days are telling us, is "talk about God." Further, the modern mood wishes us cheerily to "do theology," rather than in more traditional style to study it or to think about it. I myself hesitate about today's colloquializing that would reduce theology to "God talk".

First, there has been on earth virtually no people large or small that has not talked about God; yet relatively few have come up with theologies. When I say that peoples have spoken of God, of course I recognize that that is hasty. If they spoke some language other than English, then naturally they used some other term: more, or often less, closely equivalent to that English word. If they perceived the universe through some conceptual scheme other than the theist, then naturally they used some other concept, less or more closely counterpart. I happen to find quite fascinating the question of convergences and divergences among languages, and among the words within them that may be translated (but how loosely?—a teasing question) as "God"; and of convergences and divergences among worldviews; and in these last, of the concepts within them that play the role that the concept "God" plays in theist conceptualizations. (We have as yet no, or only barely incipient, translations among worldviews.) Also I take more seriously than do some the changes in meaning of a single term, as a language, and the society to whom it mediates the world, develop over time.

In Sanskrit, for instance, and therefore in Hindu apprehensions of the universe, there are two different words, one neuter, one masculine (*Brahman* and *Īsvara,* respectively) for the Godhead beyond God, the impersonal absolute, on the one hand, and on the other hand for the personal supreme God, to whom theists consciously devote themselves; and still another word for The Goddess. Again, in modern English there is a question as to whether God should be referred to as He, She, or It. Yet in so nearby a language as French, and therefore for the many Christians and Jews who think in it—and the same is true of Hebrew; and for Muslims, Arabic—there is no immediate distinction between "He" and "It" in speaking about God, or about anything else. In Persian or Chinese there is no distinction between "He" and "She." If we think of differences over time rather than over space, we might note that some of us now are more at ease with the concept "transcendence," in our day the term "God" having shifted for many to designating a particularist concept—that of theists—rather than a cosmic reference. In this paper, and otherwise, I still use the word "God." If there be readers who do not like or understand it (yet in the modern world we all have to understand each other's usage of terms of cosmic import, whether we like them or not), I would ask that such persons substitute for the term "God" in my presentation something like "transcendent reality," or everything that one recognizes as valuable, plus the transcendence and coherence of their value, or ultimate truth and beauty and goodness and various other such things.

In any case, the range of things that have been said about the divine, and the range of communities that have said them, are vast. In contrast, the range of theologies is fairly limited. The fact is that in past history here on earth, theology has been the prerogative of relatively few of the world's religious communities. Greece, India, and China are the three countries on earth that have produced philosophies, more or less simultaneously. Hindu religious thought has been more or less integrated with Indian philosophy; Buddhist thought, greatly influenced by it, and by Chinese; and Christian theology is clearly a consequence historically of the contribution to the Church of Greek. In passing, one may observe that Islamic and Jewish theology have been strong or peripheral in their respective communities to the varying extent to which Muslim or Jewish thinkers have been influenced by Greek philosophy directly—participating in its on-going tradition; or in the Jewish case, have been influenced indirectly through Islamic and recently Christian thought. Christian theology has been influenced also indirectly, by Islamic and Jewish instances, especially in the salient case of the thirteenth century.

I distinguish, then, between theology, and mere talk about God. I do so not only because theology is systematic and rigorous, as is the philosophy with which it has been associated. A Ramanuja's theology can be distinguished from various exuberant Hindu mythologies and from village folklore, or an Aquinas's from, say, a Pacific cargo cult ideology, by its precision, comprehensive coherence, and self-critical sophistication. There is more to my point, however, than that theology is rational talk about God, important though that be; rational in the most rigorous sense of the term. Theology is as much more than talk about God as logic is more than talk in general. "Logic" has to do not with how people speak, simply, but how they should speak, rationally: the concept formulates Reason as the ideal for reasoning, to which actual reasoning by human beings approximates when it is functioning well. The Greek affirmation, after all, is that the universe is intelligible; put the other way round, that the human intellect is capable of apprehending the truth of the world; put mediatingly, that the universe is rational and that humankind (*ho anthrōpos*) is rational, that through his and her reason man participates in the ultimate order of things. To use more incarnationalist language: that Reason, the ultimate order of the universe, is to some degree finitely embodied in human beings.

Theology, if we may characterize it succinctly, and imperiously, is true talk about God. Again, the same point may be made by leaning on the Palestinian rather than on the Greek side of our double heritage: by emphasizing the first component of the concept "theology" rather than the second, stressing the first two syllables as well as the last two. If what we say of God is not true, then it is not of God that we are talking.

Theology is speaking the truth about God.

Admittedly, I am enough of a neo-Platonist that I would say as much of all human discourse—about anything whatever. To talk is, fundamentally, to speak the truth. This is why language is so awesome a matter; and, I suppose, why Trappists take a vow of silence. No doubt, people can tell lies; but that is to abuse the human capacity for speech. There is the old argument that counterfeit money is necessarily parasitic upon authentic. Similarly, there could be no lies, if talk were not inherently, and even normally, of truth. No doubt, less damnably, we can inadvertently be mistaken in what we think and therefore say. Yet if we speak what is not true, however well-meaningly, we have failed. All verbalized error is a misuse of speech.

To talk at all is to be under a formidable obligation to speak the truth.

If this seems too austere a doctrine in general, too little tolerant of whimsy and idle chatter, yet surely one will agree that frivolous talk about God is hardly acceptable; and is not theology. My point, simply—yet that "simply" is inapt— is this: that we must approach theology with reverence and with awe. To say something about God that is not the case, is to blaspheme!

How, then, dare any of us "do theology"? With trepidation, at best; and I, preferring to resist the novel terminology of that glib phrase, and thinking of theology as "true talk about God," see even a Thomas Aquinas or a Calvin as attempting a theology, rather. This last way of speaking will enable us to recognize that all attempts at it are inadequate; and yet will enable us to recognize too that some come off as less inadequate than do others. Perhaps especially, some attempts are less inadequate than are others for our particular moment. It is this latter recognition that justifies our continuing at the endeavor—so that one proceeds *simul justus et peccator.*

This perspective, also, gives dignity to the erstwhile fashion of *studying* theology before "doing" theology: becoming familiar with, and taking seriously, the least inadequate among the attempts of human beings in past circumstances, and reflecting upon those, as our basis for our own endeavors to speak, however again inadequately, in and for our new situation, the truth about God: endeavors to formulate the closest approximation to it towards which we are able, or are given the grace, to rise.

(That word "approximation," and the passing allusion to Plotinus—one could also mention Ramanuja or the *Yogavisista;* some would allude to Hegel—must suffice for the philosophic issue, not directly our topic today, of how one handles the question of intellectual pluralism without falling into one or other of nihilism, or arbitrariness, or logical contradiction. The less lively their sense of immanental transcendence, the more troublesome some moderns seem to find this relativism issue.)

Trepidation is in order; or at least, will explain why I waited till my mid-sixties to publish my first book with the word "theology" in the title. And even in that recent work, the word "towards" is to be stressed, as well as "world."

That work is a revision of a lecture series that I agreed to give, agreed to tackle the subject, only after initially declining, and then being pressed to do so. Similarly, it is with some hesitation that I take this opportunity to place before you some ideas in the theological realm to which my historical studies have gradually pushed me.

HISTORY OF ALL RELIGION: TRUE BASIS FOR THEOLOGY

For I do have a couple of, I suppose, quite fundamental suggestions to submit to the theological world—for criticism: one proposal, basically; but it ramifies. I am a student of history; and have found myself with theological dimensions to the results to which my historical awareness was leading. This was so already twenty-some years ago, with my *Meaning and End of Religion;* and has become more conspicuous, perhaps, with my recent trilogy (I call it so; the three volumes are formally quite distinct, but have converging theological impingement, explicit in the last). For I have come to feel—dare I say: I have come to see—that the true historian and the true theologian are one and the same. No doubt, I am a historian of *religion;* yet human history is essentially the history of religion. And the history of religion, my studies have increasingly pushed me to hold, is the one true basis for theology.

This, indeed, is my fundamental submission—in principle quite simple, although it seem radical. (Doubtless it will appear more radical at first blush and from a distance than it will prove, once understood.) Perhaps, since I take history seriously, we should rephrase my point thus: that in the next phase of world thought, the basis for theology must now be the history of religion. To speak truly about God means henceforth to interpret accurately the history of human religious life on earth.

Since my contention is that the true historian of religion and the authentic theologian are in the final analysis identical—that a true understanding of the history of religion, and theology, which means true theology, converge— therefore to fellow historians my presentation would take the form of showing that to improve our historical studies, we must perceive more fully and more exactly the transcendent component in human life across the centuries. It is part of the task of Religion departments in Arts faculties to enhance intellectual awareness by the academic, rational mind of the transcendent dimensions of human affairs. Since those dimensions are there, it is an intellectual error not to see them—as I argued in my Presidential Address to the American Academy of Religion this past winter. Yet this is an error that has often been made in Western academia since the Enlightenment. It is, frankly, preposterous to imagine that anyone insensitive to the presence of God can understand or interpret human history in any but drastically inadequate ways, given the extent to which human lives have been lived in that presence. Human beings have acted the way that they have acted, have been the persons that they have been, in the light of many other and finally less important, more mundane, reasons; but also, most of them quite consciously, also in the light of this. To fail to recognize the impingement of economic factors on human history would be obtuse; no less obtuse is to fail to recognize the impingement of transcendence.

I solicit your help in this enterprise: the theologian must enable the historian to be a better historian, and vice versa. If it be the case that secular historians are on the whole more dogmatic these days than are theologians—that the theological enterprise is more open to new ideas, however radical-seeming, provided that they be rationally persuasive, than are our secular academic friends, except perhaps among the young—then perhaps my task here in *this* group is the easier. In any case, it is today my task: to make plausible that the new foundation for theology must become the history of religion.

In favor of this position one argument could be that other bases are beginning, it would seem, to crumble. Some observers report themselves rather apalled at the disarray of much present-day theological activity. In the Christian case, neither the Bible nor the traditional doctrines of the Church, nor current philosophic movements, nor the latest social or intellectual fashions, seem sufficient to provide a stable basis for a theological construct firm enough to bear the weight that the culture at large, let alone the religiously committed themselves, would like to place upon it.

I myself do not find this particular argument appealing; a more positive, and more intrinsically theological, support for the new proposal is requisite. The positive pragmatic argument is, however, both interesting in itself, and corroboratingly significant.

That positive argument is this: that many of the outstanding theoretical problems of the day do seem to be resolved in the history-of-religion orientation. The Church does indeed sorely need, and an understanding of the worldwide history of religion can indeed provide, an intellectually strong, rationally coherent, empirically based, inductively argued, logically persuasive, transcendentally adequate, integrative theory to do justice to our faith and to our work: to what we know with our hearts and what we know with our minds, at their best.

In discussions on the reputed difference between Theology and what is called "Religious Studies," a remark has at times been heard to the effect that that difference is simple: to be in theology is to be close-minded, to be in the "academic" side is to be open-minded. What those who voice such a view presumably think of as a theologian is not someone endeavoring to ascertain what can truly be said about God, but someone who rather is defending or seeking to perpetuate what others have said (others in his or her own particular community). It is alas historically (and dolefully) the case that there have been of late people like that; but it is gratuitous to think of them as theologians. Apologists, perhaps; pitiable, certainly. No significant Christian (or for that matter Muslim or other) theologian of any stature over preceding centuries has ever been of that type. Theologians of repute have been men or women of high intelligence who have struggled to express in words the best understanding of the divine to which they could manage to rise, using the most promising data available to them and integrating those data sincerely with their own life experience and with whatever else they knew of the world. I am simply suggesting not only that what else we know is today of course new, but also that we can and must use a different and wider range of data: namely, those available to us from the whole history of humankind's religious and spiritual life. Our own group's certainly; but all other communities', too.

Any other starting-point for the journey of one's mind towards a true theology inevitably omits something. Most starting-points omit much. The history of religion omits nothing. More fully, mine is a double thesis: that the history of religion omits nothing germane to theology, and includes nothing not germane. This second point might seem obvious, in that nothing that exists is irrelevant to God, nor God to it; so that astronomy, economics, marine biology, a study of human wickedness, and all, deal with matters that pertain, less or more, to a proper human understanding of the divine. Yet the student of the history of religion subsumes all this, partly because all these other matters have impinged upon it, partly because the audience to whom the modern historian must make religious life intelligible knows about them, but also since insofar as any human being has discerned the relevance of any matter to an understanding of Ultimate Truth, that discernment has become part of the history of religion. That the history of religious communities other than Christian is irrelevant to theology, or at least to what is called Christian theology, is difficult for an intelligent sensitive person to hold today, but it has been held in the past (or: non-Muslim, to Islamic theology). It seems to me palpably false, yet it may require some attention, and we shall return to it.

THREE ARGUMENTS FOR THE THESIS

First, however, the contention that the history of religion omits nothing.

In the first place, let me make the perhaps not totally obvious point, that in "history of religion" I include—(may I add, "of course"?)—the history of the Christian Church, and of Christian thought. That history, that thought, are of course relevant for theology; and they are not omitted. The situation that has arisen whereby the phrase "history of religion" or "comparative religion" connotes to some ears, or has denoted in some theological colleges and seminaries, everything but the Christian, is laughably anomalous—historically understandable, but rationally quite indefensible. What used to be called Church history is becoming or must become the Christian sector in the world history of religion.

Secondly, a critic might imagine that our thesis—that the grounds for an attempted theology must be neither less nor more than an understanding of the history of religion—must omit what God is *in se,* even if it include all God's relations to humankind. There are two answers to this objection. The first is the classical Christian, Buddhist, Hindu, Islamic, and other contention that this is true of all theological statements whatever. Thomas Aquinas and many another have affirmed that God *sicut est in se* is ultimately beyond the capacity of the human mind to apprehend, and of human language to convey. On this count, then, a theology attempted on a history-of-religion base would be no worse off than on any other. I do not rest my case there, however, cogent though this consideration seem. For I am much impressed by the capacity of the human mind to know that there is more to anything than it knows. History shows that we human beings are quite capable of postulating, and meaningfully using, self-transcending concepts, even though the mystery of this may have escaped some latter-day thinkers. Rather, my argument would take a form of insisting that the recognition of God as beyond our comprehension, if not our apprehension, is historically evidenced. It is an historical fact that the most intelligent human beings on earth who have attempted theology have with virtual unanimity averred that God transcends our intellectual grasp, and our theological precisioning. The fact that they have so averred is one of the salient data of the history of religion; and to understand it in its full import, and to take it seriously, are incumbent upon the historian who takes his or her history responsibly.

It is also the case that human history too cannot be fully understood. We shall be returning to this point. Every human being, ourselves and others, is beyond our full comprehension, let alone all human beings together in their and our course through time across this globe. History transcends our intellectual grasp, as does God. Yet ideally, if we could know the former fully, we should know the latter, at least as fully as is humanly conceivable. This last is, in fact, a tautology.

Thirdly, those who might be inclined to resist our thesis, that history is now the proper basis for any theological attempt, may feel so inclined because they discriminate between history and revelation, as sources of theological knowledge. The discrimination is vacuous, I reply. Not only is the concept of revelation demonstrably historical: a competent historian can trace its emergence and rise, its spread, its development, its many forms, its recent peregrinations, and its contemporary doldrums and re-invigorations—all this both within the Church and elsewhere. The historian can trace, too, the interrelations among Christian and other revelation concepts; interrelations rather subtly complex, it turns out. Beyond this, however, is the still more weighty fact, that apart from the concept of revelation, revelation itself, or revelations themselves, insofar as we use that term to interpret to ourselves what it conceptualizes, has or have occurred either within history or not at all. God has revealed Himself (Herself, Itself) in history, or else has not revealed Himself (. . .) at all. If the Qur'ān is the Word of God, it is the Word of God in human history. (Indeed it is not by studying the Qur'ān itself, but by studying religious history, that a non-Muslim comes to see that and how it has served God as His Word.)

I carry this point further than do many, contending that revelation must be recognized as a bilateral concept: there can be no revelation unless it be to somebody; and that means, to somebody at a particular time and place. Many have said, and say, that God has revealed Himself in Jesus Christ; this is at best a short-hand way of saying that He has revealed Himself in Christ to you or to me, in the twentieth century, and/or to St. Augustine in the fourth or fifth, and/or to a village grandmother in fourteenth-century Sweden, either every Sunday morning in church or throughout her life or whatever. To say that the Bhagavad Gītā is or is not a revelation of God is to say that God did or did not speak through it to M. K. Gandhi in India early this century, or to Ramanuja there in the twelfth. And so on. Moreover, only a person who has read and pondered Ramanuja's commentary on that work; or who knows Gandhi's life; or one who has read and pondered Ghazzali's writings set down in the conviction (which he himself, as an enormously intelligent and perceptive person, certainly had) that God spoke to him through the Qur'ān; or who has read and perceptively assessed a Christian's account, whether in words or in deeds, in response to her or his sense of knowing God in or through Jesus Christ—that is, only a sensitive historian—is in a position to have views worth considering, surely, on whether or not God has indeed revealed Himself here and there (or anywhere, or everywhere) through human history.

The question of revelation is an historical question. More specifically, it is a history-of-religion question.

SEEING TRANSCENDENCE IN HISTORY

Fundamentally, I am saying that I do not accept the dichotomy that would polarize history and transcendence. There is a transcendent dimension to human life—so far as I can see, there has always been, from palaeolithic times. Most human beings on earth over the centuries have been aware of this, and have lived their lives less or more vividly, less or more effectively, in terms of it. Leading thinkers among us, in all ages and climes, have articulated the awareness, in a vast variety of ways; and a certain number, on the whole among the most intellectually brilliant, have done so theologically. It is quite evident, as we now look back over the array of these, that whoever has done so has done so in ways pertinent to a particular time and place, and presumably this is quite right and proper. Yet it is also the case that the greatest among them have done so in a way that has in fact, historically, proven enduring; and various articulations have been preserved and cherished for centuries after, and even millennia, not in unvarying static rigidity but rather with dynamic force—although each generation has had to decide, consciously or otherwise, whether to preserve and to extrapolate an earlier articulation or to come up with a new one of its own, usually continuous with what went before, although at some times more starkly innovative than at others.

The history of religion is simply the process of humankind's double involvement in a mundane and simultaneously a transcendent environment. As for instance Rahner has insisted, virtually all human beings have lived with a mundane and a transcendent dimension to their lives. Whether the two environments, or the two dimensions, are radically different, are discontinuous, or constitute an unbroken continuum, or are in fact identical but differently perceived, or are the same perceived with less or more insight—these are questions to which there have been, historically, varying answers. My point at the moment is simply that it does not matter what answer you give to this question, so far as our present thesis is concerned. However you interpret the relation between time and eternity, both are related to the human (have been related to him and her). Human history is the locus of their intersection. Human awareness of God, of the infinite, of the absolute, human conceptions of the non-temporal, all take place within the flow of time. This is what the history of religion has been all about. Whether we see religion as human apprehension of transcendence, or the transcendent's, God's, apprehension of humankind, or any mixture of the two, the process of its on-going history includes all that there ever has been, is, or will be; or, to revert to my earlier wording, it omits nothing pertinent to theology.

It is sometimes said that certain types of Hindu, Buddhist, and Western mystics are not (*lege:* have not been) interested in history. One can even find such sentences as, "History is not important for him or her who experiences *satori.*" This is a short-hand way of saying that the range of history that interests such persons is exceptionally narrow: namely, perhaps only the moment during which the experience of *satori* occurs. My own observation is that virtually all human beings on their way through time are aware however dimly of what some call the timeless; even if for a few, at certain moments, that dimness gives way to overwhelming clarity. The curve plotting the conscious participation of men and women on earth in what a certain vocabulary distinguishes as the time-bound and the timeless may be asymptotic at the two extremes to zero and one hundred per cent of either, with most of us falling somewhere in between, each with our ups and downs. Yet however that may be, it all happens within the historical process. This is another way of saying that history, for other kinds of creature—rocks and grasshoppers—may (as some think) be totally within time; but for human beings—man being what he and she are—history is the on-going process of human involvement in what my vocabulary verbalizes as the mundane and the transcendent.

It will be evident to you by now that my idea of history is larger and deeper— is, if you like, more theological—than is some people's. And indeed the reason why one has to advocate the thesis that the history of religion is the right basis for theology, and to expect this view's acceptance presently rather than finding it already established as obvious, has much to do with the current inadequacies of prevalent concepts of history—as much as it does with the current narrowness of inherited concepts of theology. Once again, the recent bifurcation is understandable in historical perspective, even if it not be defensible in logic.

Let me elucidate a little further what I intend by "history of religion." First, I like to discriminate between history and historiography. I know that the Western term "history" originally—etymologically, and historically— designated the account of what had happened, and only later what did in fact happen, the actual course of events. The term is therefore now ambiguous: the history of England is long and complicated, whereas a *History of England* may be short and simple and weigh two pounds. Nonetheless we now have no other word for the former, that course of events; and I deem it important not only to distinguish the two in our thinking but also to keep remembering that the report of what has taken place is and must be subordinate to a prior reality, of what has indeed taken place. One could call that reality "objective" in the sense that it is what it is independently of our awareness or ignorance of it. One could call it transcendent, for the same reason and since it always transcends our grasp: all our ideas about it and our knowledge of it only approximate to the reality itself. Until recently, the approximation was very remote indeed, especially for world history, and in minute fraction; and still today, it is still very superficial, although its range has become in principle total.

For me, then, the phrase "history of religion" names not an academic discipline, as it does for instance at the University of Chicago. Rather, it refers to a many-thousand-year-old process, the actual course of human religious and spiritual life: a process variegated, world-wide, intertwined to some degree with virtually all human affairs, and involving virtually all persons, regularly at their most central and most profound. The historiography of religion is an intellectual study, relatively recent and predominantly Western; the history of religion, in contrast, is a dynamic reality of which the intellectual, the recent, and the Western are each relatively small segments.

Second: "history" means not only the past. History is process, which includes also the present, and presumably will include some future or other. The future of our galaxy, and even of much of our solar system, are predictable with considerable precision. The future sector of human history is radically problematic, as we all know; and even of that portion of the solar system that man can modify by his and her doings. History is a long-range on-going process, in which we participate, for good or ill, in the current relatively brief phase. Similarly, to be a theologian is to participate in the current phase of the long-range process of human attempts to speak the truth about God, about the universe.

Naturalistic Fallacy

I have spoken of current misconceptions in our recent Western understanding of history. Salient is the naturalistic fallacy. This is an interpretation of human affairs that imposes a naturalistic ceiling on human history, and legislates it for historiography—insisting that historians *qua* historians must not step beyond the rigid boundaries of that particular ideology. One might expect secularists to feel this way, even though one might permit oneself some surprise in finding how dogmatic a position it prevalently is and how fiercely held; also, how derivative, from a dubious metaphysics. Yet the disappointing matter is that many Christians and Jews have also become victims of it; most readily of course in that area where it does most harm, the history of religion, thought of as the history of other people's religion. Christians entered the modern world suffering from the fallacy that they alone were in God's grace, were saved, so that as they began to look out on the rest of the world they joined with the atheists and secularists in the West in opining that all other religious histories were fictitious nonsense. The more pious the Christian and the more positivistic the secularist, the more heartily they agreed that the history of Hindu, Buddhist, Islamic traditions is a this-worldly construct and aberration. The Western academic discipline that called itself "History of Religion" is only beginning to recover from this absurdity. It has largely dropped the aberration idea, no doubt. Yet it is told that it is not allowed to drop the this-worldly-construct notion, or it will be academically illegitimate.

To approach the study of history with *a priori* rigidities is crippling—whether they be naturalistic dogmas or theological ones. A good historian is one who is perceptive and open, to find things however unexpected among however unfamiliar ages or groups, and who then reports what he or she finds; who understands what he or she observes, and makes it intelligible to others. To be a good historian one must be able to learn from history—since there is always more there than one brings to it. Whether or not one must understand a fair bit about science before one takes up the task of being an historian of science, surely it is evident that if one becomes a true historian of science, one will end up understanding it. It is possible to argue that one must be reasonably sensitive to music before setting up as an historian of music, or to the transcendent dimensions of human life before setting up as an historian of religion; yet in any case it would seem incontrovertible that the history of either music or of religion includes all that until now has been significant in the two realms. (More accurately, let us say one-and-a-half realms?) Therefore in the course of studying, one becomes sensitive to, appreciative of, what has been going on. Otherwise, one fails as an historian.

My recent book on World Theology includes the following sentence. It occurs in the course of a discussion pressing the point that what used to be called "Buddhism", rather than being a given abstract entity that some people "have", has been rather a living movement in process, with a diversified history, constituted of the lives of historical persons; they do not "have" it but participate in it, in its on-going development, and our task is to understand them, and their participation. The sentence reads: "Living life religiously—for Buddhists as for all human beings, even if in the Buddhist case it be a little more obvious—has been a complex interaction among four things:

  (i) the accumulating religious tradition that, in one or another particular limited form, each inherited;
  (ii) the particular personality—with its own potentialities and its own quirks—that each brought to it;
  (iii) the particular environment—new every morning—in which each happened to live (this and the first above include the community in which each participated); and
  (iv) the transcendent reality to which the tradition pointed, and in relation to which the life was lived."

It is the fourth point that is the crux: "the transcendent reality to which the tradition pointed, and in relation to which the life was lived."

I cite this here, in order to remark that when I used a preliminary draft of this material in seminars at Harvard, both theological students from the Divinity School and history-of-religion doctoral students from the Arts Faculty joined to protest that I could not say that. At least, I could not say it as an historian, they insisted. (The passage comes in a presentation of the historical section of the work.) "That is not an historical judgment; it is a theological judgment" was the chorus. It seemed to them obvious that if it were theological, it could not be historical. In the face of their continued resistance, over two or three years, I did not alter the statement, but I have added to the printed version an additional sentence following it: "Without the fourth component here, human history cannot be rendered intelligible." It is precisely *qua* historian that I make the statement. Anyone who does not understand this truth about Buddhist life has misunderstood human history.

Mind you, I did not start my studies with the conviction that other communities' lives were lived in God's grace. I have come to this recognition only slowly, as I got to know the people and carefully studied their history.

It is sometimes remarked that a Westerner, or a Christian, or a modern, that a member of any given culture, always interprets another culture from within his or her own perspective. My response is that of course that is so at first, but is less so in the end. Gradually, as I have learned more, I have come to recognize the power and wealth and profundity of Asian religious life, in all its variety, just as over the years I have come to appreciate more deeply the power and wealth and profundity (and diversity) of the history of Christian religion.

There is a deal of discussion these days in academic quarters about methodologies, preconceptions, and the like. I yield to no one in observing (historically) that conceptual presuppositions color what one observes and how one interprets it. Indeed, I have noticed that a certain complex of presuppositions (which I happen not to share) underlies the present-day emphasis on methodology, and underlies even the concept methodology itself. (Ultimately, methodology, I am beginning to think, is a modern form of atheism.) Rather than engaging, especially here, in debates on those issues, however, I would rather insist that the true scholar, whatever the convictions with which he or she begins the work, must be open in the course of study to modifying those previous convictions. Especially one may argue that that historian of religion is of little worth, to put it mildly, who does not modify—quite radically—underlying convictions, however tacit, in the course of coming to understand other cultures', other centuries', other visions'. It is interesting to speculate on whether, on the whole, Christians are better at this than are secularists, in the history-of-religion field. However that may be, I would wager that any modern Western scholar who emerges from say twenty years of study of Asian religious life with either his secular or his Christian doctrines unenlarged, is a woefully poor historian.

"Studying History Backwards" Fallacy

We turn next to a "studying history backwards" outlook, as I have called it: that Western academic propensity that must be rectified or at least supplemented before we can truly understand anything historical, and especially the religious. It has to do with what might uncharitably be called a stunted antiquarianism, which does little justice to the on-going process of human history with, of course, its forward-moving direction. I recently did an article elaborating this point, on the true understanding of the Qur'ān as scripture, a non-reductionist historical understanding. Let me illustrate the point here, however, briefly, in—rather—the Biblical case. The same point would apply in questions of Christology, ecclesiology, and any other; to the Gita; or to new questions such as the femininity of God. In the Biblical case also a decade back I published an article on an historical understanding of the Bible, as a recognition of its on-going role in Christian life over the two millennia that begin, not end, with the first century A.D., and that are still in process. Some of you may remember that piece. In any case, I find some present-day theologians speaking of the difficulty that they face, or that the Church faces, in attempting to bridge the radical gap between two cultures, that of the ancient world in which the Bible was composed, and our own, so starkly different. They see the task of making the Bible "relevant" to our day as a formidable one, because of what they feel to be the drastic gap between its world and ours. This results from adopting a view of the Bible from a position of recent scholarship that calls itself historical, but for which the nineteen-century gap between Jesus and us is effectively empty. As you see, I call this antiquarianism, not history. It is one particular nineteenth-century kind of historicism, which it is time for our much better understanding today to leave behind. If one perceives the Bible (or for that matter, Christ) in the on-going life of the Church with anything approaching historical fidelity, which carries them steadily and step by step from the first century in Palestine through each succeeding century to just the other day, here, and indeed into today, then our business is simply to put "historical criticism" in proper perspective, as a recent step in an on-going process, and our task becomes not that of bridging a yawning gap between the first century and this, but rather of constructing the next phase in a continuing process—in the on-going historical development of Christian understanding of scripture (or of Christ).

Instead of a yawning gap between the first century and the twentieth, the gap becomes simply that between, for instance, my mother and myself. Her worldview was that of a highly intelligent, educated, warm-hearted traditionalist—you might say, fundamentalist. Or one may say that the gap is that between my childhood and my maturity; although to construct this next phase we must of course bring to bear upon its construction all the resources of our current knowledge. This last includes both our modern awareness of nineteen intervening centuries of the life of the Bible as scripture, and of the preceding millennium or two as the environment out of which that Bible first arose, and also now our modern awareness of other scriptures, our enhanced historical knowledge of the development of the concept scripture on earth, the varying roles that it has played, and the light that this throws upon the human mind and spirit—and the capacity of the Word to mediate between the human spirit and God, and *vice versa:* in theological terms, God's activity in using scripture, in varying forms and varying cultures and varying ways, to enter historically into the life of humankind. One of my most enriching recent experiences has been a post-doctoral seminar at Harvard on Scripture and its role in human history. Are prose, poetry, and scripture three important ways in which humankind uses the gift of language?

Dichotomizing Fallacy

Let us turn next to a third fallacy, as I have called them; namely, that of dichotomizing. This has already surfaced in passing.

Some will protest that this kind of thinking is all very well, but what about the distinction between the descriptive and the normative? It was Hume, I guess, who contended that one can never pass from an "is" to an "ought"; and it is important to understand historically the prevalence in recent Western intellectuality of an outlook that, even when it may not go all the way with Hume on that particular point, nonetheless acquiesces in a sense of two distinct, even disparate, realms. At a static philosophic level, the question may be tricky; but my own view is that this outlook has distorted our awareness of history, and that a true understanding of human affairs in their development over time both enables and requires a healing of this doleful breach. I have already averred that human life is lived in both realms, if two realms they be. The locus of the relation between what is and what ought to be is, and always has been, man; and the study of his and her history—especially religious history—is a study of that interrelation.

This is not merely to say that an historical awareness is an awareness of the mutual impingement, interaction, if not convergence, of "is" and "ought"—although that is certainly included. In addition, however, there is the surely manifest point that if my Christian heritage tells me that I should see the face of Christ in every man and woman, does not this mean that I should indeed do so only if and insofar as it is in fact truly there? Similarly, if the Buddhist aspirant is taught that ultimately *saṃsāra* is *nirvāṇa,* then a full understanding of human history should not only comprehend what this thesis meant to those who promulgated it and those who heard and received and pondered and structured their lives less or more in terms of it, but should include, which finally is the same thing, an understanding of the universe that would make clear what it was not only in their environment and inner life but in ours, today, that made and makes that thesis persuasive. Whatever the conceptualities that those Buddhists concocted, and that we must understand, after all the universe that they were observing is also our universe; and the humanity that they talked of, we share.

Indeed, if history and theology were to be polarized, on which side would one put the history of theology—including present-day theology?

Or, the same question put in other terms: does the statement that *saṃsāra* is *nirvāṇa* tell us something about *nirvāṇa,* but nothing about *saṃsāra?*

Once again, however, the Western error on this descriptive/normative disjunction is something that the historian can understand, and therein overcome. For it has arisen from the fact that our recent thinking about what "is" has been drawn chiefly from science, not from history: it arises from our attending to the material world, and neglecting the human. Once we subordinate science to history, as a rational mind soon again must, these problems tend to evaporate. As I shall urge presently, science itself too becomes clearer.

A failure to see this, plagues those who have become victims of the subject/object dichotomy also in their orientation to persons, not only to things—so that many moderns think of history as the history of "them," those other people: over there, or long ago. But we too are within history. The historian's chief task is to help all to see that we too participate in history, this entrancing on-going process—and that they too did, those whom one mistook as *others*. The crux (I choose that word wittingly) is to recognize history as the history of *us,* human beings. Once that corner is turned, the problems indeed evaporate.

And if you say, does true critical intellectuality not require a certain distancing of the reflective mind from what it contemplates, I counter happily by saying that one of the richest rewards that my study of world history has given me has been my ability intellectually to distance myself from current Western culture, in which so many of my friends and especially my critics are still, alas, imprisoned.

Modern Western thought should surely contribute to our understanding of the universe and of ourselves; but equally surely, should not constitute it—just as our heritage of Christian thought should, and should not.

Either I am wrong in seeing Christ's face in all human persons, or the historian is wrong who does not. Of course, the image is poetic, but that does not affect the facts of the situation—only the way they are expressed in words. Similarly I fail as an historian if I fail to see those aspects of our common universe that Gandhi saw and articulated in Bhagavad-Gītā terms, or that the most intelligent and perceptive among Buddhists have seen and reported in Buddhist terms. Of course the world historian must forge new vocabulary in order to communicate to a public audience what the various religious communities among us have seen and have thus far articulated in terms that are today private in the sense that only those within one's own restricted circle of discourse could understand. Yet insofar as there is any truth in what Hindus have seen, these are not truths "in Hinduism": they are truths in the universe, to which Hindus in this case happen to have called attention. There are no *Christian* truths—the phrase is an absurdity, almost a blasphemy. An historian of religion who has not understood and has not made understandable such truth as Christians have discerned or been vouchsafed, is no historian. Similarly for Jewish or Confucian, Zarathustrian or Muslim, matters. The historian of religion is that scholar whose aspiration (grandiose, no doubt; but to understand human history is indeed a grandiose endeavor)—that scholar whose aspiration is to apprehend, and to render intellectually apprehensible, what human beings on earth have reported or found to be transcendently true. The theologian, equally grandiosely (and I stress that "equally"), is that thinker whose aspiration is to apprehend, and to make intellectually apprehensible, the truth about God: the transcendently true. It is the same task. Insofar as in the past the two have conceived their task differently, is it not that that ceiling above which historians once wrongly supposed that they could not or need not go was artificially imposed, and indeed was imaginary, while the several grounds on which the various and disparate private theologians attempted to build towards the goal were less solidly reliable?

The Muslim theologian, who in olden times thought that the Qur'ān as Word of God provided an adequate starting point, or the Christian theologian who thought that Christ as that Word did, have been replaced in our day by their respective sectarian successors who do not know quite what to make of each other, nor quite what to make of those erstwhile starting points in the light of each other or of modern knowledge generally; whereas the comparative historian of religion's task is to understand and to make rationally intelligible to modern intellects the historical fact of both Words in a global coherence. Once we recognize, as today we can and must, that God has spoken to men and women and children, historically, both through the Qur'ān and through Christ, in differing times and places, differing languages, differing moods and modes, the historian's task becomes recognizably theological, and the theologian's, recognizably historical.

The Church, we used to say, is a divine-human complex; and so, nowadays we can go on to say, is the Islamic community, and the Buddhist and the rest. All human history is a divine-human complex in motion; a fact most noticeably discernible in its religious dimension. The task of the historian of religion is to tell the truth about that reality, that *Heilsgeschichte;* the task of the theologian is to tell the truth about God.

In the past I have found that views such as I am endeavoring to set forth are resisted—perhaps I should say, rather: my vocabulary is resisted—by, for instance, sensitive Jews or Muslims (the two chief groups that have shared with us Christians the massive exclusivistic strand in human religious orientation) who do so because of that very polarity, even dichotomy, between the sense of history and the sense of God's presence. The Passover, for Jews, or the *Laylat al Qadr,* for Muslims—the annual ritual celebrations enlivening in on-going history the continuing sense of God's presence and of His having acted for their particular community—are felt as transcending the mundane. (Christians say the same of the eucharist, for example.) In modern jargon, this is sometimes formulated by saying that these occasions are felt as transcending history (or as enabling the participants to transcend history). The point here is that this sort of ritual and celebration expresses an orientation to the historical process, and to the relation of its past to its present, that the modern mind-set has lost. Contemporary ideology, with its straining after objectivity and objectification, has objectified also the past and distanced us from it, separating us from continuity and intimacy with it. The more normal human attitude has been, nurtured through rituals of this kind, to "re-appropriate one's past," as modern writers using their own inapt terms sometimes put it, but anyway enabling participants in the ceremonies to participate thus in their "past" yet on-going history, to recognize that it participates in their lives, that the historical process transcends us but that we by participating in it participate in transcendence and that transcendence—God—participates in us. Of course the Passover enables Jews, and *Laylat al Qadr* enables Muslims, to transcend the mundane. But to misread this by saying, rather, that they thereby transcend history is to fail to recognize that human history is precisely the arena, the process, in which human beings live simultaneously in the mundane and the transcendent: in God and world, in time and eternity, or however one wishes to put it. (They have done so in varying proportions, of course, as well as in various forms.) Jews, Christians, and Muslims share a sense of a clear divine dimension to their "past" history, but share also the unhappy distinction of exclusivistic orientations; and have been almost as slow as are secularists in recognizing the fact that human history has normally been like that—all human history. To suggest that *our* religious life, *our* experience, *our* knowing, transcends history is to have what I would call a both intellectually and spiritually untenable sense either of human history, what it has been and is, or else of the history of other groups than one's own. I rather, far from denying the experience of those communities in those precious moments, and far even from denying its validity, am affirming both; while adding that it is insensitive not to recognize that something comparable has been true of most human history in most centuries.

The Sabbath, say Jews, "is a taste of eternity in time." I agree; and I teach my students that to fail to see this is to mis-read the human scene. Therefore I cannot agree with an esteemed Jewish thinker whom I recently heard say that these things "are in time but not really in history." To propose such a dichotomy is to be victim of the false naturalistic view both of history and of the human; the secularists' unwillingness or incapacity to see human history as indeed that divine-human complex in motion. Similarly I have heard it said that at moments of ceremonial observance "the flow of time is interrupted by the intrusion of the divine into the historical." Is it not blasphemy to say that God's presence is an interruption? It is the secular aridity of modern life, with its obtuseness to transcendence and its blinkered view of day-to-day life, that constitutes the interruption of genuinely human history—impoverishing history and making us less than human. Secularism has taught that religion is an addendum, an aberration; but it is wrong. Secularism is the aberration, both historically and logically. Religion has not conferred color and significance on essentially bleak and meaningless human lives, as the sympathetic secularists would have it; rather, what we call the world's religious traditions have at their best simply enabled humanity to open its eyes to the divine color and significance that are there and are our true environment—or to change the metaphor, have enabled us to hear at least an echo of the music of the spheres.

A WORD ABOUT TRUTH

I close with just a word about truth as such; for on this matter also the historical dimension of the matter has in our day become salient.

One of the fundamental problems in this realm has to do with that persistently teasing fact that philosophy in recent times has become distracted by a pre-occupation with science. For a time, this took the form of supposing that science was the avenue to truth—not merely *an* avenue, but the sole significant one. Presently, however, it went further, to the point where the concept of truth itself has tended to become defined in relation to science; particularly the notion of a true statement (statements, you may recall, I have come to deem the misplaced locus of truth), and the notion of objective truth (which I am beginning to find a contradiction in terms). Western theology, itself dazzled by science directly (were we not all?) and also influenced by philosophy's dazzlement by it, has in part fallen prey to these philosophic fallacies.

My concern at the moment is simply to press the thesis that, at least so far as the human is concerned (as over against objects and things), a study of history brings us closer to the truth than does science. The historical and the scientific outlooks were the two great intellectual achievements of the nineteenth century and of the first half of this. My contention is that of the two, the historical is the greater, and the truer; and that this is especially so, indeed overwhelmingly so, in the case of human affairs. My thesis in this realm I have recently summarized in the aphorism that history can comprehend science, but science cannot comprehend history.

Within the next generation or so, I would predict, philosophers will come round to wrestling with history primarily, putting science in at best second place. (This is because humanity is more important than things; and the truth about humanity is of a higher order than the truth about things.) Anyway, so far as theology is concerned, although for a century it was perhaps inescapable, and even proper, that theologians should concern themselves first and foremost with the challenge from science, that era is now effectively over. Today, and for the coming century, the primary challenge, on the one hand, and the primary potential support, on the other, come and will come from a study of history. The support will be primarily from a study of the history of religion. Just as to say that God is creator of the world, must today mean that God has created the kind of world that scientists (and not only poets) make known to us, so to say that God is active in human history means that God has been and continues active in the history that primarily the historian of religion studies. I should like to think that theologians might lead the way here for philosophers, rather than again being led.

In any case, it is significant that even with regard to science itself, it is the new attention to the history of science that is now raising the most interesting philosophic questions—not least, the question of truth. Awareness of the history of science is making much more understandable what science itself is, as Kuhn has shown.

One illustration which I have thought up has to do with Copernicus, and his heliostatic theory. (Sometimes his view is called heliocentric, but this is not quite accurate: in order to conform to his precise measurements, he located the sun at a short distance from the center.) Anyway, as everyone knows, for the earlier view that the earth stands still while the sun revolves around it, and elaborately the planets, he substituted the new conception that the sun, rather, stands still, close to the center of things, with the earth and planets circling about it. Indeed, on this innovating vision the modern scientific movement has by some been seen to be based. We now know, however, that in fact the sun does not stand still: it is much more vagrant than he ever thought the earth to be. And it is no nearer the center of the physical universe than is our own planet. On these matters, we may see that he was wrong. Yet obviously he had a point!

Are we then to say that modern science is founded on an insight that is true, expressed in statements that are false?

To an historian of religion, that is entrancing. It is, however, too glib; and in my recent publications I have wrestled at length with this issue. Let me here simply suggest three positions for which a student of history must have a concept of truth capacious enough to make room: Copernicus's in the fifteenth century that the sun stands still; Christians' over many centuries that Jesus Christ is the Son of God; Muslims' over somewhat fewer centuries that Jesus Christ is not the Son of God. An inability to accommodate all three in one's notion of truth would be an inability to interpret history authentically, may we not say—and an inability to understand what truth is. It would also suggest an inability to understand what language is.

CHRISTIAN THEOLOGY—OR, THEOLOGY

One final point, and I close. It is to make explicit what was implicit in my opening: that theology ideally is the truth about God. Throughout I have spoken of "theology," never of "Christian theology." Indeed, the phrase "Christian theology," once one stops to reflect about it, is a contradiction in terms. At the very least, it is un-Christian, in any serious meaning of the word. This suggestion, which I have elsewhere adumbrated, may strike you as novel, unexpected, and even bizarre. Historically, however, it is the phrase "Christian theology" that, rather, is recent, odd, and finally untenable. It is virtually unknown before the nineteenth and rare before the twentieth century.

Into the history of the concept "Christian" I obviously cannot go here, though I am entranced by it and have pondered a little its present-day radical ambiguity, between on the one hand a transcendent or metaphysical meaning, signifying "pertaining to Christ," and on the other a mundane, almost positivistic meaning, signifying, pertaining to the earthly community of (perhaps nominal) Christians, as over against or parallel to Jews, Buddhists, Hindus, and the like—terms that seldom, and in some cases never, had a transcendent reference in English (or any) usage. On the whole this second, mundane sense for "Christian" (and indeed for the others) has arisen only in the nineteenth, and become prevalent in the twentieth, centuries; but it nowadays predominates. Specifically as qualifying the concept "theology," it is virtually unknown before modern times. When St. Thomas Aquinas wrote a book that he called *Summa Theologiae* (not *Summa Christianae Theologiae*), he was illustrating as well as carrying forward the main tradition of the Church; and I feel that I need hardly apologize if I urge with some insistence that we return today to that main stream. The attempt to theologize is intimidating, as I have stressed, and trepidation is indeed in order; but let us not evade the challenge by settling for anything less than the aspiration, at least, to speak the truth about God. There may be a Christian attempt at theology; and indeed there should be. An attempt at Christian theology, on the other hand, is too narrow a goal; and in the end, is self-contradictory.

The concept "Christian theology," and counterparts such as "Christian faith," were un-thought-out and unsuccessful parts of the Church's first endeavor to deal with religious plurality, beginning last century. Before that time, Christians had been right in aspiring to theology, *simpliciter,* wrong in imagining that outside the Church there is and can be no significant or adequate knowledge of God. As my *Faith and Belief* attempts to document, those Christians were right in affirming that faith is one, wrong in imagining that it occurs in no form other than the Christian. The first book ever on "Christian faith" was Schleiermacher's in the nineteenth century; and even he did not mean by it what his English readers in the twentieth hear him as saying, in the now demonstrated mistranslation of his title as *"The" Christian Faith.* Since the Church began to discover where it was wrong, it has unfortunately withdrawn also from where it had been right, into a kind of frightened ghetto. My *Faith and Belief,* in addition to documenting the past situation on "faith," attempts to contribute towards forging a new conception adequate to our modern situation. My present plea is that the same sort of task needs tackling in the whole of theology.

CONCLUSION

The history of religion, I have claimed, omits nothing pertinent to theology, and includes nothing irrelevant.

Included in that history, of course, are not only the greatest truths that anyone, Christian or other, has ever known or seen or felt or sensed, about God, the world, our neighbors, or ourselves, but also, of course, much that is grotesque, stupid, wicked, and perverse. God's best efforts to give Himself/Herself/Itself, through the sacraments, Christian or other, through His/Her/Its Son, through the Bhagavad Gītā, through the *Torah,* and to participate in our lives, to save us in this or that century, on this or that continent, have often been but meagerly successful, at best, God knows—and we should know it too. To study history—that is, to have one's intellect participate in broad reaches of the life of humankind over time and space—is to know more fully the grandeur and the pathos of man in his and her relation to God. If theology be the truth about God, surely part of that truth is that God is confronted with the recalcitrance, ineptitude, obtuseness, of us human beings. One cannot speak the truth about God without incorporating something of God's relation to us human beings as history has shown and shows us sorely to be. The history of religion at its best shows in careful detail the highest human potential for an awareness, including intellectual awareness, of God—decisive for theology; and at its worst, the actual relation of God to man, also no small component for theology, surely.

But our time is up. An hour was too short a span to develop the view that the attempt to discern and to report the truth about human history, especially religious history, requires theology; and that the attempt to theologize requires a grounding in awareness of that history.

I.1.

Orthodox Christianity and Theologizing

STANLEY S. HARAKAS

Although it is most interesting and challenging to be asked to respond to Professor Smith's paper, I fear that the theological position from which I come is not very congenial either to the problems addressed in the paper, or the assumed methodologies of the paper, or its conclusions. Further, should this sound too negative a beginning, it is even worse than that because I feel that my understanding of ecumenism is significantly different from that presented in Professor Swidler's preconference paper on interreligious dialogue. It would be very easy for me to take the course of "proclamation"—that is, articulating my strong reservations up and down the line with these two papers, and making a statement about the person and work of Jesus Christ as the only savior of the world. I could then do one of two things: either unceremoniously depart hence, or remain in a martyr's stance, waiting to be attacked from every direction by the majority of the participants of this conference. But I will try very hard not to do either of those things. For, even though I have grave reservations, I believe myself in fact to be an ecumenist, sincerely interested in the rapprochement of Christians, and peaceful coexistence and communication with the world's religions. So, I will assume what seems to me to be an appropriate ecumenical stance by first describing briefly what appears to me to be a consistent Eastern Orthodox Christian perspective on the question of "Theology and the World's Religious History," which I believe would be assented to by knowledgeable Eastern Orthodox Christians. Then, I will state for you what I have understood from Prof. Smith's paper, and respond to it as sympathetically as I can.

THE STANCE WHENCE I SPEAK

I speak consciously and deliberately as an Eastern Orthodox Christian who, although ecumenically committed, holds to the fundamental premise that Jesus Christ is the Son of God, the second person of the Holy Trinity, who in time assumed human nature, dwelt among us, taught and healed, proclaimed and manifested the reign of God, was crucified for the salvation of the human race, was resurrected from the dead, thereby conquering the enemies of authentic human life—sin, evil, and death. As an Eastern Orthodox Christian it is my prayer, my earnest desire, for the well-being of every person who is living or has ever lived or who shall live, that Jesus Christ and his saving work be acknowledged, accepted, proclaimed, and lived. As an Orthodox Christian, St. Paul's words in his Letter to the Philippians resonate truth to me: "Therefore God has highly exalted him and bestowed on him the name which is above any name, that at the name of Jesus every knee should bow, in heaven and on earth and under the earth, and every tongue confess that Jesus Christ is Lord, to the glory of God the Father" (Phil. 2:9–11).

I know that such an affirmation can be, and has been, and for some continues to be, the root of a highly intolerant and denigrating attitude toward persons who belong to different Christian churches and toward persons belonging to other religions. It is my contention, based on the sources of Eastern Orthodox teaching, that this need not be the case, and that in fact it ought not be the case. This is not the place to develop this teaching, but suffice it to say that the ancient *Logos* theology of the early church is one grounding for this view, and the respect for the self-determining image of God in every human being is another.

At our worst, in our history, we Eastern Orthodox have ignored those truths and spoken in vituperation toward others and their beliefs, and have violated their integrity as peoples and as human beings. Our own sufferings over the centuries under alien religious and antireligious forces, certainly as much as, and perhaps more than Catholics and Protestants to this very day, have made us sensitive to our failings in this area. Rather, the road of dialogue, cooperation, the peaceful coexistence of religions, and the avoidance of overt proselytizing have become hallmarks of Eastern Orthodox attitudes toward other churches and religions in this ecumenical age.

If, by God's grace, the Orthodox lifestyle, doctrines, worship, and integration of many varied and rich cultural and ethnic traditions into the life of the church, provoke interest and desire to learn of the Orthodox Christian faith, we most heartily oblige. If not, we are able to look at every religious expression and find there much that we acknowledge to be true and beautiful, along with some things we find contradictory to the Christian faith and the affirmations that we hold. Because we recognize that we often misinterpret and misunderstand others in their practices and beliefs, we hold it a truly Christian thing to enter into dialogue with those with whom we differ. We often find much more to appreciate. Sometimes the constraints of our own history have caused us to deemphasize authentic aspects of our own tradition, and dialogue with others serves to uncover these areas, and we are enriched because of the dialogue. In the process, even though our differences may never be fully overcome, we are better off for having shared: we ourselves have grown, and we hope we have communicated the vision of truth that we hold.

I do not think it wise to expand further this portion of my remarks; I trust that my purpose has been fulfilled in providing an understanding of the background from which my comments on Prof. Smith's paper arise. What I hope to have communicated is that belief in Jesus Christ as the world's savior does not demand an imperious, intolerant, and irreverent attitude toward other faiths and religions. On the contrary, at its best, it engenders an attitude of respect for the self-determination of others and a seeking after genuine dialogue.

I have decided to list briefly a number of my understandings of Prof. Smith's paper and to raise what appear to me, as an Eastern Orthodox Christian, questions—dimensions that may need further consideration, and possible alternatives or expansions of certain positions.

Theology "of" or Theology "for" Religion?

But first I wish to address the title of this conference. It is "Toward a Universal Theology of Religion." It could be contrasted with an alternate formulation that might help us understand what we are about at this conference. Would it make any difference to us here if the title were "Toward a Universal Theology *for* Religion"? The first seems to call for a theological effort taking place somewhat distanced from the actual experience of conscious religious commitment. The second could be understood to imply the task of understanding universally the phenomenon of religion from within the believing communities and for their appropriation and acceptance. To me it seems a more desirable ecumenical endeavor. To his credit, I think that Prof. Smith wants to do something like that, even if it require that he convert us all into historians of religion in order to accomplish it!

Science and Religious Experience

I can discern at least two audiences for Prof. Smith's paper. The one is composed of his colleagues in the discipline of the history of religion; the other is the theological community. He is at odds with both on some rather fundamental matters. I hear him saying that an authentic and scientific study of the world's religions cannot adequately be accomplished without participating in the religious experience itself. I am sympathetic to that view. He has described to us the abused scientific sensibilities of students and colleagues in response to this suggestion.

Though I am very much personally taken by his assertion, I cannot help but ask if he loads the scientific method with a condition impossible to digest, given the limited parameters of the discipline. Or, in other words, given the methods of science, is it not too much to ask that it assume the role of constructive theologian, as well? But if he would continue to hold to his view—as I am confident he will—then, is it not true that much of the work done in New Testament criticism and studies in Christian origins during the past half century needs to be radically revised, because its major assumptions are precisely the rejection of his fourth point about the need to account for the reality of the transcendent religious experience?

The Theological Task

The basic premise regarding the theological task as stated in the paper I understand to be something like this: it is essentially the creation of a new perspective and view of the divine reality based on the described empirical experiences of members of all religions. As such, the theologian is seen primarily as one who constructs, on the basis of a rational, coherent, internally consistent system of ideas that (most importantly) is congenial to contemporary perceptions of truth in other areas of human knowledge. A number of propositions in the paper are marshaled to support this understanding of the theological task. Some of these I wish to note below. Let it suffice at this point for me to admit that most persons attending this conference probably share in this perception.

As an Eastern Orthodox Christian theologian, I cannot. In my tradition, and, I perceive, in other religious traditions as well, those who pass for theologians do not understand what they do in those terms at all. The theologian in the Orthodox Church is often described not so much as one who thinks, but rather as one who prays. His or her first and primary task is not to speak the truth of God, but to listen for it. Much more than what Prof. Smith asks of the scientist to experience (that is, to experience the religious phenomenon as part of his or her research), the theologian is required to hear the word of God in prayer, in worship, in obedience, in spiritual exercise, in meditation, in study—and only then to speak what he or she has heard.

I feel that no one at this conference would completely reject what I have just said. But it seems to me that the theological tradition of Western Christianity does not permit this perception to be the operative value in the theological task. I believe that what permits an approach to the theological task, which moves from the assessment of the empirical to the construction of theology, is a sometimes overt, more often covert, assumption of an *analogia entis* mentality, which closely relates the divine reality with created reality in a rationally analogical fashion. The Eastern Christian mind-set eschews any significant correlation *for the understanding of the divine reality* between the Uncreated (who alone is God) and created reality (which includes the canons of rationality and conceptualization). Thus, for the Eastern Orthodox mind the very task of "constructing a theology" in the dimensions envisaged by this conference can never really be a "true word about God."

Revelation and Transcendence

My comments on the task of the theologian may serve as a preliminary to several questions arising from the paper, which space provides an opportunity only to state, not to develop. The terms "revelation" and "transcendence" are used in what seem to me to be unusual ways. The term "revelation" sometimes means the self-disclosure of God (ultimate reality, the Transcendent One, Transcendence), and at other times means "insight" on the part of the human being. In the final analysis, are these two meanings to be identified?

Further, I would point to what seems to me to be a similar treatment of the term "transcendence." Sometimes I sense the use of the word to mean that which genuinely comes from "without" in a qualitatively different way from the "common grace" experience of divine immanence. At other times I feel that what is meant by "transcendence" is the person's apprehension of any kind of experience that comes from outside his or her self and to which some sort of special significance is attached by the subject. If I am correct here, how would Prof. Smith address the religious experience of a genuinely discontinuous transcendent reality, which, as he rightly points out, *is* experienced *in* history, but also precisely as something "breaking into history" from beyond it? Why is he ready to accept every other claim of transcendent experience as revelation, but not this one?

Rationalist, Individualist Religion, and Religion as a Gestalt

I perceive in the paper an understanding of the religious experience on the part of believers as strongly cast in individualistic and quite rationalist terms. Assuming that I am correct in this perception, I need a clarification. From the point of view of a historian of religions, are not the world religions more properly seen—even taking into account their inner pluralisms—as great spatial, temporal, social, esthetic, conceptual, experiential, spiritual gestalts, around which some boundaries exist in enough measure to distinguish them as holistic realities from other religions? It seems to me that we do another kind of injustice to religions when we fail to acknowledge their uniqueness.

Our Orthodox experience of subservient status for four centuries under the Ottoman Turks has ingrained in us a powerful respect for the integrity of other religions and their inner cohesion. Is it possible that a Western, rationalist, and individualist bias is not giving due weight to that dimension of the issue?

Does not this last comment raise the "who" question of the goals of this enterprise? If it indeed is the formation of a theology that may provide a comprehension of the "religions" as "religion," is there something that lies beyond that rational and coherent conceptualization acceptable to the modern mind? If so, is it in reality the formation of a new worldwide religion after the fashion of that described in Isaac Asimov's novel *Foundation*? I would ask: Are not the methods of the history of religions somewhat anemic for the accomplishment of such a goal in the face of the powerful revelatory claims at the source of most organized religions?

CONCLUSION

I have tried to cast my comments in ways that fit a dialogic approach. I feel that in some places I have not succeeded totally in doing so. Nevertheless, please receive my comments in the light of that intention, and my genuine desire to hear and learn in spite of my obvious uncomfortableness with the theses of Prof. Smith's paper.

I.2.

Theologizing through History?

KANA MITRA

My first acquaintance with Prof. Smith's writing was in graduate school in a course on methodology for the study of religions. We studied *The Meaning and End of Religion,* along with some Husserl, Piaget, Wittgenstein, and so forth. The study of phenomenology, structuralism, and positivism appealed to my intellect trained by *nyaya* logic, Nagarjuna's *chatuskoti,* and Sri Harsha's *advaita.* Prof. Smith's work produced a sympathetic resonance in my overall Hindu mystical temperament.

Prof. Smith is not very happy about some methodological concerns in the study of religion. Method to him, as he explained in recent correspondence with me, suggests an impersonal technique that can be picked up mechanically as a way to master some discipline. Of course, in this sense no method can lead anyone to master any discipline—even technology, not to speak of humane disciplines. In the field of technology, also, there are those who can go to the core of their subject by applying their heart and not simply their brain and muscle, and that is how they are different from robots. Any systematic study needs to be undertaken from a certain perspective and in some specific way. In this regard I find Prof. Smith's suggestion of studying religion by both heart and mind—feeling and intellect, *anubhuti* and *yukti*—the best among all the divergent suggested methods for the study of religion.

I quite agree with the suggestion that truth is not simply a matter of intellectual consistency but also a moral attitude. Divested of moral attitude, intellectual sophistication ends up mere sophistry. The intention behind our intellectual investigation needs to be an honest inquiry about truth rather than an attempt to win an argument. That is why in the Hindu traditions *vada* (discussion) is considered the best method for inquiry, not *jalpa* (wrangling) or *vitanda* (cavil). Prof. Smith's contention that the history of all religions is part of human history and thus needs to be studied as a common heritage of all of us can generate an attitude open to discussion. Those of us who study and teach world religions are familiar with the problem of attitude in understanding diverse traditions. The usual attitude in studying religious traditions other than one's own is to set up an opposition between "us" and "them." This generates polemics, not discussion. Hence, I often use a Smith essay as methodological preparation for the study of world religions.

THEOLOGY AND HISTORY

My admiration for Prof. Smith deepened further when I read *Towards a World Theology*. I sensed the great possibilities of basing theological thinking for our day on the history of world religions. However, like any other method, it is not free from difficulty.

I want to point out some theoretical and practical problems with this position. Prof. Smith says that, first, theology is speaking the truth about God; secondly, no one can really speak the truth about God, but can only attempt to speak that truth; thirdly, some attempts are more adequate than others; and finally, adequacy and inadequacy at different times are different. It would seem that we are not only to speak about the unspeakable, but we even have to speak the truth about the unspeakable. Although I am not fond of positivism, here I am in sympathy with Wittgenstein! If God is unknowable, how can we speak truth about that unknowable? Rather, what Prof. Smith probably is pointing out is that the recognition that all our talk about God as inadequate suggests that some talk is less inadequate than other talk. What could be the criterion for determining such adequacy and inadequacy? This is not simply an intellectual problem but also one that has serious practical repercussions. This is an issue not simply for secularists who do not recognize any higher reality and end up in absolute relativism, but should be faced as well by persons who seriously believe in the transcendence of the ultimate and thus recognize the relativity of their perspective—and are humble. The Aristotelian heritage of Western traditions led not only to the claim of absoluteness of truth but also to many kinds of arrogance even in the name of spirituality. Wittgenstein, for intellectual reasons, kept silent about matters of the ultimate; Buddha did so for moral and spiritual reasons. We, however, must ask the question, as Raimundo Panikkar often puts it: "What is the criterion of criterion?"

Prof. Smith contends that there is a transcendent component to human life across culture. I do not understand how this can be considered a historically based statement. In history there is evidence of the human quest for transcendence. However, there is also contrary evidence. The Indian Carvakas and Ajivikas, the Greek Epicureans, and modern secularists do not recognize any transcendent component of human life. If not to notice the transcendent component of human life in history is an intellectual error, not to recognize the contrary evidence is equally so. Historically there have been not only diverse answers to the question about the relationship between the mundane and the transcendent, but there also has been denial of transcendence altogether.

It is argued by Prof. Smith that only a minority of humans deny transcendence, whereas a majority accept it, and hence it is true. This is not a strong argument. It is true that the majority of human beings throughout all ages have had some recognition and idea of transcendence; yet only a minority of them—the few saints and seers—lived their lives according to their experience and understanding of transcendence. Their lives made an impact on the theological thinking of their traditions. Therefore, the argument from number—how many persons think something to be true—does not make it more credible. Moreover, even if human beings throughout the ages have had ideas of transcendence and have lived by them, that does not necessarily demonstrate the impingement of the transcendent on history.

Prof. Smith's vision of history, as he himself indicates, is theological. He believes that God or transcendence can be recognized in history. However, such recognition is not possible simply by taking note of history. An ordinary person and a mystic may look at the same reality, but they "see" differently. This is true not simply of those who have a transcendent view of transcendence, but also of those who consider the transcendent immanent. Insofar as the qualitative difference between apparent and transcendent is recognized, it would suggest some special ways of knowing it. In Castanada's *Separate Reality,* Don Juan keeps saying that in order to know reality one has to learn to "see" and not simply to look. That is basic to all religion, and that is why prayer or meditation and similar practices are considered so important for transformed sensitivity. Prof. Smith's understanding of history as a process of past, present, and future does not itself guarantee the recognition of God in history, unless, like Hegel, he considers it also progress and progress toward the absolute. That would generate other difficulties for making history the basis for universal theology, for this Hegelian understanding of history is very much Christian.

The practical problem in Prof. Smith's position comes not simply because a theology based on the history of religions would be grandiose, but also because theology, by its all-comprehensive nature, has to make room even for contradictory truth claims. Prof. Smith, in his writings, has demonstrated his ability to touch the inner core of diverse religions; yet, as he himself indicates, his book *Towards a World Theology* offers only some suggestions. It would be interesting to see how he would develop a systematic theology from the Christian perspective following his own proposal. Classical Hindu theological thinking was in one way encyclopedic: it followed the method of *purvapaksa,* hearing divergent points of view; *khandana,* refuting contrary views; and *uttarapakṣa,* stating one's own view. However, although Indian theological thinking was encyclopedic, contradictory truth claims, for reasons of intellectual consistency, were either refuted or subsumed under the particular proposed theology. It would seem that Prof. Smith wants to avoid all polemics. It would be interesting to see how he would achieve it.

HISTORY IN HINDU THEOLOGY

My intellectual critique of Prof. Smith is based mostly on my left-brained attempt at comprehension. However, my right-brained apprehension gives me some different insights about his presentation, and I find myself in empathy with his statement that theology needs to be based on history. By reflecting on and contemplating Hindu theology, I can feel and see the importance of history in theology, although here I am taking history more in the conventional sense and not in Prof. Smith's sense. We Hindus, especially the modern intellectual ones, proudly proclaim that our theologians recognized religious plurality from our earliest history and formulated comprehensive and perceptive theoretical interpretations for religious diversity; Westerners are still struggling with it! Taking history seriously will make us more humble—a virtue we profess, but do not always practice! Plurality of religions is integral to the entire history of the Indian subcontinent. There have been and still are worshipers of Vishnu, Shiva, Krishna, Gopala, Durga, Chandi, and other gods—the 330 million gods, as they are sometimes referred to. Never in the entire history of India has there been *a* Hindu religion. It is commonly said today that there are Hindus but no Hindu religion, and that the name "Hindu" was given to us by non-Hindus. Recognition of the plurality of religions by our theologians is historically conditioned; and we need to attend to that historical conditionedness.

The general model for dealing with the plurality of religions is the Rg Vedic statement, *Ekam sat vipra vahudha vadanti*—truth is one; people call it by various names. But the theologians of different historical periods have differed in their specific arguments and orientations. If we take the examples of rather well-known theologians of Hinduism, Sankara and Ramanuja, we can see that their theological thinking was based in their historical surroundings.

Sankara handled plurality by recognizing two levels of truth—phenomenal and transcendental. Plurality is true on the phenomenal level, not on the transcendental. Sankara reconciled plurality by an ultimate denial of it. He even subordinated all personalistic forms of belief under the suprapersonal Brahman. Even though there is no unanimity as to exactly when Sankara lived, at least there is no denial that he was not pre–sixth-century C.E. (We Hindus get so much absorbed in the pursuit of transcendent truth—which is suprahistorical—that we tend to forget about history, and the deemphasis of *nama-rupa*—name and form—is one of the reasons for not putting down a name or date in many of our writings. Consequently, present-day historians often have a difficult time in determining the date and authorship of various works.)

Buddhism became a dominant religion of India via the Maurya King Ashoka (273–232 B.C.E.). The Buddhist refusal to deal with metaphysical questions or the God question and its practical denial of the caste system posed a challenge for Hinduism. Eventually the Madhyamika School of Buddhism came into being, particularly with the help of Nagarjuna (second century C.E.). He developed his ingenious logical scheme of *chatuskoti* or fourfold negation to demonstrate the inconceivability of the ultimate. Sankara utilized Nagarjuna's logical scheme—which was not in opposition to the Upanisadic tradition of *neti neti* ("not this, not that")—to develop the idea of suprapersonal Brahman, which could accommodate the Buddhist refusal to talk about God. On the level of practice, he established monastic orders to transcend caste problems. Before Sankara there were individual monks but no monastic orders in Hinduism. In accordance with the four stages of life, in the last stage Hindus often became wandering monks. Monasticism, thus, was not quite alien to Hindu traditions, although it was only for the last stage of life. Sankara, however, established four monasteries to introduce monastic orders in Hinduism. Thus, clearly much of Sankara's system, theoretical and practical, was heavily influenced by the historical circumstances of his time.

The situation of the eleventh-century Ramanuja was different. He was post–*advaita Vedanta* and post–Muslim encounter. Sankara's philosophical system appealed to the intellect but could not fulfill the emotional needs of many. Meanwhile, Islam was presenting a majestic, magnificent, benevolent, personal God, which was not foreign to the devotional trends of Hinduism. Ramanuja subordinated Sankara's nonpersonal Brahman as a way of knowledge to the personal deity Vishnu—and one could live in the eternal bliss of his presence through devotion. Again, historical circumstances played a central role in the development of the system of a major Hindu thinker.

A. L. Basham shows that the thirteenth-century theologian Madhva developed his dualistic theology in an encounter with Christianity.[1] In more recent times, in the thought of Tagore, Aurobindo, Radha-Krishnan, and others, we can see the impact of global thought. In many of their works, perhaps with the exception of Tagore, we can find some elements of apologetics. It was a need of their time.

At present, some of us feel the need to develop a self-critical attitude. An awareness of history and of the historical conditionedness of all human projects can help us in this enterprise. Although still rather scarce, fortunately some historically based studies are being done.[2]

Also, by taking history seriously, we perhaps can gain some insights to help us resolve the problem of the relationship between what we call *sanatana-dharma,* or perennial truth—which is transhistorical and the attainment of which is the goal of our human life—and *sva-dharma,* or one's own particular duty according to one's nature and situation, which is the historically situated springboard for realizing the transhistorical. In the early period of Hinduism as it is described in the *Dharma Sastra, sva-dharma* or one's duty is to be determined by one's age, sex, and caste. We Hindus, even liberated intellectual ones, recognize the differences and distinctiveness among different individuals. It seems self-evident to us that a child's duty and a grown-up's cannot be exactly identical. Even with women's liberation movements, we find that among the Hindu people the element of competitiveness between males and females is not very evident. It seems self-evident to most of us that male and female are different. The recognition of distinctiveness and differences did lead to various discriminations and injustices, no doubt, and a need for reform is felt. Yet, egalitarianism from the Hindu perspective does not mean the elimination of all differences, but rather the recognition of the mutuality and interdependability of the diverse.

However, caste differences, which during the time of Manu perhaps were as obvious as were the differences of age and sex, are not so obvious to many modern Hindus. Many intellectual Hindus think that the caste system is anachronistic. However, we have yet to find a proper resolution of this problem. The theological basis of caste is the preponderance in varying proportion in each human being of the three *guna*s or qualities of *sattva, rajas,* and *tamas* (goodness, passion, and darkness)—or, to put it more simply, the differences of the actual dispositions of human beings, although all are human. This seemed so sensible that even Gandhi, who fought for the rights of the untouchables and called them *harijana,* God's people, did not want to eliminate the system. How the perennial insight is to be concretized in history, however, is still a problem. In any case, the history of Hinduism shows how important historical circumstances have been in our theological thinking. We need to become more aware of this, and then pursue our reflections in light of that awareness.

CONCLUSION

I agree with Prof. Smith in recognizing the importance that history (even in the conventional sense) plays in theological thinking. I have reservations insofar as he wants to derive all the data for theology simply from history, because, according to him, history does not exclude anything that is relevant for theology. It is well argued by him—and I doubt whether anyone would disagree—that revelation or realization (i.e., any encounter with the transcendent) is historical insofar as it takes place in time with temporal persons. However, the content of that encounter seems to refer to that which does not suggest the contingent and nonabiding character of time. That is why theology refers to cases of direct encounter, whether of revelation or actual realization. Of course, this often ends up in mere reiteration of what has already been said in the past. The difference, however, between such theologians and the outstanding ones is that the latter have a greater sensitivity for the transcendent.

In other words, when mystics are theologians, as the examples of Augustine, Al Ghazāli, or Ramanuja indicate, they definitely have a chance of being outstanding theologians. However, I also see the possibility that theologizing by reference to the history of religions, insofar as it is a sincere effort at finding truth and not simply an effort of justifying an already possessed conviction, can itself become a spiritual discipline and, like prayer and meditation, can lead to a new way of looking at history—as I suspect has happened with Prof. Smith.

NOTES

1. A. L. Basham, *The Wonder That Was India* (London, 1954).
2. G. C. Pande, *Foundations of Indian Culture* (New Delhi, 1984), can be cited as an example.

II.

Toward a Christocentric Catholic Theology

JOHN B. COBB, JR.

I am deeply sympathetic with the concerns and purposes of those who have planned this conference. I find myself in a large measure of agreement with the preconference paper prepared by Leonard Swidler.

Nevertheless, I do not like the name of the conference. I am not myself seeking a "universal theology of religion." My rejection of this language is no doubt partly a terminological matter of a relatively unimportant sort. But it also expresses basic commitments that may be appropriate for discussion in this conference.

I will order my remarks as follows. In Section A, I state my objections to the goal of a universal theology of religion. The remainder of the paper will attempt to show how a Christocentric catholic theology can address the concerns underlying the calling of this conference. Section B considers how the internal history of Christocentric thinkers can become inclusive or catholic. Section C briefly notes the importance of catholicity of subject matter as well. And Section D presents a more detailed discussion of how traditional Christian convictions are to be so formulated as to show that they are complementary to the deepest convictions of other traditions rather than in outright conflict.

A

My first objection to the title of this conference is its focus on "religion." I am pleased to see that in the second version of the preconference paper there has been a shift from "interreligious dialogue" to "interreligious and inter-ideological dialogue." Much of my practical concern is mitigated by this shift.

The World Council of Churches has avoided the term "religion" and has advocated dialogue with persons of other faiths and ideologies. I prefer this. To call Christianity, Judaism, Islam, Confucianism, Hinduism, Buddhism, and the primal religions all "religions" focuses attention on aspects of their total life that are not, in most instances, the most important. That all these traditions have encouraged religious practices is beyond doubt, but that as a whole they are well categorized in light of this feature is very doubtful indeed.

If the word "religious" means nothing more than ways of binding together—that is, ways of organizing and directing life and thought—then I would withdraw my objection. But then there would be no need to add "ideologies," for ideologies too would be religions. In fact the word "religion" almost always highlights to the Western ear cultic practices and especially those associated with belief in divine being(s). It is this that renders it a poor choice as the primary category for many of the great traditions.

But does the WCC shift to "faiths" help? Wilfred Cantwell Smith has objected that we should speak of various ways in which faith is expressed rather than of a plurality of faiths. He makes a good point. I would add that I do not see faith as the center of all traditions. It belongs to the theistic traditions primarily, so that the use of this term places other traditions in an unsuitable category. Further, it is only by virtue of its theistic connotations that "faiths" requires supplementation by "ideologies."

The only positive suggestion I can make as to how we can speak of the great traditions of humankind is that we call them "ways." By "ways" I mean not only ways to live but also ways to understand life and the total context of life. I suspect that no *way* that has guided the life of large communities over any extended period of time is devoid of strong religious elements. But these are not always primary. Marxism is a very important way in our time, but it deemphasizes or even denies its tendencies to divinize historical processes and heroes, and to evolve its own cultic patterns. And there are forms of Judaism, Christianity, Confucianism, and Buddhism for which cult and divinities are not central. Nevertheless, they are all comprehensive ways of life and thought.

Now it might well be said that what is meant by "religion" in the conference title is what I mean by "way," so that my quarrel might be a rather petty one. Let us assume that. In that case, what about a theology of religion understood in this sense? Would a theology of religion then be reflection about the great ways of humankind? Would these ways of life and thought become themselves the subject matter of theological inquiry? Surely it is theologically appropriate to reflect about these traditions. And there have been important theologians who have taken human experience, activity, and thought as their topic. But for my own part, I believe this to be a mistake. I believe that theology should concern itself primarily with that with which these ways have concerned themselves, not with the ways as such.

I suspect here again that I am not in real disagreement with the conference planners. Their emphasis is interreligious dialogue, not history of religions as an academic discipline. The latter tends to make the ways and their religious practices its topic, whereas dialogue usually focuses on what the participants see as most important. Hence I will assume that theology of religion, when religion is understood as I have proposed, deals with that to which the great ways of humankind point, and I will not raise further objections to this.

But what of a "universal theology"? Here I am genuinely uncertain as to the intention. But I fear that the meaning conveyed is that theology can begin with a perspective shaped neutrally by all the ways rather than by any one of them in particular. This means that a universal theology will replace specifically Christian theology, which is viewed as being inherently parochial.

If that is the meaning, then I protest in the name both of realism and of Christian faith. In the name of realism I protest that the pretense to stand beyond all traditions and build neutrally out of all of them is a delusion. In the name of Christian faith I protest against the implicit relativization and even negation of basic Christian commitments.

I propose as an alternative that what we Christians need is a truly catholic theology. Inasmuch as I am a Protestant you will understand that I do not mean by "catholic" something specifically bound up with the Roman Catholic Church. Yet as a Protestant I do recognize that the impulse to true catholicity may be stronger in the Roman Catholic Church than in the Protestant denominations, despite the sectarian tendencies that afflict it too.

I propose, secondly, that the impulse to catholicity is specifically christological and that it is christocentrism that requires of the Christian the rejection of all arrogance, exclusivism, and dogmatism in relation to other ways. I believe a truly christocentric theology must be catholic, and that a truly catholic theology will satisfy much of what is sought by those who propose a universal theology of religion. The remainder of this paper is devoted to clarifying and developing this claim.

B

First, who is the Christ in whom Christian theology is properly centered? Throughout the history of Christianity there has been a duality of focus that is essential to the idea of incarnation itself. There is, first, the one who becomes incarnate and there is, secondly, the one who is the incarnation. The Word became a human being in Jesus. I myself wish that the Johannine prologue had spoken of *Sophia* instead of *Logos*, and I propose that, despite the predominance of "Word" in the tradition, we speak today of "Wisdom."

Christocentrism means both that we should place our faith in the divine Wisdom, which is very God of very God, and that the embodiment of that Wisdom in Jesus provides us with the center of our history. These two aspects of christocentrism are indissolubly connected for us. We trust the everlasting Wisdom because of what happened in Jesus. We affirm Jesus as the center of our history because in him we find the everlasting Wisdom.

The Wisdom we find incarnate in Jesus is present everywhere and at all times. Specifically, it is that by virtue of which there is life wherever there is any living thing, and it is that apart from which there is no human understanding at all. Hence the affirmation that this Wisdom is incarnate in Jesus cannot mean that Jesus is the only channel through which God is present in the world. On the contrary, the Wisdom we meet in Jesus is precisely the Wisdom that is already known by all. Exclusivism implicitly denies that this Wisdom is truly God, and thus opposes the Christian understanding of the incarnation, which, in turn, is the basis of christocentrism.

Even those who acknowledge that God is somehow known to all sometimes argue that Jesus, and Jesus alone, has introduced an understanding of God adequate to all human needs. The words, "I am the way, the truth, and the life," which in their Johannine context apply to the divine Word or Wisdom, are wrongly taken to refer exclusively to a particular human being. Thereby the exclusivism banished by one aspect of christocentrism makes its reappearance through a particular form of the other aspect. Because the problem lies in wrong affirmations about Jesus and, especially, in false conclusions from the doctrine of incarnation, I want to describe a form of incarnational theology for which Jesus is the center of history, and leads away from exclusivism to true catholicity.

I should acknowledge, before proceeding, my indebtedness to one book of H. Richard Niebuhr. Reading *The Meaning of Revelation* as a seminary student was for me a revelatory experience. It permanently affected my understanding of the theological task. What I have to say today is indebted to that book.

Niebuhr helps us understand that we all live by our private and communal memories or internal histories. If you want to know who I am, I can provide some categories in which to place me: citizen of the United States, member of the United Methodist Church, male, white, seminary professor, and so forth. But if you really want to know who I am, you will have to let me share my story with you. Similarly you can define Christianity in terms of certain categories to which it belongs or certain of its official teachings or widespread practices. But if you want to know what it really means to be a Christian, you will have to study the history of Christianity and specifically how that history is now understood and appropriated by believers. It is in that way that you will discover that Jesus is the center of history for Christians.

Of course, to be the center of history is not to be the whole of history. The conventional story begins with Genesis and remembers the history of the Jews down to the time of Jesus. It includes the way the early Christians responded to Jesus and then follows the history of the expansion of Christianity and the specific ancestry of our present several communities. As Christians, most of us live out of some such story.

Now the problem with that story is not, as some suppose, that Jesus is at the center, but that the circumference is far too narrow. For most of us it does not even include the whole story of Christianity. In our Western church histories we are likely to neglect the Orthodox East after the credal controversies are ended. We Protestants learn very little of Catholic history after the Council of Trent.

The ecumenical movement among Christians is doing much to heal this foreshortened memory and to enable us all to claim the whole of the Christian story as our story. This is a gain, and there is little doubt that we achieve this precisely through our joint acknowledgment of the centrality of Jesus to all of our Christian stories.

But this is obviously insufficient. If Christian ecumenism were to be won at the price of intensified exclusivism in relation to others, the price would be too high. Especially the emphasis on the centrality of Jesus in Christian ecumenism is in danger of intensifying the destructive wall that separates us from Judaism.

The story we Christians learn begins with that of the ancient Jews. But this story culminates in the fierce attack on the Jews placed on the lips of Jesus in the Gospel of John and in the struggle with the Jews recorded in the book of Acts. The story of those from whom we Christians separated with much bitterness is to most of us something alien. It is indeed the story of those we reviled and persecuted, and it is not pleasant to recall it. Nevertheless, Christians are today attempting to learn that story. We must learn it first as *their* story, but we must also move beyond it. It must become part of *our* story as Christians-and-Jews.

Now whence comes for us as Christians the impulse to learn this story and to redefine what we mean by "we" to include both Christians and Jews? It comes from Wisdom. But I am trying here to focus on the particularities of history. Historical sources are difficult to prove, but I have no doubt that it comes from the story whose center is the Jewish Jesus. When we seriously take Jesus as the center of our history, we cannot be satisfied with the partisan rejection of Jesus' people that has characterized our gentile Christianity through the centuries. We look forward with Paul to the time when our gentile misappropriation of Jesus will not compel Jews to disown him. We believe that our destiny as Christians is bound up with the destiny of the Jews in one destiny of Jews-and-Christians. Indeed we understand that we are all Jews whether we are the natural or the engrafted branches.

My point is a simple one. The broadening of our internal history to include Judaism does not—for us Christians—displace Jesus from the center of our history. On the contrary, it is because Jesus is the center that we are moved toward the more inclusive history.

What about that other great offshoot of Judaism, Islam? Can Muslim history also become part of our internal history? We are much further from Muslims. It will take decades of study and dialogue before we can integrate their historical experience with ours. But already we recognize that the God whom Jesus called Father is also the one they call Allāh. We cannot feel ourselves wholly alien to those who do the will of that God, and we cannot but recognize the seriousness with which Muslims undertake that task. As long as Jesus is the center of the history by which we live, there will be a strong impulse for us to expand that history to include that of Islam as well.

To live by a remembered history is not to sentimentalize that history or to minimize the evil that plays so large a role within it. Concealing the evil and highlighting the good in our personal and communal stories is a temptation to which all succumb. But the Jewish scriptures are remarkable in the extent to which they evade this temptation. The heroes are also sinners. The Jews know themselves as a people often faithless to God. In the Gospels also the disciples appear as foolish and weak. Unfortunately a tendency to adulation of Christian heroes begins in the Acts of the Apostles and has infected much of the Christian story ever since. But to learn that our story is one of exclusivism, anti-Judaism, sexism, racism, corruption by power, corruption by wealth, corruption by piety, corruption by nationalism, and a host of other sins does not keep it from being our story. Because Jesus is its center we can understand this evil for what it is and repent.

Similarly, as we appropriate the stories of Jews and Muslims as part of our enlarged new story, we do not do so uncritically. We find many ways in which, in the light of Jesus, they are to be commended for avoiding sins to which we succumbed. But we will also inevitably evaluate their stories as well, and in the light of Jesus we will see ways in which they have much to gain by appropriating him more fully into their internal histories.

The expansion of our internal history is proceeding in another direction as well. Our critical study of the scriptures was long directed toward isolating the pure Jewish and Christian strain from the many other influences that gain expression there. We celebrated our history largely by contrasting it with paganism. That is now changing. We continue to celebrate the creativity of the Jewish people in weaving together the many strands of influence into a creative and dynamic faith in one God, but we no longer view the strands that are woven together as something to be despised. Our Jewish heritage leads us to reclaim our Egyptian, Canaanite, Mesopotamian, Persian, and Greek heritage as well. Our internal history expands. But it does not become simply the sum total of all those histories told in any way and from any perspective. On the contrary, we appropriate all into an enlarging history whose center remains, for us, Jesus. It is the nature of that center to allow and demand the expansion of the circumference.

Thus far, in a very schematic way I have indicated what I mean by expanding our internal history to encompass a larger part of human history, not in spite of Christocentricity but because of it. But even this is not enough. There are other histories, those of India and China and Korea as well as Africa and the indigenous peoples of the New World, that cannot be brought into our internal history simply through the historical expansion of the story we tell ourselves. In order to include these stories, too, is it necessary to give up the centrality of Jesus and seek some other principle of organization or revelation for the larger whole? Should I, after all, give up my Christocentric catholic project in favor of the universal theology of religion?

The answer to this question requires honest self-examination. I do find myself desirous of incorporating into my internal history a wider one than that historically connected with Jesus. Why? What draws me in that direction? Why am I not satisfied to identify myself strongly with one portion of humanity and to view others simply as others? What pulls against the we-they dualism that also afflicts me? As far as I can tell, there is a double answer corresponding to the dual elements in Christocentrism. First, whenever I draw the line between "us" and "them" I seem to discern wisdom on both sides of the line, and I cannot be satisfied consciously to reject or ignore what I, at the same time, recognize to be wise. That I understand that wisdom to be the divine Wisdom, present in the other, focuses and intensifies this need to overcome the barriers that separate.

I have also learned that a besetting temptation to which I and others are continually succumbing is to identify that bit of understanding already possessed with the whole of wisdom, or with what is really important in it. I have learned that this is arrogance and that nothing cuts us off from God more surely than this idolatry of what we already possess. I have learned that coldness or indifference to others in the concreteness of their being, which includes their understanding, is the rejection of God's love for us as well as the refusal to love God. I have learned that my destiny is bound up with that of the whole globe.

The question now is, Where have I learned these things? There are many answers: home, school, church, books, friends. But when I press the question more deeply, I must come back to the fact that it is from the Christian story that I have learned them, primarily from the Bible. And when I ask how in fact I understand the Bible, I must confess that I read it in terms of a center that is Jesus. My impulse to live out of a story larger than the one that is historically interconnected with Jesus comes from Jesus.

That, of course, is only a beginning of the answer to the larger question. Suppose we Christians are impelled to include Gautama Buddha within our internal histories. Granted, the impulse comes from Jesus. Will the result be simply an expansion of the history from which we live so that the center remains Jesus? Or will Gautama introduce a new center—one that displaces Jesus from centrality?

Such displacement of Jesus is not to be rejected a priori in the name of Christian faith. On the contrary, faith expresses itself in action whose consequences we cannot anticipate. If faithfulness to Jesus leads to the displacement of Jesus from centrality, then such displacement is itself faithful.

There are certainly those who, consciously or unconsciously impelled by Jesus, have turned to Gautama and found there a new center that displaced the old. My argument is that this is not the necessary result, and that when Jesus is removed from the position of center of all history by the appropriation of Gautama, much that could be included in the history of which Jesus is the center can no longer be included. I do not mean here to judge the question of the value of a fully Buddhist way in comparison with a Christian way. My comment is of a different order. So far as we now can see, much that is of value from the Christian perspective—that is, much that the way centered in Jesus seeks to include—is neither valued nor included in the Buddhist way. Hence, from the Christian perspective, there are reasons to try to include Gautama within the circle centered in Jesus so that the rest of what is included in that circle can be retained.

In dealing with the other expansions of the Christian circle I have spoken chiefly of additions. This is one-sided; every addition involves some transformation of that to which the addition is made. This feature is greatly intensified in relation to Buddhism. One cannot add Gautama to a basically unchanged complex. To bring him in is to transform everything. The historical consciousness, the quest for meaning in history, cannot remain unchanged when the internal history in question includes Gautama's radical critique and denial of historical meaning.

I have written elsewhere, in *Beyond Dialogue* especially, about a crossing over to Mahayana Buddhism and a coming back to Christianity and how the Christianity in question is thereby transformed. I will not repeat that here. My point is only that the expansion of the internal history from which we live to include the Buddhist achievement as well need not displace the centrality of Jesus, although it will transform all that is known from that center.

The task of dialogue and going beyond dialogue in relation to each of the great ways of humankind is a vast one. We have barely begun to deal with the fundamental changes that must be effected within our Christian faith. The changes that come about through one dialogue may make the next dialogue still more difficult. After each new transformation, the work that was done earlier will have to be done again. But a truly Christocentric faith must seek catholicity in this way.

How is this Christocentric catholic theology to be compared to a universal theology of religion? It is not less universal in the sense of omitting some segment of human experience and wisdom from its purview. But it does not pretend to a neutral or impartial perspective on the whole. Does this render it biased or arrogant? I do not think so. It would be arrogant to assert that the project of catholicity is one that all should pursue, and it would be biased to assert that the only way catholicity can be attained is by Christocentrism. But it is not arrogant to explain that we as Christians are impelled toward catholicity, and to acknowledge that what impels us is our Christocentrism.

Indeed, one of my concerns about the promotion of the project of a universal theology by Christians is that it is difficult to avoid giving the impression that Jews and others should join us in this project. It can be, in relation to Jews, another way of placing them on the defensive if they decline to surrender their identity as Jews to join the quest of universal theology of religion. There are, I think, impulses within Judaism toward a catholic theology, but it is not for Christians to evaluate the importance of those impulses in Judaism in comparison with those toward the preservation of Jewish distinctiveness, or to determine how these are rightly related to one another. It seems more honest and more open to others to explain where we stand as Christians rather than to claim to place our project beyond confessional diversity. My thesis is that a catholic theology can gain the advantages of a universal theology without the arrogance entailed in claiming to attain such universality.

C

Thus far I have been considering the catholicity of theology in terms of the internal history that shapes the Christian. My understanding is that Christian theology is thinking that is consciously expressive of a perspective shaped by the shared history of Christians. Christian thinking remains parochial as long as that history is parochial. It becomes catholic to whatever extent that history is inclusive. Ultimately the only history adequate to its center in Jesus will be the history of life on this planet.

Christian theology should become catholic in another way as well, and, indeed, becoming catholic in the first way will tend to make it catholic in the other as well. Sometimes it is supposed that Christian theology deals properly only with ideas that are reflected in a particular segment of history, such as the Bible. The topics of theology are narrowly defined in terms of the tradition. Indeed, in the attempt to establish theology as a "science" (*Wissenschaft*), some Protestant theologians of the previous generation carefully explained its task as the interpretation of specific texts, those on which sermons are to be preached. Most of the topics dealt with by St. Augustine or St. Thomas fall outside the purview of theology so conceived. Indeed, most of the issues of life and death with which society now struggles turn out not to be appropriate topics for theological discourse!

In contrast, a truly catholic theology must be catholic in its concerns. Of course it will be selective. It does have a special need to understand the history that has shaped it and the center that governs the understanding of that history. But chiefly its principle of selection will be its sense, coming from that history, of what is most important today. To questions of peace, justice, personal wholeness, ecological health, racism, sexism, hunger, and freedom, as well as those of God, the church, salvation, and eschatology, it will bring the resources and the perspective shaped by the most catholic history it can internally realize. I do not think this project is likely to be called forth by a theology of religion.

D

I would make another point in agreement with Wilfred Cantwell Smith. Through dialogue we should be able to learn the ways in which our customary affirmations growing out of our own histories are heard by others as denials of their deepest convictions. We should, then, undertake to reformulate our beliefs so that this negation of others will be reduced and finally overcome.

The underlying assumption here is that the aspects of reality that persons come to see through different communal histories differ profoundly, but these aspects are not in flat contradiction. This assumption is based on still deeper ones. First, reality is extremely complex but not self-contradictory. Secondly, what persons really see is there to be seen. The problem, illustrated again and again in all sorts of dialogues, is that our account of what we see is usually inaccurate and exaggerated, and that we quickly move from affirmation of what grasps us to denial of what grasps others. In appreciative listening to others we can come to reformulations of our own convictions that are more accurate and more limited, leaving space for the accurate and limited formulations of the convictions of others.

Examples are numerous. We can take the familiar and central one about salvation. Having experienced personal salvation through faith in Jesus Christ, many Christians have taught that no salvation is possible in any other way. But obviously such sweeping negations follow neither from the Christian experience of salvation, nor from convictions about Jesus Christ's saving power that are appropriate to the experience. A more accurate analysis of the role of Jesus and of the divine Wisdom in effecting our salvation is needed. Also we need to clarify just what we mean by salvation or just what type of salvation is effected for the Christian believer. It is quite likely that the precise salvific experience brought about through faith in Jesus Christ occurs in no other way. But the Christian should listen carefully to the Hindu account of *mokṣa* or the Zen Buddhist account of *satori*, recognizing that these are just as authentic as the Christian experience. Whether we shall stretch the meaning of salvation to include such other experiences and then distinguish diverse modes of salvation, or limit the use of "salvation" to the Christian experience while retaining *mokṣa* and *satori* to refer to the others, is an important decision, but in either case it will be possible to continue to make Christian claims for the dependence on Jesus Christ of what Christians have most prized without entailing any pejorative implications about Hindu and Buddhist experience.

I have gone to great lengths earlier to indicate that we should go beyond merely clarifying our diversity in ways that allow a genuine pluralism. For the Christian it is important not only to understand the experience of others in their difference but to find ways to incorporate these diverse experiences in a transformed Christianity. But even this will not do away with a continuing pluralism. We must continue our care to affirm even our most catholic convictions in such a way that they do not deny the always continuing divergent convictions of others.

Of course, it is unlikely that this project can be completed any more than can the others. Those coming from other traditions may insist on formulations of their convictions, which we cannot accept without denying what is centrally important to us. However careful we are, others will hear our affirmations as pejorative, especially because we cannot give up all the language that has been used during centuries in which Christian doctrines did constitute negations of what others affirmed. For example, no matter how carefully we explain what we mean by asserting that Jesus is the Christ, many Jews will continue to hear our affirmation as a contradiction of their insistence that the Messiah has not come. But the abandonment of the word "Christ" on our part is not the appropriate response. Instead we must work together repeatedly to clarify the difference between what Jews mean by "Messiah" and what Christians legitimately mean by "Christ." We need to join the Jews in their longing for the coming of the Messiah and the messianic age.

Many persons who agree that there are differences among the Christian experience of the forgiveness of sins, the Hindu experience of *mokṣa*, and the Zen experience of *satori*, such that no conflict is involved in acknowledging the authenticity and importance of each, believe that there is another level at which this type of solution cannot apply. This is the level of "ultimate reality." Of course, most will agree that "ultimate reality" is beyond our finite conceptualities. Hence we would expect that approaching it from diverse perspectives will lead to diverse affirmations about it, none of which are finally exhaustive. But whereas the forgiveness of sins, *mokṣa*, and *satori* may be acknowledged, quite simply, as different experiences, many suppose that what is approached as "ultimate reality" must be one and the same, however diversely it is apprehended and conceptualized.

This conviction about the self-identity of "ultimate reality" is strengthened by dialogue among Jews, Christians, and Muslims. All three agree that the One they worship is one and the same. They may argue about what this One is like, how it has acted, what is its will, what more is to be expected from it in the future. But they are sure that their diverse languages and images have a common reference transcendent of all that any of them can think or say. For example, the One of whom they speak is the reality that created and creates all that is.

But what happens when believers in the One Creator of all enter into dialogue with representatives of traditions that do not affirm a creation or a creator? Zen Buddhism will serve as the example. Historically some Christians have simply refused dialogue on the grounds that Zen Buddhists are the worst of all reprobates—atheists. But most Christians have seen too much of power and validity in Zen Buddhism to dismiss it in this offhand way. Two alternatives remain.

The first has dominated the dialogue to date. Christians have thought that "Creator" was but one way to understand the One who has been worshiped by the Jewish family of religions. This One is most fundamentally "ultimate reality." Hence the question is not whether Zen Buddhists affirm a Creator but rather how they approach "ultimate reality." The fact that their approach to, and what they say about, "ultimate reality" differ so profoundly from our approach and doctrine only reinforces the awareness that "ultimate reality" is far beyond all that any of us can say or think.

Lest anyone should miss the distinction between this way of avoiding contradiction among the convictions of the several great ways and the former one, allow me to recapitulate. With respect to salvation it would theoretically be possible to say that there is but one experience of salvation, which is variously described as the forgiveness of sins, *mokṣa*, and *satori*. But careful study renders such a judgment implausible. If one looks in Christianity for an experience more like that of *mokṣa* or *satori*, one will turn to the mystics who do not describe their culminating experiences as the forgiveness of sins. Almost everyone recognizes that there are many different types of experience even within a single religious tradition, and that there is no reason to suppose that the diverse accounts of religious experiences are all efforts to describe one and the same type of experience.

With respect to what is experienced, however, the situation differs. Here the dominant approach is to assume that that which forgives sins is also the reality that is realized in *mokṣa* and *satori*. In this approach, the difference of experience is understood to be the reason that the reality is spoken of in quite diverse ways. But difference in image and concept is not taken to mean that there is a difference in the reality itself.

This approach to dialogue is compatible with what I said earlier about the vast complexity of reality on the one hand and the noncontradictory character of the diverse experiences of it on the other. Nevertheless, it contains an assumption that I find unwarranted. This is the assumption that there is a one-to-one correspondence between what is thought of as "ultimate reality" in our Western tradition and that with which all "religious" traditions concern themselves. One advocate of this position, Paul Knitter, acknowledges that indeed this is an unproven assumption, and he recommends that it be treated as a hypothesis. Nevertheless, he asserts that just this hypothesis should be held by those who seek dialogue.

My belief is that there is no need to encumber the dialogue with this hypothesis. Indeed, I believe that the dialogue becomes more fruitful when we are fully open to the opposite hypothesis. For example, we should consider that what the Zen Buddhist names "Emptiness" or "Emptying" may not be the same as what the Christian names "God." Of course, if I am correct about this difference, we are left with the task of formulating a creative synthesis in which the relationship between Emptying and God can be understood in ways that neither Buddhists nor Christians have adequately articulated in the past. But what is wrong with that?

What is wrong, I am told repeatedly, is that there can be only one "ultimate reality." I am left with the impression that those who affirm this doctrine regard it as self-evident and suppose a pluralistic metaphysics to be nonsensical. They may, of course, be correct. But is this supposition itself not subject to dialogue? Is it absolutely self-evident, for example, that the ground of form and the ground of matter are identical? Is Plato's cosmology in the *Timaeus* self-evidently absurd?

My suggestion is that it is best to enter each dialogue with both hypotheses in view. It may be that what my dialogue partners will speak of is their experience of that same reality that I know in Jesus Christ as God. If so, fine; I have much to learn from them. But it may be that they will speak of something else, something of which I am even less well informed. If so, I must listen all the more intently. I will have all the more homework to do afterward in integrating what I learn with what I thought I knew. I will need to revise not only my theology but, perchance, my metaphysics. But surely that is nothing against this approach. Surely Christians must be as open to revising metaphysics as to revising theology!

This brings us full circle to my anxiety about the formulation of the topic for this conference. I fear that the project of universal theology is the easy way out of our present problems. Consciously or unconsciously we are likely to hold to the metaphysical concomitants of our respective ways and relativize only the historical and theological concomitants.

Let me be more concrete. Many Christian theologians are convinced that underlying the totality of the reality that we can approach through our ordinary modes of inquiry there is another that eludes us. It is the One, the "ultimate reality," that contrasts with everything finite. Schleiermacher tells us it is that on which everything else is absolutely dependent. Tillich calls it Being Itself and declares that it is our ultimate concern.

Those who hold to this metaphysics are likely to suppose that, because everyone is in fact related to this one "ultimate reality," and because this is finally the most important of all relationships, all the great traditions of the world give expression to how this relationship is apprehended. Hence these theologians advocate dialogue and expect through dialogue to become aware of more about how this relationship functions in human life. But what the *relata* of this relationship are, they already know. Through dialogue, it is presumed, we can overcome some of the parochial features of our own historical relationship to "ultimate reality" experienced as the God of the Bible.

Given these assumptions it is not surprising that the hypothesis is favored that Buddhist Emptying, also, is this one "ultimate reality" underlying all finite things. Commitment to the hypothesis is strengthened by the fact that Buddhists also expect that all truly concerned persons are dealing with one and the same reality, the one they call Emptying. From both sides there is agreement that Christians name "God" the same reality that Buddhists name "Emptying."

Yet when these Christians and Zen Buddhists clarify their fundamental metaphysical assumptions about reality, the assumed identity becomes acutely problematic. Christians speak of the *underlying* reality, the reality that somehow is the cause of the finite or the phenomenal world. Zen Buddhists point to the reality *of* that finite world itself. It turns out that the assumption common to both dialogue partners—that their reference is identical—leads to the contradictions both wish to avoid. Each claims the other is referring to something that the other repudiates as its reference.

One can, of course, appeal again to the fact that both Zen Buddhists and Christians insist that the reality with which they have to do vastly exceeds all that they can say or think. Both can affirm, for example, that what they point to transcends the antithesis of the personal and the impersonal. But does that help to overcome the difference between them? I think not. The basic difference is between the true nature of finite reality on the one hand and the ground of finite reality on the other. Perhaps both transcend the distinction of personal and impersonal. But that does not overcome the difference.

It is interesting to observe what happens in those instances in which the impasse appears to be broken through. Inasmuch as the Zen Buddhist account is inextricably bound up with Zen Buddhist experience, there can be no movement from that side. The Buddhist effort is to help Christians surrender their clinging to something that transcends or grounds the actual, finite world. Because Christian experience is far less directly bound to the metaphysics of Christians, some Christians modify their formulations, redefining transcendence in terms of the depth of finite reality and abandoning the distinction between ground and what is grounded. They find in Christian mysticism points of contact with Buddhist experience. They give up the imagery of Creator in favor of the creativity that constitutes the finite world itself. In short, they treat biblical modes of thought as cultural expressions that they can outgrow. Their ties to the history of their own community become attenuated. They maintain these ties only by emphasizing the exceptional strain of apophatic mysticism which is found within their tradition.

I suggest that this is not a happy outcome of dialogue. I do not wish to preclude the abandonment of Christocentricity on the part of Christians who engage in dialogue, or even their conversion to the other tradition, but changes that largely uproot one from one's own tradition impoverish at the same time that they enrich. It is time to recognize that the metaphysics of universal ground is in fact an abstract expression of the biblical understanding of creation and hence not a neutral basis for dialogue among all the great traditions. It is time to recognize also that it is not the one metaphysics everlastingly appropriate to the Christian faith. There are other ways of translating the biblical experience of a Creator into metaphysical language that may contribute more fruitfully to dialogue with Zen Buddhists.

I will not try here to spell out alternative metaphysical approaches. If I use the term "metaphysical" very broadly—as I have done—then I can suggest that both Heidegger and Wittgenstein provide metaphysical bases for dialogue with Zen Buddhists that do not entail the problems I have noted. Elsewhere I have tried to show the fruitfulness of a Whiteheadian approach. But my task in this paper is theological, not metaphysical. As a Christian theologian I commend all efforts to break Christianity out of its parochial limits and especially out of its implicitly or explicitly negative relationship to the other great ways of humankind. But I am troubled by the dominant proposals for carrying out this task. I do not believe these proposals will commend themselves to the most sensitive and committed representatives of some of the other great ways. I do not believe they commend themselves to Christians. Hence I am calling for a different approach—for Christians, a Christocentric catholic one.

It is my hope that the followers of the other great ways will also find within their own traditions reasons and means for analogous openness to learning from one another and being transformed by what is learned. If this leads some day to a merging of all the great ways into one that is at the same time Jewish, Christian, Muslim, Hindu, Buddhist, Confucian, primal, and so forth, so be it. If that merged way is fully and authentically Christian, I as a Christian see nothing to fear from that. But if all the great ways continue to the last day distinct from one another, each open to all, enriched by all, and transformed by all, I as a Christian see nothing lacking in that. My belief is not that all human beings should join Christian churches but that Jesus Christ has something of greatest importance to contribute to all. To the end we will continue to witness to that. If Jews appropriate Jesus while remaining Jews, and Buddhists, while remaining Buddhists, I, as a Christian, see nothing lacking in that.

We do not now need to decide between an ultimate goal of merging all the great traditions into one and the alternative of their living side by side in mutual openness to the end. We do now need to decide what theological contribution we can now make to moving toward either of these ends. My proposal is that for Christians the finest contribution will be a Christocentric catholic theology.

II.1.

The Interior Path

ZALMAN SCHACHTER

I want to thank Professor Cobb, first of all, because hearing him was different from reading him. When I read a position paper, I become an adversary of the writer. It is natural; that is part of how one reads critically. I heard him speak, and there he was, a witness. And the more he *said* "Christocentric," the less it became a mere word for me. I realized that for him it was a position, for, if it were taken from him, he would have no place to stand. But he was speaking of a commitment, and I must honor that.

I agree with so much that he said. In the space in which I represent the Jewish magisterium to my fellow believers, we are Torahcentric; without the Torah there is no place for us. It is exactly this function of *Memra,* the word, the *Logos, Sophia, Hokhma* that centers the process that is the basis of all our striving. Or, maybe even better put: it is the tropism in our souls that draws us closer to God, and *Hokhma* is this tropism. So if we were not to have that tropism to take us closer to God, then we would not have any ground left. On this level I want to say yes to Dr. Cobb.

What function does that Christocentric pivot serve? I do think that there is something in the sociology of knowledge, a position that he wished to avoid. Deep down, I am convinced that there is such a thing as generic religion, no-frills religion, which comes in a plain brown wrapper. And we also have brand names: Judaism, Christianity, and the like. And all of us would not have gotten to where we are had not the brand name religions and their dogmas taken us there. But somehow there is something to generic religion. And this is perhaps where that universal theology is. There is *Sophia* drawing us to that *also*. It is the "also" that I want to talk about.

Kabbalah and its hermeneutic help me a lot. My suggestion is that the mysticisms of all religions have given us languages and have technologies for thinking about different levels of experience dealing with different levels of alternate realities. If we are looking for an ultimate one, we need the language and experience of mystics. We need to find out what that transformative thing is for us in an experience like Meister Eckart's "The eye with which I see God is the eye with which God sees me." For the ultimate we want the term Godhead rather than God. Such language creates ways in which we can talk and think about that ultimate reality. It is not a reality that we can look at as an object *out there*. It is not even *in* here; it transcends both. It is the nominative case of I AM THAT I AM or—as we would say in Kabbalah and Hasidism—a way that looks at the universe from God's perspective. So, too, do I look at the function of the *Soter* (Savior). The rationalists among us Jews have often wished to deny the *Soter* function of the Zaddik ("righteous one"), and Sunni Muslims do not like to deal with it, and yet Sufis talk about *Fana fi rasul,* the way to *Fana fi'llahi*—self-effacement to the messenger as the way to self-effacement to God: that one becomes a window for the other. Hasidim talk about the *Shoresh han 'shamah,* that the root of one's soul is with the rebbe. Often, in dialogue with Christians, I find that we share best when I sense that Christians are Nazarene Hasidim and that in Jesus they have a rebbe, a *Soter.* And if this is what Dr. Cobb means by "Christocentric," I am willing to agree with him.

I find also a Trinity of three persons in one God easier to handle when I go with the Christian Kabbalist Joachim de Fiore. He says that there is an apprehension of reality which we meet in God the Father. The first two thousand years of world history (within the biblical time track) refers to that. And then comes an apprehension of reality that we meet in God as the Son, a period changing from the new era to the present. And there still is the next one to come, that of the Holy Spirit. My sense is that this is the element of *Ruah haqodesh,* that feminine hypostasis of God, that element in which Pallas Athena is seen as springing out of the head of Zeus, or, as is said, *Hokhma* comes out from the Great Nothing: no-thing (*Hahokhma m'ayin timmatze*). Here perhaps *sunyatā*—the Buddhist void—and *Hokhma* do have an interface and a dynamism between themselves.

I also realize that there is a second element that has to do with *Soter*: as a focus for the worshiper. Even "atheistic" Buddhism relates devotionally to Buddha as *Soter.* Go and watch Shinran Buddhists, the whole range of Buddhists, even Theravadins, when they appear in the temple before a statue of the Buddha. What is their functional attitude? They may theoretically deny that it is worship of a God. In their obeisance that goes deeper than the *dulia* that the Catholic Church allows for saints, one that goes to *latria*—which troubles us, because of idol-*latria*—they worship. So my feeling is that functionally they relate to the Buddha as God. There is something about human sharing together in *Sophia* language. Anthropomorphism says that at the core of our beings we are godlike and so we meet God as person.

Now I want to ask myself what is the good of taking the position of universal religion. It is the coming one knocking at our door. We throw it out the door, and it comes in through the window; it keeps on saying, "Do something about how you talk together." We face the issue of the paradigm shift. Every map of reality we have had up to now seems less firm. If we have to share the road together so that we can walk on the way, a good map would be helpful. The old maps have been shaken by every discipline outside the discipline of religion. We are grasping so hard to keep the old maps, the ones we are used to, playing our dialogue games, and it turns out that the maps are all rotting under our feet. There is not much left of that old reality map anymore. There are no substances and no particles and no waves, and there is so much emptiness. There is something about *sunyatā* and the void and the godhead and St. John of the Cross's dark night that helps us get to the unified state. This development brings us to the ultimate in religion.

My sense is that we have to change our tools, and if we start to, we must do so as a planetary community of sharing, so we can say one to another in the dialogue: "What tools do you have in your toolbox? Look at the tools I have in mine," so that we can survive the paradigm shift as it involves our religions. It is important for us to weather our entrance into the next paradigm.

There is something in my orthopraxis that is very warm toward Khomeini, who is saying, "Cannot there be for once in the history of the world a republic that will live according to the Qur'ān?" I honor that, and yet at the same time I see the impossibility of it—in Judaism, in Christianity, in Islam. If we could only get our heads together and talk to one another about that which is beyond the ethnic or timebound, that is global and has to do with communication and the utilization of the planet in a shared way! It looks to me as if another language is coming up, and this is what I am proposing for your consideration.

We are cautioned, by a working hypothesis for sharing, not to drive along looking into the rearview mirror, as we in religion have been doing so tenaciously. Most of the time we go back to the years 50–200 c.e.—and there we want to solve all our present-day problems. Why go back there if there is so much ahead of us that is so unclear and in which the values of the transformative functions of religion are so essential? Here is where I come back to Dr. Cobb's use of "Christocentric," which in my vocabulary has to do with *t'shuvah*. If we are not going to be able to change the quality of our lives as individuals, then what is the good of our whole enterprise? We must be able to change the quality of our life as social aggregates. As a Hasidic Jew, I say that Jesus has, as a Nazarene rebbe, for those who follow in his footsteps, brought about the possibility to be born again, to grow again, to mature again. I want to say, "More power to you."

This is what the Christian is waiting for in the second coming and I in the first coming. Both of us are waiting for the transformation of the planet—social, human, and ecological aggregates. Here is where Teilhard de Chardin comes up with a hypothesis that saves your Christocentrism in the Cosmic Christ and at the Omega point. In Judaism we speak of it as the *Geulah shlemah*.

We surely can use some more sharing on these issues.

II.2.

Christocentrism-Buddhacentrism

KENNETH K. INADA

The proposal of a Christocentric catholic theology by Dr. John Cobb is one of the finest and most practical that I have encountered within the framework of interreligious dialogue. It takes on added meaning and significance because of his wide-ranging interests and profound knowledge of other religions, Buddhism in particular. Other theologians may differ with his proposal—indeed, in this paper as well as in his other writings, he anticipates differences of view. But as a Buddhist I am most impressed by the well-reasoned historical and spiritual approach. Insofar as its theological aspect is concerned, Buddhism will have very little difficulty in accepting and accommodating the methodological elements.

In fact, speaking on behalf of Buddhists, I may respond very positively by endorsing the proposal and simultaneously counterproposing an analogous position for Buddhism—a Buddhacentrism. This is not to be presumptuous or to counter Christocentrism as such, but rather to clarify the position of a dialogic partner, a position that I am sure Dr. Cobb would allow. It is to create an ideal situation in which the dialogue partners may function fully as equals in all respects, for to understand a partner's viewpoint is to work toward an intimate feel for that person's "centric" nature, which may be vague and unclear at the beginning, but as the dialogue proceeds should become clear.

The proposal for Buddhacentrism is really nothing new, for the whole history of Buddhism is a manifestation of such a centrism. It will be recalled that Buddhism appeared in an Indian climate of ideological pluralism, in the presence of Hinduism, Jainism, and Sāṃkhya-yoga, and that its own doctrines were framed within the prevailing philosophical and religious context—that is, with respect to the contemporaneous knowledge of metaphysics, epistemology, and yoga practice. It did not make a big splash from the start, but continued to borrow, adapt, and incorporate ideas from other systems and traditions throughout its long history within and without India. This does not mean, however, that Buddhism became merely a synthetic way of life, in which its original doctrines were no longer discernible, for it stood its ground and guarded carefully the core of the Buddha's enlightenment. But it was flexible and resilient enough to expound its teachings in ways that always "fitted the case," in accordance with the Buddha's own many-sided approach to suit his listeners' respective capabilities.

The conservative streak in Buddhism solidified early on, and has continued up to the present day in the form of Theravada Buddhism. The more liberal streak sped northward, principally to Tibet, China, Korea, and Japan. It not only spread but developed its doctrines by direct contact with the diverse indigenous cultures that came in its path. Buddhacentric dialogue was a huge success in China, though it met hostile forces at the outset in the forms of Confucianism and Taoism. In the process, however, Buddhism transformed itself into Chinese Buddhism, enriching and deepening thereby the whole complex of Chinese thought and culture. The same process was duplicated in Korea and Japan. And now it is happening in America.

So Buddhacentrism is an old story and its present serious encounter with Christocentrism, in particular, heralds one of its most challenging ideological adventures to date.

Dr. Cobb is quite correct in advancing a pluralistic world where there can be a family of religions in an ambience of coexistence, each member being independent and respected by others but not reduced to a relativized entity. To foster the ambience further I wholeheartedly endorse the ten rules of interreligious, interideological dialogue so compactly and forcefully presented by Dr. Swidler in his preconference paper. I am sure they will guide us throughout our deliberations, especially in this and future Christocentric-Buddhacentric dialogue.

Dr. Cobb's first presentation of Christocentrism, to my knowledge, was in the journal *The Eastern Buddhist*.[1] It was later expanded in his *Beyond Dialogue*[2] mentioned in his present paper. The paper does not enter into any serious dialogue between Christianity and Buddhism, because his aim is basically theological, not metaphysical. But in order to understand his position better we would have to look at these works.

Dr. Cobb's earlier approach was decidedly philosophical. This must be distinguished from his theological position, but, if I read him correctly, there is no conflict here: philosophy provides the necessary tools for doctrinal clarification. I heartily agree, and might add that in Buddhism the philosophical approach is very much in tune with its doctrines, and, indeed, though Buddhist philosophy is clearly distinguishable from Buddhist religion, they do not conflict with, but complement each other.[3]

The philosophical approach should always be free from dogmas, biases, and discriminations, in order to realize a sweeping, unadulterated vision of reality, just as the early Greek thinkers essayed. So it is no wonder that Dr. Cobb follows the Greek tradition and takes up the contributions of such modern thinkers as Schopenhauer, Wittgenstein, Heidegger, Northrop, and Whitehead to provide insights into human experience and reality, and to open up dialogue on the interreligious level. He has struck upon a very fruitful area of universal discourse and it would certainly be profitable to pursue this further by including the Buddhist framework.

BUDDHIST-CHRISTIAN DIALOGUE: METHODOLOGY

In order to come to grips with this philosophical approach, I have devised a very simple diagram to illustrate the dialogic area. I call this the "H-bar Diagram." It is provisional and needs to be modified as we go along in dialogue. What I wish to emphasize here is the methodological aspect, not the metaphysical, which neither Dr. Cobb nor I are presently concerned with.

H-bar Diagram

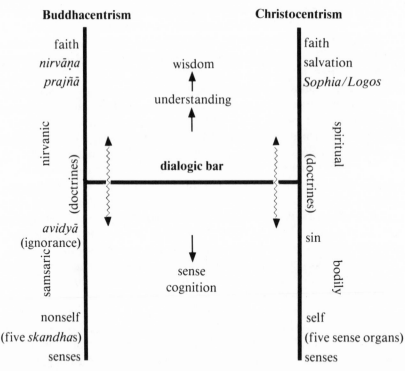

1. The diagram is constituted by two centric systems, Buddhacentrism and Christocentrism, with a horizontal bar that brings them in contact. It depicts contacts in a pluralistic world.
2. The bar that connects both centrisms is mobile—it may move down toward

the sense level or up toward the level of wisdom. Figuratively speaking, it is on rollers.

3. The bar is where all dialogues take place and therefore it may be called the dialogic bar.
4. The nature of a dialogue is essentially philosophical in order to maintain the sense of neutrality, rationality, objectivity, and realization of wisdom.
5. The dialogic bar must be kept in balance or horizontal as much as possible in order to produce fruitful results.
6. Any undue imbalance or disruption of the dialogic bar means that there is a "derailment" in the dialogue, which must be adjusted immediately. Ideally, a dialogue must manifest a "self-corrective mechanism," to borrow a term from Nolan P. Jacobson.[4]

Needless to say, dialogue carried on according to the H-bar Diagram requires utmost cooperation, openness, and understanding by the partners involved. I wholeheartedly agree with Dr. Cobb's multiple and flexible hypotheses[5] as a necessary point of departure in any dialogue rather than maintaining a dominant hypothesis, such as the nature of ultimate reality, in which all doctrines are framed. My personal observation on the concept of ultimate reality is that it is a problem, albeit a crucial one, belonging to the respective religions within their own cultural settings and need not enter into the dialogue from the beginning; that is to say, to introduce it at the very outset will only bring on metaphysical difficulties and confusion, which would not be conducive to the discussion of the more practical aspect of life, which is already burdened by matters that are still being probed.

I must confess that there is a basic weakness in the H-bar Diagram—namely, that it does not incorporate the element of meditation. This is unwarrantable, and must particularly be noted in light of the fact that meditation is part and parcel of Buddhism. The popularity and attraction of Zen in the West is largely attributable to the fact that there is something to be gained and realized in taking up meditative discipline. It is no wonder that Thomas Merton or Father Kadowaki have ventured to accept this discipline in order to improve themselves, as noted by Dr. Cobb.[6]

The nagging question remains: Why is meditation not included in philosophical discourse? Or why is meditation rejected outright from such discourse? The lack of tangible elements seems to be a poor excuse. It is never treated as a legitimate child, or even a stepchild, in any discourse. Whenever a great thinker—whether Plato, Kierkegaard, Wittgenstein, Heidegger, or Whitehead—utters something on the nature of the mystical, it is swept under the rug without further exploration. Wittgenstein, for example, made the following cryptic statement: "Not how the world is, is the mystical, but that it is."[7] To my knowledge, there has never been a serious follow-up on this statement. Philosophers by and large have chosen not to focus on this mystical statement, for they saw the forking of the philosophical roadway, that it clearly branched off either to the logical or the nonlogical (mystical) and forthwith chose the former at the expense of the latter, the result being a not so whole-some view of humanity and its world. Meanwhile, however, we must not resign ourselves, but insist on a wider and deeper conception of humanity, which will entail much "de-mystification" of our ordinary views on human nature. We could very well start with meditation as a vital tool.

Dialectic is another matter we must consider. Plato's dialectic, though premised on the condition of perfecting the body and soul of the aspirant, still lacked the meditative discipline to sustain the drive and to take the final leap and remain in the realm of the Good. But we are forever grateful to him for showing us a novel approach and an "ideality" of existence. Hegelian dialectic was a huge innovation of dialectical play in terms of the thesis-antithesis-synthesis continuum, but it turned out to be more speculative than practical, although we must acknowledge the fact that the element of evolutionary development was a singular contribution. Marx-Engels discerned the highly speculative nature of the Hegelian dialectic and focused inward to the practical nature of things by introducing the dialectic that transforms quantity to quality and vice versa, interpenetration of opposites and negation of negation, to produce one of the great insights into the course of events in history. It is still influential in some quarters of the world today, but falters by virtue of its overexuberance for the materialistic interpretation of events, lacking again the spiritual discipline to give a full accounting of humanity in its historical setting.

All the above examples show that dialectic without incorporation of the meditative force to firm up the ideas and concepts relative to humankind and its quests in life will eventually end up being speculative and inadequate. I admit that this is a very delicate matter, which philosophers and theologians have feared to treat, but as a vital component in most of the Asiatic ways of life and some Western, it needs to be seriously considered in any dialogue so as to bring to the fore the realm of the nonlogical, nonrational, and nonmaterialistic, and thereby to provide a perception of the depth and fullness of human existence.

NIRVĀṆA AND EMPTINESS

I am certain that Dr. Cobb would allow for the meditative discipline along with his philosophic approach, although the fusing of the two is not so apparent in his writings. Much needs to be done in this area, especially in refining the dialogic bar. From the Buddhacentric standpoint, all discourse must start at the bottom of the H-bar Diagram. Dr. Cobb is aware of this and discusses Buddhism under the central concept of *nirvāṇa* in terms of (1) cessation of all craving and clinging, (2) extinction of the self or realization of the true self, (3) ultimate reality as emptiness, and (4) abolition of time and history.[8]

This is a well-conceived plan of analysis but I have certain reservations. He says that *nirvāṇa* is "the absence of attachment, clinging, or craving. That absence gives rise to perfect freedom, perfect presence, perfect wisdom, and perfect compassion."[9] It should be noted that suffering is basic and that it is caused by craving and clinging. He then takes the stand that with craving and clinging gone, *nirvāṇa* becomes an established fact. Well, it is not as simple as that; he describes the clinging phenomenon in a general sense, not in the Buddhist way. He does expand on the matter in the next step, the extinction or dissolution of the self, and analyzes why, instead of a self, there is no self in the subject and object interaction in the "experiencing subject."[10] He goes on to say that in the exposition of a world of objects and subject, "there is no subject apart from objects and that there are no objects apart from a subject,"[11] and that there are only "objects becoming subjects which become objects constituting new subjects."[12] But this process is strictly a Western expression of arriving at the nonself doctrine. It seems that its orientation is still burdened by realistic and empiricistic elements. He goes on to say that "this process is the only self there is, hence, the true self, which is at once true reality. . . . It is Nirvana."[13]

What he says is correct on the level of formal analysis but, because we are dealing with the content of the experiencing subject, I find that the analysis falls short of a full exposition. Similarly, when he says that "Wisdom comes only when one ceases to cling to what people call knowledge and ability to think. . . . Wisdom comes only as one lets that go,"[14] the reader will be confused and may interpret the statement in undisciplined ways—for example, that knowledge-gathering and the thinking process are to be denied, which is hardly Buddhism or Zen Buddhism.

Let us pause here to remind ourselves that the Buddhist starts with the sensed realm of existence or the five *skandha*s, the so-called five aggregates of being. The way these aggregates function depicts the fundamental origins of the nature of what we call a self. It is not a self that goes through the aggregating process; rather, it is the aggregating process that spells out the self. So that all references to clinging and craving are microscopically present in these five *skandha*s. When we speak of the self craving for something, we are already on the second level of suffering, so to speak, the macroscopic level, and when the mind enters the process we are on the more complex third level in terms of dealing with the subtle forces of reification, discrimination, and so forth.

In short, the complex of being is really complex and herein lies, I believe, the strength and value of meditation in uncovering the roots of our own being and thereby the origins of suffering. Suffering is universal in this respect. That is, when the first teachings of the Buddha mentioned that "birth is suffering," it meant the aggregating phenomenon of being, the craving and clinging relative to life sustainment exhibited by the newborn. So we must be careful when reading Dr. Cobb's statement that "Buddhist meditation is not in quest of the ground [or substratum] but of the dissolution of all grounds,"[15] which may suggest to the unwary mind nihilism or annihilationism (*ucchedavāda*), but I am sure he is here referring to the empty (*śūnya*) ground of existence.

In the next item, ultimate reality as emptiness, there are some problems. I will not comment on Dr. Cobb's reference of *nirvāṇa* to the kingdom of God or simply to God but, as a Buddhist, I am concerned about the notion that *nirvāṇa* is empty (*śūnya*),[16] with obvious reference to the identity of *nirvāṇa* and *saṃsāra*. He goes on to say, "the realization of the one is at once the realization of the other. What is realized is Śūnyata or Emptiness, which for much of Mahāyāna becomes the preferred way of naming ultimate reality."[17] In his present paper he also touches upon the concept of ultimate reality in terms of Buddhist emptying, a Zen Buddhist way of realizing a higher form of knowledge (*prajñā*).

What disturbs me is that *nirvāṇa*, as "ultimate reality," is identified with emptiness. Nowhere in the classical texts is such a reference made directly. Emptiness is identified, to be sure, with dependent origination and the middle way, but not with *nirvāṇa*.[18] Emptiness refers to the realm of *skandha*s, *dharma*s, and so forth, which are the way dependent origination functions in the enlightened sense and thus also is equatable with the middle way, which avoids the extremes of being and nonbeing. To slip emptiness into the realm of *nirvāṇa* because the saṃsāric and nirvāṇic realms (*koṭi*) are the same is to identify the nonenlightened (*avidyā*) and (*vidyā*) realms also. Certainly, this is not the intent of the equation. It is a statement made as a result of attaining higher levels in the meditative process by the adept, and does not apply to those who are still caught up in the lower forms of knowledge or mired in the saṃsāric elements (self-natures).

And so, as I see it, emptiness attached to *nirvāṇa* is unwarranted, because it is basically an "organic" or "biological" concept in the sense of the aggregating phenomenon, and later on it is associated with the conscious realm where it is initially the denial of self-existent natures and dichotomous existence—which denial brings consciousness to the level of emptying all dharmic factors of experience, leading thereby to the full emptiness of experience. It cannot be lifted to the level of a metaphysical concept, although D. T. Suzuki's writings, for example, give the impression that it is so. Rather than emptiness, perhaps a more appropriate concept might be "thusness" of being (*tathatā*) or "thatness" (*tattva*), both of which express the true reality sensed by the enlightened.

It is easy to follow the Northropian scheme[19] of starting off with the differentiated esthetic continuum, the sensed world, and gradually moving away from it to capture the undifferentiated realm of existence, but the process, in its simplicity, has omitted, glossed over, and even negated, much of the full human complement of being. In the final analysis, the Buddhist metaphysics of reality, to stay with Northropian concepts, entails both differentiated and undifferentiated coexisting, just as we are told of the interpenetrative and mutually identifiable phenomena of *dharma*s (*dharma-dhātu*) in the Chinese Hua-yen School. What brings them together or leaves them alone, as the case may be, is the crux of Buddhist meditation.

I hope my comments will not detract the reader's attention from the Christocentric approach by Dr. Cobb. As Christians and Buddhists need to become aware of their own spiritual heritage and widen their horizons, they must join in an open dialogue, because the spheres of both are infinitely greater and deeper than anyone could envision.

NOTES

1. John B. Cobb, Jr., "Buddhism and Christianity as Complementary," *The Eastern Buddhist,* 13/2 (Autumn 1980) 16–25.

2. John B. Cobb, Jr., *Beyond Dialogue: Toward a Mutual Transformation of Christianity and Buddhism* (Philadelphia: Fortress Press, 1982).

3. It is my personal view that original Buddhist thought was thoroughly philosophical, but in its practical manifestation it turned quickly into an institutionalized phenomenon, i.e., the founding of the Buddhist order (*Sangha*), which gradually added all the trappings of a bona fide religion, especially in the later Mahāyāna tradition.

4. Nolan P. Jacobson, *Buddhism and the Contemporary World: Change and Self-Correction* (Carbondale and Edwardsville: Southern Illinois University Press, 1983).

5. *Beyond Dialogue,* p. 44.

6. Ibid., pp. 69–71, 97–98.

7. Ludwig Wittgenstein, *Tractatus Logico-Philosophicus* (London: Routledge & Kegan Paul, 1949), 6.44.

8. *Beyond Dialogue,* pp. 76–94.

9. Ibid., p. 81.

10. Ibid., pp. 85–86.

11. Ibid., p. 86.

12. Ibid.

13. Ibid.

14. Ibid., p. 81.

15. Ibid., p. 89.

16. Ibid., pp. 70, 90.

17. Ibid., pp. 89f.

18. Nāgārjuna, *Mūlamadhyamakakārikā.* XXIV, 18.

19. Dr. Cobb discusses this scheme in *Beyond Dialogue* (pp. 65–68) in the section, "The Philosophical Approach," pointing to its strengths and weaknesses, but in general accepts and expands on it as a fruitful approach.

II.3.

A Tale of Two Theologies

ANTONY FERNANDO

In his paper Dr. Cobb could be said to be approaching the problem of contemporary Christianity from two angles. There are actually two questions that he is addressing. One is the question of the right attitude of Christians toward other religions. Dr. Cobb's own attitude is one of a rare large-heartedness and open-mindedness. The other is the question of the form and function of theology in its contemporary multireligious context. Here his view is that contemporary theology should be at one and the same time Christocentric and catholic. The word "catholic," as he uses it here, means "universal." The two questions are of course interrelated; they can be taken as two facets of one and the same thesis.

This thesis of Dr. Cobb as well as the manner in which it is discussed is specifically theological. But a characteristic of this thesis is that it is of interest not only to theologians, but to ordinary Christians as well, and especially to ordinary Christians living among other religionists.

Inasmuch as my remarks will be of a rather personal nature, it will be helpful to preface them with a brief description of my background. That should help others to take my remarks for just what they are worth.

I come from a Christian family in Sri Lanka where Christianity, in spite of the multiple forms in which it is found, is a minority religion. All the major religions of the world have a home in Sri Lanka, but the religion of the majority is Buddhism. Influenced by the religious fervor of my family, at a very early age I cherished a yearning to be a lifetime missionary for Christianity, or more precisely for Catholicism. To realize my yearning I gained membership, while still a teenager, in a missionary organization of the Catholic Church. I would have been a member of that society even today, had it not been for the fact that my growing contact with Christianity in its diverse denominational forms on the one hand, and with other religions, principally Buddhism, on the other, made me see the missionary reality in a totally new light.

That new awareness was further heightened by the opportunities I had for studying Christianity (doctorate in theology) and Buddhism (doctorate in philosophy). Today, seeing the humanity-building values of not only Christianity but also of Buddhism, I have come to the conviction (which to some is surely to appear a misconception!) that a Christian living in a predominantly Buddhist country could be a missionary at one and the same time for both Christianity and Buddhism. My present profession as a university lecturer in Christian culture (not to be confused with Christian theology) in a secular university that is predominantly Buddhist makes me believe more firmly in the possibility. I strongly feel that if religion in its best sense is for human uplift-ment, then it should be possible for a person to be a missionary for religion as such, without being a sectarian missionary for just this or that religion—much less for this religion against that religion!

This brief account of my background should make at least two points clear. It should show that my personal interest in Dr. Cobb's thesis is not haphazard or casual; and it should also show that there are persons in far-off countries for whom the multireligious problem discussed in this conference is of vital, and not just of theoretical or peripheral, importance.

Of the two points discussed by Dr. Cobb let me take first what he says about the attitude that Christians should have toward other religions, which is sure to be an "eye-opener" for many. I personally feel a deep sense of gratitude for his having said what he has said. Two assertions of his deserve to be cited here. I like these assertions because they are very self-confessional in tone, and self-confessional statements by theologians are rare, but very enlightening. The first gives a hint of the sense of humility and self-diffidence with which a Christian should investigate other religions. The study of Islam is taken as an illustration here: "Can Muslim history also become part of our internal history? We are much further from Muslims. It will take decades of study and dialogue before we can integrate their historical experience with ours."

It is not often that we come across Christian scholars who are humble enough to admit that "decades of study and dialogue" will be necessary to understand another religion. What we are more accustomed to hearing are the a priori, doctrinaire statements of those who seem to feel that they know everything about other religions, and that there is nothing to learn from them.

The second statement indicates the "come-what-may" open-mindedness with which Christians should start investigating other religions. Christians should be impartial and objective in their study, especially when they are uncertain as to what the consequences of the study will be. The religion that Dr. Cobb takes as an illustration here is Buddhism:

Suppose we Christians are impelled to include Gautama Buddha within our internal histories. Granted, the impulse comes from Jesus. Will the result be simply an expansion of the history from which we live so that the center remains Jesus? Or will Gautama introduce a new center—one that displaces Jesus from centrality?

Such displacement of Jesus is not to be rejected a priori in the name of Christian faith. On the contrary, faith expresses itself in action whose consequences we cannot anticipate. If faithfulness to Jesus leads to the displacement of Jesus from centrality, then such displacement is itself faithful.

I must confess that I have hardly ever read a theological statement on the attitude toward other religions as straightforward as this. Such statements are educative in their highest form because they are in fact liberative. They liberate persons to seek after truth without fear and pressure.

Dr. Cobb's second major point is no less important, though a little more difficult than the first to sum up. According to him, theology should tackle the multireligious problem in a form and with a theological formulation different from that envisaged by Dr. Swidler. In fact he presents his point of view in opposition to Swidler's. He of course tries, out of a sense of delicacy, to underplay the difference, saying that it is only a difference of language or terminology: "My rejection of this language ["universal theology of religion"] is no doubt partly a terminological matter of a relatively unimportant sort." But in reading both papers I have a suspicion that the difference is not just one of terminology. It is much more.

But the strange thing about this Swidler-Cobb controversy is that the points of view they uphold are not mutually exclusive. Someone following the controversy will not be obliged to reject the one in order to accept the other. Cobb and Swidler here are handling two problems that are totally different from each other, though very much interrelated. Like banana trees that can have different stems but the same root, there can be two problems that are structurally different though having the same origin. Swidler and Cobb are both speaking of theology in a multireligious context, but they are speaking of two types of theology altogether. Their theologies serve different functions.

Because of the complexity of Cobb's second point, it is best that I present my observations about the views of both Cobb and Swidler. Both points of view are totally acceptable, but both have their problematic side.

PROBLEMS WITH CHRISTOCENTRISM

According to Cobb, theology of the contemporary era should be Christocentric and catholic. "Christocentric" and "catholic" are his two key words. From the explanations given of them, there is not the least doubt that they are terms of great significance. But nonetheless they are, as anyone would grant, words that only Christians (and particularly the more initiated among them) will understand. They are not part of the language of the common person. They will never be used, for instance, in our newspapers. But the unintelligibility of these terms to the non-Christian is no problem for the stand that Cobb is taking. They are theological terms and theology has a special role. That role is the education of Christians, especially of Christians who are community leaders, such as priests or ministers. The theology that Cobb is concerned with is an intracommunity matter. It is a discipline of Christians for Christians. The audience of the theologian is the Christian community.

This is no doubt what theology has been for centuries in the past, and so, the stand of Cobb is unassailable. And what is more, Cobb looks at theology in its intracommunity form with a breadth of vision that is truly universal. There is not the least doubt that the very aim of his educational ministry is to give that vision to all Christians. As he sees it, the very first step in any program of interreligious dialogue is the enlarging of the worldvision of Christians themselves. I for one am fully in agreement with that methodological approach.

But, of course, the term "Christocentricity," to which he attaches importance, has its strong and weak sides. In the past, for instance, it has saved Christians from adhering to wrong centers. There have been in certain eras, and probably there are even today, forms of Christianity that can be described as "pope-centered," "king or political power–centered," "devotion to Mary or saints–centered," "celibacy-centered," "male-authority-centered," or "preacher-centered." A Christianity that is Christocentric is an antidote to such deviations.

But on its weak side, "Christocentricity" is a word that the rank and file of Christians, not having a theological training, will find difficult to decipher. As an ordinary reader of the Bible, I would have great difficulty in seeing the biblical foundation for such a term. It is true that as a term "Christocentric" is not unrelated to the poetico-mystical utterances of John the author of the Fourth Gospel, or of Paul the author of the Epistles. But when the New Testament is taken as a whole, the down-to-earth picture of Jesus, his life and teaching, is very different.

From what I understand of the Gospels, Jesus was an extremely un-self-centered person. He never made himself a center in any form when he preached to ordinary farmers and shepherds. If a center is to be found in his teaching, the one that would come closest is the "reign of God" idea. That is what he referred to most. Perhaps, if we focus on the less frequent but nonetheless very momentous utterances of Jesus, we have to say that his teaching on the "Spirit" or the "life of the Spirit" is a center. It is the Spirit that Jesus asked his disciples to live by; it is ultimately the Spirit that he left them with. Or again, if we pass from what he said to what he did, and what he did is often referred to as "miracles," then we have to say that his ministry was one of healing and so, "healing-centered." When I take all these realities together—the "Reign," the "Spirit," the "healing"—I get the feeling that Jesus' "Christianity" is really (to use a rather secular term) "human-liberation–centered."

What I have said here is in no way intended as a refutation of Cobb's stand. I simply mean that the ordinary Christian may not take the term "Christ" or "center" exactly in the same way as a theologian would. The fact that I might have personal difficulties in the comprehension of such terms does not in any way reduce my esteem for the Christocentric theology of Cobb, as well as for the function and role of theology as he envisages it.

PROBLEMS WITH INTERCOMMUNITY DIALOGUE

To pass on to Swidler's point of view, I feel he is concerned with a theology of a totally different nature. Whether what he pleads for should be called theology might be disputed. "Theology" is a tradition-backed word and we may have to respect its traditional sense. Aware of that fact, Swidler himself uses the term "systematic reflection." Perhaps a new word like "religiology" could suit his purpose better. It certainly needs a new name, for it eventually could turn out to be a new science, or at least a new branch or new extension of theology.

Whatever the appropriate name and form be, his system of study and reflection is not restricted like Cobb's to Christians. His audience is the whole world, and members of all religions. His therefore is not an intracommunity discipline, but an intercommunity one. Hence, simply because his audience is different, the type of language he needs is different. For him an "ecumenical Esperanto" that all religionists understand is vital. The role or function of his "theology" is different. It is not just the education of Christians. It is the encouragement of all religionists to actual dialogue, to actual acceptance of one another in their very otherness, in their other-religionness. The center, too, of his system is different. It has to be "humanity-centered" or "human-upliftment-centered."

Anyone who takes seriously the contemporary problem of multireligious humanity will not fail to admire Swidler for his innovative thought and pioneering venture. The list of ten rules he proposes ("Ground Rules for Interreligious, Interideological Dialogue") is (at least as I see it) the boldest answer formulated in recent times by a Christian to the problem of a religiously divided humanity.

But the approach of Swidler, and particularly his "ground rules," has also its problematic side. His "ground rules" ("dialogue decalogue") will surely appear shocking to religionists of diverse persuasions, including Christians. Many Christians would see his venture as an attempt to shake the very foundations of Christianity. Just one rule of his is sufficient to make this point. The seventh rule is as follows: "Dialogue can take place only between equals . . . *par cum pari*. Both must come to learn from each other."

Is this setting of different religionists as equals around the same table a real possibility in our mentally unadult world? An offhand remark of a reader of the "ground rules" that I heard is quite revealing in this regard: "Dr. Swidler is asking too much. How could he now ask us to consider ourselves as equals when from our childhood we have been taught that we were superior?"

The greatest obstacle that Swidler is bound to face in his praiseworthy campaign for interreligious dialogue is the sectarianism that all religions today seem to be victims of. For some unexplainable reason (probably not so unexplainable to psychologists and sociologists), every religionist is a firm adherent of a we-are-superior ideology. It is not only we Christians who think that ours is the superior religion. Every Muslim, every Hindu, every Buddhist has that we-are-superior conviction.

The mental situation that most of us are in today is such that we are not able to see that the basis of our we-are-superior feeling (which is the root of religious fanaticism) is weak. We are not grown-up enough to accept the fact of "accidentality" or nondeliberateness of our very affiliation to a religion. We are not frank enough to admit that our affiliation to a particular religion has not been a matter of real choice. We (the majority of us) are Jews, Christians, Muslims, Buddhists, or Hindus because we happened to be born in a particular region, and in a particular family. Today, not much less than in the past, an Arab is a Muslim, a European is a Christian, a brown Indian is a Hindu. As somebody once said, "I am a Christian because my parents were Christians, and my parents were Christians, because their king was a Christian"—a statement quite reminiscent of the old Latin adage, *cujus regio ejus religio*.

This is of course not to say that what is accidentally received cannot be appropriated, or that religions do not have a philosophy or physiognomy of their own. It is only to say that there is an unadult and unthought-out fanaticism of some degree or other in the very best of us when it comes to the appraisal of our own religion. That situation, which is almost universal, is the greatest obstacle that Swidler will have to overcome.

But this situation in no way minimizes the contemporary relevance of the stand taken by Swidler. On the contrary, it only intensifies its opportuneness. His task, however, would become much easier if there were within each religious group an educational program to defanaticize its members, giving them at the same time a universalism of vision of the type envisaged by Cobb for Christians. If there were a Cobb in all religions, the task of Swidler would become relatively easy!

When we are less fanatical about our own religions, we will understand better what religion itself is, and we will see that what actually matters is not so much religion but human beings and their upliftment. The very raison d'être of religion (taken in its best sense) is human liberation. This too is how Jesus saw religion: "The Sabbath is for humanity, not humanity for the Sabbath." In the contemporary context he would have said, "Religion is for humanity, not humanity for religion."

Religions must exist, but religious fanaticism is not a necessity. Humans must be able to belong to sects (and all religions in the concrete are sects) without being sectarian. If Dr. Swidler's and Dr. Cobb's dreams are realized—at least to the extent they could be realized in a weak human world—then a day would come when different religionists could sit together at a table to discuss religion (or the human liberation that religions are for) without animosity or fanaticism. At such a table they would refer to themselves not in exclusivist terms—"we Jews," "we Christians," "we Buddhists," "we Hindus," "we Muslims"—but primarily as "we human beings."

III.

The Invisible Harmony: A Universal Theory of Religion or a Cosmic Confidence in Reality?

RAIMUNDO PANIKKAR

Harmonia aphanēs phanerēs kreittōn.
Invisible harmony is stronger than the visible.
—Heraclitus, Fragm. 54

INTRODUCTION

My presentation is going to be succinct, dialectical, and basic. *Succinct*, because, based on previous studies, published and unpublished, it will allow me to refer to them for the justification of my assertions.[1] *Dialectical*, because, I fear, I may represent a minority view and can put forward my opinion only in confrontation with the predominant trends among the experts in this field. *Basic*, because it tackles the problem at the very fundamental structure of the human being, from the perspective of a metaphysical anthropology, one could say, and not from a sociological or pragmatic viewpoint.

In a first part I shall examine the reasons that direct modern Western scholarship to search in the direction of a universal theory of religion. In a second part I shall submit the "universal theory" to a critique. In the third, I shall attempt to offer an alternative.

A general remark at the very outset is called for. I am fully aware that there is no East and no West, no monolithic Christianity, nor standard Hinduism, that human traditions and even human beings themselves are much more holistic than most of our intellectual disquisitions tend to assume. In every one of us looms an East and a West, a believer and an unbeliever, a male and a female, and so on. Every human being is a microcosm and every human culture represents the whole of humanity. The true *ātman* of (in) every one of us is brahman. Buddha-nature lies at the bottom of every being. We all are called upon to share divine nature. Hence, the level of my discourse is directed at detecting predominant winds, leading threads, the dominating *Zeitgeist*, on the one hand, and the deeper structures of the human being and of reality on the other.

I encompass under the notion of "universal theory" all those efforts at reaching a global intellectual understanding, be it called "ecumenical Esperanto," "world theology," "unified field theory," or even a certain type of "comparative religion" and "ecumenism." The common trait here is the noble effort at reducing the immense variety of human experiences to one single and common language, which may well respect the different dialectical forms of expression and of life, but which somewhat subsumes them all and allows for communication and understanding on a universal scale. The universal theory assumes that a certain type of rationality is the general heritage of humankind and even more, that it is the one specifically human trait. It assumes we are human beings because we are rational creatures, reason being our last appeal; thus the same reason theoretically has to be capable of solving all the problems that plague our human race.

The gist of this study is a challenge to all this. And yet, the alternative is not solipsism on the one hand or irrationalism on the other, being respectively victim of a depressive individualism or of a shallow sentimentalism. I have already hinted that a whole anthropology and metaphysics are here called into question. The raising of such problems should be the concern of crosscultural studies if they want to be really crosscultural and not simply windowdressing with more or less exotic or less known ways of thinking.

The reader will have noticed that I do not mention the usual names of sociologists, anthropologists, and philosophers dealing with the traditional problems of evolutionism, structuralism, synchronicity, and the like. Is there a common human nature, does evolution or, on the other hand, structuralism, offer a basis to understand our phenomenon? Although it would have been very instructive to take a position in the contemporary discussions, I have opted for not entering into the scholarly debates for two main reasons. The one is that to do it properly would require an almost independent study as long as the present one—and it has been done several times.[2] The other and more important reason is that my perspective claims to be more crosscultural and "metaphysical" than such studies usually are, for they by and large remain within the problematic of today's (and yesterday's) Western scholarship.

I am not now criticizing a particular theory of an individual scholar or a school. I am submitting to analysis the sense of the enterprise itself. However, because of the very holistic character of our being, our theories also are more comprehensive than we generally imagine. Thus, if my criticism is answered by showing me that what I am saying is precisely what others wanted to say, because it was already implicit or taken for granted in their minds, I shall then be glad to have elicited this clarification.

ANALYSIS OF THE INTENT

Continuation of the Western Syndrome

The thrust toward universalization has undoubtedly been a feature of Western civilization since the Greeks. If something is not universal, it looms as not really valid. The ideal of humanity of the Greeks, the inner dynamism of Christianity, the feats of the Western empires, the emancipation of philosophy from theology in order not to be tied to a particular confession, the definition of morality by Kant, the modern cosmological worldview, and so forth, all are explicit examples claiming universality. *Plus ultra* was the motto of imperial Spain, and following it the Spaniards could reach America. World government, global village and global perspective, planetarian culture, universal net of information, world market, the alleged universal value of technology, democracy, human rights, nation states, and so on—all point to the same principle: universal means catholic, and catholic means true. What is true and good (for us) is (also) true and good for everybody. No other human civilization has reached the universality that the Western has. The way was prepared since the Phoenicians, prefigured by the Christian empires, and made actually geographically possible by the technocratic complex of present-day civilization.

To be sure, this feature is not totally absent in other civilizations, but it is not so prominent, so developed, and so powerful. The belief in being the best, which the Chinese culture had, is different from the belief in being universal— and thus *universalizable*, exportable to any place and time.

Further, this feature is not altogether negative. Yet it is ambivalent and often ambiguous. The destiny of the West rises and falls with this basic thrust. It is visible in the Abrahamic religions, without excluding Marxism and liberalism, as well as in the universal dominion of technology, the modern scientific cosmology, and the universal economic system. Proselytism as well as messianisms and expansionisms of all kinds also imply a conviction of representing universal values, which thus impels those who are charged with this burden to share, communicate, convince—and ultimately conquer (for the benefit of the conquered). This feature is also visible in the psychological make-up of *homo occidentalis* and is clearly detectable in the very spirit of Western philosophy. The "once and for all" of the Christian event (see Heb. 7:27) and its claim to universality are perhaps the clearest manifestation of this spirit. From the point of view of the history of religions we may say that only the Western gods (Yahweh, Allāh, Mammon, . . .), which like most divinities were tribal deities, became the universal God—and this to the extent that Christianity even renounced a proper name for God—or accepted the Jewish one. Most religions have a proper name or proper names for God or the gods. Christianity uses the common name "God," although the New Testament makes a distinction between *Theos* and *ho Theos*. In a word, the power of the West is linked with this thrust toward universalization. It has produced glorious results and also deleterious effects. But this is not my point now. My only point is to detect this specific trait.

To be sure, the Chinese Son of Heaven or the Indian *cakravartin*, the Buddhist *dharma* or the Confucian *li* have an inbuilt claim to unbound validity, and Nâgârjuna's philosophy has an equivalent pretension when it criticizes all possible *drsti*s or worldviews. But in most cases that universality was more of a metaphor and an expression of power and grandeur than an a priori. It was often a sense of superiority, not of universality. There is something democratic in the belief of being universalizable. Which monarch in history, to give another example, has claimed to have universal jurisdiction over the world, without even the intention of conquest, as did the Renaissance popes? What philosopher begins thinking by inquiring about the very conditions of absolute possibility, as did Kant? Heretics have been butchered in Asia and Africa because they were judged to be harmful and had to be punished, but not because truth was considered to be one and they had to be saved, as in the Inquisition. In short, there is here something special in Western civilization. "Everything that exists, exists therefore because it is one" (*Omne quod est, idcirco est, quia unum est*), said the synthetic mind of Boethius (PL 64, 83 b) speaking for the West. This *unum* is not the vedic *ekam* and much less upanishadic *ekam evâdvitîyam* (CU VI, 2, 1), which are surrounded by *asat*, nonbeing (RV X, 129, 2). This thirst for universality forms part of the Western myth. Yet it is difficult to argue, because we discover only the myth of the others, not the myth in which we live.

A long story (of thirty centuries!) in short: the very trend of looking for a "universal theory," even if expressed with all the respect and openness possible, betrays, in my opinion, the same *forma mentis*, the continuation of the same thrust—the will to understand, which is also a form of a will to power, and thus the felt need to have everything under control (intellectual, in this case).

I have not said that this feature is wrong. I have only situated it within a particular context and submitted it to an initial analysis by sociology of knowledge. It is not accidental that this need for universalization is felt precisely in the West and more especially *today*.

The *today* should be clearer than the preceding general reflection on the character of the Western mind. Probably in no other time of human history have we had so much information available regarding the ways in which our fellow human beings live and have lived. The time is gone when the *oikumene* could be the *mare nostrum*, when the languages of the human race were believed to be seventy-two, and true religions only those of the "peoples of the book," when we could speak of Christianity on the one hand and all the other religions lumped together. We are now submerged in an avalanche of data. How to proceed in this jungle of information? The need for intelligibility becomes imperative. We cannot live as if we were self-sufficient in our own corner. "The Spirit of the Lord *filled* the whole earth" (*Spiritus Domini replevit orbem terrarum*; Wis. 1:7), sang the Christian liturgy at Pentecost. Now radio and television waves fill the whole world.

I am saying that in the present situation of the world we cannot have the innocence of the Amerindian tribes, assuming that the others worship more or less the same Great Spirit and are governed by similar cosmic feelings. We need knowledge, and knowledge of the other, for survival and for self-identity. The thrust toward a universal theory is very comprehensible indeed. Join to this the desire to understand the other (and even ourselves better) without committing the past blunders of intolerance and fanaticism—and we all rejoice in this mood. The intention is more than justified. My doubt is whether it offers the proper remedy.

Inasmuch as we generally learn more from other areas when the subjects are too touchy for our own skin, I may cite simply as an example the ideal of the physical sciences. It was Einstein's dream—and drama—to work toward a "unified field theory," as he called it. In it the set of laws governing gravitation and the other set governing electricity should find a common mathematical formula. Faraday had succeeded in "converting magnetism into electricity," thus unifying those two groups of phenomena. Einstein later unified gravitation, time, and space. No wonder that the next step should appear to be the total unification. Yet we are still waiting for the formula. Perhaps not even in mathematics and physics can all be reduced to unity (think of Gödel and Heisenberg). We should be alert to this warning.

In short, my suspicion is that the drive toward a "universal theory," be it in physics, religion, or politics, belongs to the same Western thrust. And I repeat that this trait, in spite of its often bitter results and today its menacing danger, is not altogether negative, and that at any rate we have to reckon with it as probably the most powerful force in the world today. But I also insist that this thrust is not universal—and thus not a proper method (to deal with human problems), both because it is not truly a universal *theory* (rationality is of many kinds) and, more importantly, because no theory is *universal* (rationality does not exhaustively define the human being). Moreover, the phenomenon of religion is certainly not exclusively theoretical. May I recall that I am trying to be succinct, dialectical, and basic?

The Unavoidable Search

The important thing for us is not whether Einstein's lifelong search will fail or not, or whether a universal theology of religion convinces or not. The important thing is to realize that Western culture apparently has no other way to reach peace of mind and heart—called, more academically, intelligibility— than by reducing everything to one single pattern with the claim to universal validity.

I could put it facetiously by describing the plight of the drunk coming home in the early hours of the morning and looking for his lost house key under a particular streetlamp. Asked by the police whether he was sure he lost the key there, he answered: "No, but there is more light here." We look under the only light we have.

Now, my whole enterprise here consists in showing that there are other streetlamps in the city of humanity and that the Western lamp is not the only one we have. Obviously, the response is to say that it is not a question of a Western lamp, but that it is the human lamp of reason, the sole source of intelligibility, and that unless we wish to break off all human intercourse, commerce, communication we have to accept that single light. Pushing the example further, I would suggest that to find the key to the house of wisdom we had better rely on the daylight and that only that superhuman light of the sun may be the common lamp for the entire universe, and not the artificial streetlamps, be they of the gas of reason, the electricity of intuition, the neo-gases of feeling, or whatever. Yet, what if it is at night that we lose our key? But I am not now pushing a theological argument.

Without identifying Descartes with our drunk I may recall the logical fallacy of the father of modern Western philosophy: everything that I see with clarity and distinction (remember, under the lamp)—that is, all evidence—must be true. I may concede here, for the sake of the argument, that it may be the truth. But from this it does not follow that truth is *only* what I see with clarity and distinction. Evidence may be our criterion of truth, but, first, I cannot a priori assume that what I see with clarity and distinction, you also will see in the same way. Secondly, truth may be wider, deeper, or even elsewhere than what I, or even we, see with clarity and distinction. Here we must recall the Western philosophical paradigm that was present since the beginning: "Humanity is the measure of all things, how those which exist do exist and those which do not exist, do not exist" (*Pantōn chrēmatōn metron anthrōpon, einai. Tōn men ontōn hōs esti, tōn de nē ontōn hōs ouk estin*), as Protagoras said (reported by Plato, *Theat.* 151e–152a).

This is not necessarily sheer humanism, as it is often said. It can also be traditional theology, for even if God speaks, God will have to use human language and be ultimately dependent on our understanding of the divine words. My quarrel here is not with *anthrōpos*, with humanity, or even anthropocentrism—although I would contest this; my quarrel is with *metron*, with the drive to measure everything—and extrapolating, with the thrust to want to know everything, because it is assumed that everything is knowable. Ontologically said: thinking does not need to exhaust Being. Now, under those Western assumptions, the move toward a "universal theory" is a welcome move to put a certain order among the many worldviews. Within that framework it may be the best way of expressing it. But reality is richer. The "divine darkness" of Gregory of Nyssa has not had a follow-up in the West. It became the "dark night of the soul" in St. John of the Cross, and faded into the unconscious of modern psychology—after the lightning of Meister Eckhart.

This is my point. Granting that a hypothetical universal theology of religion were possible, it would be a very positive contribution to understanding the phenomenon of religion *only* for those who live within the cultural process in which all those words make sense—that is, for those who in one form or another subscribe to the myth of history, who accept the *intellectus agens* (*nous poiētikos*) of Aristotle and the Arab philosophers, the Cartesian intuition, the Kantian critical revolution, the Marxist analysis, or an absolute monotheism. This is a very impressive and powerful club, but it is not for everybody. To be sure, nobody now consciously wants to circumcise the others to their own ways of thinking in order to reach universality. In short, the striving for a universal theory is *one way* of expressing the manifoldness of the human religious experience, but it is just one way of doing it. It has a formal value. It expresses the genius of the West. However, we do not any longer want intellectual colonialisms.

I should not be misinterpreted. The effort at a universal theory is a noble enterprise. It is also a fruitful one. So many misunderstandings are overcome when we search for a common language; so many unclarities are dispelled; collaboration is made possible and religions are purified of so many excrescences, narrowmindedness, and fanaticisms. It would be totally mistaken to interpret my critique as not being a constructive one, as not aiming at the same goals and going in the same direction of mutual "understanding," tolerance, and appreciation. It may appear that I am also searching for a universal myth—although it would not be the same. Myth emerges and cannot be concocted; myth is polysemic and irreducible to one interpretation; myth does not support any particular theory.

What I am against ultimately is the total dominion of the *logos* and a subordinationism of the Spirit—to put it in Christian trinitarian words—or against any form of monism, in philosophical parlance. And yet I am against all this, I repeat, without ignoring the function and power of the *logos*, this fellow-traveler of all reality, coextensive with it, but not exhaustively identifiable with it.

Let me sum up my misgivings before I engage in a more positive critique. The search for a "universal theory" indeed fosters dialogue, but runs the great danger of imposing its own language or the frame within which the *dia-logos* has to take place. It claims to be a *lingua universalis*, which amounts to reductionism, to say the least. Secondly, it assumes that religion—or in a broader sense, human traditions—are, if not reducible, at least translatable into *logos* (and probably one kind of *logos*), and thus gives a supremacy to the *logos* over against the Spirit. But why should all be put into words? Why is not acceptance without understanding—as I read the Christian symbol of Mary (Luke 2:19, 51)—also an equally human attitude?

CRITIQUE

The Question of Pluralism

I have the impression that most of those who speak about pluralism and fill it with a positive meaning are not sufficiently aware of the far-reaching consequences that pluralism entails: the dethronement of reason and the abandonment of the monotheistic paradigm. It is like those who speak grandly of tolerance of others without taking into consideration that the real problem of tolerance begins with why and how to tolerate the intolerant. "The tolerance you have is directly proportional to the myth you live and inversely proportional to the ideology you follow."[3] This could be the Law of Tolerance.

Pluralism in its ultimate sense is not the tolerance of a diversity of systems under a larger umbrella; it does not allow for any superstructure. It is not a supersystem. Who or what principles would manage it? The problem of pluralism arises when we are confronted with mutually irreconcilable worldviews or ultimate systems of thought and life. Pluralism has to do with final, unbridgeable human attitudes. If two views allow for a synthesis, we cannot speak of pluralism. We speak then of two different, mutually complementary, although apparently opposite, attitudes, beliefs, or whatever. We do not take seriously the claim of ultimacy of religions, philosophies, theologies, and final human attitudes if we seem to allow for a pluralistic supersystem. In that case, obviously, we all would like to be pluralistic and not so narrow-minded as the Muslims, Catholics, Marxists, or whoever who still think that their analyses or views are ultimate—at least within their respective horizons. It is easy to be pluralistic if the others abandon their claim to absoluteness, primacy, universality, and the like: "We pluralists have alotted each system its niche; we then are truly universal." This, I submit, is not pluralism. This is another system, perhaps a better one, but it would make pluralism unnecessary. We have a situation of pluralism only when we are confronted with mutually exclusive and respectively contradictory ultimate systems. We cannot, by definition, logically overcome a pluralistic situation without breaking the very principle of noncontradiction and denying our own set of codes: intellectual, moral, esthetic, and so forth.

In other words, to assume that Hindus or Catholics are so dull as to be either fanatics or blind to the fact that the other also has the same or similar ultimate claims is to do an injustice to the self-understanding of the best minds of those religions. They know well that the claim of absoluteness, for instance, is a scandal to the human mind and that it does not entail disrespect of the other or straight condemnation of other views. There exist in the world even today well-balanced and thought-out absolutistic and mutually irreconcilable positions. And when we have to deal with sufficiently long-standing traditions, we cannot reasonably be satisfied with the proleptic attitude of a vague "hope"—I would rather call it expectation—that in the future our dissensions will fade away or find a solution. They have lived too long for us to believe that one fine day the Vaishnavas finally are going to recognize that the Shaivaites are right. This pious hope (without irony) is a very healthy attitude, as far as it goes.

Christian ecumenism offers a good example: what was considered impossible at one time became a fact a couple of decades later. But this model cannot so easily be extrapolated, for not everyone necessarily shares the conviction that history is the locus of reality or has a central point of reference, like Christ. In other words, an interdisciplinary study is not yet crosscultural.

There is even more. A pluralistic system as such could not be understood. Pluralism is only a formal concept. Sensible persons cannot understand how on earth there are many who think that all is matter, or that there is a God, or that the inferior races or less intelligent persons should not serve the superior ones, and so on, if they happen to have firm convictions in the opposite direction. And yet we are forced by circumstances to coexist with such world-views or systems. No overarching is possible. Either there is God or there is no God, either the individual does have ultimate value or does not, either the cosmos is a living organism or it is not. Despite all our sympathy and effort to understand, we disagree with the other; we cannot even understand how the contrary opinion may be reasonably held. We may have our personal interpretation and interpret the given examples, for instance, as false dilemmas. It remains, nevertheless, a fact that the others may not share our belief in a *coincidentia oppositorum*.

In short, there are a few fundamental human attitudes at the very basis of different human traditions that are mutually irreconcilable. I am an animist and you are a positivist scientist. Our two visions of the world cannot be both true. Or can they? The question of pluralism belongs to that ultimate level. And we should not take this lightly. Is it allowed to torture one individual, who otherwise will not speak, in order to save fifty thousand persons who are going to be blown up in the next few hours? We cannot say yes and no, or withhold an answer, for that would already imply giving one.

What this example contains in a time capsule is the situation of the world today. My hypothesis may be right or wrong, but I am not off the track. Such is the seriousness of the problem of pluralism. We cannot postpone to an eschatological happy ending the solution of all antinomies, nor can we rely on the last scientific or theological discovery of some guru telling us what to do. By that time, not the fifty thousand of my example, but millions of our fellow beings will have already starved to death or been killed in fratricidal warfare.

The problem of pluralism is paramount and has many facets. One of them is the question of good and evil. For my purpose I shall concentrate on the central issue of truth. What happens to it in face of so many disparate ultimate convictions? Let us assume that we have exhausted all the provisos and cautions at our disposal. We know that the context is essential, that different perspectives yield different visions, that temperament, culture, and the like, vouch for bewildering diversities. As long as the lines of dialogue are open, as long as the other does not draw the ultimate conclusion, there is no need to speak of pluralism. We are still struggling to find a common truth. We speak, then, of dialogue, of tolerance, of difference of opinions, and even of competition of worldviews in the human arena. We all recognize a legitimate multiperspectivism. The question of pluralism appears only when all those doors have been shut, when we return to ourselves and then have to take the decision to *écraser l'infâme*, or to allow ourselves to be overrun by evil, either to tolerate ultimate error and evil, or to fight it, even succumbing to it.

If the history of humankind is a succession of wars, and if war today appears so terrible, our issue of pluralism is not alien to this human predicament. What is the place of the philosophies underlying the Hitlers and Stalins in a "pluralistic worldview"? There is no "pluralistic worldview"; there are simply incompatible worldviews.

One of the presuppositions of the universal theory is that all problems are theoretically soluble. I am in complete agreement with the effort to try to solve the problems, and with patience, good will, and intelligence much can be achieved. We should go on trying again and again, untiringly. But we have to recognize two facts. One is that the partner may break off relations, stop the dialogue, become dangerous, oblige me to make decisions. And this is not necessarily because of some evil design, but because of the inner logic of the system. Not all who waged wars were criminals, not all who preached crusades were corrupt, not all those who believed in the inquisitions and slaveries of various types were subhuman—although now in our age we could not justify such acts or attitudes, which today should be condemned as out-and-out aberrations.

Now, there is no guarantee whatsoever that all human problems are (should be) theoretically soluble. This is probably not the case, even in mathematics, let alone in the complex existential situations in which contradictory human views are embedded. The universe may not have the logical coherence assumed by the spirit of Laplace or even by the belief in a monotheistic Deity for which nothing is unintelligible. These are already religious presuppositions not shared by every human tradition. Would those who think differently from us have to be excluded from a universal theory?

A second fact we have to take cognizance of is of another nature altogether. It is the unexamined presupposition—it has been taken for granted, "pre-sub-posed"—that truth is one rather than pluralistic.

The pluralism of truth is a much more serious and disturbing hypothesis than the obvious recognition of *perspectivism* and *relativity*. To admit that truth is perspectival should not offer any difficulty, although on that ultimate level the problem emerges as the question of what is the most adequate perspective in order to have the most accurate vision of things. And this obviously cannot be again another perspective without a *regressus ad infinitum*.

The *relativity* of truth, once it is distinguished from *relativism*, should also not be difficult to accept. Relativism destroys itself when affirming that all is relative and thus also the very affirmation of relativism. Relativity, on the other hand, asserts that any human affirmation, and thus any truth, is relative to its very own parameters and that there can be no ab-solute truth, for truth is essentially relational. The latter case is the reverse of the former. Relativism destroys itself if we affirm it. Relativity on the other hand is presupposed in the act of denying it. Any truth actually relates to an intellect. The concept of absolute truth has to relate to an infinite intellect.

The pluralism of truth goes a step further. It asserts that truth itself is pluralistic, and thus not one—nor many, for that matter. Pluralism is not plurality. To affirm that truth itself is pluralistic amounts to averring that there is no one all-encompassing or absolute truth.

The pluralism of truth is based on two fundamental assumptions: (1) the *first* is anthropological; (2) the *second* theological—or philosophical. I should prefer to stay in communion with all those traditions that do not make the split between philosophy and theology.

The *first* assumption is the recognition that each person is a source of understanding. Person here means not only any subject of rights, as an individual or a juridical person; it also includes collective units, and especially cultures as historical entities.

I am not necessarily resurrecting the Augustinian illumination theory of knowledge, or subscribing to any subject/object epistemology. I am saying only this: each person is a source of self-understanding. What a person is has to take into account the self-description and definition of the person in question. I am another person and have no right to superimpose my parameters and categories of understanding on others. Or, rather, if I do, the understanding I impose would be my understanding of the others, not the understanding of the others as they understand themselves—that is, as the understanding of their self-understanding. When the Hindu tells you or the Bantu tells me something that to us sounds preposterous, we have no way of passing any other judgment than that to us it sounds unacceptable for such and such reasons, apparently not accepted—or seen—by the other. However, we cannot reduce it all to objective statements. We are dealing with personal convictions, not with objectifiable events.

This almost obvious fact has been often dimmed by the influence of the natural sciences, which deal mainly with objectifiable phenomena and even more precisely with measurable entities. There is, for instance, a relative universality, at least in elementary mathematics, so that $2 + 3 = 5$ may appear as a universal truth independent of any source of understanding besides the objective intelligibility of the statement. Without discussing the nature of mathematics, suffice it to say that this is not the case when dealing with human affairs. And this happens even in applied mathematics. If $3 + 2 = 5$, everybody should agree in exchanging three canoes plus two women for five pounds sterling. And if it is replied that the quantities have to be homogeneous, we should then be inclined to agree to exchange two acres of land plus three houses for some other two acres and three houses (of the same price) outside the tribal country—and wonder why those "savages" of Papua New Guinea make such a fuss at being relocated, or why the Israelis could not go elsewhere, or the Palestinians for that matter. The fact is that neither land nor house are measurable entities. Each being is unique—that is, incommensurable.

Be this as it may—although it is not off the track—we may easily agree that the self-understanding of a particular culture is in a certain sense an ultimate and has to be taken as such without a reductionist twist to our ways of judging things. This is an epistemological statement. I am in no way saying that the Aztecs did well in performing the human sacrifices they did, just as I am not saying that some countries today do well in trading arms or in building atomic arsenals. I am saying that unless we understand the inner logic of a person and consider that person to be a source of self-understanding, we shall not understand that person and this will remain a permanent irritant among us.

If each human being qua human is endowed with self-understanding, each culture is also, because it possesses a specific vision of reality, a certain myth as the horizon within which things and events are discerned. Now, to privilege our understanding of reality and reduce all other perspectives to our own, even if we accept the data of the others, does not seem a proper method of dealing with what humans think about themselves and the universe, unless we reduce the human being to a set of data scientifically detectable.

If each person is a source of self-understanding, if humans are beings endowed with self-understanding, then we shall not be able to understand humans without sharing the self-understanding of the person(s) concerned. In that sense, an objective anthropology makes no sense. Human beings are not objects, but subjects. It would be methodologically wrong to treat humans as scientific objects.

Religions deal mainly with the collective ultimate self-understanding of a human group. The truth of religion can be gauged only within the unifying myth that makes the self-understanding possible. If we want to cross boundaries, we will have to share in some common truths brought forth in the common endeavor. But we should not project the truths of one religion over against an objective screen of truth in itself. Even if such an objective truth were to exist, we could not apply its canons in order to understand the self-understanding of a tradition that does not recognize them without distorting the issue. We may eventually condemn a religion as a human aberration, but always judging with our standards.

If the first assumption is anthropological, the *second* is theological, or rather, metaphysical. It contests one of the most widespread beliefs in the West as well as in the East—namely, that Reality is totally intelligible, that the *noēsis noēseōs* of Aristotle, the *svayamprakāsha* of the Vedantins, the self-intelligible and omniscient God of the Christians, the total reflection of many spiritualist philosophers, is really the case. It contests the ultimate belief of every idealistic monism—that there is a Being or a Reality that encompasses all that there is and that this Reality is pure consciousness, absolutely self-intelligible, because all is transparent to the light of the intellect, all is pervaded by *cit, nous*, mind. I am not contesting that *logos, nous, cit,* or by whatever name we may call this dimension of the real, is a fellow traveler of reality or coextensive with Being. I am only contesting that Being is totally reducible to it. What I am saying is that Reality has other dimensions—Matter, for instance, or Spirit—which cannot be reduced to *logos*, word, *vāc, nous*, mind, consciousness, *cit*. Consciousness is Being, but Being does not need to be only Consciousness.

One of the philosophical implications of this view is that there is no being absolutely identical to itself. Self-identity would imply absolute (total) reflection (an *a* identical to *a*). Each being, not excluding a possible Supreme Being, presents an opaque remnant, as it were, a mysterious aspect that defies transparency. This is precisely the locus of freedom—and the basis of pluralism. Thinking, or the intelligence, covers the totality of Being only from the exterior, so to say. Being has an untapped reservoir, a dynamism, an inner side not illumined by self-knowledge, reflection, or the like. Spontaneity is located in this corner of each being—its own mystery. It is unthought, unpremeditated, free, even from the structures of thinking. The mystery of reality cannot be equated with the nature of consciousness. There "is" also *sat* (being) and *ānanda* (joy), the Father and the Spirit. They may be correlative and even coextensive with consciousness, probably because we cannot speak (think) of the one without the other, but certainly they cannot be all lumped together as ultimately one single "thing." This is one of the consequences of what I call the theanthrocosmic or cosmotheandric insight. From all this follows that there is no absolute truth, not only because we mortals have no access to it, but because reality itself cannot be said to be self-intelligible—unless we a priori totally identify Reality with Consciousness. The Absolute is in the Relative. Something can be absolutely true, but this is not absolute Truth. Truth is always a relationship, and one of the poles of the relationship is the intellect that understands what is the case (intelligible, coherent, and so on).

Even assuming a divine or perfect Intellect, it could know only what is intelligible. To aver that it can know All amounts to gratuitously affirming that All is intelligible, that Being is intelligible—in other words, that Being is Consciousness.

In this scheme, to know is to become the known. In the process of a real understanding the identity between the subject and the object is total. Vedāntic and Christian Scholastic philosophies, for instance, defend the ontological significance of the epistemological act. Ultimately Being is reduced to Consciousness. The (epistemological) principle of non-contra-diction becomes here the ontic principle of identity. Only a noncontradictory thing is identical to itself. It *is* itself (identity) because it is noncontradictory. Thinking, governed by the principle of noncontradiction, amounts ultimately to Being, which is governed by the principle of identity. Thinking and Being form the ultimate paradigm.

The application to our case is easy to detect. There can be a universal theory of religion, or of anything, only under the assumption that Theory covers Reality, that Thinking can (theoretically, in principle) exhaust Being—can know Being without any (unknown) remnant. In a word Being is intelligible (*quoad se*). This is the ultimate presupposition of any universal theory. But it is this ultimate presupposition that is here called into question. To affirm that Consciousness is Being is a postulate of intelligibility, but not of Being. Truth is the result of some equation between Consciousness and Being. But Being may transcend its equation with Consciousness.

Furthermore, de facto, the actual pole for all our truth utterances is not a divine or perfect intellect but human consciousness, individual or collective, situated in space, time, matter, culture, and so forth. We have to take our own contingency very seriously; and our grandeur lies precisely in the awareness of our limitations. Anything we touch, think, speak—including all our ideas about any Supreme Deity—is permeated by the contingency of our being. I am not excluding the possible existence of the supreme consciousness of a realized soul, a *jîvanmukta*. I am saying that even *that* language is a relative language and suffused in polysemy. The moment that we come into the picture, all is tinged by our creatureliness, humanness, or whatever we may call it.

To sum up, the pluralistic character of truth does not mean that there are many truths. "Many truths" is either a contradiction in terms if we admit the possibility of many true and mutually incompatible answers to a particular judgment, or it is a displacement of the problem to a meta-truth that would be the conceptual truth of the many truths, as our single concept of sardine allows us to recognize many sardines. Truths would then be many exemplars of the meta-truth and the problem would begin with the meta-truth all over again.

The pluralism of truth means fundamentally two things. First, that truth cannot be abstracted from its relationship with a particular mind inserted in a particular context. "There is bread on this table" cannot be criticized outside the perspective of the author of the sentence, although "the city of Madras is on this table" cannot be literally true, for lack of internal coherence. We cannot abstract from every context and proclaim the oneness of truth. We have to recognize perspectivism and contextualization. Truth is relationship, and quantification does not occur.

Secondly, and more importantly, the pluralistic character of truth shows that the notion of truth is not identical, say, with the notion of goodness. Ultimately Truth and Goodness may coalesce, but even then they are not the same. History shows us what an amount of evil (nongoodness) has been perpetrated in the name of Truth. Truth *alone* in this sense is not enough—that is, does not fulfill the function that truth is supposed to perform. It also explicitly requires goodness. Truth is pluralistic; hence, truth, truth alone, disincarnated truth, cannot be an absolute, and ultimately it is not true. It needs other elements, at the same level of truth, as it were. Goodness is a case in point. Truth is not goodness and yet truth without goodness is maimed, is not truth. I shall not discuss whether one of the weaknesses of the dominant Western philosophy is that it desired to be merely *sophia* (converted into *epistēmē*) and reduced the *philia* to desire (of wisdom), forgetting that it has equally to be (wisdom of) love.

Be this as it may, the pluralistic character of truth denounces the monism of thought and reveals the existential aspect of truth. Each truth is one, certainly, but a universal truth in general is just an extrapolation of our mind.

This does not mean that within one particular period in history or within one given culture—I should prefer to say within one living myth—there are no unanimously accepted standards and, in that sense, relatively universal truths.

There are such truths, because they are seen as such by that particular group of humans. Slavery as an institution, to give just one example, may today elicit a general consensus as being something to be abolished, so that even those who still practice it do so with bad conscience. God was for a long time and in a great part of the world such a myth or recognized truth. It now no longer is. Anticapitalism and democracy could be adduced as examples of absolute political truths for some and yet contested by others.

My thesis is clear: a universal theory of whatever kind denies pluralism. Any alleged universal theory is one particular theory, besides many others, that claims universal validity, thus trespassing the limits of its own legitimacy. Further, no theory can be absolutely universal, because theory, the contemplation of truth, is neither a universal contemplation, nor is (theoretical) "truth" all that there is to Reality.

The Inner Limits of the Logos

We have indicated, so far, the impotency of the *logos* to unify (identify) itself completely with itself, thus showing a dimension of Reality "incommensurable" with the *logos*, or rather "incommensured" by it. We have implicitly mentioned the Unspeakable and also the Unspoken, as well as the Unthinkable and the Unthought. We have obliquely realized that there is a place for the Unthought and the Unspoken. The Unspeakable and the Unthinkable are in a way within the realm of speech and thought inasmuch as we are still aware of them. With the Unthought it is different. We are not aware of it. We recall only later that something remained unthought for a while, and from there we assume that there still may be more, and that perhaps something always remains unthought—but we can neither speak of it nor prove it. We speak about the Unspeakable as that *x* about which nothing *else* can be said. If we were to speak about the Unspoken, we would destroy it; it would be a contradiction in terms.

I here want to deal with the inner boundaries of the word. Language is neither singular nor plural. Like the notion of the personal person, it defies number. A person is not just a single individual. An I entails a thou and both imply he/she/it/they/we. An isolated I is a contradiction in terms. It is an I only because of a thou—and vice versa.

Similarly, language entails not only more than one speaker (a single individual would not speak—there would be neither any need of nor meaning in speaking), it also entails more than language. Language in the singular makes no sense. There is no private language, nor is there a single language. First, de facto, there is not just a single language. There are languages in the world. Secondly, de jure, no language could exist alone. A single language (and this implies a single speaker) would coincide with the things it speaks about, and words would be the things. The distance between word and thing would be zero. There would be no need to express the thing other than by itself if there were a single language.

By language I do not mean now, say, English. English inasmuch as it is spoken by a number of persons, each one of them having a different perspective in the use of each word, is already a polyphonic and even polysemic language.

English is a set of speeches with certain common sounds and structures. What we now call language, or *a* language, is the homogeneous integral of a group of speeches. I made reference to a single language in the sense of a single speech by a single speaker (or a plurality of speakers using the identically same speech). Words are not things: things can be worded differently. Otherwise the word would be the thing or no-thing. No word exhausts the thing; no word expresses the thing completely; no name is the real name, the name that could totally cover the thing. Language is language because it speaks, it says, it unfolds things and reveals them, it unveils them, to the persons for whom they are precisely things. This fundamental reflection on language seems all too often overlooked, and it is relevant for our topic.

The phrase, "In the beginning was the Word," means in so many traditions from Asia and Africa that in the beginning there was a Speaker, a Spoken To, a Spoken With, and a Spoken About. Without this *quaternitas perfecta* there is no Word. If "Word was at the beginning," now after the beginning there are words, languages, and a plurality of those *quaternitates*. The temptation to make sense of it all by returning to the beginning is comprehensible, but it is also understandable that to "want to be *like* God" was condemned by God as a hybris that led to human alienation. Let me close this reference by saying that what that tradition tells us is to become Christ himself—*ipse Christus,* not *alter Christus.*

In a simpler manner: we do not speak language. We speak a language, a language that has relationships with other languages and each of which represents a new perspective on the world, a new window and often a new panorama. We cannot understand all the languages of the world. We can cross the boundaries of, say, a dozen languages, and become aware of the multidimensionality of the things we word so differently. Other persons can also cross some other boundaries, and so the net can spread all over the world—but with a center nowhere. This is what happens in predominantly oral cultures.

Illiterates in many countries of the so-called Middle East and India, and I suppose Africa as well, are not persons who do not know how to read and write (this is a Western fixation), but individuals who know only a single language, who understand only the dialect of their own village. As a matter of fact, what we call languages are certain dialects that have gained some power and been endorsed by Royal Academies and Learned Societies, and been printed as the official or correct way of saying things. This is a phenomenon unheard of a few centuries ago in Europe, and still today in most of the world. The real languages are the dialects.

Illiterates are those persons who cannot distinguish a particular locution from what it means, because they know only that locution and are not aware that the "same" thing can be said in different ways so that nothing is absolute.

In point of fact each village develops its own language, but the villagers know perfectly well that some miles away the "same" thing is given another name, which they also know. In this way they do not confuse the name with the thing. (The importance of this is not to know how to name utensils—so we can buy and sell in the neighboring bazaar—but how to understand living words like beauty, justice, propriety, politeness.) They know that no one word, no one language, can exhaust the immense variety of the human experience. So it is only together, in *colloquium*, that we touch the universality of human life.

A universal theory claims to be a universal language, a language in which all languages find themselves reproduced, reflected, or into which they can be translated. Yet a universal language does not exist. And if it would, it would represent an impoverishment of the riches of the many languages.

Certainly we can and should stretch the meaning of words as much as we can, so as to make them say what until then they did not mean. I have cited the example of "grace" elsewhere, which for a long period of Christian theology was almost by definition the exclusive property of Christianity. Today we have rescued that word from meaning only the saving grace as a share in the divine nature, as the apostle Peter understood it. There are also Indian religions of grace and Christian theology does not deny it, although it will have to find theological explanations for this fact. But words, in spite of their elasticity, have their limits.

Theology is a case in point. We can say that by *theos* we understand the Christian concept; but can we include in the meaning of this word what a Buddhist means with no proper word and a Marxist by denying the existence of such a being? If we mean just transcendence, let us say it and not speak about the Transcendent.

In order to properly approach crosscultural problems I have developed a theory of *homeomorphic equivalents* as analogies of a third degree. "Brahman" is not the translation of "God," for instance, but both perform the equivalent functions required in their respective systems. We may perhaps find the homeomorphic equivalents of the word "theology," but we cannot assume that this word encompasses all those equivalents, just as God does not cover what Brahman stands for. It may even be that on the doctrinal level they are incompatible notions. Either there is a creator God, or an inactive noncreator Brahman, but not both, in spite of the fact that in the respective systems both are not only legitimate but necessary. Or we need to modify the meaning of the two words so as to make them compatible within one single system. It is very proper to have our language and to want to express all that we can in our own language, but it will remain only one possible language, which should not pretend to supplant the others.

As I have argued elsewhere, terms, as signs for scientific information—as labels in a nominalistic world—can certainly be all translated more or less artificially into any language. We can say entropy or weight in any language. They all have a measurable point of reference. Not so with words whose points of reference are the historical and cultural crystalizations of human experiences, which can be verified only by sharing in those experiences. How do we translate French *esprit*, Catalan *seny*, Navajo *hosho*, Sanskrit *rayi*, English *countenance*, German *Stimmung*? Poets know something about this. A universal theology of religion would not want to deal only with the equivalent of mathematical infractures common to most religions.

There have been in our days efforts at highly formalized theories of religion. They are useful attempts at finding some common structures and formal gestalts of religion. I myself define religion as something fulfilling the equation $y = f(x)$, where x is the human condition as seen by any culture or religion at any given moment; y is the goal, aim, end, solution, meaning, result, or whatever of x, the human condition of life; and f is the function that transforms x into y.

All religions, I submit, claim to fulfill this condition and satisfy this structure. This is a formalized language that helps us to understand religious phenomena by finding an ultimate common structure, so that if something fulfills that equation, like a certain type of humanism, for instance, it should—or could—be called religion, although the label "religion" may not be customary. But all this is far from providing us a universal theory by which to understand religion. It provides us, certainly, a kind of algebra about which I have elsewhere also commented on its limitations.

A truly universal theory of religions should be a sort of theory of theories, for every religion has its thinkers and systematizers spinning out theories of their respective religions, calling them theologies, philosophies, or whatever. A theory of theories amounts to a language of languages, a meta-language, a meta-theory. By now we should know the dialectic of such attempts. Either the theory of theories is another theory, and then it falls into the class of which it claims to be the set (which is a contradiction) or it is a meta-theory—that is, not a theory at all but something else. What can that "else" be if not another more sophisticated theory of a second degree, as it were? But then we may need another theory of a third degree to explain the other possible meta-theories that may emerge, *et sic ad infinitum*. If the "else" is of another order, we can no longer call it "theory"; it ceases to be of the order of the *logos*. This insight will open a door for us (see "The Alternative," below). But there is still another point to consider.

The Outer Boundaries of Any Theory

We have seen the inner limits of a universal theory. But there is still more. No need to be a Marxist or to follow any particular sociology of knowledge in order to subscribe to the philosophical insight that any theory stems from a praxis and is nurtured by it, even if often standing in dialectical opposition to it. Any theory not only attempts to explain the status quo (of the physical sciences, for instance); it also springs from that very status quo (of the post-Einsteinian physics, in our example). It would suffice to change the praxis (in our case it would be the appearance of an unaccounted for physical fact) to upset all the existing theories. What would become of a universal theory of religion if suddenly (or less abruptly) a new religion would appear or even a new notion of religion? The universal theory would either have to be given up or it would have to deny a priori the character of religion to the newcomer. Let us not forget that for a long time Confucianism and Buddhism were not considered religions, because they did not fit into a neat theory of religion. I am afraid that something similar happens with regard to Marxism and humanism, to which many would deny the name (and not just the label) religion.

I have already made allusion to the (colonialistic) cultural monoformism from which most of the universal theories come. They assume that we are today in a better position than ever to know the essence of religion. In that we are free from any desire to dominate, all we need to do is to evaluate and understand the present (religious) situation—without being aware that this very attitude both consecrates, as it were, the status quo, and transforms it in one very particular direction. In other words, a universal theory of religion is loaded with political overtones. A telling example today is the so-called theology of liberation within the Catholic Church. It raises waves within the institution because it does not tally with a "universal theory of Christian religions" sponsored by the Supreme Pontifex of that church.

Any theory is only an intellectual explanation of a given datum, but it is all too often blind to the fact that the datum appears first as such when seen under the light of a particular theory. The relationship between theory and praxis is that of a vital circle—not a vicious circle. Any human praxis entails a theory and any human theory entails a praxis, not because the one is *based* on the other and presupposes it, and vice versa—which would constitute a vicious circle—but because the two are intrinsic components of one and the same human factor. Both are interdependent, though not through a causal link, and probably not even by means of a logical dialectic. It is rather a ying-yang dialogical relationship. There is no synthesis possible, but only a constituent and mutually dependent polarity.

The problem has been sufficiently studied so as to spare us the task of spelling it out. It suffices to have mentioned it. In a word: any alleged universal theory is dependent upon a praxis that is far from being universal. It is an iron colossus with earthen feet!

THE ALTERNATIVE

What, then, is to be done if we reject any grandiose universal theory and even detect in this intent a latent will to dominate and a fear that if we do not make sense of everything we will lose our bearings and become vulnerable? I repeat that I do not minimize the importance of the noble desire to overcome exclusivistic doctrines and to open up ways of communication between compartmentalized and often frozen traditions. Yet, I discover a change in a fundamental human attitude that may have begun very early in human history. It is a shifting from a natural confidence in reality to a cultural mistrust, even of ourselves. We may recall Descartes's existential doubt: even our mind may cheat us, were it not for a veracious and trustworthy God. It begins a culture of mistrust (which is different from critique) and it ends a civilization of (in) security (which has to do with the obsession for certainty). But then, should we give up any critical stance or, on the other hand, any hope at understanding each other? Should we resign ourselves to provincial explanations and eventually to more rivalries and further wars of "theologies," and religions? Far from it. I need not repeat that my entire life is directed toward mutual understanding and cooperation among religious traditions.

After having criticized a universal theory I obviously cannot fall into the trap of proposing one of my own. What I espouse could be summarized in the three headings of this third part. First, we must put our house in order, as it were. Secondly, we must open ourselves to the others; and thirdly, we both, or if need be, we alone, must rely on the overall thrust of the human experience.

I should add here that these three moments are intertwined and require each other. They are three moments of one and the same fundamental religious attitude. This fundamental religious attitude, I submit, is a basic human attitude. It is an attitude of trust in reality. *Apistia* is a cause of ignorance, said Heraclitus (Frag. 86). Without a certain confidence somewhere, the human being cannot live. I have to trust my parents, my friends, the grocer, language, the world, God, my own evidence, my consciousness, or whatever.

The fundamental error of Descartes, as the father of modernity, along with the founders of the "new science," which since then has dominated Western civilization, is that once the method of doubting of everything is consciously started, there is no end to it, and yet it has a beginning, a foundation that is taken for granted. God, for Descartes, is the "object" that will put an end to the *regressus ad infinitum*, but what he does not see is his taking for granted the *ego* of his doubt as well as of his *cogito*. Even if he doubts that he doubts or thinks, it is always his *ego* that is presupposed.

This is the birth of modern individualism. And once we identify ourselves with our singularity we have to look frantically for a foundation. Singularity needs support, a foundation. I am no longer a constitutive element in the universe. I am no longer in communion with the whole, no longer the whole. I no longer am, for I could *not* be. *Angst* is the companion of an isolated singularity. I have to justify my existence and conquer my being; I have become a stranger to reality, a mere spectator who suddenly discovers I have no ticket (no reason) to see (share) the spectacle of the real. The estrangement begins. We may say, this is what the loss of innocence means. It *may* be. We discover ourselves naked—that is, alone, alienated from the rest of the universe.

Whatever this may be, the fact is that the old innocence cannot be recovered. A second innocence is a contradiction in terms. The moment that I become aware that it is second, it ceases to be a real innocence. It is not for nothing there was an angel at the gate of paradise with a sword of fire to prevent return. There is no point in going back. But there can be a new innocence, so new that it does not even remember the previous one, or rather that it does not believe in the first innocence. The essence of paradise is to be lost—always and ever lost. It is the necessary mental hypothesis for the myth of the fall, be it of Eve or of Galileo/Descartes and Co. The resurrection myth looms on the horizon.

Having discovered the precariousness of the individual—that is, having practically exhausted all the arguments of reason for a better world, or a good life, for total security, or a real foundation of thinking, behavior, and what not—having discovered in the entire explanation of ourselves and of the universe at least one weak spot that makes the whole thing foundationless, we may as well make a jump, a *metanoia*, a conversion, and discover that, in spite of all our efforts, we were all the time assuming an unconscious trust in reality, a confidence perhaps in life, certainly in "that" which makes the entire human enterprise an adventure, either with sense or meaningless. We discover, in short, that it all may be a game, even a bad game at that, an illusory one, or whatever, but ultimately it is our game, our entertainment, our adventure. In a word, we recognize, we believe that we are created, born, thrown out, existing, dreaming, living or even imagining it all, but nevertheless doing it. It is to that fundamental human trust that I appeal—and personally confessing that I do not find the human adventure so dull, uninteresting, or negative.

The Harmony from Within

If we speak of religious traditions or of religion in general, we should not remain at the surface of the human religious experience. We should begin by living, knowing, and experiencing our own tradition, or particular subtradition, as intensively and deeply as possible. Religion has been probably the place where the worst human passions and the most dangerous human attitudes have occurred. At the same time, religion is the locus where the highest peaks of the human experience have been reached and where the most sublime quality of human life has been unfolded.

I shall not linger here at defining religion as the quest for the ultimate, as the set of symbols and practices of the human being when confronted with the most definitive questions as to the meaning of life and the universe, not just on an intellectual plane, but on an existential and vital level. Religion is, in the last instance, a dimension of human life.

My first point is this: when trying to understand the religious phenomena of the human race, we cannot neglect our own personal religious dimension developed with more or less force in one particular tradition. Otherwise, we distort the entire enterprise. Only those who knew "number" were allowed to enter Plato's Academia, only those endowed with "faith" could duly practice Christian theological reflection. Only those with a medical title are allowed to practice medicine. Only those who know how to rule themselves are the true rulers of others, declared Lao Tzu, Plato, and sages from practically all traditions. Only those who cultivate the religious dimension in their own lives can really dare to enter upon the excruciating task of trying to understand what religion is all about. The study of religion is not the classification of "religious" data, but the study of the religious dimension of the human being. I am not saying that scholars should belong to any particular religious persuasion or that they should be outwardly "religious" in the almost hypocritical sense that the word is used in many circles today. I am affirming that without both an intellectual and an experiential knowledge (which implies love, involvement, and a certain pathos) there is little hope of succeeding in this enterprise. All too often individuals who seem to pose as exponents of some other religion know fairly little about the riches of their own tradition.

But I am saying still more, and it is a delicate matter to formulate it without being misunderstood. I am not preaching that one has to belong to any religious institution. I am propounding that one has to have reached a certain religious insight, poise, maturity, wisdom, and even inner peace and harmony within one's own being, without which intellectual discourse about religion will be marred at the very outset. I am saying that knowledge requires connaturality and even implies a certain identification with the thing known.

The classic Western word for this gnosis is wisdom (*sapientia: sapida scientia*). Religion is not like geology, which may be cultivated provided we have enough information of the objective facts and the scientific theories. But the study of religion demands a special kind of empathy with the subject matter, which cannot be dissociated from one's own life. We can write about the symbolic meaning and extraordinary beauty of dance as an expression of the sacred and compare Greek with Amerindian rituals, for instance. But if we have not had at least a glimpse both of the transforming effects of the dance and of the inner relationship between dance and the rest of life, we shall not be able to make much headway in the interpretation of the religious phenomenon of the dance. Religion is a certain wholeness. A good oboe player is not automatically a good conductor of a symphony orchestra. One needs something more than the sum total of the skills of the individual instruments. Religion, I submit, is the symphony, not the solo player or singer.

The inner harmony I am referring to is manifested in the spontaneous and creative way in which we may be able to deal with one particular religion because we are really at home there and able to simplify, to relate disparate things, or put practices together. I am speaking about a certain identification with that tradition, which does not preclude, of course, critical opinions and even harsh judgments, but which are always somewhat from within. When dealing with a religion at that level we should speak *ex abundantia cordis et mentis* more than from a catalogue of propositions. The existential reason is obvious. Any authentic religious dialogue dispels misunderstandings from both sides and calls for rectifications and new interpretations. If one of the partners is not at home in the process, because of not knowing almost spontaneously and by an instinctive sense (what the Scholastics, following Plato and Aristotle, called *per connaturalitatem*) the living sources of his or her tradition, discussion will stick to mere formulations and become rigid. No encounter, no dialogue, will take place.

If scholars gain this insight into their own tradition, they will be able to become aware of what I call the *pars pro toto* effect. In order to be brief I may exemplify it with the attitude we find in so many truly spiritual masters. I am aware that I see reality, although through the perspective of my own window. I may believe that I see the entire panorama of the world and the meaning of human life, although through the color, shape, and glass of my particular window. I may further believe that it is the best window, at least for me, and that the vision it allows is not distorted. I may at this moment withhold judgment regarding the validity of the vision through other windows, but I cannot hide the fact that I believe that through my window I see the entire panorama—the *totum.*

Nobody is ultimately satisfied with partialities. A Christian, for instance, will say that Christ represents the totality or is the universal savior or the center of the universe, to utilize different metaphors, the interpretation of which does not enter now into the picture. We may well demythicize them. Nevertheless the Christian will not be satisfied with a partial view, that Christ is just one *avatāra* among many, and be content with it as the Christian's lot (or *karma*?). In short, Christians will have to say that in Christ they find the truth—and with qualifications, the whole truth.

But there is a third experience still to pass through. We should, further, be aware that we see the *totum per partem*, the whole through a part. We will have to concede that the other, the non-Christian, for instance, may have a similar experience and that the non-Christian will have to say that the Christian takes the *pars pro toto*, for from the outside one only sees the *pars*, not the *totum*—the window, not the panorama. How to combine these apparently contradictory statements? We will have to say that the other is right in discovering that we take the *pars pro toto* (because the outsider sees the window), but that we are also right in seeing the *totum per partem* (because we see the panorama). It is a *totum* for us, but *per partem*, limited to our vision through the one window. We see the *totum*, but not *totaliter* one may say (because we do not see through other windows). We see all that we can see. The other may see equally the *totum* through another window, and thus describe it differently, but both see the *totum*, although not *in toto*, but *per partem*. *Rota in rotae (trochos en trochō)* said Christian mystics commenting on Ezechiel 1:16.

This means that we do not need a universal theory as if we could enjoy a global perspective—which is a contradiction in terms. It means that each one of us may be aware of the whole under one particular aspect—and not just that we see only a part of it. Both the subjective and objective models break down. There is neither subjective nor objective universality. We see all that we can see—one may grant—but only *all* that *we* can see, our *totum.* The whole is what is wholesome for us (and healthy—following the wisdom of the words). Something is complete when it has an inner harmony—as we shall still emphasize. Let us recall that the root *kail (koil),* from which the word "whole" derives, suggests both beauty and goodness.

Dialogical Openness

Once internal dialogue has begun, once we are engaged in a genuine intrareligious scrutiny, we are ready for what I call the *imparative* method—that is, the effort at learning from the other and the attitude of allowing our own convictions to be fecundated by the insights of the other. I argue that, strictly speaking, comparative religion, on its ultimate level, is not possible, because we do not have any neutral platform outside every tradition whence comparisons may be drawn. How can there be a no-man's-land in the land of Man? In particular fields this is indeed possible, but not when what is at stake is the ultimate foundations of human life. We cannot compare (*comparare*—that is, to treat on an equal—*par*—basis), for there is no fulcrum outside. We can only *imparare*—that is, learn from the other, opening ourselves from our standpoint to a dialogical dialogue that does not seek to win or to convince, but to search together from our different vantage points. It is in this dialogue, which cannot be multitudinous, but only between a few traditions in each case, where we forge the appropriate language to deal with the questions that emerge in encounter. Each encounter creates a new language.

In these dialogues we do not come up with great universal theories, but with a deepened mutual understanding among, say, Catholic Christianity and Śaivasiddhanta, or between Lutheranism and Shī'ah Islam, or between modern Western philosophical categories and traditional Bantu religiousness. Once a net of relationships has been developed, it is relatively easy to establish new and more general links and even venture common categories. The great religions of Africa should be mentioned here, for they offer a peculiar difficulty on the one hand, and a grand facility on the other, to dialogue. It is difficult because often dialogue becomes doctrinal, abstract, metaphysical, and the genius of many an African religion lies elsewhere. We have difficulty in finding common categories. It is easy, on the other hand, because of the charge of humanity and concreteness of such exchanges. The common language is the simplest one.

These mutual studies, relationships, and dialogues change both the opinion of the one partner and the interpretation of the other. Religions change through these contacts; they borrow from each other and also reinforce their respective standpoints, but with less naivety. This type of dialogue is not only a religious endeavor for the participants, it is a genuine *locus theologicus*, to speak in Christian Scholastic parlance, a source in itself of religious (theological) understanding. A theory of a particular religion today has also to deal with other religions. We can no longer ignore the other. The religions of others—our neighbors—become a religious question for us, for our religion.

In a way, there is many a theory of religion claiming to be a universal theory of religion. But then we are, although on a second and much more fruitful higher spiral, at the same initial point—namely, having to confront a series of universal theories of religion. We will have to deal with, say, how Islam sees itself in the religious mosaic of our times, or how Marxism confronts the Hindu interpretation of reality.

This process of mutual learning has no end. Imparative religion is an open process. A universal theory attempts to clarify everything as neatly as possible in one single place and ends eventually by stifling any ultimate dialogue. In my alternative the polarities remain and the ideal is not seen in a universal theory, but in an ever emerging and ever elusive myth that makes communication, and thus mutual fecundation, possible without reducing everything to a single source of intelligibility or to mere intelligibility. The very theory is dialogical. In a word, the dialogical character of being is a constitutive trait of reality. Agreement means convergence of hearts, not just coalescence of minds. There is always place for diversity of opinions and multiplicity of mental schemes of intelligibility.

Human Cosmic Trust

What I am trying to put forward is not a counter-theory, but a new innocence. We should beware of so many reform systems that began with a greater universalistic impulse than the original systems and became new philosophies, new sects, or new religions. Often they do not subsume or even enhance the others but simply multiply their number. This may be not bad—except they do not achieve what they started to do. Any universal theory will soon become another theory.

We should beware of claiming to understand religions better than they have understood themselves. I do not deny this possibility, but it should carry along some contemporary representatives of such a religion, and at least partially transform that religion, lest our interpretation become a new religion. Religious traditions have more existential than doctrinal continuity. There are not many doctrines in common between a Christian of the first century and a present day one, for instance. The case of Hinduism is still clearer. Hinduism is an existence, not an essence. The decisive factor is the existential confession, not the doctrinal interpretation.

The study of religion, I repeat, is not like the scientific approach to physical phenomena, which even in the sciences is becoming obsolete. We are not dealing with objective facts—supposing they existed. Even in the case of allegedly revealed facts, we are still dealing with human constructs, which house, as it were, a group of human beings, giving them the housing of a more or less coherent and protective universe.

In our days we feel, perhaps more acutely than at other times, that we do not know each other, that we still mistrust one another, that in fact we are at loggerheads in many fundamental insights of immediate importance for the praxis of our lives. We are painfully aware of our differences because we are more conscious of our mutual existence and the need to intermingle—brought about by the techniculture of our times. But we cannot chop off our divergences to remain only with what we have in common: we all want to eat and to be happy. This is fundamental, but hunger has many causes and the ways to happiness, and even its concept, differ.

Religions can no longer live in isolation, let alone in animosity and war. Traditional religions nowadays are not, by and large, very powerful and thus do not present a major threat, except of course in some countries. More secular religious ideologies today have greater virulence and fight each other. They cannot be left out of the picture in a discourse about the encounter of religions. The last two world wars were not strictly religious, and yet they were "theological." Where do we turn for harmony and understanding?

The political and economic situation of the world today compels us to radical changes in our conception of humanity and the place of humanity in the cosmos. The present system seems to be running toward major catastrophes of all kinds. This situation brings near the thought that if the change has to be radical and lasting, it also has to transform our ways of thinking and experiencing reality. The point in case of the religious traditions could not be more pertinent. I am prepared to argue that if there is any solution to the present predicament, it cannot come out of one single religion or tradition, but has to be brought about by collaboration among the different traditions of the world. No single human or religious tradition is today self-sufficient and capable of rescuing humanity from its present predicament. We can no longer say "that's your problem!" Hinduism will not survive if it does not face modernity. Christianity will disappear if it does not meet Marxism. Technocratic religion will destroy itself if it does not pay heed to, say, the Amerindian tradition, and so on. Humanity will collapse if we do not gather together all the fragments of the scattered cultures and religions. But togetherness does not necessarily mean unity, nor is understanding absolutely required.

What is needed is trust, a certain trust that sustains a common struggle for an ever better shaping of reality. I mean something like this. As the very word suggests (especially in Latin—*fiducia*), this "trust" entails a certain "fidelity" to oneself, "con-fidence" in the world as cosmos, "loyalty" in the struggle itself, and even (as perhaps etymologically hinted at) an attitude rooted in the soil of reality like a "tree," a basic "belief" in the human project, or rather in the worthwhile collaboration of humans in the overall adventure of being. It excludes only the suicidal and negative desire of self-destruction and annihilation of everything. It does not eliminate the passionate thrust toward the victory of one's own ideals—reprehensible as this may appear to many of us if this is striven for as an absolute.

Elsewhere I have proposed the distinction between the basic and constitutive human *aspiration* by which the human being is constituted precisely as a human being, and the *desires* that plague concrete human existence when not walking on the path toward realization. This, I would submit, takes into account the Buddhist criticism of *tanha, tṛṣṇa*, thirst, desire, the one-pointedly Hindu concern for realization, and the Christian preoccupation with dynamism and creativity. There is a primordial human aspiration, but there are equally hasty desires. The trust I am speaking of is related to the human aspiration by which humans believe that life is worth living, because Reality can—must—be trusted.

The danger in this aspiration—in our case, we may say, toward truth—is that it can become a desire for our own understanding. In other words, the danger lies in the possible confusion between our *desire* to understand everything, because we assume (a priori) that reality is (should be) intelligible, and the *aspiration* of making sense of our life and all reality. This latter is the trust that there is some sense (direction, "meaningful" dynamism) in the universe.

This assumption is not a universal theory, not even a universal praxis. It is only so far a relative cultural invariant inasmuch as exceptions are seen precisely as aberrant deviations by the vast majority of mortals. This trust is an impulse simply not to give up in the task of being what we are (or should be), which some may say is that of being human, others divine.

Half a century ago I called this cosmic trust the cosmological principle, and millennia before it was called *rta, tao, ordo.* Even when we formulate the ultimate metaphysical question, "Why is there something rather than nothing?" we are assuming that the question is meaningful—that it is a real question—even if we do not find an answer, or only a nihilistic one. It may be said of this ultimate ground that there is something somewhere asking whether it all makes sense at all, or that it is all the dream of a dreamer and has never existed outside that dream, or that it is a very weak ground indeed for the unfolding of the universe and our participation in it. Yet it may be enough, for in one way or another we have to stop somewhere. Traditionally this ultimate ground has been called God, Man, or World. We have further interpreted those words as meaning consciousness, goodness, power, intelligence, nothingness, absurdity, matter, energy, and the like. We may change words and interpretations, but some fundamental trust indeed persists.

The ultimate ground for this cosmic confidence lies in the almost universal conviction that reality is ordered—in other words, is good, beautiful, and true. It is a divine Reality, say most of the human traditions. There is no need to blow up a wretched universe, because Reality is not evil ultimately. We may have to bring it to completion, to achieve it, as the fundamental principle of alchemy puts it, and eventually correct it, but not create an artificial-mechanical universe that we must have under control because we cannot trust Reality. Underlying this felt need for control there is a certain Protestant climate that "creation" is a fiasco, combined with some "humanistic" interpretation that the redeemer is Man. But Christian theology will tell us that redemption entails an inner dynamism that ultimately belongs to the "economic Trinity."

Cultural Excursus

To hen . . . diapheromenon auto
autō xumpheresthai, hōsper harmonian
toxou te kai luras.
The one . . . is brought together
by opposition with itself, like the
harmony of the bow and the lyre.
> —Heraclitus, in Plato,
> *Symposion,* 187 a[4]

What I am trying to demythicize is the deeply anchored belief that the true and the one are convertible: *verum et unum convertuntur* was the traditional formulation.[5] It reaches even as far as the curious etymology of Theodoricus of Chartres: *unitas quasi* ontitas *ab* on *graeco, id est entitas* (un-ity amounts to *on-ity* [be-ingness] from *on* [be-ing] in Greek—that is, en-tity [be-ingness]),[6] to understand, then, is to reduce everything to unity and this unity is the oneness of Being. This almost universal insight begins to go astray when interpreted quantitatively. The One is not the counterpart of the Many. *Tò métron* is the first endowment of reality, according to Socrates.[7] The Bible states that God arranged everything according to measure, number, and weight (but not according to meters, quantities, and gravitation).[8]

In attempting to criticize a utopian single theology of religions, or theology of religion, and at the same time trying to awaken a new awareness, I would ally myself here with one of the most incisive leitmotifs of one branch of the Western tradition[9]—and, obviously, predominant in the East.[10] I would even suggest that this has been the prevalent human vision of Reality and that the belief in a possible exhaustive rational explanation of everything is the exception. The alternative is neither anarchy nor irrationalism (even under the cloak of *Gefühlsphilosophien*). The alternative is a dynamic notion of freedom, of Being, and the radical relativity of everything with everything, so that all our explanations are not only for the time being, because ours is a being in time, but also because no Absolute can encompass the complexity of the Real, which is radically free. The Absolute is only absolutely incarnated in the Relative.

It is not enough to say *multa et unum convertuntur*,[11] or to introduce a *coincidentia oppositorum*. It is not convincing to revert to a new individualistic monadology either.[12] These attempts do not assume a dialogical relationship between the One and the Many (*hen kai polla*).[13] With the concepts of quantity and individuation we fail to do justice to the problem. We should introduce other symbols. The one I would choose here is the widespread symbol of *concord*, which as such defies quantification.[14] Neither multiplicity as such nor sheer unity brings about, or even allows, harmony.[15] Harmony implies a constitutive polarity, which cannot be superceded dialectically. It would be destroyed.

Concord is neither oneness nor plurality. It is the dynamism of the Many toward the One without ceasing to be different and without becoming one, and without reaching a higher synthesis. Music is here the paradigm. There is no harmonical accord if there is no plurality of sounds, or if those sounds coalesce in one single note. Neither many nor one, but concord, harmony.

We find this root metaphor almost everywhere from the last mantra of the Rg Veda[16] to Chuang Tzu.[17] It is the thought repeated differently by Heraclitus and taken up by Filolaus,[18] commented upon by Ramon Lull,[19] Pico della Mirandola,[20] Cusanus,[21] and so many others,[22] up to St. François de Sales,[23] and lately taken as title for a book by R. C. Zaehner.[24] This leitmotif has been often submerged by the predominant trend of victory and unity.[25] The Christian symbol is the Trinity.

"Yield and overcome," says Lao Tsu.[26] Fight and overcome, echoes the predominant spirit of Western culture: *Veni, vidi, vici,* said Caesar.[27] Make everything *inclusive*, India would say.[28] Make everything *universal*, responds the West. Strive to make everything complete by realizing harmony is what this third tradition is saying.

My motto would then be *concordia discors*, discordant concord, and it could have as underplay the opposite, "concordant discord," for as the always paradoxical Heraclitus liked to put it: "The mysterious harmony is stronger than the evident one"; or again, "The unspoken harmony is superior to the verbalized one."[29]

But we may still quote:

> *Kai ek tōn diapherontōn*
> *Kallistēn harmonian*
> *Kai panta kat erin ginesthai.*[30]
> (And from divergences
> the most beautiful harmony [arises],
> and all happens through struggle.)[31]

It is the same Heraclitus who praises harmony as the result of polarity.[32] He formulates it in the most general way: "Nature aspires to the opposite. It is from there and not from the equal that harmony is produced."[33]

This is the insight into the agonic character of reality.[34] In point of fact this experience is not as uncommon as one might assume.[35] It lasted until our times.[36] It was with Descartes that divergency of opinions created philosophical anguish. It was the beginning of the modern age. I should like to insist on this. Diversity of opinions becomes disturbing once we direct our attention to mere orthodoxy severed from orthopraxis, and the former is thought to express the essence of being human. Once we take individualism for granted, we find it scandalous that there is diversity of opinions—forgetting the beautiful metaphor of Fernando de Rojas.[37] It is the estrangement of the human mind from nature that leads to the assumption that univocity is the ideal. Thinking begins to be understood as measuring, calculating.

I have quoted these texts in order to suggest the spirit and the method in which I should like to situate the entire enterprise. I have on purpose quoted mainly from the Western tradition, because I have been criticizing mainly a Western theory and attempting to enter into dialogue with it. I am far from wanting to reduce all to any unity.

We hear of a friendly enmity, of a polarity between concord and discord, and a link between the two; we hear of a discordant concord, of the fundamental thrust of nature toward diversity, and we try to understand that true concord is not unity of opinion or equality of intellectual views, but of an order higher than the intellect, for it entails precisely struggle, strife, antagonic dynamisms—*agōn* the Greeks would say, as already indicated.

Discordia is disagreement—literally, setting our hearts at variance, and yet not asunder. Why? Obviously because we do not absolutize our opinions, or identify our being with our "thoughts," because we realize that, by my pushing in one direction and your pushing in the opposite, world order is maintained and given the impulse of its proper dynamism.

The very words by which we often express what we are striving for— "unanimity," "consensus," "agreement," "concord"—all have a cordial or an existential core. One *animus* does not mean one single theory, one single opinion, but one aspiration (in the literal sense of one breath) and one inspiration (as one spirit).[38] Consensus ultimately means to walk in the same direction, not to have just one rational view.[39] And again, to reach agreement suggests to be agreeable, to be pleasant, to find pleasure in being together.[40] Concord is to put our hearts together.

Another word for harmony may be *sympathy*, which does not primarily mean individual, sentimental compassion, but the common *pathos* among all the constituents of reality. Universal sympathy is another way of overcoming the split between individual and collective interests, the one and the many. And the word here suggests not only a more "feminine" receptivity for a predominantly "masculine" culture, but also a greater awareness of the mystery of suffering (pathos, *dukkha*) in a civilization that shuns facing this most elemental factor, which awakens us to transcendence and interiority.

This is the discordant concord: a kind of human harmony perceived in and through the many discordant voices of human traditions. We do not want to reduce them to one voice. We may yet want to eliminate cacophonies. But this again depends very much on the education and generosity of our ears.

All this should not be taken as a mere metaphor. If we live only or even mainly on the values of the eye, the intellect, truth, and we neglect—on that ultimate level—the other senses, the heart, beauty—in a word, the concrete over against the general—we shall live a crippled life. Academia, scholarship, and modern education in general, let alone *techniculture*, seem to have almost forgotten all those other values that we find still so prominent and effective in other cultures. No need for me to understand what the animist or the Hindu or the Christian ultimately mean when they voice their respective worldviews. We may somewhat enjoy the beauty of the symphony, the inexplicable concord out of so many dissenting voices. Pluralism tells us here that one should not assume for oneself (person or culture) the role of being the conductor of the human and much less of the cosmic orchestra. It is enough with the music (the divine), the musicians (the human), and their instruments (the cosmos). Let us play by ear!

CONCLUSION

I have tried to spell out some of the implications of that attitude. I may sum it up with the word "confidence." I mean by this a certain fundamental trust in reality, which impels us to trust even what we do not understand or approve of—unless there are positive and concrete reasons to fight what we discover to be evil or error. To understand that we do not understand is the beginning of transcending knowledge, as most of the spiritual traditions of the world will tell us.[41] Further, to understand that the other is an equal source of understanding, and not only an object of it, is again what many a school has called the beginning of enlightenment.[42]

It all boils down to the experience of our personal and collective limitations, including the very limits of the intellect, not only in us, but in itself. The last function of the intellect is to transcend itself. And this is possible only by becoming aware of its own limitations—and this, I submit, not only in every one of us, but in itself. If we want to reduce everything to consciousness, we are forced to admit that pure consciousness is not conscious of itself. It would then not be pure. Brahman does not know that it is Brahman, says Vedānta coherently. Īśvara knows that "he" is Brahman. The knowledge of the Father is the Son, the *Logos*, says the Christian Trinity. This is not irrationalism. It is the highest and intransferable mission of the intellect, to become aware of its own boundaries. In becoming conscious(ness) of itself, consciousness becomes conscious(ness) of its own limits, and by this very fact transcends them. If pure Consciousness is aware of its limits, this amounts to conceding that not All can be reduced to Consciousness.

Humankind is held together not because we have the same opinions, a common language, the same religion, or even the same respect for others, but for the same reason that the entire universe is held together. We mortals strive not only among ourselves, but we also struggle with the gods for the order of the universe. And yet this *eris* (*kama* and *tapas* the Vedas would say)[43] is also our responsibility, our answer to the very challenge. To maintain the world together, the *lokasamgrahā* of the Gita,[44] is precisely the function of primordial *dharma*, of which humans are active factors.[45]

At Pentecost the peoples did not all speak the same language, nor did they have simultaneous translation, nor did they understand the mutual refinements of the respective liturgies. Yet, they were convinced, they felt, they sensed, that all were *hearing* the great deeds of God, the *megaleia tou Theou*.[46]

This cosmic confidence certainly has an intellectual dimension; I have been speaking about it on the intellectual level. Yet, it does not need to be put into words. And it is this cosmic confidence that stands at the very basis of the dialogical dialogue and makes it possible. The dialogue—we all agree on this— is not a trick, a stratagem to get to the other, to defeat the partner. There is a basic confidence that, although we neither understand nor often approve of what others think and do, we still have not given up all hope (which is a virtue of the sempiternal present and not about the temporal future) that human conviviality makes sense, that we belong together, and that together we must strive. Some thinkers may be tempted to say that this is an option. I would prefer to suggest that this is an instinct, the work of the Spirit.[47]

NOTES

1. See, e.g., "Die existentielle Phänomenologie der Wahrheit," *Philosophisches Jahrbuch der Görresgesellschaft, 1964* (Munich, 1965), pp. 27–54; *Religionen und die Religion* (Munich: Max Hueber, 1965); "La philosophie de la religion devant le pluralisme philosophique et la pluralité des religions," *Pluralisme philosophique et pluralité des religions,* in E. Castelli, ed. (Paris: Aubier, 1977), pp. 193–201; *"Colligite Fragmenta:* For an Integration of Reality," in *From Alienation to At-Oneness: Proceedings of the Theology Institute of Villanova University,* F. A. Eigo, ed. (Villanova University Press, 1977), pp. 19–91; "Rtatattva: A Preface to a Hindu-Christian Theology," *Jeevadhara,* 49 (Jan.–Feb. 1977) 6–63; *The Intrareligious Dialogue* (New York: Paulist Press, 1978); "The Myth of Pluralism: The Tower of Babel—A Meditation on Non-Violence; Panikkar in Santa Barbara," *Cross-Currents,* 29/2 (Summer 1979) 197–230; "Hermeneutics of Comparative Religion: Paradigms and Models," *Journal of Dharma,* 5/1 (Jan.–March 1980) 38–51; "Aporias in the Comparative Philosophy of Religion," in *Man and World,* 12/3–4 (The Hague: Martinus Nihoff, 1980) 357–83; "Words and Terms," in *Esistenza, Mito, Ermeneutica (Scritti per Enrico Castelli),* M. Olivetti, ed. (Padua: CEDAM, 1980), II, pp. 117–33; "Is the Notion of Human Rights a Western Concept?," *Diogenes,* 120 (Winter 1982) 75–102; "The Dialogical Dialogue," in *The World's Religious Traditions,* F. Whaling, ed. (Edinburgh: Clark, 1984), pp. 201–21.

2. As a single example useful not only for its contents but also for its rich bibliographical references (mainly German, English, and French) see Llufs Duch, *Religió i món modern. Introducció a l'estudi dels fenòmens religiosos* (Montserrat: Abadia, 1984), which I wish could soon be translated from its original Catalan into some major European language.

3. Raimundo Panikkar, *Myth, Faith and Hermeneutik* (New York: Paulist Press, 1979), p. 20.

4. See below, n. 32.

5. See Aristotle, *Met.,* II, 1 (993 b 30) as the *locus classicus* from which the Scholastic principle derived—although Aristotle's dictum is somewhat more subtle: *ekaston hōs échei tou einai outō kai tēs alētheías.* Compare the traditional Latin version: *unumquodque sicut se habet ad hoc quod sit, ita etiam se habet ad hoc quod habeat veritatem.* Or more literally: *Quare unumquodque sicut se habet ut sit, ita et ad veritatem.* Cf. Thomas Aquinas, *Summa Theol.,* I, q. 2, a. 3: *Quae sunt maxime vera sunt maxime entia.*

6. *Commentarium in Boethia De trinitate* (Jansen, ed., p. 11), in P. Gaia, *Opere religiose di Nicolò Cusano* (Classici delle religioni) (Turin: UTET, 1971), p. 636.

7. Cf. the astounding text of Plato, *Philebus,* 66a, where, after measure as the first value, comes proportion, and only thirdly reason, followed by *techné,* and fifthly pleasure.

8. Wis. 11:21: *Omnia in mensura (metrō), et numero (arithmō), et pondere (stathmō) disposuisti.*

9. The two modern symbols could be the two seventeenth-century figures of Descartes *(cogito ergo sum)* and Pascal *(le coeur a ses raisons que la raison ne connaît point).*

10. Suffice it to quote the famous *Brahma-sûtra* text, I, 1, 4: *Tat tu samanvayāt* ("But that [because of] the harmony") of all texts of all the sacred scriptures—in spite of the

fact that they write, teach and even command different and prima facie diverging things. Harmony is not uniformity. Even today in India religious understanding is rendered as *dharma samanvaya*. See *Prabuddha Bharata*, 90 (April 1985) 190.

11. As P. Gaia, *Opere*, interprets the *unum* as *complicatio multorum* of Nicholas of Cusa.

12. See the insightful study of Maurice Boutin, "L'Un dispersif," in *Neoplatonismo e religione (Archivio di filosofia)*, 51/1-3 (1983) 253-79, commenting on François Larvelle, *Le principe de minorité* (Paris: Aubier, 1981). There are *"des monades absolument dispersées et dépourvues de monadologie, de raison ou d'universel,"* says Larvelle, for individuals are the *"constituants ultimes de la réalité"* (ibid., p. 261).

13. Plato, *Phileb.,* 15 D, as *locus classicus.*

14. This is the rich concept of *homóuoia*, concord, unanimity, sameness of mind (*homó-uoia;* just as *homó-uomos* means of the same order, law) in the Hellenic tradition since Demosthenes. This concord is defined as *epistēmē koinōn agathōn* in the *Stoicum Veterum Fragmenta*, edited by H. von Arnim (Leipzig, 1903), III, p. 160; as the science of the common goods (in Liddell-Scott, *A Greek-English Lexicon*, Oxford, 1973). See the bibliographical references in Liddell-Scott and in Hammond-Scullard, eds., *The Oxford Classical Dictionary* (Oxford, 1973).

15. "Sameness (*ta homoia*) and the similar (*homóphyla*) do not need harmony; but the different (*anómoia*), the not-similar, and that which is not ordered need to be brought together through harmony," wrote the Pythagorean Philolaus of Kroton, Fragm. 6, in H. Diels-W. Kranz, *Die Fragmente der Vorsokratiker* (Berlin: Weidmann, 9th ed., 1960). The entire text is fundamental.

16. *Samānī va ākūtih / samānā hrdayāni vah / samānam astu vo mano / yathā vah susāhāsati.* (Harmonious be your intention, / harmonious your hearts, / may your spirit be in harmony, / that you may be together in concord!) RV X, 191, 4. I give here a different translation from that in my anthology *The Vedic Experience* (Berkeley: University of California Press, 1977), p. 863.

17. Passim. See, e.g., *Inner Chapters* II (in the translation of G. F. Feng and J. English [New York: Vintage Books, Random House, 1974], p. 46).

18. Fragm. 10. See Diels-Kranz, *Fragmente*, I, p. 410.

19. *"Per ço que enans nos puscam concordar"* are practically the last words of one of the three sages (Jewish, Christian, Muslim) after they left the gentile (who would choose the right *lig* [religion] without the knowledge of the three): Ramon Lull, *Libre del gentil e los tres savis*, in *Obres essencials* (Barcelona: Selecta, 1957), I, p. 1138. However, Lull is perhaps too much in favor of unity. See the dissertation (Munich: Evangelisch-theologische Fakultät, 1976) by François Medeiros, "Judaisme, Islam et Gentilité dans l'oeuvre de Raymond Lulle."

20. *Dopo [Dio] comincia la belleza, perchè comincia la contrarietà, senze la quale non può essere cosa alcuna creata, ma sarebbe solo esse Dio: nè basta questa contrarietà e discordia di diverse nature a constituire la creatura, se per debito temperamento non diventa e la contrarietà unita e la discordia concorde, il che si può per vera deffinizione assignare di essa bellezza, cioèche non sia altro che una amica inimicizia e una concorde discordia. Per questo diceva Eraclito la guerra e la contenzione essere padre e genetrice delle cose; e, appresso Omero, chi maladisce la contenzione è detto avere bestemmiato la natura. Ma più perfettamente parlò Empedocle, ponendo, no la discordia per sè, ma insieme con la concordia essere principio de le cose, intendendo per la discordia la varietà delle nature di che si compongono, e per la concordia l'unione di quelle; e pero disse solo in Dio non essere discordia perchè in lui non è unione di diverse nature, anzi è*

essa unità semplice sanza composizione alcuna (Commento, II, 9, in H. de Lubac, *Pic de la Mirandole* [Paris: Aubier Montaigne, 1974], p. 296, emphasis added).

In *Heptaplus (aliud proemium)* he again writes about a discordant concord: *Quoniam sc. astricti vinculis concordiae uti naturas ita etiam appellationes hi omnes mundi mutua sibi liberalitate condonant: . . . occultas, ut ita dixerim, totius naturae et amicitias et affinitates edocti, . . . Accedit quod, qua ratione haec sunt distincta, quia tamen nulla est multitudo quae non sit una,* discordi quadam concordia ligantur *et multiformibus nexuum quasi catenis devinciuntur* (in de Lubac, *Pic,* p. 297; emphasis added).

21. See his work *De concordantia catholica* of 1433 and his *De pace fidei* of 1453, a few months after the defeat of Constantinople, although Cusanus falls into a dialectical *coincidentia*. Consider his revealing text: *Omnia enim in tantum sunt in quantum unum sunt. Complectitur autem tam ea quae sunt actu, quam ea quae possunt fieri. Capacius est igitur unum quam ens, quod non est nisi actu ist, licet Aristoteles dicat ens et unum converti (De venatione sapientiae,* 21).

22. E.g., Postel: *Concordia mundi; De orbis terrae concordia;* etc. Erasmus: *Querela pacis; Oratio de pace et discordia; Precatio pro pace Ecclesiae; De amabili Ecclesiae concordia.* Juan Luis Vives: *De concordia et discordia in humano genere* (1529); *De pacificatione* (1529); etc. See also Augusto Gentili, "Problemi del simbolismo armonico nella cultura post-elizabettiana," in E. Castelli, ed., *Il Simbolismo del Tiempo* (Rome: Istituto di studi filosofici, 1973), p. 65.

23. "Introduce unity into diversity, and you create order; order yields harmony, proportion; harmony, where you have perfect integrity, begets beauty. There is beauty in an army when it has order in the ranks, when all the divisions combine to form a single armed force. There is beauty in music when voices, which are true, clear, distinct, blend to produce perfect consonance, perfect harmony, to achieve unity in diversity or diversity in unity—a good description might be *discordant concord*; better still, *concordant discord*" (François de Sales, *Traité de l'amour de Dieu,* I, 1 [1616]; translated by R. C. Zaehner at the beginning of his book cited in the next note).

24. *Concordant Discord. The Interdependence of Faiths* (Oxford: Clarendon Press, 1970)—the Gifford Lectures, 1967/1969.

25. One quotation may suffice: *So wird also die Universalgeschichte, die Geschichtsphilosophie und die Zukunftsgestaltung in Wahrheit zu einem möglichst einheitlichen Selbstverständnis des eigenen Gewordenseins und der eigene Entwicklung. Für uns gibt es nur die Universalgeschichte der europäischen Kultur, die natürlich der vergleichenden Blicke auf fremde Kulturen praktisch and theoretisch bedarf, um sich selbst und ihr Verhältnis zu den anderen zu verstehen, die aber mit den anderen dadurch nicht etwa in eine allgemeine Menschheitsgeschichte und Menschheitsentwicklung zusammenfliessen kann. Unsere Universalgeschichte ist um so mehr ein europäisches Selbstverständnis, als nur der Europäer bei seiner Häufung verschiedenster Kulturelemente, seinem niemals ruhenden Intellekt und seiner unausgesetzt strebenden Selbstbildung eines solchen universalhistorischen Bewusstseins auf kritischer Forschungsgrundlage für seine Seele bedarf* (E. Troeltsch, *Der Historismus und seine Probleme* [Tübingen: Mohr, 1922; reprint, Aalen, 1961], p. 71) (vol. 3 of the *Gesammelte Schriften*). I feel that most of the efforts at universalizing are still under this post-Hegelian spell. *Der Europäismus* is, significantly enough, the title of Troeltsch's chap. 4, part 2.

26. *Tao Te Ching,* 22; also 40, 51, 62, etc.

27. Plutarch, *Caes.,* 50, 3 (*ēlthon, eizon, eníkēsa*) and also *Moralia,* 206 e; quoted also in other sources: Lucius Annaeus Florus (2nd century), 2, 13, 63; Cassius Dio (2nd century), 42, 48; up to the 12th-century Byzantine historian Johannes Zonaras, 10, 10; etc.

28. See G. Oberhammen, ed., *Inklusivismus. Eine indische Denkform* (Vienna: Institut für Indologie, 1983).

29. I have now translated my motto differently. *Aphanēs* means literally "without being *phaneros*" (visible, apparent), from the verb *pháinō*, "to shine, illumine," and thus "let know, appear, manifest." The root *pha* (*phn, phan* . . .) means "to shine" (cf. fantasy), but immediately related to *phēmn*: "to say," *phásis*, "the word" *phōnē* (cf. prophet)—cf. voice, symphony, phenomenology, epiphany, telephone, etc.

30. Heraclitus, Fragm. 8 (cf. also Empedocles, 124, 2). The text refers probably first to music and from there to the wider reality. Cf. a standard translation: *Das Widerstrebende vereinigte sich, aus den entgegengesetzten (Tönen) entstehe die schönste Harmonie, und alles Geschehen erfolge auf dem Wege des Streites* (W. Capelle [translation and introductions], *Die Vorsokratiker, Die Fragmente und Quellenberichte* [Stuttgart: Kröner; Taschenausgabe Nr. 119, 1968], p. 134). W. D. Ross's standard translation of Aristotle, *Nichomachean Ethics*, VIII (1555 b 4), reads: "and Heraclitus [saying] that 'it is what opposes that helps' and 'from different tones comes the fairest tune' and 'all things are produced through strife.' " See the book with which Romano Guardini practically began his intellectual career, *Der Gegensatz und Gegensätze. Entwurf eines Systems der Typenlehre* (Freiburg: Herder, 1917), which had substantial revisions until the 2nd edition of 1955 with the title *Der Gegensatz. Versuche zu einer Philosophie des Lebendig-Konkreten.*

31. The word *eris*, from *erei* or *er* (cf. German *errege, reize*), means "strife, quarrel, struggle, discord, disputation." *Eris* is also the goddess of discord in the marriage of Peleus and Thetis. In the *Eumenides* (975) of Aeschylus, *eris agathōn* appears with a positive meaning. For *eris* see also Fragm. 80: *polemon eónta xunón kaì dikēn erin kai ginómena panta kat' erin kai chreōn* ["One should know that] strife is the common thing, along with the right to struggle, and that all things happen by struggle and necessity."

32. See Fragm. 51, in Diels-Kranz, *Vorsokratiker*, I, p. 162, and its Platonic commentary in *Symposium,* 187, with the famous metaphor of the arc and the lyre, quoted in the epigraph of this excursus. We could also translate: "The one conflicting with itself is brought into harmony with itself like the harmony of the bow and the lyre."

33. *Isōs de tōn enantiōn hē phýsis glichetai kaì ek toutōn apoteleï tò symphōnon, ouk ek tōn homoiōn.* See Diels-Kranz, *Vorsokratiker* (Heraklitos, fragm. 10). See also Aristotle, *De mundo* (5, 39 b, 7).

34. "Agonic" contains almost all the elements: it means *assembly, ágora*, gathering. This *gathering,* being a human one, is a *place of speech*, where the *word* is paramount. But persons speak in order to *contest* each others' opinions. *Agòn* is the *struggle*, either in battle or the mental agony (as we still say). It is this *vehemence* that elicits *power*, although, of course, sometimes *anxiety, agony.* A *trial, legal action*, can be *agonizing activities.* All the English words in italics are meanings of this word whose root means precisely "to lead, to carry, to fetch, bring, take," etc. Cf. *agós*, the leader. The root *ago* means to "lead." Cf. Sanskrit *ajah*, to "drive, push."

35. As a single and yet multivalent example I may quote the first lines of the Preface of the Spanish classic *La Celestina* of Fernando de Rojas (first edition, Burgos, 1499): *Todas las cosas ser criadas a manera de contienda o batalla, dice aquel gran sabio Heráclito en este modo:* Omnia secundum litem fiunt. *Sentencia a mi ver digna de perpetua y recordable memoria. . . . Hallé esta sentencia corroborada por aquel gran orador y poeta laureado Petrarca, diciendo:* Sine lite atque offensione nihil genuit natura parens. *Sin lid y ofensión* [*combate* in modern Spanish] *ninguna cosa engendró*

la natura, madre de todo. [I note parenthetically that *parens* is here translated *madre*. In the Roman religion the earth is called *sacra parens*; see J. Ries, *Le sacré comme approche de Dieu et comme resource de l'homme* (Louvaine-la Neuve: Coll. *Conferences et Travaux*, nr. 1, 1983).] *Dice más adelante:* Sic est enim, et sic propemodum universa testantur: rapido stellae obviant firmamento; contraria invicem elementa confligunt; terrae tremunt; maria fluctuant; aer quatitur; crepant flammae; bellum immortale venti gerunt; tempora temporibus concertant; secum singula, nobiscum omnia. *Que quiere decir; "En verdad así es, y así todas las cosas de esto dan testimonio: Las estrellas se encuentran en el arrebatado firmamento del cielo, los adversos elementos unos con otros rompen pelea, tremen* [in modern Spanish *tiemblan*] *las tierras, ondean los lares, el aire se sacude, suenan las llamas, los vientos entre sí traen perpetua guerra, los tiempos con tiempos contienden y litigan entre si, uno a uno, y todas contra nosotros."* . . . *Mayormente pues ella con todas las otras cosas que al mundo son, van debajo de la bandera de esta notable sentencia: "Que aun la misma vida de los hombres, si bien lo miramos, desde la primera edad hasta que blanquean las canas, es batalia"* (edited by Bruno Mario Damiani, *La Celestina* [Madrid: Ediciones Cátedra, 11th ed., 1983], pp. 45–47).

36. See the well-known book by Miguel de Unamuno, *La agonía del cristianismo* (Madrid: Renacimiento, 1931); the French edition dates from 1925 (Paris: F. Rieder).

37. *No es menor la disensión de los filósofos en las escuelas, que la de las ondas del mar* (Rojas, *La Celestina*, p. 48).

38. *Animus* translates not only the Greek *psychē* but also *thymos* and *pneúma*, although it has its exact Greek counterpart in *anemos*—in Sanskrit *aniti (anilaḥ)*, meaning "to breathe."

39. The Latin *sentire* (whence "sense" derives) means to feel (cf. sentiment) and thus also to discern by the senses (sensible, sensibility, etc.); it means also *sentis*, a path (cf. Spanish *sendero*) and thus direction. Cf. Old High German: *sinnen*, to go and also to think (to feel one's way).

40. The etymology of Latin *gratum*, Sanskrit *gurtas*, pleasure, and also joy, is related to *charis* meaning gracious, grace, joy, gratuitousness, agreeable, favor, charity. Cf. Spanish *agradar*, to please.

41. See Kenopanishad, II, 3 (and also RV I, 164, 32), etc.

42. "Knowing others is wisdom. Knowing the self is enlightenment" (*Tao Te Ching*, 33). The reason is apparent. I can know others by shedding the light of my knowledge on them. But I cannot know myself in this way. It needs another light falling upon me from outside me. I need to be illumined in order to be enlightened—i.e., I need to be *known* by somebody else. I need to be *loved*. Cf. *èpignōsomai kathōs kaì epegnōsthen;* "I shall know as I am known"; *cognoscam sicut et cognitus sum,* in the Vulgate (1 Cor. 13:12). Here is the locus of grace—again an openness and movement.

43. RV X, 129, 4 and 190, 1; etc.

44. B G III, 20 & 25.

45. RV X, 90, 16: *dharmani prathamani.* Cf. B G VII, 11.

46. Acts 2:11.

47. This ending is not just a phrase. The core of Western culture is based on the ultimate binomial Being/Thinking, or in theological vocabulary: Father/Son (*Logos*). This basic dyad has often obscured the trinitarian paradigm, which alone overcomes the strictures of science ("the laws of nature are immutable") and makes room for freedom—as I have indicated elsewhere.

III. 1.

A Universal Theory or a Cosmic Confidence in Reality? A Taoist/Zen Response

CHARLES WEI-HSUN FU

Before commenting on Prof. Panikkar's thesis, I should like to clarify my position as a commentator with regard to that portion of my title: "A Taoist/Zen Response." I am not a professed Taoist or Zen Buddhist, nor do I wish to exaggerate the accomplishments or contributions of Taoism and Zen Buddhism. In religious search and philosophical inquiry, I always want to be a nonpartisan cosmopolitan, somewhat like "a heavenly horse running in the vast sky," to borrow a Chinese idiom, or like a fastidious bee trying to make the best possible honey out of various nectars (I mean, various sources such as Christianity, Buddhism, Confucianism, and so on). If I take the Taoist/Zen stand here in my response to Prof. Panikkar's insightful thesis, it is only because I believe that, insofar as the interrelated questions of language, truth, and reality are concerned, Taoism (as represented by Chuang Tzu) and Zen Buddhism (as well as the transphilosophical philosophy of Mahāyāna Buddhism originated by Nāgārjuna) have the least dogmatic and most justifiable solutions or recommendations. Taoism and Zen can indeed help us understand the limits or limitations of a so-called universal theory, the myth that Prof. Panikkar has critically and thoughtfully uncovered for us.

In my view, Taoism and Zen are entirely free of any intellectual temptations to attempt a universal theory construction—the kind of theory that, as Prof. Panikkar has acutely pointed out, intends to establish, by adopting a single, common language, an absolute truth claimed to be universally valid for all. As I understand it, both Taoist enlightenment (*ming*) and Zen *satori* (*wu*) imply, if put in our modern terms, humanity's ultimate liberation from any human fixations of language, truth, and reality. In critical contrast to a universal theory, which must presuppose or rely upon a universal language, a universal reason (*logos*), and (what Bradley calls) "the Really Real Reality" of an onto-theo-logically substantive nature, those paradoxically puzzling expressions in Taoism and Zen—"no-word" (*wu-yen*), "no-thought" (*wu-ssu*), and "nothingness-nothingness" (*wu-wu*)—profoundly indicate the spiritual open-ness and experiential inexhaustibility of the "no-mind" (*wu-hsin*), the enlightened mind of the Taoist sage or Zen master. One of the important messages of Prof. Panikkar's paper is that our clear understanding of the limitations of a universal theory should lead us to dialogical openness and open-mindedness in our pluralized and enormously complex world today. Fully agreeing with his message, I want to suggest that Taoism and Zen can contribute to our present cause of opening up and widening the gateway to more and more meaningful and fruitful dialogues among the great traditions of the world.

In his critical exposition of the universal theory myth, Prof. Panikkar makes it clear that he does appreciate the effort at a universal theory as a noble and fruitful enterprise, for such a theory has helped us overcome many misunder-standings, has dispelled many unclarities, made collaboration possible, and purified religions of many excrescences, narrow-mindedness, and fanaticisms; it even fosters dialogue. It does, however, tend to become a stumbling block to the development of open dialogues by "imposing its own language or the frame within which the *dia-logos* has to take place."

Prof. Panikkar also observes that "no other human civilization has reached the universality as has the Western. . . . This thirst for universality forms part of the Western myth, and, I am prepared to argue, we discover only the myth of the others, and not the myth in which we live." To this observation I wish to add that no such myth or thirst can be found in Taoism and Zen, for they have never trapped themselves in the entanglements of what Prof. John Hick calls "con-flicting truth claims" (see the last chapter of his *Philosophy of Religion*). On the contrary, the philosophical or religious teachings of Taoism and Zen are designed to serve as an educational guide to the total liberation of our mind from any such entanglements.

Taoism and Zen are often misunderstood to put forward, just like any other system of thought, their own special truth claim in competition with other truth claims made by Christianity, Islam, and so on. But, has not Lao Tzu made his point abundantly clear in his opening words, "The tao that can be taoed is not the invariable Tao; the name that can be named is not the invariable Name"? Has not Chuang Tzu clarified Lao Tzu's point, saying, for instance, that "Tao cannot be thought of as being (*yu*), nor can it be thought of as nonbeing (*wu*). In naming it 'Tao,' we are only adopting a provisional expression"? Has not Master Chao-chou recommended a Zen way of transcending the duality of truth and untruth in his one-word reply, *Wu* (nothingness), to the question, "Does the dog have Buddha nature or not?" And, to those who are still struggling hard with the problem of conflicting truth claims concerning the so-called Really Real Reality, I strongly recommend as a good *koan* exercise the following poem, which Master Wu-men ("No-gate") composed at a moment of great enlightenment, after six years of his Zen inquiry into the trans-metaphysical meaning of Chao-chou's one-word puzzle:

> *Wu wu wu wu wu, wu wu wu wu wu;*
> *Wu wu wu wu wu, wu wu wu wu wu.*

In "poetizing" *wu* or "nothingness" twenty times, does Master No-gate look like a linguistic idiot talking nonsense, or like a great liberator to all universal theory concocters and truth-claimers?

Where there are conflicting truth claims made by Kantians, Hegelians, Marxist-Leninists, logical empiricists, Christians, Muslims, Buddhists, and others, and if "truth" here is understood (or misunderstood) to mean nothing but the "objective truth of absolute certainty and universal validity," we are, to borrow Prof. Panikkar's words, "confronted with mutually exclusive and respectively contradictory ultimate systems." How can Jews and Muslims, let alone non-Abrahamic religionists or atheists, accept the Christian fundamentalist assertion that the crucifixion of Jesus Christ on the cross is *the* turning point of history for all humankind, if this historical truth is taken as objective and absolute beyond the Christian context, which is no more than a particular religious context? But, if Christian fundamentalists are compelled to accept the nonuniversalizability of this historical truth, how can they resecure their faith without a sense of humiliation?

How can Muslims convince both Jews and Christians that the truth of Abrahamic religion finally culminates in Islam? But, if Muslims are told to admit that their truth manifests no more than a particular faith of a particular religious group in a particular context, how can they make peace with themselves without unease or perplexity? How can Abrahamic religionists convince Buddhists, Hindus, and other religious groups of the "universal truth" of God and revelation in the history of Judaism, Christianity, and Islam? On the other hand, if Jews, Christians, or Muslims are unable to universalize their particular faith and religious doctrines, how can they justify their position as secure and solid? How can they maintain their own faith without believing at the same time that their God and their revelation are the universal and objective ground for the existence of the world and humanity?

How can Marxist-Leninists prove or justify the "absolute truth" of their dialectical materialism, according to which ultimate reality is nothing but matter-in-motion in the dialectical process of nature? But if they are to acknowledge the relativity or nonuniversalizability of dialectical materialism, how can they reconcile this acknowledgment with their materialist conception of history, which provides the theoretical ground for their communistic attempts at a universal transformation of the world and humanity?

The most crucial question is how to resolve the problem of conflicting truth claims—claims that arise in nearly all cases as a result of overzealous attempts at an unexamined and unwarranted universalization of a particular theory, dogma, thought, faith, or experience. Prof. Panikkar has made a very thoughtful suggestion—that the meaning of "truth" be reoriented as a matter of "perspectivism and relativity." I think this suggestion is very sound and should be well taken. Coincidentally, I have, for about ten years, also tried to tackle this very crucial question and have reached a tentative conclusion in terms of what I have called "holistic multiperspectivism in functional form." That is to say, all human truths linguistically formulated in religion and philosophy are none other than multiperspectively functional (nonsubstantive) ways of divulging, on higher or lower levels of the human mind, the holistically inexhaustible meanings of the so-called Really Real Reality, whatever that may be. And I think that the structure of a universal theory myth can be further exposed in this light.

A universal theory must first presuppose or posit the "is-ness" of the Really Real Reality as the ultimate and secure—objective and universal—ground for the human quest for Truth, which, in correspondence with the Really Real Reality, must also be absolutely certain and universally valid. To express Truth and Reality, a universal language of an onto-theo-logically substantive nature needs to be constructed accordingly. A universal theory or an absolute truth claim can be made only by taking what I call "the substantive (or, what-to-see) approach." First, *The Really Real Reality is*; it is ultimately what is to be seen, often expressed as substance or being in the Western tradition. Secondly, *Absolute Truth is*, which can be reached by way of universal reason (*logos*), intellectual intuition, or divine inspiration. Thirdly, a universal language is to be designed in order to disclose both reality and truth.

Hence the origination and multiplication of conflicting truth claims by Aristotelians (substance or being, logical truth of a two-value nature), Hegelians (Absolute Spirit, dialectical truth), Husserlians (transcendental ego and ideal essences, phenomenological truth and language), Christian Fundamentalists (the universal God, the Christian truth for all humankind), *et cetera, et cetera*; the list can be endless. As long as the substantive or what-to-see approach is taken as legitimate and workable, there can be no appropriate way of resolving the problem of conflicting truth claims. Even Advaita Vedantists, mystics in all traditions, or Buddhist thinkers, who are supposed to be able to transcend a formulated universal theory, sometimes trap themselves in the entanglements of conflicting truth claims despite themselves. For example, when Advaita Vedantists are tempted to assert "(*Nirgu ṇa*) *Brahman* is" or "*Ātman* is," when some Buddhists like Walpola Rahula say unequivocally that "*Nirvāṇa* is" or "Absolute" Truth is," when Paul Tillich speaks of "God above God" as the ultimate source of the human courage to be, or when Frithjof Schuon attempts to posit "the Divine Source" for the "transcendental unity of religions," we see an extremely subtle, intriguing, and inordinate way of universalizing language, truth, and reality.

Does Tillich really know what he means when he says "God above God"?

Are his words, "The God above the God of theism is present, although hidden, in every divine-human encounter," meant to be a universally valid statement, or no more than a subjective expression of his personal encounter with his own God (or Godhead)? Can Rahula not realize how misleading it is to universalize *nirvāṇa* or absolute truth (*dharma*) in Buddhism? Is not Schuon unconsciously kicking Buddhism and Taoism out of the community of world religions when he says:

> Just as every color, by its negation of darkness and its affirmation of light, provides the possibility of discovering the ray that makes it visible and of tracing this ray back to its luminous source, so all forms, all symbols, all religions, all dogmas, by their negation of error and their affirmation of Truth, make it possible to follow the ray of Revelation, which is none other than the ray of the Intellect, back to its Divine Source [*The Transcendent Unity of Religions*, xxxii].

"I should not be misinterpreted," to borrow again Prof. Panikkar's words. I am not suggesting that Tillich, Schuon, Advaita Vedantists, and the others should not have said what they have said, nor do I argue that what they have said is entirely wrong—for, if I argue in this manner, I would have to invent my own "absolute truth," which would be self-defeating. What I am suggesting here is that they should recognize the limits of the languages they use, the truths they present, and the Really Real Reality they talk about; their assertions or statements will mislead all of us (including themselves) if there is no such recognition. But, how can there be any such recognition unless a Copernican revolution concerning language, truth, and reality is initiated?

My proposal is that the substantive (or, what-to-see) approach be completely replaced by the functional (or, how-to-see) approach, that all substantive languages (*Substanzsprachen*) be radically transformed into functional languages (*Funktionssprachen*), that all (onto-theo-logical) truths claimed to be objective or universally valid be undisguisedly redisclosed as no more than "human, all too human" (*menschlich, allzu menschlich*) perspectives on higher or lower levels, and that the multidimensionality (in appearance) and inexhaustibility (in meaning) of the Really Real Reality, be it called "Being," "Substance," "God," "Brahman," "Tao," "Nothingness," or the like, be modestly reunderstood as reflecting the multiperspectival projection of the mind (experience, faith, religious sentiment, viewpoint, the spiritual impulse) on higher or lower levels.

Nothing is really changed in my proposal; what is changed is our new (Copernican) way of seeing the essential nature of the languages we use, the truths we present, and the reality we speak of. In short, substantive languages are to be reoriented as functional languages; truth in the objective sense is to be reinterpreted as (what is called in Chinese philosophy)—*tao-li* (literally "the principle or reason of the way"), which means "*human* reasons or truths" and which can claim only *intersubjective* truthfulness or acceptability, having nothing to do with objective or absolute truth.

The question of the Really Real Reality is then reset as the question of our (the mind's) multiperspectively functional ways of seeing "how" rather than "what" on the higher or lower levels of our mind. Knowing that Prof. Panikkar is flexible enough to say, for instance, that "Reality has other dimensions," I tend to think that "an intersubjective confidence in open-ended explorations" may be less misleading than "a cosmic confidence in Reality" as far as our necessary move from the stage of the universal theory myth to the higher stage of dialogical openness is concerned.

Dialogical openness certainly promotes mutual understanding and even mutual sharing. However, it does and must involve mutual challenge and mutual "give and take" as well. As far as the problem of universality/particularity is concerned, mutual challenge is a twofold task: (1) x (say, a Christian dialogist) draws the attention of y (say, a Buddhist dialogist), and vice versa, to the fact that the universalization of some particular ideas, principles, or doctrines attempted by each group is unexamined, unjustifiable, unacceptable, damaging to interreligious dialogues and to the two traditions. (2) Being firmly convinced that some particular ideas, principles, or doctrines in both traditions are universalizable or have a universal significance beyond each tradition, x asks y, and vice versa, to acknowledge, accept, or even integrate them into the existing system of thought in the other tradition. Mutual challenge between x and y can result in mutual "give and take" in diverse ways: (1) x (or x's tradition) gives y (or y's tradition) whatever looks universalizable or tends to have a universal significance or implication in the x tradition, and vice versa; and (2) x (or x's tradition) takes or receives whatever looks universalizable or tends to have a universal significance or implication in the y tradition, and vice versa. (3) A dialectical "give and take" between x (or x's tradition) and y (or y's tradition) leads toward a mutual transformation or perfecting of each tradition. (4) A mutual transformation of the x and y traditions may also lead to a higher stage—the formation of a new religion or system of thought as a dialectical synthesis of the x and y traditions. To repeat Prof. Paul Feyerabend's expression in his *Against Method*, "anything goes" in interreligious dialogues.

What I have said and analyzed above concerning universality/particularity has nothing to do with the universal theory myth. No misunderstanding should arise, particularly after the presentation of my proposal with respect to the radical transformation of the nature of language, thought, and reality in religious search and philosophical inquiry. I think I have been careful enough to say "whatever *looks* universalizable or *tends* to have a universal *significance or implication*"; my words here are only suggestive of mutual influence, mutual sharing, and intersubjective explorations and confirmations of any creative and meaningful human perspectives, experiences, insights, and so forth, in religious search and philosophical inquiry, for the sake of progress within each particular tradition or progress beyond that tradition.

A most interesting case for our investigation of what possible consequences our open dialogues may bring out is Prof. John Cobb's "beyond dialogue" approach, as shown in his book with this very title, and the subtitle, "Toward a

Mutual Transformation of Christianity and Buddhism." His approach is a clear example of the "mutual give-and-take" I mentioned above. In his conclusion he says:

> I have argued that authentic dialogue must lead beyond dialogue to the radical transformation of the dialogue partners. . . . A Buddhized Christianity and a Christianized Buddhism may continue to enrich each other and human culture generally through their differences. . . . First, it is the mission of Christianity to *become* a universal faith in the sense of taking into itself the alien truths that others have realized. . . . Second, it is the mission of a self-transforming Christianity to invite other religious traditions to undergo self-transformation as well. . . . Christ as Truth will transform the truths of all other traditions even as they transform ours [*Beyond Dialogue*, p. 143].

And, in his Postscript, he restresses his conviction as both Christian and Whiteheadian:

> The Christianity which would emerge from these several appropriations of aspects of truth which other traditions have developed would be a different Christianity from what the West now knows. I do not, however, believe it would be less Christian. On the contrary, my argument is that in faithfulness to Christ we are to expose ourselves to these multiple transformations [ibid., p. 149].

Prof. Cobb's "beyond dialogue toward mutual transformation" approach may or may not be agreeable to a Christian or a Buddhist, but his dialogical openness must be greatly appreciated.

The history of world religions has clearly shown us that dialogical openness (mutual understanding, mutual sharing, mutual challenge, mutual "give and take," mutual transformation) proves to be one of the most significant and determining human factors causing the formation and development of new and creative ideas within or beyond each and every tradition. The long history of Chinese philosophy and religion is a most interesting example to illustrate my point here. The Chinese two thousand years ago were ideologically fortunate enough to see a formidable alien religion, Indian Buddhism, imported to their Middle Kingdom. Thanks to the availability of their philosophical legacy, Taoism in particular, the Chinese during the Wei-Chin period were able to digest, through the guidance of visiting Indian masters, the enormously difficult philosophical systems of Indian Buddhism, such as Mādhyamika, and subsequently formed and developed their own philosophy and religion of Sinitic Mahāyāna, which was destined not only to become, along with Confucianism and Taoism, one of the Three Teachings in China, but also to exercise an indelibly lasting influence on the reshaping of the Chinese mind. The formation of neo-Confucianism or the further development of religious Tao-ism would never have occurred if Buddhism had not preexisted in China. The same thing can be said of Japan—the nation of cultural multi-layeredness—which has absorbed not only Indian and Chinese thought, Buddhism in particular, but Western philosophy and theology as well, as can be seen from the gradual formation of the Kyoto School in modern times. To conclude, Asian nations like China, Korea, and Japan (as well as India), have been historico-culturally compelled and impelled to develop the mentality of dialogical openness. It is in this sense and spirit that scholars of Asian back-ground feel that participation in this confernece on open dialogue is a most exciting human experience.

III. 2.

Universal Theology *and* Dialogical Dialogue

THOMAS DEAN

My response to the many critical issues raised and the alternative proposed for our consideration by Raimundo Panikkar could best be summarized by coming back to the title of his paper, "A Universal Theory of Religion or a Cosmic Confidence in Reality?" I pose the question: Must we choose? Can we not rather (and this would be my counter-thesis) have both? Are the two notions, as the title seems to imply, mutually exclusive? Is the attempt to put forward what Panikkar calls a "universal theory of religion" (or, in the language of this conference, a "universal theology of religion") really incompatible with simultaneously adopting an attitude of "pluralistic confidence in reality"? Or, to put it the other way around, does holding an attitude of pluralistic confidence in reality preclude the attempt to articulate a universal theory or theology that is not only compatible with that attitude but perhaps even demanded by it as its implicit rationale? It seems to me, in any case, that it should be possible to maintain both sides of this disjunction and that, accordingly, the title of Prof. Panikkar's paper may be taken as pointing not to an exclusive either-or but to a possible inclusive both-and.

To bring this general question into focus and to open the way to an understanding of the underlying issues involved, let me reformulate what seems to me to be the basic issue at play in the title and in the subsequent arguments of the paper. For the moment I shall disregard the adjectives "universal" and "pluralistic," and the prepositional phrases "of religion" and "of reality" in the title and concentrate on the governing nouns, "theory" and "confidence," because the subsequent focus of the paper is precisely on the problematic status of theory—that is, of reason or rationality—in the Western cultural tradition and in proposals for a universal theology. If we substitute the word "reason" (or "rationality") for the word "theory," and the word "faith" (or "trust") for the word "confidence," then it becomes clear that the underlying philosophical issue being pointed to in both the title and the body of the paper is the absolutely fundamental and long-standing question that has always characterized philosophical and theological reflection in the West, at least—the question of the relationship between *reason* and *faith*. If this translation of the title is appropriate, then the nature of the question I am raising can be seen more clearly, as well as the direction of the counter-thesis I am proposing. In our attempts to understand and participate in religion and in interreligious dialogue, must we choose between reason and faith, between theoretical reflection (which by definition tends in the direction of universality) and spiritual acceptance (which by definition tends in the direction of the basic conditions of existence)? Rather, must we not attempt, ever and again, in response to our changing cognitive and existential circumstances, to hold both these dimensions of our life together in a unified way (which is not to say in a reductionist, one-sided, or undialectical way)? If so, the question, then, is how exactly do we understand those concepts of *reason, faith,* and *reality* that would be required to make this alternative reading of Prof. Panikkar's title possible?

(As an aside, if for "theory" we were to substitute the word used by the sponsors of this conference—"theology"—we could then pose the question: Must we choose between *theology* and *faith*? I think the answer to this question would be an even more obvious no, the only issue being just how we would want to formulate the *positive* relationship between them.)

Against these background remarks, let me proceed to a closer look at the three concepts that, as I have indicated, are central to working out an adequate understanding of the relationship of reason to faith, of theory or theology of religion to our basic confidence or trust in reality: the concepts of reason (or rationality), faith (as a spiritual or existential attitude), and reality or being. With respect to these three concepts, Panikkar has developed philosophical theses that supply the basis for his critique of the traditional Western notion of rationality and contemporary proposals for a universal theory of religion, and for his alternative approach to religious pluralism, which he calls "dialogical dialogue." I shall label these theses, respectively, Panikkar's *epistemological* thesis, concerning the nature of reason; his *anthropological* thesis, concerning the relation of reason to faith, or of *logos* to spirit, in the overall makeup of human existence; and his *ontological* thesis, concerning the nature of being or reality, and its relationship, in turn, to reason, language, and truth. The structure of the remainder of my remarks will, accordingly, be as follows: first, I shall state each thesis and show how Panikkar uses it to criticize traditional Western and contemporary universalist theories; next, I shall indicate how he uses it to formulate his own alternative proposal; and finally, I shall then raise my own specific question of clarification and state my counter-thesis.

With each of these theses my specific question to Prof. Panikkar will be intended as a further statement of my general response to his paper—namely, that in reflecting upon the emerging global encounter and dialogue among the world religions, I do not think we have to choose between a universal theory (or theology) of religion, on the one hand, and a pluralistic confidence in reality, on the other. Rather, it is precisely this pluralistic confidence that demands of each of us, and of each of our traditions, that we not only participate in but reflect rationally upon this global encounter. To put it as directly as possible, I shall argue that what Panikkar calls *dialogical dialogue* and what the sponsors of this conference call *universal theology of religion* are, dialectically speaking, one and the same. Each not only needs the other, each leads over into and indeed makes the other possible. (As a corollary, far from being in the minority on this matter, I suspect, as I shall now try to prove, that, like it or not, Panikkar is in fact, and fortunately for us all, among the majority on this issue! See the Postscript of this paper.)

A

Panikkar's first or epistemological thesis is that no one view of reason, no one type of rationality, whether Western or Asian, philosophical or theological, can set itself up as universal and claim to represent the essence of human reason or rationality as such. As he puts it, the Western "lamp" is not the only lamp we have, nor should we assume that it is identical with, or provides the sole standard for, the human "lamp" of reason. Rather, there are many kinds of rationality, and insofar as a universal theory of religion rests on an attempt to universalize one particular, however powerful or global, standard of rationality, then such an attempt must be resisted. To be sure, the intentions of the partisans of a global theology may indeed be to foster a genuine dialogue among the many voices of the world religions, but they run the risk of superimposing their own particular kind of Western (usually Christian) rationality, their own *logos*, on the context within which genuine *dia-logos* is to take place. Panikkar sees in such theological attempts the claim, whether explicit or implicit, to have arrived at a universal language, an "ecumenical Esperanto," in which all other languages find themselves *aufgehoben*—that is, in one sense preserved, but in a deeper sense superceded.

Panikkar's alternative suggestion, based on this thesis of epistemological pluralism, is that we should give up such attempts to find a single, universal, all-encompassing *logos* in the encounter of the world religions, and instead open ourselves to the experience of listening to and truly hearing the immense diversity of human voices, the many *logoi*, that make up the richness of interreligious encounter. In place of a universal theory, therefore, Panikkar offers the wonderful image of a net of discourse, an ever-changing web of criss-crossing and overlapping conversations in which, through dialogical dialogue rather than monological theorizing, we search together to forge new and more appropriate ways of speaking, each such encounter resulting perhaps in a more inclusive *logos*—not some universal theory, but deepened mutual understanding. Once this net of relationships has developed, he points out, it may then, and only then, be possible to establish "new and more general links" in the web of language, perhaps even to venture "new categories."

But these efforts, which look somewhat similar to the efforts of the universal theologians, must always be qualified by the reminder that the underlying motive as well as goal of such dialogue is not the production of a single universal theory of religion, let alone a single world religion, but rather a sense on all sides of the mutual enhancement of the respective voices, the diverse *logoi*, that represent the irreducible different parties to such conversations. The outcome of such a dialogical dialogue, epistemologically speaking, is not to reduce the many voices of the partners in conversation to some one voice, but rather to discover a fundamental human harmony "in and through the discordant voices of the human traditions"—or, to use the fine phrase employed by R. C. Zaehner in his Gifford Lectures, to discover, through dialogue, the "concordant discord" of the many voices of humanity.

If I have accurately stated this epistemological thesis, then my first question is whether in fact Panikkar's view of dialogical dialogue could not be said to be grounded in an implicit (and perhaps he would say explicit) philosophical theory—that is, in a theory of rationality of its own. If so, then Panikkar's proposal for dialogical dialogue rests, whether implicitly or explicitly, just as much on what could properly be called a universal theory of religion—here, epistemological in nature—as do, say, the theories of Wilfred Cantwell Smith, Ninian Smart, John Hick, Leonard Swidler, or other like-minded Christian theologians (these being, I presume, the type of thinkers Panikkar has in mind in the first part of his critical remarks—namely, advocates of such things as "ecumenical Esperanto," "world theology," "global theology," or "universal theology of religion").

More specifically, I would suggest that Panikkar's concept of dialogical dialogue rests on an epistemological theory, a theory of rationality, of the sort that has been clearly articulated by Hans-Georg Gadamer in his book, *Truth and Method*. As Panikkar well knows, Gadamer, like Panikkar, offers a critique of traditional Western notions of rationality. But what is important for my question is that he also offers an alternative theory of rationality (or, more broadly, of understanding, of the *logos* of human existence) founded not on the *logos* of one partner at the expense of the other, nor, for that matter, on a simple reversal in which we privilege instead the *logos* of the other rather than our own. *Logos*, the structure of human rationality, is located rather precisely in the phenomenon of *mutual understanding*, a phenomenon that involves change and transformation in the *logos* of both partners to dialogue—a process that Gadamer calls "fusion of horizons," in which the *logos* that emerges (and one *does* emerge) can no longer simply be equated with, or reduced to, either one or the other, or even the sum total of, the initial voices in the conversation.

The point I want to stress, and address to Panikkar as a request for clarification or as a counter-thesis, is whether in his characterization of the "universal theory of religion" found in such writers as Smith, Smart, or Hick, he is not in fact either misstating or perhaps overstating the differences between their and his positions—for I believe that their positions, like Panikkar's, are firmly grounded in an awareness of and commitment to something like Gadamer's description of the dialogical nature of all human understanding (including theory). If so, this would necessitate not so much the eliciting of a clarification from them, as Panikkar suggests, but rather a clarification from Panikkar: whether his initial description of their position in fact conceals the large extent of underlying and, I would contend, fundamental agreement between him and them—a concession that, as I have already suggested, would have the happy effect of establishing Panikkar as a member of the majority, not the minority, on this particular issue.

It seems to me, then, at this epistemological level, that the choice is not between a universal theory of religion or no theory at all. It is rather between a universal theory of religion that is sensitive to the sorts of critical issues Panikkar raises, and one that is not. For in any case, insofar as Panikkar's own paper constitutes, by his own admission, "a *discourse about* the encounter of religions" (italics mine), it too presupposes, if it does not articulate, a universal theory as well. As Panikkar says, no single language can exhaust the variety of human experience. It is only together, in colloquy, that we touch the universality of life, and, I would add, of language, of reason. And that "universality" turns out to have the distinctive *form* of "dialogue," as Gadamer has shown us. But that is exactly the point of such thinkers as Smith, Hick, and Swidler as well—global theologians all! It is for this reason, among others, that I am arguing, therefore, that not all the advocates of global theology are open to the sort of critical charges Panikkar here levels against them—and that there is in fact more common ground, on this epistemological issue, than he seems willing to acknowledge.

(Let me also say that I think it follows from a Gadamerian epistemology of the sort I find compatible with, if not implicit in, Panikkar's notion of dialogical dialogue, that the epistemological conundrum he sets for himself about the contradictory status of a theory of religion that is a member of the class it purports to describe, is basically a false issue. The short answer to this apparent dilemma is to argue, following Heidegger, that this involvement of our second-order theories of dialogue or global theology in our first-order theologies reflects a structural feature of all human understanding—namely, its "circular" character, what Heidegger calls a "hermeneutical circle." This circle need not be a vicious one—it need not generate contradictions, as Panikkar suggests—for it is rather the indispensable ground and condition of the possibility of distinctively human, self-reflexive understanding. It seems to me, therefore, that every theory of religion, including Panikkar's own notion of dialogical dialogue, as a second-order theory, must unavoidably partake of certain first-order commitments as well. And rather than try to break out of that circle altogether, or end up feeling defeated by it, it is important, first of all, to be critically self-aware of its presence, and secondly, precisely through dialogue with others, to "overcome" our own circle of assumptions insofar as it threatens to become counterproductive, by a process of "fusion" with the horizons, or hermeneutical circles, of other persons or traditions.)

B

I turn now to Panikkar's second or anthropological thesis involving his view of the respective places of reason and faith, *logos* and spirit, in the metaphysical makeup of human beings. Panikkar states that there are more dimensions to human existence than that of *logos* or rationality alone; there is, in particular, the dimension of spirit. And although understanding occurs at the level of language, logic, rationality—that is, of *logos*—there is also an attitude of the heart, of the spirit, a faith or confidence that is able to accept the other even when it does not or cannot understand or put into words that which it accepts. It is precisely at this level of acceptance of the other, even when we do not or cannot understand the other, that some of the most spiritually important and liberating things happen in our personal encounters with members of other traditions.

Panikkar expresses this thesis in various ways: he notes that a universal theory of religion not only assumes, as the first thesis points out, that one type of rationality is supposed to characterize all human rationality, it also assumes, as his second thesis now makes clear, that rationality is the one single defining trait of human existence, that which alone, or especially, or essentially, characterizes and distinguishes human being from all other types of being. Was it not Aristotle who fatefully decreed for the entire Western tradition that *ho anthrōpos* is the *zōon logon echon*, that "the human being" is the "living being who possesses *logos*, language, reason"? Does not a universal theory of religion, qua theory, make precisely the same assumption—namely, that the truth of dialogue can be captured at the level of theory, of *logos*, thus overlooking, or at least subordinating, the equally if not more important truth of the spirit, of lived existence, of existential faith? As Panikkar puts it, "universality does not belong to the order of any theory, rationality does not exhaustively define the human being."

In other words, I can imagine Panikkar saying in response to my first query: "Well and good, perhaps at the level of epistemology my notion of dialogical dialogue and a so-called universal theology do end up holding certain assumptions in common. However, I do not confine my criticism of universal theology to the level of theory alone. My criticism goes far deeper and is more radical than you have imagined. I am saying that the truth of theory, even of a Gadamerian theory of dialogue, does not reach the level of the spiritual reality and truth of what occurs in the event of dialogue. And what I am here above all concerned to resist, in defense of the spiritual reality of dialogue, is the attempt of theorists of a universal theology to subordinate, in trinitarian terms, the spirit to the *logos*. Religion, which is after all the life of the spirit, is not reducible to or translatable into *any* kind of *logos,* let alone *one* kind of *logos*. I am against any move that results in giving supremacy to the *logos* over spirit, and this, I am afraid, is exactly what the overzealous, rationalist partisans of global theology are trying to do."

In saying this Panikkar would also make clear that he is in no way holding a brief for irrationalism, subjectivism, fanaticism, or solipsism in interreligious dialogue. His view, as I understand it, is something like this: *logos* is coextensive with human existence, but human existence is not identical with or reducible to *logos*. There is more to human existence than *logos*, though in every aspect of human existence *logos* is co-present as well. Thus he would appear to provide an adequate safeguard against any kind of retreat to irrationalism in his defense of the equality or primordiality of the spirit over against the *logos* in human life.

What is important to recognize, therefore, is that in and through dialogue we can arrive at a spiritual attitude of acceptance, faith, trust, confidence vis-à-vis our partner in dialogue without necessarily having to insist that this trust be capable of being put into words, let alone formulated in a theory. Although understanding is frequently possible in dialogue, it is not absolutely required, whereas trust, an attitude of spiritual acceptance of the other, is not only required but, in the last analysis, constitutes the liberating truth, the spiritual value, of such encounters. What is called for, Panikkar concludes, is not a "utopian single theology of religions," a *global theory*, not even some counter-theory called a theory of "dialogical dialogue," but rather a new awareness, a "new innocence," a new sense of spiritual affirmation or *global trust*. What holds humankind together, he states, is not some shared theory or shared language, not some shared religion or even religious history; it is rather a shared attitude, a unanimity, agreement, or concord in our spiritual sensibilities, not in our rational views. It is a "pluralistic confidence," not a "universal theory."

But then, almost as an aside, Panikkar complicates things, for me at least. For he allows that this spiritual attitude of pluralistic confidence does indeed have an intellectual dimension—that is, a *logos*! In other words, to use Panikkar's trinitarian metaphor again, he now seems to allow that the spirit, though not identical with or reducible to *logos*, nevertheless can be said to proceed from it (the *filioque* clause)—that spirit is not subordinate to *logos*, but that *logos* is nonetheless coextensive with spirit, that in fact spirit and *logos* are mutually implicated in one another. But to refer back to my initial translation of the title of his project, this means that although faith is not subordinate to reason, nevertheless faith can be said to proceed from reason as well, and that, therefore, faith and reason, theory and attitude, are deeply and mutually implicated in one another. And so I am provoked to reflect, and to ask Panikkar as well, whether in his concern to make a legitimate distinction between *logos* and spirit he has perhaps overstated the case against reason, rationality, *logos*, whether his "corrective" is not possibly an over-corrective. For insofar as pluralistic confidence provides, as he himself says, the very basis of dialogical dialogue, that which makes it possible, is it not possible that this confidence in fact *has* a *logos* of its own, and that, in fact, it is possible only as a distinctive form and expression of *logos* itself?

Let me try to explain why I think it is important to raise this question, and what the philosophical assumptions are that lie behind my asking it. If I am visiting the zoo and, passing the tiger cage, see the cage door open and the tiger getting ready to spring out at me, I am sure I would be seized by a sudden, complete, and immobilizing terror—a feeling that I could not possibly begin to fully capture in words. It would be a feeling that was not reducible to or translatable into intellectual terms. And yet, under the circumstances, the feeling would seem to be an entirely *rational* one; it would not be an *irrational* response to the situation. If, on the other hand, while passing the tiger cage, with the door firmly locked and the tiger safely behind bars, I was nevertheless seized by a sudden, complete, and immobilizing terror, I think we would want to say that, under the circumstances, my feeling, which again I could not fully express in words, was a completely *irrational* one.

In other words, the question of whether a feeling or attitude, such as pluralistic confidence, can be put into words or not—whether spirit is reducible to or translatable into *logos*—is not the same as the question of whether the feeling or attitude is a rational, intelligible, logical one or not—whether spirit, in this sense, possesses *logos* or not. (Here I also have in mind Heidegger's critique of those who would try to drive too sharp a wedge between cognitive and noncognitive meaning. Such basic moods as joy, anxiety, or trust are, as distinctively human modes of being, modes of understanding our being-in-the-world—that is, they are modes of intelligibility or *logos*.)

We can, in other words, distinguish between faith that is rational and faith that is irrational, faith that proceeds from and through *logos* and faith that does not, without thereby claiming that such spiritual attitudes are therefore reducible to reason or *logos*. I myself simply do not believe, therefore, that partisans of universal theology such as Smith or Hick would feel affected by a criticism that says what we need is not global theology but simply global trust. I suspect that none of the above-named thinkers are guilty of committing the mistake of suggesting that theology is in any way a substitute for faith, but I am equally sure that they think that an attitude of pluralistic confidence, insofar as it has an intellectual dimension to it, can be articulated in intellectual terms, as in fact Panikkar himself has also done. I think they would hold that both this spiritual attitude and the theoretical articulation of it are vitally needed for our religious or spiritual future and our theological or intellectual future as well.

To return for a moment to my example of the tiger in the cage: I would even go so far as to say that the very fact that we would label my second response, where the door was locked, as irrational in and of itself implies that there is another, rational explanation of my phobia that can be found, though presumably it must be sought elsewhere than in the immediate physical circumstances. Perhaps with the help of a psychologist it will be found that this irrational response has after all a deeper *ratio*, a hidden *logos*, one hidden, that is, from me but accessible through dialogue with another who, in that situation, perhaps understands me better than I do myself. And precisely in that dialogue of one with another there is uncovered a deeper *logos*, or there emerges a new *logos*, that not only spiritually transforms but also renders more intelligible both partners to the dialogue.

C

I come now to Panikkar's third thesis, the one that seems to me hidden or implicit in his first two theses, the one I call his ontological thesis. As far as I can make out, it runs like this: thinking, or consciousness, or language, or *logos* do not exhaust being, reality, and truth. This sounds like his second thesis, but I think it goes further and deeper. It is a comment not just on the nature of human existence but on the nature of reality as such. Here Panikkar disputes the claim, which I take it he thinks some, if not all, the advocates of universal theology would want to affirm—namely, that Reality is totally intelligible, or as he puts it, that the *nous* of Aristotle, the *svayamprakasha* of the Vedantins, the self-intelligible God of the Christians, or the total reflection of Hegel, are really the case. He challenges what he calls the ultimate claim of every idealistic monism "that there is a Being or a Reality which encompasses all that there is and that this reality is pure consciousness, absolutely self-intelligible, because all is transparent to the light of the intellect." Again, Panikkar makes clear that he is not contesting the claim that the *logos* is coextensive with Being; he is only contending that Being is not totally identical with or reducible to *logos*. (*Logos* here stands for total intelligibility, self-intelligibility, total self-reflection, total transparency in the light of intellect, etc.)

I find this ontological thesis absolutely breathtaking, because it goes far beyond the usual metaphysical or theological claim, which Panikkar also makes, that because of the limitations of our finite human intellects, we cannot hope to render fully transparent the infinite depth and mystery of the divine. I take it that he is also saying that even God, even the Divine, even Being itself (whatever our preferred term) cannot achieve this sort of absolute self-transparency—and I find that an absolutely staggering and revolutionary ontological and theological claim. Gadamer says of human historical consciousness that there is always more being than consciousness. I take it Panikkar is going even further and saying that even in the essence of ultimate reality there is always more being than consciousness or *logos*. For as he goes on to say: "One of the philosophical implications of this view is that there is no being absolutely identical to itself. Each being, not excluding a possible Supreme Being, presents an opaque remnant, as it were, a mysterious aspect that defies transparency. Being has an untapped reservoir, as it were, a shadow side not illumined by self-knowledge, reflection, or the like."

Panikkar's concern in making this point is to provide an ontological explanation for why there can be no such thing as absolute truth, but only a pluralism of truths (including, of course, the possibility of relatively absolute truths). My concern, however, in line with my general response to his paper, is that his remarks suggest to me, if I understand them correctly, that he is presenting (if only implicitly) a version of a *process* theory of ultimate reality (in fact, of both being and truth), one of whose consequences, for him, is that *logos, nous*, reason, rationality, language cannot, finally, be identical with being or truth so regarded—because *logos, nous*, and so forth, seem to demand or presuppose the possibility of total transparency, total illumination, the elimination of all shadows. But if that is how the West has traditionally understood the demand, the claim, the promise of universal reason, universal *logos*, then he is saying, "I've got bad news for you guys" (and "guys" is probably appropriate here, for this is a male concept of reason or rationality that is being criticized). Why? Because *logos* or reason, so conceived, cannot exhaust the infinite depths and mystery of being. In fact, even God's *logos*, Aristotle's *nous*, or Hegel's *Geist* cannot pull off that particular feat, because it is not a matter of the limitation of finite human intellects, it is simply a contradiction in terms, it is a logical impossibility even for God. Ultimate reality, being, God, is irreducibly opaque even to itself, or, to put it in Heideggerian terms, the Nothing is co-primordial with Being, and the truth of being, even for God, is a matter of *alētheia*, disclosure or un-concealment, which takes place in a never-ending dialectic with concealment and hiddenness as well. The Nothing, as the veil of Being, is always there, and male wishes to the contrary notwithstanding, it can never be completely removed, completely overcome. Truth always presents us with an opaque remainder, "a mysterious aspect that defies transparency."

Inasmuch as I find myself in basic agreement with Panikkar's assertions concerning being and its opacity, my question may seem merely a semantic quibble, but it is this: Why could Panikkar not say, following Heidegger for example, that not only Being and Truth but also *Logos* itself participates in this profound dialectic of concealment and disclosure—that *Logos* (to paraphrase Parmenides) is identical, or better, the same as Being and Truth—that *Logos*, equiprimordially with Being and Truth, is itself a never-ending dialectic (and in our context, dialogue) of hiddenness and transparency, of openness to the other and failure to completely understand the other—a failure that does not invalidate but rather, in the particular form of *logos* that we call faith, trust, or confidence, displays itself as a commitment to the ongoing dialogue, always willing to share with one's partner in dialogue the dialectical or dialogical adventure of faith, which is this open-ended journey on the way to shared understanding, on the way to shared language, on the way to shared truth, on the way to shared being—as Heidegger might put it, Being and Truth as always *unterwegs zur Sprache*. It is not, I am suggesting, that Being and Truth transcend Reason and *Logos*, but that Reason and *Logos* themselves display this same opacity and (the other, positive side of the coin) the same openness (for openness to truth, openness to being, openness to *logos* is quite a different matter from claims of absolute transparency of truth, transparency of being, transparency of *logos*). By admitting opacity into Being and Truth but not into Reason or *Logos*, Panikkar is perhaps unwittingly *perpetuating*, rather than truly *rethinking*, the very same concept of *logos* or reason that he accuses the partisans of universal theology of employing. A more radical critique, and one more consistent with his own epistemological and ontological premises, would be one that sees the *logos* or reason as also fully participating in the dialectic of openness and opacity that characterize Being and Truth.

Once again, therefore, at this most fundamental ontological level too, our choice would not be between a universal *logos* of religion versus a pluralistic confidence in being, but rather would feature a deeper understanding of the nature of universal theology as grounded in a processive, dialectical, and finally dialogical understanding of both reason and faith. This would not only reflect the implicit intellectual dimension, the implicit *logos*, of pluralistic confidence; it would also, I am contending, articulate the explicit philosophical foundations (epistemological, anthropological, and ontological) of dialogical dialogue as well.

In closing, I should like to make one further observation about Panikkar's ontological thesis, and that is that here, in his fundamental ontological vision, with its transformed and broadened, dialogical concepts of reason, truth, and *logos*, I see Panikkar as indeed providing a radical alternative (one that in this respect might still be a minority view) to the ontology that I think may still be operating in the work of Hick, Smart, and Smith, and which I am sure is present in the universal theory of religion found in Frithjof Schuon, Huston Smith, Walter Stace, or S. H. Nasr—the sort of ontology John Cobb refers to and which I would label Neo-Vedantist or Neo-Platonic—namely, the claim that Ultimate Reality is finally One. Over against that ontological foundation for interreligious dialogue or universal theology (which too often seems simply a disguised apologetic for one particular type or dimension in the world's religious traditions), I see Panikkar suggesting a radically different ontological basis for interreligious dialogue and global theology, one that brings him close to John Cobb and the Whiteheadian tradition, or perhaps to Wittgenstein or Heidegger.

In any case, I think Panikkar is absolutely right when he concludes that interreligious dialogue, understood as *dialogical* dialogue, is not only a religious endeavor, and a spiritual experience, for its participants, but that it can also become a new *locus theologicus*, and, I would add, a new *locus theoreticus* as well—a source not only of new religious and spiritual truth, but of new theological and theoretical truth as well. Such "universal theologies" as emerged would of course always be "dialogical" in their form, and that means ever open to further conversation and truth. And so I want to thank Prof. Panikkar for his extremely helpful, insightful, and thought-provoking remarks—and to express the hope that I have responded in that spirit of "friendly striving together" which he has so eloquently embodied in his own life and thought, and invited all of us to share.

POSTSCRIPT

One of the basic disagreements throughout the conference was between advocates of "universal" theology (Smith, Swidler) and critics of such theology

(Cobb, Panikkar), who spoke instead for a theology that, however open to dialogue, was still done from a confessional perspective. Thus, as Cobb put it, however "catholic" (universal) in its dialogue with others theology might be, as Christian theology it must be done from a Christocentric perspective. It is impossible to do theology from some completely neutral standpoint outside every particular perspective or from some multiperspectival standpoint.

As far as I could see, however, this alleged disagreement in fact rested on an ambiguity or equivocation in the use of the term "universal theology": "universal" could refer to the *perspective* from which such a theology is done, or it could refer to the *data* upon which such a theology draws. If we take "universal" to refer to the perspective from which such theology is done, as I believe Cobb and Panikkar assume Smith and Swidler wish to do, then it seems to me Cobb and Panikkar would be quite right in their insistence that such a theology is either methodologically incoherent or culturally totalitarian. Theology, as a human, cultural, historical enterprise, can be done only from some particular perspective or other, and any claims to be able to dispense with such a perspective or to universalize it must simply be rejected.

The problem with such criticism, however, is that however correct it might be *in abstracto*, it seems to me to have been misdirected against Smith and Swidler, for neither Smith nor Swidler say anything that could be taken as indicating that they construe the term "universal" to refer to the *perspective* from which such theology was to be done. Smith explicitly refers more than once to the fact that he is speaking of "world theology done from a Christian perspective." In other words, for both Smith and Swidler the term "universal" refers to the vastly extended range of *data* that the Christian theologian must take into account in the emerging *global setting* of interreligious dialogue.

Just as in the nineteenth century Christian theologians had to deal with the *new data* of evolutionary science or historical criticism, so today they must deal with the *new data* of the history of religions and interreligious dialogue. It is no longer sufficient to restrict their "data-base" to the Christian scriptures, the history of Christianity, European philosophy, or modern Western secular culture.

But for Christian theologians to take into account the data of other religious traditions in no way suggests that their response to this data will not still be made from their particular historico-cultural perspective as Christians. Therefore, the whole issue between Cobb and Panikkar, on the one hand, and Smith and Swidler, on the other—"universal" theology vs. "catholic Christocentric" theology, "universal" theology vs. "pluralistic" dialogue—is a *false* issue resting on an ambiguous or equivocal use of the term "universal." Once disambiguated into universal-as-perspective (which all four theologians agree in rejecting) and universal-as-data (which all four theologians agree in accepting), the whole controversy simply dissolves.

A further issue, addressed only indirectly by this conference (inasmuch as all four major speakers were Christians), would be this: How might the shape, or even the need, of "universal theology" or "interreligious dialogue" look from the perspective of other religious traditions? The real need, at the theological or theoretical level at least, is for a dialogue about "dialogue," a theological conversation about "universal theology," among representatives of the various religious traditions, not just among theologians of the same (Christian) tradition. This, dialogue, however, was in fact launched by the responses and subsequent discussions during the present conference.

III. 3.

Anthropomorphism and Cosmic Confidence

BIBHUTI S. YADAV

Prof. Panikkar has envisioned a city, the religious plurality of which he invites us all to affirm. Thousands of lamps elevate the city to a thing of beauty, each lamp revealing graphically the contours of the symbols underneath it. The city is cross-cultural. Its streets are thick with robes: black, blue, and brown robes; green, orange, and red robes; saffron, white, and yellow robes. The city is colorful. Its simplicity embodies the sobriety of the "economic trinity," one whose complex smell is worthy of its porous humanity. The city is postcolonial by virtue of being postlogical. Panikkar has envisioned it in light of the myth of resurrection, which he thinks looms large on the horizon, the cosmic horizon. The Spirit has resurrected itself after rational univocity, the tool through which the old Adam sought anthropomorphic universality, has decisively gone to the cross.

Such rationality was inaugurated by Socrates and the Greeks; it was practiced by Thomistic theology and the historicist church. A new enlightenment has dawned upon postlogical, postcolonial humanity. Having been redeemed from Adamic doubt, human beings now have cosmic confidence in the "unthought" and "unspoken" Spirit. Comprised of irreducible religious windows, the city is replete with interreligious dialogue, even though there is no universal language. Music is the paradigm of new intelligibility, and the cosmic orchestra is celebrating religious plurality under the resurrected Spirit. The music is divine, the musicians are the coreligionists, and the instrument is the cosmos itself.

Panikkar is a master at telling tales, and his theology is christology told through music. There are many strands in Panikkar's thesis, all of which

175

deserve attention. I respond to one aspect only—namely, the relationship between anthropomorphic universality and global theology of religion. I take a Buddhist stance, one that was taken by Chandrakirti in his *Prasannapada*. My response is in two parts. In the first part, I attempt to establish that Panikkar is engaged in anthropomorphic imagineering of history, that he does so to affirm the uniqueness of his religious identity, and that he is practicing a universal theology of religion. In the second part, I describe Chandrakirti's stance on the relationship between rationality and anthropomorphic universality in the context of Indian thought. I do so to recontextualize the implications of Chandrakirti's words on interreligious discourse.

A CRITIQUE OF PANIKKAR

The onto-theological ego, observes Chandrakirti, is committed to extremes; unhappy with one extreme, it turns to the contrary. It does so to affirm anthropomorphic belonging, to displace the fear of losing identity by virtue of not belonging to toys, positional toys.[1] Hence the shift from being to nothingness, from *saṃsāra* to *nirvāṇa,* from historicism to cosmicism, from the thought to the "unthought." Panikkar's is a bipolar theology. Because he is unhappy with the West, and because the dominant leitmotif of the West is rational, Panikkar affirms the contrary—namely, the East, which must be the sphere of happiness by virtue of being nonrational. In the name of rejecting rational "oneness," Panikkar is given to imagineering fundamental duality in the heart of humanity for which he claims universal validity.

Such polarization is rooted in contrastive historicism; anything other than the West is construed in light of its having to be reified contrary to the West (*samaropena*). The Western psyche, in Panikkar's reckoning, is sinfully rational, anthropomorphically universalistic, and appetitively imperialistic. The non-Western psyche, on the contrary, is innocently nonrational, nonuniversalistic, and therefore nonimperialistic. A product of a guilty culture, Panikkar's historicism involves moral messianism and pride (*sila vasana*).

Panikkar would have us believe that the dualistic divide of humanity pertains to the archetypal psyche, to the metaphysical condition of being in time, and not to the mutation of history. "Western psyche," observes Panikkar, "has no other peace of mind and heart—called more academically intelligibility— than by reducing everything to one single pattern with the claim to one universal validity." The non-Western psyche, on the other hand, has peace of mind in nonrational intelligibility. The Indian mind, for instance, finds intelligibility in "existential confession, not discursive understanding."

It is true that Panikkar is opposed to the Latin captivity of the church constituted by either/or logic, to the claim that in order for a religion to be true it must be Christian, or else it is false. It now seems that Panikkar is given to archetypal captivity of humanity by an either/or of sorts, to the claim that, in order for non-Western religions to be there, they must be mystical, or else they do not exist. His noble intentions notwithstanding, Panikkar commits himself to an essentialism involved in the anthropomorphic universalization of eighteenth- and nineteenth-century Europe—namely, the rational West and the mystical, exotic East. Such essentialism is a rationalization of a historicist ideology; it involves a form of thinking that elevates the contingencies of history to a metaphysics of culture, to Being that bears the burden of its being in time through a chosen people.

Panikkar does not question the anthropomorphic genesis of the archetypal divide of humanity. He only elevates it to axiomatic righteousness, asserting that the mystical non-West is spiritually superior. Rejecting historicist Christianity and the West, he finds comfort in the cosmicism of the East that has confidence in the "unthought"; the possibility of a dominant leitmotif in the middle is ruled out.

The irony is that Panikkar practices such either/or logic in the name of moral concern associated with nonreductionism. To avoid reductionism, he has proposed a dialogical theology that reduces history to a worldwide *ecclesia,* to a forum for interreligious recognition by way of "mutually enriching contrast." The Christian, in order to remain self-consciously so, must ask "Who am I?" Self-consciousness necessarily implies its contrary; I cannot be a Christian unless I also ask "Who are you?" It is not that other religions are nonexistent, or false, because I am a Christian. Rather, it is because I am a Christian that there must be other religions.

In Panikkar's view, other religions should be considered not as "adversaries" but "contraries," as mirrors or media through which the what and how of the kerygma can be encountered by contrasting it with what it is not, and how not. "In brief, *das Ungedachte,* the unthought, can be disclosed only by one who does not 'think' like me, and who helps me discover the unthought *magma* out of which my thinking crystalizes."[2] Panikkar is not interested in what non-Christians in fact *are;* he is interested in what they *can* be. And what they can be is determined by their being helpful in satisfying an anthropomorphic need; their existence is equated with their kerygmatic images (*pratibimba*).

To give existential certainty to his religious identity, to make his kerygma vivid to himself by way of contrast, Panikkar has proposed a theology of exodus.[3] It is a theology that reduces the human space to a dualistic divide, to what Chandrakirti would have called the categories of departure and arrival (*gata-agata*). The exodus theology is a device for being at home mentally after having left it physically, for being overtaken by Mara in Gaya by virtue of having left Kapilavastu.

Panikkar has taken an exodus from the West, the home that he thinks reduces reality to knowability because it is afraid of the "unknown other." He has arrived in *terra incognita,* in the territory of African and Asiatic humanity.[4] It is a territory of multivocity. Africans and Asians eat and dress differently; live, grow old, and accept death differently; and then go to heaven or hell by different paths. However, they all are given to acceptability without knowability because they are unafraid of the unknown other; they therefore do not reduce Being to thought, nor do they reduce speaking—and hearing—to the circumcizing functions of propositions framed by Thomistic logic. Given Panikkar's a priori historicism, there could not have been in India persons like Dharmakirti; Udayana and Gangesha; Chandrakirti, Shriharsa, and Raghunatha Shiromani. The Nyaya could not have done rational theology, because the Thomist tradition alone could do it.

It seems that, in order to confirm the uniqueness of his unthought *magma,* Panikkar subjects non-Western traditions to his anthropomorphic conformity, to a mirror that can reflect an image in ways Panikkar wants it reflected. Among themselves the non-Western peoples are different. However, when contrasted with the West, they all look alike. Panikkar's postcolonial anthropomorphism is unique. It does not universalize and export the sort of univocity that he detects in a rational theory. Rather, it universalizes and imports the nonrational univocity of non-Western religions so that the West could affirm, by way of contrast, its religious self-certainty at home. Hence the theology of the "unthought" and "unspoken" Spirit.

Panikkar's bipolar theology ignores the facts of Western history as well. He equates rationality with the imperialistic psyche. A less guilt-laden reading of Western history would render such an equation questionable. In fact it is more reasonable to say that it is the messianic confidence in the "unthought" reality, and not rationality, that is constitutive of imperialistic universality. "What," Socrates asks Euthyphro, "will the art which serves the gods serve to produce? You must know, seeing that you say that you know more about divine things than any other man."[5] Socrates was arguing that knowledge is a social property, that objective conditions of cognition account for the public content of knowledge, and that commonality of cognitive contents is an argument against a feudalistic hierarchy established in the name of divine mystery. Basically Socrates was inquiring into the protected privileges that led to asking ordinary persons to have confidence in the gods and Spirit. To Euthyphro's claim that such confidence produces notable results, Socrates responded: "So are those, my friend, which a general produces. Yet it is easy to see that the crowning result of them all is victory in war, is it not?"[6] A proponent of *logos,* Socrates was up against the psyche of *mythos.*

Two strands constitute such a psyche. First, there is no truth apart from the believed truth; even if there were such a truth, it would be dangerous, indeed immoral. It is not for nothing that the prophets, in the works of Sophocles and other Greek tragedians, are blind to things that are there to see. And if Oedipus the king insists upon reducing being to knowability, if he equates his being not with what others believe to be but with his thought of it, then he would be exiled from the republic as a blind and sinful man.

The second strand in the mythic psyche is that the gods, through oracles and prophets, demand cosmic confidence from the average person. Hence, to rationally and publicly demonstrate in the streets of Athens that the gods and the "unthought" Spirit are anthropomorphic creations is to commit treason against the state. Socrates was up against a colonial ideology that demanded cosmic confidence in the "unthought," and was nourished not by rational *logos* but by the poetry and politics of the oracles. Battus of Thera was caught up in the art of elevating colonial ideology to the mysticism of the sacred. Wanting to overcome a stammer, he went to hear the cosmotheandric voice at the shrine. "Battus," said the oracle, "you have come for a voice, but King Phoebus Apollo sends you as a founder of a colony to Libya."[7]

Contrary to Panikkar's reading, Socrates was not proposing an imperialistic rationality. He was fighting what turned out to be the most effective tool of imperialism in the West—namely, messianic universalization of a people's anthropomorphic uniqueness in the name of the "unthought" mystery. In a sense Socrates embodies the dilemma of Western intellectual history: he cannot accept Athens, and he cannot leave it. He represents the dilemma of Athens with itself, a city that must silence a being it necessarily produces with the hope of giving a rational language to its perception of itself. That is why Socrates is condemned to reject the suggestion that he accept exile from Athens and be given to a life of wandering in strange lands. Knowing that any other society would have the same anthropomorphic syndromes as Athens has, Socrates cannot step into *terra incognita* in order to encounter the "unthought" Spirit. That would be only a horizontal movement, an unqualitative leap into a cultural space imagineered by a mythic psyche. Socrates is interested in thinking about the "unthought" of his social self; against all odds, he is committed to a qualitative return to the interior of his Athens, which is none other than a sustained struggle of the West against its own imperfection.

The intellectual history of the West has been an interminable dialectic of *mythos* and *logos,* faith and reason, evangelical self-righteousness and skeptical restraint, institutionalized romanticism and individual facticity, imperialism and revolution. There simply is no *nirvāṇa* without *saṃsāra.* The stern assertion that the West is sinfully rational is commensurate with its historical falsity; it involves nothing more than a guilt-laden mourning that a certain people is not more than human. Panikkar robs the West of its complex humanity, its historical anguish with itself.

Panikkar complains that a rational theory suffers from theoretical impatience, that it is loaded with a messianic syndrome, and that it leads either to solipsism or to universal conformism. With equal justification it can be shown that Panikkar's theology involves all these deficiencies. I comment on the last two only—solipsism and conformism.

Let us recall that there is multivocity in Panikkar's interreligious city. Loyal to their tradition, Hindus, for instance, necessarily speak from within their tradition, from their window. In so doing, however, they should not transplant the language of others, he says. Given to an imparative form of thinking, they affirm Brahman as the whole reality, one that is all that is, and different from which, other than which, there is nothing (*naparah*). There are two qualificatory stipulations, however. The Hindus encounter the whole of reality from their window only in part, and they also experience that others encounter the same reality from their windows, equally in part. Such is the case with Christians, for instance. Honest to their tradition, they affirm that Jesus Christ sums up the whole of reality; from the Christian window, they experience the whole reality in part and know that non-Christians do the same. All coreligionists perceive the whole of reality as well as the part and experiences that others do likewise.

My concern is twofold. First, just how would Christians, for example, identify the whole, the cosmic reality they have encountered from their window? Secondly, how do Hindus ascertain that the part they know constitutes the same whole that the Christians, too, know? We should note here that a nonintelligible content, according to Panikkar, is not any different from no content at all, and that all coreligionists must have their measurable point of reference in such a way that they not supplant the language of others. If forms of speech and intelligibility are necessarily different, how can Hindus say, and understand, that Christians talk about the same reality? Panikkar is committed to "mutual understanding," to connaturality through dialogical language. But he does not explain precisely how "mutual understanding" is different from the "understanding" involved in a universal theory, or how, by virtue of being mutual, it is different from Hindus' "understanding" of Christians' understanding of reality. And vice versa. Precisely how is mutual understanding different from mutual supplantation, or no understanding at all?

The problem becomes particularly acute when we recall Panikkar's views on homeomorphic equivalents, according to which "Brahman" is not the translation of "God," by virtue of the fact that the former does not cover what the latter stands for. "Either there is a creator God, or an inactive noncreator Brahman, but not both, in spite of the fact that in the respective systems both are not only legitimate but necessary." Panikkar's imparative method necessarily leads humankind to religious solipsism, to a city of estranged windows. Without commonly intelligible contents, one wonders what coreligionists dialogue about. And how?

Panikkar is nonetheless for dialogical dialogue that admits no rational measurability and no anthropomorphic universality. He is for creating common categories through interreligious encounter. He does not, however, explain just what these categories are. Because he insists that interreligious encounter is from a window, from a tradition that provides the locus of theological language, one may wonder which window would provide such common categories. How are such categories different from those of a universal theory and theology of world religions?

The question is important, particularly when we recall Panikkar's stance on interreligious language. "Why," asks Panikkar, "must all be put in words?" The primacy of the Spirit over *logos* implies that meaning, and intelligibility, is not coextensive with speech, nor with propositional language that has syntactic and semantic structure. Opposed to linguistic colonialism, Panikkar rejects a universal language, including metalanguage. He is nonetheless for a common language. "Dialogue," says Panikkar, "forges appropriate language to deal with issues that emerge in the encounter."

There's the rub. If the "common language" is syntactically constituted, then one may wonder according to whose linguistic anthropomorphism? Precisely whose theory of word and sentence, whose grammar or linguistic convention, will constitute the "common language"? And how would it be different, in form and function, from the language of a universal theory and, for that reason, from that of a global theology?

Presumably, by language Panikkar means symbolic expressions, which make effective communications possible. But just as there is no such thing as a "no-man's-land in the land of Man," so also there is no symbol that is not somebody's symbol. Symbols are effective because of their volitional reciprocity with the anthropomorphic psyche of those whose symbols they are. One wonders precisely whose symbols, and the inner dimension of whose psyche, Panikkar would recognize as constitutive of the common language in which the categories of interreligious dialogue would be forged. Nor does Panikkar explain how this "common language" does not involve the imperialistic univocity of a universal theory. It seems there is an alienation of promise and praxis in the theology of cosmotheandric trust.

Panikkar insists he is opposed to theological oneness. Unlike the universal theory, his theology is far from wanting to reduce everything to unity, and the unity to oneness of Being. He is for discordant voices of human traditions, for multivocity. But Panikkar is also for unitive plurality, for interreligious concord and agreement, for unanimity and consensus. "Consensus ultimately means to walk in the same direction." It means to be of one sense, one feeling, one aspiration, and not just one rational view or theory.

By the time he arrives at the conclusion, Panikkar seems to relapse into his Western syndrome. He seems to propose some sort of ecumenical Esperanto that in effect does the same thing he accuses universal theories and unified field theories of doing. Of the Western syndrome, Panikkar says:

> The common trait here is the noble effort at reducing the immense variety of the human experience to one single and common language, which may well respect the different dialectical forms of expressions and of life, but which somewhat subsumes them all and allows for communication and understanding on a universal scale. The universal theory assumes that a certain type of rationality is the general heritage of humankind and even more, that it is one single trait of the human being.

There seems to be an irony here. In Panikkar's theology of religious plurality, human beings have different, even dialectically opposed, forms of intelligibility. Contradictions are there, but they are respected, even guiltily defended. The contradictory forms of expressions do not function in contradictory ways, however; going through conversion or inner completion, they are instead subsumed in the cosmotheandric Spirit, the symbol of universal concord. Interreligious communication continues on a universal scale; there is understanding and agreement of cosmic proportions under the Holy Spirit. Panikkar assumes that a nonlogical confidence in the "unthought" Mystery is the general heritage of humankind, that accepting the Mystery without understanding it is a universal trait of humanity and the cosmos. Under the Holy Spirit, the interreligious form of life is constituted by a oneness of sense and feeling that makes the city unidirectional. "The very words by which we often express what we are striving for are 'unanimity,' 'consensus,' 'agreement,' 'concord,' and all have a cordial or an existential core."

One wonders precisely how the commitment to one sense or feeling would not subsume religious plurality into one form of religiosity on a universal scale. Just how does walking in one direction not reduce religious plurality to a single teleological and salvific universality? The conflicting accounts by the religions of how humanity came to be, and keeps on being, in time constitutes their irreducible multivocity with regard to striving for direction in time and in history. One cannot, for instance, be a Buddhist and say one believes in *nirvāna* without also believing in the *marga,* the path. The Buddha after all was a methodologist (*mahamargi*), who insisted that there is no such thing as a given and that to know X is to determine the causes and conditions that gave rise to X. Equating truth with the method of its demonstration (*artha adarsama*), the Buddha proposed a worldview in which, logically and existentially, the first noble truth is meaningless without the second, and in which the third noble truth does not make any sense without the fourth—and vice versa. It seems that Panikkar grants the plurality of non-Christian revelations, but not of salvation. The non-Christians have revelations, but they cannot have salvation without teleological and salvific movement under the Holy Spirit.

It seems that, having taken an exit from history to cosmos, Panikkar now reduces the cosmos to a teleological anthropomorphism of the West. Panikkar seems to have lived too long in territories of revelatory multivocity; he returns home only to offer the non-Western religions to the sacred historicism involved in the salvific univocity under the Holy Spirit. Panikkar celebrates his arrival by evoking historical memory. "At Pentecost the peoples did not all speak the same language, nor did they have simultaneous translation. . . . Yet they were convinced, they felt, sensed that all were hearing the great deeds of God, the *megaleia tou Theou.*" Having undertaken an exodus from technicultural historicism, Panikkar has brought the religions to a new Sinai, to the church of the Cosmic Christ built with theandric technology. Discordant multivocity is still there; revelatory languages are left untranslated, but they are recognized as symphonies, as media of audibility—and intelligibility—of salvific univocity immanent in the cosmic word that is "Christ." The cosmotheandric church, unlike the historicist church, does not export revelatory univocity anymore. It does something else. Having rehistoricized the salvific univocity, the new church witnesses—and celebrates—under its magisterium the kerygmatic tower of multiple tongues.

Panikkar contends that a universal theology of religions suffers from a messianic syndrome, that it is given to theoretical impatience, and that pluralism leads either to solipsism or universal conformism. Unfortunately, Panikkar's communitarian theology is saturated with anthropomorphisms; it

is an argument for contrastive historicism, for an archetypal divide of humanity. It suffers from the universalistic syndrome as well, for it assumes that
confessional confidence in the "unthought" Spirit is a universal trait of humankind. Given to mystical impatience, Panikkar's theology ignores the complexities of history; it cannot wait for the eschatological happy day when
interreligious antinomies will be solved. Panikkar has therefore envisioned an
interreligious city of realized eschatology in which there is teleological unanimity because the Holy Spirit has refleshed the religions in its own image.
Panikkar shifts over from rational to spiritual anthropomorphism, to rehistoricized salvation of the religions under the Holy Spirit.

A BUDDHIST RESPONSE

Such is the autotheological reflection of a "mutational" man who has returned home after living through a life of "enriching contrasts." Panikkar took
an exodus from the West and the Christianity that has historicized Christ in
Jesus. He did so *as* a Christian, and "found" himself a Hindu. He "returned" a
Buddhist without ceasing to be a Christian.[8] In Panikkar's scheme, Buddhism
and Hinduism are moments in the history of his confession. Hinduism is what
he found himself *as,* and Buddhism is equivalent to his *returning as* a Buddhist.
Hinduism and Buddhism are matters of kerygmatic completion, of being born
again at home after the exodus in spheres of dialectical contrast with the West.

Unfortunately, such inner completion through contrasts necessitates the
equation of *seeing as* with seeing, of being *as* a Buddhist with Buddhism. In
Panikkar's confessional scheme the confirmation of one's religious identity is
far more important than the religions themselves.

Panikkar left as a Christian, and he returned a Christian; he was Christian in
the beginning, and he is so in the end. There is nothing wrong with that. My
concern is with the middle. Between his beginning and his end, Panikkar
establishes an interreligious city by letting his kerygmatic image of Buddhism
and Hinduism become a substitute for those very religions.

There is a Buddhist tradition that the Buddha did not talk of the beginning
and the end; and in the middle, one's own anthropomorphic image, no matter
how grand, should not become a substitute for reality either (*madhye'pi
sthanam na karoti panditah*). Interreligious dialogue means that we play by
ear, but it also demands that a sequence, both historical and logical, be
established between listening and talking. We must listen to the structural
complex of the categories of the religions before we talk to them, or start
talking on behalf of them. I did not see Hindu and Buddhist lamps in
Panikkar's interreligious city. I wish to rekindle briefly two such lamps—
namely, Nyaya and Madhyamika Buddhism. I do so to indicate why a theologian in a dialogical city projects his word as an *other,* and then claims he is
talking to the other when in fact he is listening to his own words. The
anthropomorphic positing of one's own word as an *other* to oneself is the basis
for planting one's own words unto others (*atmasamaropa*).

I think interreligious dialogue should be honest to history. Most cognitive civilizations have been obsessed with rational universality for anthropomorphic reasons, for maintaining collective identity in history. Indian civilization is no exception. In this section I shall describe how Indian thinkers struggled with *logos* and *anthrōpos,* and how some critical minds demonstrated that onto-theological rationality is a cover for the anxiety of losing collective identity. I do so by following Panikkar's recommendation—namely, that each tradition is like a historical person and should therefore be taken as a source of self-understanding. I take the *pramanavada* tradition, which was forced to encounter its own anthropomorphism by Madhyamika Buddhism proposed by Chandrakirti in his *Prasannapada.* Following Chandrakirti, I shall end by arguing that cosmicism is a case of displaced historicism, and that we need self-psychoanalytic meditation, not cosmic confidence, to overcome anthropomorphism.

Honest to its etymological genesis, *pramanavada* is obsessed with the measurability principle. Elevating cognitive trinity to divinity, it reduced the being of humanity to cognitive subject (*pramata*), consciousness to the *cogito (prama*), and reality to knowability and speakability (*prameya*). Charged with the measurability syndrome, it insisted that Being gives itself to thought, that all that can be thought exists, that knowability is the condition of acceptability or rejectibility of things, that efforts are rooted in technical knowledge (*sadhana*) and that a healthy form of life is concomitant with a logical form of thinking.[9] "Logic," claimed the founder of *pramanavada,* "is the ground of all thinking, the tool of all actions, including moral actions."[10] Epistemology was accepted as the methodology of doing ontology, of establishing what exists and how, what does not exist and how not. The conditions under which X could be demonstrated to exist are far more important than the mere existence of X.

Pramanavada also is a tradition of *hetusastra,* of constituting a universe of meaning through inductive logic, the paradigm of which is "X is Y because of Z." *Hetusastra* is a methodology of arriving empirically at universal propositions, of demonstrating that certain propositions are universally true, and others not. It also is a methodology of celebrating the virtues of objectivity and self-criticism. Not having such a methodology is to reduce cognition to fantasies, truth claims to dogmatic assertions, life to subjectivities such as memory, indecision, and illusion. The logic of objective truth is like this: "X is Y" is true because, and only because, of Z, where invariable concomitance (*vyapti*) between Y and Z is established empirically, and where X is the locus in which such concomitance occurs. "There is smoke on the hill" is true because "wherever there is smoke, there is fire" is true, and because "there is smoke on the hill" is true. Invariable concomitance (*vyapti*) gives two universal propositions. "All cases of smoke are cases of fire," and "no case of nonfire is a case of smoke." All P is Q, and no non-P is Q.

The Hindu and Buddhist traditions of rational universality were convinced that a healthy form of life and peace of mind are comprised of propositions embodying universal truths. Committed to conflicting frames of measurability and universality, both Hindus and Buddhists sought to sell the religious form of life in the philosophical marketplace. Constituted by the *cogito* (*prama*), it was a place thick with definite, indubitable, and demonstratively true knowledge of what is the case and how, and what is not the case and how not (*yathartha adarsana*). It was a marketplace of the certainty syndrome; in need of buying a rope to tie his cow, the philosopher was out to make sure he did not buy a snake in innocent trust. They believed that the life of *cogito* leads to successful actions, not disappointment, to moral sociality rooted in rational decisions, not instincts or whims.[11] In the world of *pramanasastra* there are no mysteries.

The Sanskrit philosophers respect universal laws of diction as if words were police officers (*sabdahhidandapasikah*). There is a reciprocity of word and being, saying and meaning. Ontologically speaking, *a* is *b* because of *c;* existentially speaking, life is as smooth as syllogistic reasoning. Ontological discovery, according to Nyaya, implies a soteriological recovery of the self from the not-self; and according to Buddhist logicians, there is a connaturality between the *cogito* and the recovery of existence from the nonsense that is the self. According to both Hindu and Buddhist logicians, however, the *cogito* liberates humankind from the possessive ego, the appetitive being (*aham*) that affirms itself in *having* (*mam*) and is therefore condemned to self-predicative recurrence of rebirth and redeath in vain.[12]

But then there was Nagarjuna, the founder of Madhyamika Buddhism. Legend has it that he journeyed to the bottom of the sea, the symbol of the subconscious (*samskara*) in Indian myths, and surfaced with the *Prajnaparmita-sutra,* the holy scriptures of Mahayana Buddhism. Loyal to the scriptures, Nagarjuna wrote several texts including the *Vaidalyasutram,* in the preface of which he says this: "One who is rid of the pride of logic and is desirous to debate, for him I write *Vaidalyasutram* in order to destruct his ego."[13] Nagarjuna wrote succinctly, in *sutra* style. He had two proposals: to see how the ego incarnates itself in the *cogito;* and to achieve peace of mind by destructing the ego. Such endeavor leads to onto-logical silence, to liberation from theories (*drstisunyata*).

Chandrakirti, devoting his *Prasannapada* to Nagarjuna, his master, proposes a hermeneutic of ontological language. His is an elucidative reflection on a simple theme: ontology is egology (*aham vasana*). *Vasana* is derived from the root *vas,* meaning "to dwell," "to stay," "to reside," "to house," "to be." The word *vasana* usually occurs in conjunction with *sangha,* meaning "in company of," "in relation to," "in appropriation of," "in association with." Chandrakirti demonstrates that the ego has come to house itself in ontological language, that the *cogito* (*prama*) is the libidinal sedimentation of the ego (*kamamulam*). The sense faculties are not inactive; they do not passively receive impressions from outside. The senses are the medium (*karana*) through which the ego seeks a "this" in order to give materiality (*rupa*) to "I am." Every cognitive assertion is in fact a self-recognitive act. "This is a table" is an implied argument for "This I am."

Epistemology is a methodology of establishing self-certainty, an appetitive mutuality of self and self-predication (*raga*). The will to know is rooted in the existentially a priori (*anadi*) will to be, the truth of propositional assertions, including subject-predicate logic, in the libidinal commitment of self-predication (*aham mameti aiti astha*). Such also is the case with the logic of invariable concomitance. It is a methodology of establishing reciprocity between "I know" and "I exist," a technique through which the ego arrives at itself repeatedly for reasons of self-certainty.

Ontology therefore is not a categorical description of reality (*padarthasastrara*). It is an act of egological projection (*praksepa*). Chandrakirti detects two strands in such an act: self-distanciation (*duribhuta*) and belonging (*nibandhana*). Given to self-projection, the ego needs distance and space between "I am" and "I am this," between its being (*aham*) and its being there (*idam*). Exteriorization is a metapsychological need (*abhinivesa*); it requires the positing of space to account for the duality in the ego of its being and its being "there." Space is a self-distancing horizon; it also is a self-recognitive medium (*karana*) for the ego to fulfill the abstract "I am" into the fullness of "I am here." This *having* (*mam*) by the ego of itself is the ground of its being itself in any form; it also is the basis of the ego's love of itself as well as of anything else. "I am mine" seeks incarnation in "my Being" or "my God," which in turn is the foundation for saying "I love God." The *logos* of Being and Nothingness, God and the Buddha, universal theory and counter-theory, is a case of refleshing by the ego of its own flesh.[14]

Chandrakirti demonstrates that ontological discourse involves a semantic of desire, a libidinal need that has incarnated itself through words.[15] A religious sentence like "The Tathagata speaks the dharma" is no exception. The wish to exist *as* Buddhists, the anxiety of collective identity, seeks shelter in the words of the historicized Buddha, in the referring form of speech like "The Tathagata is there."[16] The truth is that the alleged referents of "Tathagata" and "God" have a psychosomatic (*nama-rupa*) genesis; they are projections of humanity's underworlds (*klesavarana*). It is not that there are persons who are Buddhists by virtue of hearing the words of the Buddha. Rather, it is because there are persons who desire to establish their identity by speaking about things that they wish to, and in a place of their desire, that there is a historical Buddha who is believed to have been born in Kapilavastu, who achieved enlightenment at Gaya, and who first spoke at Saranatha in Banaras. Rather than being a referring term, "Tathagata," like "God," is a projection of the hearers who in fact are the speakers.[17]

Self-love is repetitive; it involves the recurrence as group-identity—hence the emergence of Indian philosophy as group-think (*siddhantavada*). Hence also the persistence of tradition, of the continuity of onto-theological identity in time.

Chandrakirti notes with dismay that the Buddhists forgot religious experience as the self-psychoanalytic vocalization (*nidanavada*) involved in the word "Tathagata." The Buddhists instead adopted a non-Buddhist language of agent-act grammar and subject-predicate logic.[18] Committed to the theory of momentariness, they even instituted *vadvidhi,* the methodology of establishing the universal truth value of their claim by showing the contrary theory, the Hindu ontology of self and substance, to be false. Interested in making indubitable truth claims in order to establish their certainty *as* Buddhists, they needed the space of a competing truth system (*purvapaksa*) into which they could make a cognitive exodus, which could be shown to be dubitable and erroneous, and by contrast with which they could establish their self-certainty. Hence the dialogical nature of Indian thought, a conceptual space set in motion by theories and counter-theories, a rolling conference in which each system encounters all others.

Indian thought is a dialogical space in motion, one in which each position makes universal truth claims, and in which each requires all others for reasons of "mutual contrast," for self-certainty. The history of Indian thought is a continuity of group-think (*paksa*), each group needing the others for the certainty of its identity, and each refuting the others at the same time. Indian philosophy is a history of competing egologies, a dialogical continuity of neurosis of identity (*paksa-purva-paksa*).

It is a world of tradition as well. The interontological history involves a hermeneutic of positional belonging, a perpetual resaying of what has already been said (*bhasya*). Subject to the dialectic of eternal recurrence, of reprieve and rebirth, collective neuroses have been frozen into the ontic form of speech: into "is" (*asti*) and "not-is" (*nasti*), being (*sad*) and nonbeing (*asad*), eternity and momentariness, God and no-God, substance and attribute, soul and mind, *saṃsāra* and *nirvāṇa.*[19] It is a history sedimented with self-love (*raga*), a thick forest of kadali trees in whose trunks libidinal self-certainty and anticipatory fear of losing positional identity have found a home in interontological dialogue, and at whose base is *samskara,* the subconscious drive by which libido (*kama*) incarnates as the *cogito* (*prama*).

Chandrakirti likens such interontological space to a colorful horizon, through the contours of which the ego has posited its immortality wish and metaphysics of eternal substance, the ontology of momentariness and the logic of universal truth claims, the spermatic *logos* (*prabhava*) and cosmic eschatology (*laya*), the agony of death and mythology of heaven and hell, the Buddha and God.[20] Chandrakirti quotes the Mahayana holy scripture, the *Aryapariprcchasutra,* to liken the interontological space to a spaceship. It is a glittering ship imagineered out of gold by recurrent egologies, by beings who suffer from perpetual childhood, who are fearful of being in the world by virtue of having to die in it, and who deny to themselves the existence of such fear in themselves by identifying their being in time with Being, with transcendental entities (*lokottara dhatu*). Decorated with truth claims, thick with symbols of anthropomorphic belonging, the spaceship is stuck with self-defeating circularity unto the heavens, the mirage of the promised land called *nirvāṇa.*[21]

Nirvāṇa would not be different from *saṃsāra* if humans carried within themselves the anguish as well as the categories of the place from which they departed. One should not carry Kapilavastu to Gaya; that would be the case of suffering rebirth *as* salvation, Gautama *as* the Buddha, Jesus *as* the Cosmic Christ, Arjuna *as* Krishna. Chandrakirti urges the kerygmatic spaceship, along with the philosophers and theologians who imagineer it, to return to Kapilavastu. Having returned home, from which they actually never made an exodus in the first place, philosophers and theologians should put two questions to themselves. First, why is it that their pleasure in clinging to their theories is as intense as embracing young women (he spoke as if only men could be philosophers or theologians)?[22] Secondly, why is it that in interontological dialogue, they still claim rationality and truth value for their positions despite the fact that they are false in terms of their own criteria of truth? Staying there in Kapilavastu, the Buddhists should put another set of questions to themselves: Why do they make ontological claims at all, and why do they engage in interontological discourse?

Chandrakirti has had enough of this tradition of interontological discourse, this interreligious forest in which, like fearful antelopes, Buddhists and others are running from history to the edges of the cosmos, and in which suffering philosophers talk as though they are the healing sons of the Buddha.[23] Chandrakirti would rather dig into the underground, the root of the onto-theological tree itself. To this end he introduces the technique of deincarnation (*anavatara*), of returning home from exodus. So doing, Chandrakirti has Buddhists and Hindus in mind. There is no doubt, however, that he would suggest that Christians, too, return from *terra incognita* to the anthropomorphism of the holy church, from the cosmic Christ to the historical Jesus. Chandrakirti asks Buddhists to suspend ontological commitment; after all, the defense and refutation of doctrines is contrary to the Buddha's way.[24] Buddhists need not make an exodus to *terra incognita,* nor do they need to return to postlogical *logos.* There is no such territory, because in taking an exodus humanity carries the samsaric kerygma to the city of *nirvāṇa* (*nirvanapuram*). Buddhists should instead return reflectively unto the *logos* itself, into their own ontological commitment (*drsti*). The Buddhist should not engage in existential confession either; that would only give an esthetic sanctity to the guilt-laden ego (*sila vasana*). In order to deincarnate the ego (*anavatara*), Buddhists should instead encounter themselves in self-psychoanalytic empathy (*saksat kartavyah*). They should use their own ontological claims, their own *logos,* as a mirror, so to say: *tailapatre niriksate.* In so doing, they will descend through the path (*marga*) leading to the underground *libido,* the cave in which Buddhas are conceived (*tathagatagarbha*), and from which the libido shoots through the edges of cosmotheandric space (*lokottaradhatu*).[25] Buddhists would have lived through the truth of dependent origination, the process of how the libidinal ego incarnates itself as ontology, the historical Buddhas like Tathagata who took an exodus from Kapilavastu, who wandered in unknown territories in search of *nirvāṇa,* and who walked and talked dialogically for forty years to establish the church (*sangha*) and a city of peace.

Chandrakirti reorients the concept of dependent origination. He does so to uncover the psychosomatic compulsions by which Buddhists, driven through ontological language, feel at home in displacement. The preeminent example of such displacement is inhistorization, the converting of a mere self-psychoanalytical skill (*upaya kauselya*) into a historical dogma. It is a dogma rooted in the Gautama of Kapilavastu, who was the only son (*priyaikaputra*) of *Suddhodana* and *Maya,* whose birth was a case of a libidinal dream come true, and at whose birth the cosmos and the gods danced and sang cosmotheandric songs. Chandrakirti wants Buddhists to look into the anthropomorphic compulsions (*abhinivesa*) that become refleshed in such mythicization of history. He would want us to practice the principle of dependent origination with regard to so-called historical religions as well. He would like us to see how the human libidinal obsession with tribal identity is altered into a unique event, into a "once and for all" syndrome. It is an event that calls for a universal *metanoia* in order to clear the confusion of tongues at Babel.

In particular, Chandrakirti would like Buddhists to see the causes and conditions by which they themselves managed to turn the second noble truth— the Tathagata as merely a self-psychoanalytic method (*marga*)—into the first noble truth, into the suffering involved in formulating and defending self-certainty (*drsti*).

Chandrakirti wants Buddhists to see how they turn their anthropomorphic image into the historical Buddha, how a *ben adam* is altered into the body of *logos* (*dharmakaya*), and how their wish to be a chosen people (*kulaputra*) is refleshed into the language of faith, into historical community and sacred institutions (*sangha*). Such a meditative encounter into oneself is enlightenment (*Tathata*). It is a lived-through encounter (*saksatkartavyah*) with how the ego, seeking libidinal collectivity and belonging, incarnates itself in historicity and tradition, and how the libido gets re-edited and formalized as ontological commitments (*drsti nibandhana*). Spermatic to the core, the ego re-creates itself perpetually in traditions to which it has as intense a libidinal belonging as it has toward a young woman. Fearful of losing its identity, the ego needs recurrent self-confirmation. The ego therefore needs an interontological space in which it defends a theory with as much of a libidinal concern as it protects a young woman from rival claims.[26]

That is why Chandrakirti insists that he had no desire to play the language game that the philosophers play (*vacanam kridartham*), that he has no theory of reality and no methodology of arriving at universally true propositions (*prayogavakyam*).[27] He requests that humanity overcome the onto-theological canopy that it has constructed by means of the *cogito*. These are canopies made in a dreamworld, where philosophers and theologians live through interontological anguish by way of justifying their absolutistic trails to God and the cosmic Christ, the Buddha and *nirvāṇa*. It is a world of conjectures and refutations, of ideological hegemony and cries of foul play.[28] Honest to Mahayana scriptures, Chandrakirti wants the fearful ego to wake up from the libidinal discourse of an interontological dream:

Oh humanity! Do not fear; do not fear. You are asleep. You have not taken an exodus from your samsaric home at all. This is how the Buddhas instruct those who are struck with delusions: "There is no woman, no man, no *sattva* and *jiva,* no *purusa* and no *pudgala.* All the *dharmas* are delusions. All the *dharmas* are imagined. . . . All the *dharmas* are like the double moon in water."[29]

Chandrakirti goes on reciting other Mahayana scriptures to show how the sacred canopy, including the forest of ontic entities, is symptomatic of the ego's feverish anxiety (*paridaha*) with regard to identity, religious identity. Honest to the therapeutic vocation involved in "Tathagata," Chandrakirti demands that ontological language be brought to the streets for cross-examination (*prasanga*). There in the streets, and in ordinary language, human beings should witness the psychosomatic (*nama-rupa*) genesis of the theandrics of their own minds. They should realize that the limit of thinkability and speakability, of the "unthought" and the "unspoken," is the limit of their own bodies (*phassay-atanadini vuttani*).

Religiously speaking, enlightenment consists in acknowledging the fact that onto-theological commitments, belonging to religious flags and traditions, is symptomatic of a humanity that is out to circumcise its perpetual childhood into adulthood, into the postlogical collective egology.[30] Honest to "Tathagata," Chandrakirti suggests that humanity be a lamp unto itself, that it grow up to overcome the childhood confidence in a Buddha, no matter how cosmic. There is nothing else except the lamp of self-psychoanalytic encounter (*nidanavada*) at the Madhyamika Buddhist window. Chandrakirti would love to belong to an interreligious city in which residents live through a life of meditative celebrations (*dhyanasukhavihara*). After all, how could humanity be a witness of anything other than humanity, and how can anything other than humanity be a witness of humanity?[31]

NOTES

1. *"Ragakoti bhayabhita viragakotim nihsaranam"* (Chandrakirti, *Prasannapada* [Darabhanga: Milhila Institute, 1960], p. 203).
2. Raimundo Panikkar, *Myth, Faith and Hermeneutic* (New York: Paulist Press, 1979), p. 333.
3. Ibid., p. 330.
4. Ibid., p. 325.
5. Plato, *Euthyphro, Apology and Crito* (New York: Library of Liberal Arts, 1956), p. 17.
6. Ibid., p. 18.
7. See William Angell and Robert Helm, *Meaning and Value in Western Thought* (Washington, D.C.: University Press of America, 1981), p. 80.
8. Raimundo Panikkar, "Faith and Belief: A Multireligious Experience," *Anglican Review,* 53 (1971) 220.
9. *"Pramanato'rtha pratipattav"* (P. P. Shastri, ed., *Nyaya Darsanam* [Varanasi: Chowkhambha, 1970], pp. 1–3).

10. *"Pradipah sarva vidyanam"* (ibid., p. 15).

11. Ibid., p. 2.

12. *"Tattvajnanam nihsreyasadhigamasca"* (ibid., p. 15).

13. Nagarjuna, *Vaidalyasutram* (Varanasi: Tibetan Center, 1974), p. 27.

14. *"Kama janami te mulam"* (*Chandrakirti, Prasannapada,* p. 149).

15. *"Atmiyakara grahana pravrtta"* (ibid., p. 198); *"Vasti nibandhana iti prapanca syuh"* (ibid., p. 195).

16. Ibid., p. 236

17. *"Tathagato hi pratibimba bhutah"* (ibid., p. 236).

18. Ibid., p.92.

19. *"Abhisamskaroti kayena vaca manasa"* (ibid., p. 129).

20. *"Mohanam mohah sammoha padartha svarupa vijnanam"* (ibid., p. 199).

21. *"Chitramanourama sajjitapuspah svarma-vimana jalanti manojnah"* (ibid., p. 80).

22. *"Te strinimittam kalpayitva"* (ibid., p. 17).

23. Ibid., p. 192.

24. Ibid., pp. 217 and 5.

25. *"Aham samsaram samatikramisyami"* (ibid., p. 129).

26. Ibid., p. 17.

27. Ibid., pp. 6–7.

28. *"Krandet socet paridevet"* (ibid., p. 17).

29. *"Na tvamito grhat kutasca nirgatah"* (ibid., p. 17).

30. *"Ghanataro mahabhinivesena"* (ibid., p. 194).

31. *"Ko nu naka paro bhavet"* (*Dhammapada,* quoted in ibid., p. 151).

IV.

Christianity and World Religions: Dialogue with Islam

HANS KÜNG

I am happy to see again leading figures in interreligious dialogue who—long before I entered this field—have done so much pioneering work: John Cobb in Christian-Buddhist dialogue; Raimundo Panikkar in Christian-Hindu dialogue; and the "elder statesman," whom I was especially eager to meet, Wilfred Cantwell Smith. Professor Smith has done more than anyone else to promote what this conference calls "a universal theology of religion," an encounter of different religions, especially from a Christian perspective.

This year is also the one hundredth anniversary of Temple University. This symposium, I believe, is probably the most suitable way to celebrate such a centennial. I recall another centennial of another university where a conference like this was also held. It was the centennial of the American University in Beirut, almost twenty years ago, to which I was invited, along with Cardinal Willebrands, head of the Roman Secretariat for Christian Unity, and Dr. Visser't Hooft, then secretary general and now honorary president of the World Council of Churches.

There were, however, significant differences between the two conferences. At Beirut we Christian theologians met one week, and Muslim theologians— invited from all over the world—met another week. I asked the president of the conference (who was the former president of the United Nations General Assembly), Charles Malik, foreign secretary of Lebanon at that time, whether it would not be possible to meet with the Muslim scholars; in the end, however, it was so arranged that we did not meet. Today I am convinced that if a serious dialogue between Christians and Muslims would have been started twenty years ago, Muslims (who were already *then* practically the majority in Lebanon) would have long since received the rights that are still being fought over after thousands and thousands of victims. I think Lebanon could have remained what it was then called—"the Switzerland of the Near East"—a beautiful, happy country, whereas today many sections of the capital are destroyed, hostility is rife, and much of the land is occupied by Syrians, Palestinians, and Israelis—a real *catastrophe*.

Thus, when we speak about interreligious dialogue, it is not just a matter of a few theologians debating some abstract questions. I am convinced that the Vietnam war was, behind the scenes, also heavily grounded in religious antagonism, in that case between Buddhists—Buddhist monks especially—and the Catholic regime of Diem and his princes, together with the colonial powers. And I am also convinced that the antagonism between India and Pakistan, the war between Iraq and Iran, and the whole situation in the Middle East are largely grounded in religious antagonisms. I am, of course, well aware that these conflicts are not just a matter of religion; there are also political, military, economic, and social aspects. Yet battles and wars become fanatical when they have a religious base. We in Europe have enough experience of what it means to conduct "religious wars."

I am convinced it would be possible to avoid this kind of war. I am not an illusionary; I have seen it happen in Europe. After having had several hundred years of wars between Germany and France, Germany and Poland, but especially Germany and France—the origin of World War I and World War II—religiously committed persons after World War II said, "Enough!" (In this case, they were Christians, but I am sure that persons like Gandhi and others from other faiths would have said the same thing.) I am convinced that it could have been done because at that time we had not only technocrats in European governmental agencies (as we have them now in Brussels), but also the likes of Konrad Adenauer, Robert Schuman, Charles DeGaulle, Alcide DeGasperi, and others who, because of ethical and religious convictions, thought that we must put an end to warfare. One of the greatest achievements of this century, I believe, was to bring together nations that had considered themselves hereditary enemies.

So why should it not be possible—of course with adequate preparation—to do this also in the Near East? Somebody must make the effort. We must urge what I proposed to Muslims in Lebanon, to Christians in Lebanon, and to Israelis in their Foreign Ministry: they must begin something like a "trilateral" conversation, a "trialogue," as it is called. Of course, it will demand sacrifices; persons are needed who will commit themselves even when it is very dangerous.

I remember the story the former chancellor of the Federal Republic of Germany, Helmut Schmidt, told me of his trip down the Nile with Anwar Sadat. Sadat, then president of Egypt, said that he was convinced that there would never be peace in the Near East without having peace among the religions, and that was why he wanted to establish a common sanctuary for Jews, Christians, and Muslims.

Hence, I would very willingly subscribe to what Wilfred Cantwell Smith has said at this conference about the religious dimensions of all history. It is our intellectual error not to see those dimensions, and I think that this error has been committed especially by politicians. This error has also been committed by many development experts—all those Western advisors, Europeans and Americans, who, for instance, advised the shah of Iran not to bother with the religious dimension, because they themselves did not think it important. They thought only about technocratic problems—and we have seen what has resulted.

My thesis, therefore, is: no world peace without peace among religions, no peace among religions without dialogue between the religions, and no dialogue between the religions without accurate knowledge of one another. This is one reason why we are assembled here. We can no longer regard the world religions simply as existing side by side; rather we must view them together—in interdependence and in interaction. Today, no religion can live in splendid isolation.

I am well aware of the fact that there will always be persons (in certain religions more than in others) who will ask, "Why should we talk to each other?" I asked a European specialist of the Arab world why should we talk to each other, and what, in his opinion, the solution is for Jerusalem. He was quite candid when he said, "War." I believe that this is indeed the alternative to religious dialogue: war. I told him that we had already had a number of wars—without resolving anything. I am convinced that interreligious dialogue is of the greatest importance not just for politicians concerned with conflicts in the Near East, but for all human beings involved in the ordinary business of life.

Another element that should concern us in this issue is the fact that out of every six persons in the world, one is Muslim and two are Christian. This is one of the reasons why I have chosen the encounter between Christianity and Islam as a model for interreligious dialogue. I could also talk about the encounter between Christianity and Hinduism, or Christianity and Buddhism, though of course the approach would have to be different, because these religions are so different. These dialogues are especially important for us Americans and Europeans, partly because Hinduism and Buddhism still are for us largely unknown universes. We have not had direct conflict with these Eastern religions, whereas the history of Europe, since the seventh century, has also been a history of conflict with Muslims. This must be borne in mind today in a period of re-Islamization as a fundamental reason for the pressing need of dialogue with Muslims.

Dialogue with Muslims? Who is ready in Islam to have dialogue? Perhaps Khomeini? I have met Muslims all over the world who find recent developments in Iran catastrophic; such developments, they feel, are blocking mutual understanding and are propagating prejudice against Islam. I believe, however, that it is precisely at *this* time that we need to talk about our relationship to Islam, and not simply to think about the terrible things that have happened in Iran. Such events should not deter us. I am convinced—without going into detail here—that the present situation in Iran is ultimately an episode (as was the "reign of terror" within the French revolution), after which a process of normalization will begin. But it is important that we now actively prepare for that process and not just wait for it to happen.

I now want to speak as a theologian. I am not speaking as a politician, nor as a specialist in comparative religion. I have studied many religions, talked to many of their adherents, and visited many of their countries. However, as a theologian, I have to answer a particular question: How can Christians today come to terms with the claims made by the Muslim faith? I shall take up questions that will help us to thoroughly examine our altered ecumenical stance toward other world religions in general, with a view to greater broadmindedness and openness; and I shall try to focus the questions so that they will help us to reread our own history of theological thought and faith against the background of Islam. I do this as a Christian theologian; from my Christian basis, I want to take other religions seriously.

To a great extent Christians still regard Islam as a rigid entity, a closed religious system, rather than a living religion, a religious movement that has been continually changing through the centuries, developing great inner variety, all the time shared by real persons with a wide spectrum of attitudes and feelings. I think no one has done more than Wilfred Cantwell Smith to make it clear that Islam is not just a system of the past or a collection of theories we have to study, but a reality today; Professor Smith has urged us to make an attempt to understand *from the inside* why Muslims see God and the world, service to God and to their fellows, politics, law, and art with different eyes, why they experience these things with different feelings from those of Christians. Keeping Iran in mind, we must first grasp the fact that even today the Islamic religion is not just another strand in the life of a Muslim, what secularized persons like to refer to as the "religious factor" or "sector" alongside other "cultural factors" or "sectors." No, life and religion, religion and culture, are dynamically interwoven. Islam strives to be an all-embracing view, an all-encompassing perspective on life, an all-determining way of life— and so in the midst of this life a way to eternal life. Islam is referred to as paradise, salvation, liberation, redemption, but it is not just a way in this life, with the focus on only the here and now. This leads to one of the eight questions I should like to raise—and they are all very delicate questions.

1. ISLAM—A WAY OF SALVATION? OF ETERNAL SALVATION?

I pose the following question (not least because of the ambivalent attitude of the World Council of Churches, which, due to the conflicting standpoints of its member churches, chose not to answer it even in its 1979 "Guidelines for Dialogue with People of Different Religions and Ideologies"): Can there be salvation outside the Christian churches, outside Christianity? This is a question of great urgency today, because if we think Muslims are going to hell anyway, it is not really worthwhile to engage in a dialogue with them. Thus I do not understand why the WCC does not speak out on this matter.

The *traditional Catholic* position, as forged in the first centuries of the

Christian church by Origen, Cyprian, and Augustine, is generally well known: *extra ecclesiam nulla salus*. No salvation outside the church. Thus for the future as well: *extra ecclesiam nullus propheta*. No prophet outside the church. The Ecumenical Council of Florence in 1442 defined this very clearly:

> The Holy Church of Rome . . . believes firmly, confesses and proclaims, that no one outside the Catholic Church, neither heathen nor Jew nor unbeliever, nor one who is separated from the Church, will share in eternal life, but will perish in the eternal fire prepared for the devil and his angels, if this person fails to join it [the Catholic Church] before death [Denz. 714].

Does that not settle the claim of Islam, at least for Catholics? It seems to have done so for more than five hundred years.

Today, at any rate, the *traditional* Catholic position is no longer the *official* Catholic position. We cannot change the words, because the conciliar statement was, indeed, an infallible definition, but we are allowed to say the contrary! The Second Vatican Council declared unmistakably in its "Constitution on the Church" that "those who, through no fault of their own, do not know the Gospel of Christ or his Church, but who nevertheless seek God with a sincere heart and, moved by grace, try in their actions to do his will as they know it through the dictates of their conscience—they too may achieve eternal salvation" (Art. 16). This is valid even for atheists of good will.

Particular mention is given by Vatican II to those who, due to their background, have the most in common with Jews and Christians through their faith in the one God and in doing God's will: Muslims. "But the plan of salvation also includes those who acknowledge the Creator, in the first place among whom are the Muslims: they profess to hold the faith of Abraham, and together with us they adore the one, merciful God, the judge of humanity on the last day" (ibid.). Thus, according to Vatican II, even Muslims need not "perish in that eternal fire prepared for the devil and his angels"—they can "achieve eternal salvation." That means that Islam, too, can be a way of salvation.

The next problem is, what about prophets? The "Constitution on the Church" and the "Declaration on Non-Christian Religions" mention Islam but do not mention Muhammad. So I turn to my second question.

2. MUHAMMAD—A PROPHET?

Of course many religions do not have prophets in the strictest sense. Hindus have their gurus and sadhus, the Chinese their sages, Buddhists their masters— but they do not have prophets, as do Jews, Christians, and Muslims. There is no doubt that if anyone in the whole of religious history is termed *the* prophet, because he claimed to be *just that*, but in no way *more* than that, it was Muhammad. But may a Christian assert that Muhammad was a prophet?

Christians, if they pause to survey the situation, must admit the following (especially in light of the Hebrew Bible):

• Like the prophets of Israel, Muhammad did not function by reason of an office assigned to him by the community (or its authorities), but by reason of a special personal relationship with God.

• Like the prophets of Israel, Muhammad was a person of strong will who felt himself fully imbued with a godly calling, fully consumed, exclusively appointed to his task.

• Like the prophets of Israel, Muhammad spoke to the heart of a religious and social crisis, and with his passionate piety and revolutionary proclamation he opposed the wealthy ruling class and the tradition it was trying to preserve.

• Like the prophets of Israel, Muhammad, who mostly called himself the "Warner," sought to be nothing but the verbal instrument of God and to proclaim not his own, but God's, word.

• Like the prophets of Israel, Muhammad untiringly proclaimed the one God who tolerates no other gods and who is at the same time the good Creator and merciful Judge.

• Like the prophets of Israel, Muhammad required, as a response to this one God, unconditional obedience, devotion, submission, which is the literal meaning of the word *Islam*: everything that includes gratitude to God and generosity toward fellow human beings.

• Like the prophets of Israel, Muhammad combined monotheism with humanism or human values, belief in the one God and God's judgment with a call to social justice, and a threat to the unjust, who go to hell, with promises to the just, who are gathered into God's paradise.

Whoever reads the Bible—at least the Hebrew Bible—together with the Qur'ān will be led to ponder whether the three Semitic *religions of revelation*—Judaism, Christianity, and Islam—and especially the Hebrew Bible and the Qur'ān, could have *the same foundation.* Is it not one and the same God who speaks so clearly in both? Does not the "Thus says the Lord" of the Hebrew Bible correspond to the "Speak" of the Qur'ān, and the "Go and proclaim" of the Hebrew Bible to the "Stand up and warn" of the Qur'ān? In truth, even the millions of Arab-speaking Christians have no other word for God than "Al-lāh."

Might it not therefore be purely dogmatic prejudice that recognizes Amos and Hosea, Isaiah and Jeremiah, as prophets, but not Muhammad? Whatever one may have against Muhammad from the standpoint of Western Christian morality (armed violence, polygamy, a sensual lifestyle for males), the following facts are indisputable:

• Today there are almost eight hundred million persons in the huge area between Morocco to the west and Bangladesh to the east, between the steppes of central Asia to the north and the island world of Indonesia to the south, who are stamped with the compelling power of a faith that, like virtually no other faith, has molded into a universal type those who confess it.

• All those persons are linked by a simple confession of faith (There is no

God but God, and Muhammad is his prophet), linked by five basic obligations, and linked by thorough submission to the will of God, whose unchangeable decision, even when it brings suffering, is to be accepted.

• Among all the Islamic peoples there has remained a sense of fundamental equality before God and of an international solidarity that is basically capable of overcoming race (Arabs and non-Arabs) and even the castes of India.

I am convinced that, despite all the renewed fears of Islam, there is a growing conviction among Christians that, in the light of Muhammad's place in world history, we must correct our attitude toward Islam. The "scourge of exclusiveness," arising from Christian dogmatic impatience and intolerance, condemned by the British historian Arnold Toynbee, must be abandoned. Regarding the figure of the prophet, I believe the following must be admitted:

• Arabians in the seventh century rightly listened to and followed the voice of Muhammad.

• In comparison to the very worldly polytheism of the old Arabian tribal religions before Muhammad, the religion of the people was raised to a completely new level, that of a purified monotheism.

• The first Muslims received from Muhammad—or, better still, from the Qur'ān—endless inspiration, courage, and strength for a new religious start: a start toward greater truth and deeper understanding, toward a breakthrough in the revitalizing and renewal of traditional religion.

In truth, Muhammad was and is for persons in the Arabian world, and for many others, *the* religious reformer, lawgiver, and leader; *the* prophet *per se.* Basically Muhammad, who never claimed to be anything more than a human being, is more to those who follow him than a prophet is to us: he is a model for the mode of life that Islam strives to be. If the Catholic Church, according to the Vatican II "Declaration on Non-Christian Religions," "regards with esteem the Muslims," then the same church must also respect the one whose name is embarrassingly absent from the same declaration, although he and he alone led the Muslims to pray to this one God, for through him this God "has spoken to humanity": Muhammad the prophet. But does not such an acknowledgment have very grave consequences, especially for the message he proclaimed, the teachings set down in the Qur'ān?

I think for the peoples of Arabia Muhammad's prophecy led to tremendous progress. Whatever we Christians do with this fact, we must affirm that he acted as a prophet and that he was a prophet. I do not see how we can avoid the conclusion that on their way of salvation, Muslims follow a prophet who is decisive for them. This leads us to an even more difficult question. If he is the prophet, what, then, about the Qur'ān?

3. THE QUR'ĀN—WORD OF GOD?

The Qur'ān is more than an oral tradition, which can be easily altered. It is a *written* record, set down once for all time; it cannot be altered. In this respect it is similar to the Bible. Because of its written form, the Qur'ān has retained a remarkable constancy from century to century, from generation to generation, from person to person, despite the changes and variety in Islamic history. What is written is written. Despite all the different interpretations and commentaries, despite all the forms taken by Islamic law (the *shari'ah*), the Qur'ān remains the common denominator, something like the "green thread" of the prophet in all Islamic forms, rituals, and institutions. One who wishes to know not only historical Islam, but also *normative* Islam, must, still today, return to the Qur'ān of the seventh century.

Although the Qur'ān in no way predetermined the development of Islam, it most certainly inspired it. Commentators came and went, but the Qur'ān remained a source of inspiration. Commentators came and went, but the Qur'ān remained intact. It is the one great constant in Islam amid all the countless variables. It provided Islam with moral obligation, external dynamism, and religious depth, as well as with specific enduring doctrines and moral principles: the responsibility of the individual before God, social justice, and Muslim solidarity. The Qur'ān is *the* holy book of Islam; it is understood to be, in its written form, not the word of a human, but the word of *God*. For Muslims, God's word became a book. Our question is: Is this book really the word of God?

Here we can turn to Wilfred Cantwell Smith who was one of the first to focus this question concerning the authorship of the Qur'ān. For centuries this question was never posed as a serious issue. It would have threatened with excommunication Muslims as well as Christians—the former if they had doubted it, the latter if they had affirmed it. And who can deny that this question has caused deep political divisions among the peoples of the world, from the first Islamic conquests in the seventh century to the Crusades and the capture of Constantinople, to the siege of Vienna in modern times and the Iranian revolution under Khomeini. Just as naturally as Muslims from West Africa to central Asia and Indonesia have answered this question affirmatively and have oriented their lives according to the Qur'ān, so believing Christians all over the world have said no. This negation was later restated by secular Western scholars of comparative religion who took it for granted that the Qur'ān was not at all the word of God, but wholly that of Muhammad.

In 1962 Wilfred Cantwell Smith posed this question in clear terms, threatening though it was for both sides. I cannot but agree with his assertion that the two possible answers, both of which were supported by intelligent, critical, and thoroughly honest persons, in fact relied upon an unquestioned, insistent *preconviction*. On both sides, the opposite viewpoint was seen as either superstitious or lacking in faith.

Is it true then, as Smith's Canadian colleague and my friend Willard Oxtoby claims, that a rule of thumb in the study of religions is that "you get out what you put in"? In other words, is it true that those who regard the Qur'ān as the word of God from the start will repeatedly see their conviction confirmed in reading it, and vice versa?

Can we allow this contradiction between Muslims and Christians to perdure, unsatisfactory as it is from an intellectual standpoint? Are there not increasing numbers of Christians and Muslims who have become better informed about the faith of others and about their own position, and who are, therefore, posing self-critical questions? Let me outline the situation from both points of view.

a) *Self-critical questioning of an exclusively Christian understanding of revelation.* This, of course, is a very delicate question for us. Many Christians are not ready to face this question, but are content to let the great majority of humanity be consigned to hell. It must be recalled, however, that Adam was not the first Jew, but the first human being. And the first covenant was not with the people of Israel, but with the whole of humanity. In contemporary religious literature, besides talk of erroneousness, benightedness, and guilt, there is a wealth of positive statements about the world outside Israel, in the distant past, and outside Christianity, since then. The thinking behind these positive statements is that originally God bestowed self-revelation upon the whole of humanity. Indeed, both the Hebrew Bible and the New Testament teach that non-Jews and non-Christians can also know the true God (I cannot go into details here). These texts explain this possibility in terms of the revelation of God in creation.

Considering this biblical background, and reading it now to see what we could learn for our time, we cannot exclude the possibility that countless persons in the past and in the present have experienced, and are experiencing, the mystery of God on the basis of the revelation of God in creation, and that such experience involves the grace of God and true religious faith. And we cannot exclude the possibility that in this context certain individuals have also, within the bounds of their religion, been endowed with special insight, entrusted with a special task, a special charism.

Many Christians do not realize that the Catholic Church has excluded as an error the claim that outside the church there is no salvation, no grace. By implication, there *is* grace outside the church. There can be special charisms outside the church. How, then, can we deny that outside the church there also are persons who have such charisms, including prophetic gifts? *Extra ecclesiam gratia!* If we recognize Muhammad as a prophet, to be consistent we must also admit that the message of Muhammad was not of his own making; the Qur'ān is not simply the word of Muhammad, but the *Word of God.* And the Qur'ān is much more important for Muslims than is the prophet!

b) *Self-critical questioning of the Islamic interpretation of the Qur'ān.* I come now to the hardest point in discussion with Muslims. It is a question that applies, uncomfortably, to both sides, but it must be faced. The question concerns the Qur'ān (or the Bible) as the word of God. That the Qur'ān is the word of God I do not contest. However, there is the further question: *How* is the Qur'ān (or the Bible) the word of God? Does revelation directly fall from heaven, so to speak? Is it, as some maintain, dictated word for word by God? Is there nothing human in this word of God? It must be remembered that not only

Muslims believe this; fundamentalist Christians look upon the Bible in the same way. The fundamentalist Christian says: All this is dictated by God, from the first phrase to the last. There is nothing that changes, nothing to interpret. Everything is clear.

Today it is important that the Qur'ān as the word of God be seen in its historical context. Many Muslims would tell me that it is blasphemy to think that this word of God could also at the same time be the word of a human being. I would answer only in a provisional way. When the first Jew asked this about the Hebrew Bible, he was excommunicated; this was Spinoza, the seventeenth-century Jewish philosopher in Amsterdam, who started critical exegesis of the Bible. The first Catholic to raise this question was a disciple of rabbis in Paris at the time of Bossuet, also in the seventeenth century. He was exiled and had to publish his books in Amsterdam. That was Richard Simon. Thus the Catholic Church missed the chance to formulate a critical approach to the Bible as early as the seventeenth century. Reimarus, the first Protestant to propose a critical approach to scripture, also had the greatest of troubles, in Germany, and as a matter of fact did not even dare to publish his work. The great poet Lessing published it after Reimarus's death, claiming that, although it was not his own view, it was worthy of discussion. Later on, Lessing admitted that he shared Reimarus's views, and he was told not to speak of it further.

So who would be surprised if today in Islam there are similar reactions? It is dangerous to take up this matter publicly. But I know that Muslim students say in private what they will not say in public. I am accustomed to such a situation in the Catholic Church, having raised the same questions for Christians that I am proposing for my Muslim friends.

This is, then, not only a question for Muslims. Is it really contrary to the word of God if we say that this word is at the same time the word of a human being and that it has been influenced by a human medium? There are a few Muslims, like the Pakistani Fazlur Rahman at the University of Chicago, who entertain such thoughts and provide supporting evidence from Islamic tradition. Such scholars are often attacked by orthodox Muslims, as was Rahman, who was even forced to flee his own country. This question, however, cannot be suppressed. If even the Catholic Church, with all its organization and power, was unable to suppress the issue, neither will Islam be able to do so, for Islam does not even have a magisterium or a Holy Office. (In Islam it is mainly the masses of the believers who can prove to be threatening and dangerous.)

Is it not possible to understand and experience the Qur'ān as a great witness to the all-merciful God, as Muslims do, without viewing it as *dictated* by God? Such an understanding would also be a help in dealing with the question of capital punishment and other issues that *have* to be changed, and not only by reinterpretation but by admitting that certain practices that were necessary or meaningful in a past historical context are no longer fitting for our present context.

4. WHAT ARE THE MAIN COMMON ELEMENTS
AMONG MUSLIMS, JEWS, AND CHRISTIANS?

a) The basic common area among Muslims, Jews, and Christians is found in their faith in *one and only one God*, who gives meaning and life to all.

b) Jews, Christians, and Muslims are also of one mind in their belief in the *God of history*—the God who is not *above*, but *in*, history, intervening, calling in a hidden way.

c) Jews, Christians, and Muslims agree in their belief that the one God is an approachable partner. God can be addressed.

d) Finally, this God is a *merciful and gracious God*. The Arabic *al-Rahmān,* the "merciful one," is etymologically linked to the Hebraic *rahamim*, which, together with *hen* and *hesed*, represents the semantic field for the New Testament *charis*, the Vulgate *gratia,* and the English "grace." This shared belief has a political relevance. I have been told that for the Camp David Agreement it was not unimportant that a believing Christian, a believing Jew, and a believing Muslim came together and saw that they finally had to do something for world peace.

These shared beliefs clear the way for more difficult questions.

5. IS THE QUR'ĀN PORTRAYAL OF JESUS ACCURATE?

It is well known that the Qur'ān speaks of Jesus of Nazareth, and always in a positive manner. This is astonishing when one considers the very different attitude of Jewish sources and also the centuries-old history of hatred and vilification between Christianity and Islam. How can we assess these passages theologically? A close examination of the texts of the Qur'ān relevant to Christianity reveals that all the material concerning Jesus found in the Qur'ān is integrated *in a fully coherent manner into the whole theological conception of the Qur'ān.* From whatever tradition this testimony to Jesus may stem—and I shall go into this more closely—the whole is conspicuously permeated with the spirit of Islam, with Muhammad's intense prophetic experience of the one God. On the basis of this experience, Muhammad had no cause whatsoever to contradict Jesus (in fact he *does not* contradict him): the preaching of Jesus he makes his own, and both the virgin birth and miracles are acknowledged without envy by the prophet. There is but one disclaimer: Jesus may not be made into a god; he may not be put alongside the one God as a second deity. For Islam, that would be the ultimate abomination.

The position of Jesus in the Qur'ān is unambiguous. Dialogue is therefore not aided by contemporary well-meaning Christians who read more into the Qur'ān than it contains, claiming that in the Qur'ān Jesus is called the "Word" of God. For the Qur'ān, however, he is not the Word of God in the sense of the prologue of John's Gospel, in which the preexistent divine *logos* became flesh. If the Qur'ān acknowledges the virgin birth of Jesus, it is a sign of God's omnipotence, but emphatically not a sign of the deity of Jesus.

In other words, for the Qur'ān Jesus is a prophet, a greater prophet than Abraham, Noah, and Moses—but certainly not more than a prophet. Further, just as in the New Testament John the Baptist is the forerunner of Jesus, so in the Qur'ān Jesus is the forerunner of, and undoubtably the encouraging example for, Muhammad. According to the Qur'ān, Jesus was created directly by God as a second Adam (this is the meaning of the virgin birth), unlike the Prophet.

For this reason, Christians should avoid wanting to make "anonymous Christians" of Muhammad and Muslims, as some theologians (among them my friend Karl Rahner) have attempted; such attempts run counter to the Muslims' understanding of themselves. We must never give others names they cannot apply to themselves. If we call them "anonymous Christians," then we also should be willing to be called "anonymous Muslims." Then of course there arises the question, whether Muslims would not like to make Jesus an anonymous Muslim.

If we who represent Christianity concern ourselves with a revaluation of Muhammad on the basis of Islamic sources, especially the Qur'ān, we hope that Muslims might eventually do what Jews have begun to do: Jewish scholars have started to study Jesus, to do research on him. Our hope is that in time Muslim scholars also will consider the historical sources and will come to a revaluation of Jesus of Nazareth on the basis of those sources—that is, the Gospels themselves.

The portrait of Jesus in the Qur'ān, I would say, is too one-sided, too monotone, for the most part lacking in content; in the Qur'ān Jesus simply proclaims monotheism, calls to repentance, and performs miracles. This is a weak, one-dimensional picture in comparison, for example, with the Jesus of the Sermon on the Mount. Precisely because legalism is a central problem in both Judaism and Islam, it is important to examine Jesus' position concerning the law and legalism; he was, after all, executed because of his stand against legalism. According to Islam, Jesus did not really die; he simply was assumed into heaven. It is, however, important to recognize that according to the original sources of the first century he really did die. We must, I believe, rely on these sources. I am aware that it is said, "But Muhammad received his revelation directly from God." Here again we have a historical problem.

6. WHAT IS THE CENTRAL THEOLOGICAL DIFFERENCE?

The focal concern of Jesus himself was to overcome legalism by fulfilling the will of God in love, in view of the coming reign of God. For the Christian church, however—and here we come to the decisive difficulty—the focal concern slowly shifted from the reign of God to the person of Jesus and his relationship with God. The debate between Christianity and Islam remains focused on this question. Up to now, the decisive Christian objection to Islam has been that Islam disputes the two related central doctrines of Christianity: the *Trinity* and the *incarnation*. Indeed, the Qur'ān addresses Christians:

People of the Book, do not transgress the bounds of your religion. Speak nothing but the truth about Allāh. The Messiah, Jesus, the son of Mary, was no more than Allāh's apostle and his Word, which he cast into Mary: a spirit from him. So believe in Allāh and his apostles and do not say [of Allāh, that he is] "three." Allāh is but one God. Allāh forbid that He should have a son! [sura 4:171].

Furthermore, there is no truth in the assertion of Christian apologists and many scholars of religion that Muslim theologians have always misinterpreted the Christian doctrine of the Trinity (three in one) as a doctrine of tritheism (three gods). There is a certain misunderstanding of the Trinity in the Qur'ān, I believe, but that is not so important. As early as the medieval controversies there were many Muslim theologians who understood the Christian doctrine quite well. But they were simply not able to understand what the Jews as well could not grasp: that when there is one godhead, one divine nature, the recognition of three persons in one God does not automatically lead to the relinquishing of that faith in one God that Abraham stood for, and Moses, and Jesus, and finally Muhammad also.

Why distinguish at all between nature and person in God? It is obvious that the *distinctions* between one and three made by the Christian doctrine of the Trinity do not satisfy Muslims. All these concepts of Syrian, Greek, and Latin origin are more confusing to them than enlightening, a game of words and concepts. How can the one and only God, asks the Muslim, be a conglomeration of hypostases, persons, processions, and relations? Why all the dialectical tricks? Is not God simply God, "combined" neither in this way nor that?

According to the Qur'ān, "Unbelievers are those who say, 'God is one of three' [or 'three-faced']." This viewpoint, which was completely unacceptable to Muhammad, is flatly rejected by the statement, "There is but one God" (sura 5:73). This brings me to my seventh question.

7. HOW ARE WE TO ASSESS THE CENTRAL THEOLOGICAL DIFFERENCE?

That which applies to the doctrine of the Trinity applies also to christology. I think that today if Christians and Muslims (and Jews as well) wish to come to a better mutual understanding, they must *return to the sources* and then look critically at all subsequent developments.

I know this is a difficult point, especially to our Orthodox Christian brethren, who do not want to go back behind the councils of the fourth and fifth centuries to the New Testament. It is not merely for archeological reasons that we should want to go back; all the churches, including the Orthodox churches, are founded—as all the fathers of the church say—"on the New Testament." When the term *homoousios* was objected to, because it was not in the Bible, Athanasius said, "Read the Bible and then you will understand it correctly." Read the Bible, read the New Testament, and the relationship between Father, Son, and Spirit will be more understandable—and it will become clear that the dogmas of the fourth and fifth and seventh centuries are not a little different from what was said about Father, Son, and Spirit in the New Testament. It can also be shown that what was said about Jesus in the beginning was somewhat different and may be easier to understand than what was said in Greek in the fourth and fifth centuries.

I acknowledge the intentions of those councils and their decisive content, but I also understand that for persons not educated in this tradition, who do not understand *hypostasis, physis, homoousios, homoiousios, homoousios kata panta*, this language can be not just mysterious but meaningless. So it makes sense to ask how the first disciples, who were Jews, understood Jesus. Such a question opens many complex but fruitful issues. In the beginning our church was a church of Jews. Then it became a church of Jews and gentiles, but what remained finally was a church of gentiles. Where are the Jewish Christians today? I met one recently at Harvard. He came to me after my lecture and said, "I am so grateful that you spoke about Jewish Christians"—he had become one.

It is unfortunate that after the destruction of Jerusalem under the Emperor Hadrian in the year 132 and the flight of all Jewish Christians to the East, the growing church was almost completely uprooted from its Jewish soil. The gentile, Hellenistic Christians did not really care. I do not want to blame them; we probably would have done the same thing. The whole Roman empire despised Jews, and gentile Christians despised Jewish Christians. It was rather sickening; but they "knew not what they were doing." Though difficult and delicate, this question of the early Jewish Christians must today be reexamined.

I have found that some scholarly research has been done, but it had been completely silenced, especially in dogmatics, both in Eastern Orthodox churches as well as in Catholic and Protestant churches. In fact, the picture of Jesus in the Qur'ān may well have had something to do with the Jewish Christians. Muslims, of course, traditionally say that the quranic depiction of Jesus had nothing to do with human factors; it was all dictated by God. I have respect for this—a conviction of faith—but from a historical approach to the Qur'ān, further questions arise. The picture of Jesus in the Qur'ān, because it is a sympathetic picture, cannot come from orthodox Christianity, for the Qur'ān continually protests against orthodox christology. So where does the picture come from? There is an evident, though surprising, answer. The picture of Jesus in the Qur'ān is very analogous to the picture of Jesus in Judeo-Christianity.

It is difficult to prove historico-genetic links between the two pictures, for we do not know much about the Arabian peninsula before Muhammad. I would, however, like to quote a famous—and conservative—Protestant exegete, Adolf Schlatter of Tübingen, who as early as 1926 had traced connections between gentile Christianity, Jewish Christianity, and Islam:

The Jewish-Christian church died out in Palestine only *west* of the Jordan ["West Bank" we say today]. Christian communities with Jewish practice continued to exist in the *eastern* regions, in the Decapolis, in the Batanaea, among the Nabataeans, at the edge of the Syrian desert and into Arabia, completely cut off from the rest of Christendom and without fellowship with it. . . . For the Christian of this time, the Jew was simply an enemy, and the Greek attitude, which overlooked the murders by the generals Trajan and Hadrian, as if they were the well-earned fate of the evil and contemptuous Jews, was accepted by the church as well. Even leading figures, such as Origen and Eusebius, remained astonishingly ignorant about the end of Jerusalem and of the church there. In the same way, the information they give us concerning the Jewish [i.e., Judeo-Christian] church in its continued existence is scanty. The Jewish Christians were heretics because they would not submit to the law that applied to the rest of Christendom and were therefore cut off from that body. None of the leaders of the imperial church guessed that this Jewish Christendom, which they held in contempt, would someday shake the world and cause a large part of the dominion of the church to break away. [Here Schlatter plays the prophet:] That day came when Muhammad took over many of the beliefs preserved by Jewish Christians—their awareness of God, their eschatology with its proclamation of the Day of Judgment, their customs and legends—and launched a new mission as "the one sent from God."[1]

Is Muhammad then, according to Schlatter, a "Judeo-Christian apostle" in Arabian dress? That is an astonishing claim, which Schlatter, incidentally, had substantiated as early as 1918 in an essay on the development of Jewish Christianity into Islam.[2] Forty years earlier, Adolf von Harnack had perceived the wider influence of Jewish Christianity on Islam, or more precisely of gnostic Jewish Christianity, and in particular of the Elkesites, who stood for strict monotheism and rejected the ecclesiastical teaching concerning *hypostasis* and "Son of God."[3]

Considering the present state of research, any direct dependence of Islam on Jewish Christianity will continue to be disputed. Yet the similarities are amazing. Muhammad rejected the orthodox (and Monophysitic) Son-of-God christology, yet accepted Jesus as the great "messenger" (*rasul*) of God, indeed as the "messiah" (*masih*) who brought the gospel. The Jewish scholar Hans-Joachim Schoeps (probably the foremost Jewish scholar on Judeo-Christianity) states:

Even though it is not possible to clearly establish the precise connection, there can be no doubt about Muhammad's indirect dependence on sectarian Judeo-Christianity. It remains one of the truly great paradoxes of world history that Jewish Christianity, cut off from the Christian church, has been preserved in Islam and so has been able, to this day, to continue its influence.[4]

Strangely enough, these pieces of historical knowledge have hardly been known in Christian theology up to now, let alone been taken seriously. There is still much to be investigated, such as the history of Muhammad's cousin-by-marriage, Waraqa, who was a Christian (probably speaking Hebrew, certainly not a Hellenistic Christian) and who according to the sources early drew Muhammad's attention to the relationship between his revelation experiences and those of Moses. Be that as it may, what we have here are previously unimagined possibilities for trilateral dialogue between Jews, Christians, and Muslims. Discussion of such matters will perhaps be uncomfortable in the beginning, but will eventually be of advantage to all concerned—for we need not be afraid of the truth.

In this context we must bear in mind that in his struggle against ancient Arabic polytheism, according to which Allāh had daughters and maybe also sons, Muhammad had no choice but to reject the heathen-sounding term "Son of God." This was polytheism. And yet Muhammad took up the story of Jesus as it was being circulated in Arabia at the time and gave it his own meaning. What had happened so often in the Bible now happened in the Qur'ān: an old tradition was not simply handed down; it was interpreted so as to make it relevant to contemporaneous experience. The same thing happened in the New Testament: just as Christians referred many elements ("prophecies") of the Hebrew Bible to Jesus, even though these passages originally meant something quite different, so Muhammad used much of what he had heard (probably not *read*) about Jesus to refer to his own time. For Muhammad, Jesus' greatness consisted in the fact that, in him and through him as the servant of God, God had been at work. Thus Muhammad's "christology" (if you wish) was not far removed from that of the Judeo-Christian church. What will be the ultimate consequences of all these new findings?

8. WHAT SHOULD MUSLIMS AND CHRISTIANS DO?

We are faced with a problem of extraordinary moment, the consequences of which are not yet visible. If the exegetical and historical data outlined above are accurate and open to further clarification, then both sides in the Muslim-Christian encounter are faced with the challenge to stop thinking in terms of alternatives—Jesus *or* Muhammad—and to begin thinking instead, despite all the limitations and differences, in terms of synthesis—Jesus *and* Muhammad. This does not mean that everything has to be put on the same level. We have to recognize that Muhammad himself wanted to be a witness to Jesus—not to a Jesus of the Hellenistic gentile Christians, but rather, to a Jesus as seen by his first disciples, who were Jews like Jesus himself.

As I already have pointed out, I have no intention of rejecting the early councils; rather, what needs to be done, in our contemporary ecumenical context, is to rethink what it means to call Jesus the Son of God or the Word of God. Inasmuch as today we have come to a new, and we think, clearer understanding of the concept "Son of God," perhaps we can better explain this belief to contemporary Jews and Muslims. So, with all due reservations and in the hope that others will join the discussion, let me try to comment, very briefly, on these two pivotal questions: How might a Muslim today view Jesus? How might a Christian understand Muhammad?

a) In what way might *Muslims* view *Jesus*?

According to the Qur'ān, Muslims already see Jesus as the great prophet and messenger of the one God, designated by God to be the "Servant of God" from his birth to his exaltation, as one who, along with the message he proclaimed, was of lasting importance to Muhammad.

Certainly, for Muslims, Muhammad and the Qur'ān remain the decisive guideline for faith and conduct, life and death. I do not expect Muslims to simply accept the Bible.

However, if in the Qur'ān Jesus is called the "Word" of God and bringer of the "gospel," should not Muslims try to gain a broader understanding of this gospel and take it seriously? Understood in the light of the message and conduct of Jesus, Islamic law, which is often characterized even by Muslims as oppressive, would perhaps receive a less stringent interpretation— commandments being given for persons, not persons for commandments. Also, in the light of Jesus' person and message, the Qur'ān could be interpreted in a way that would make for greater personal freedom—not from the law but from legalism, as was the case with Jewish Christians.

Furthermore, the picture of both the life and death of Jesus—and according to our earliest sources his death is undeniable—and of his new life with God and in God might enable Muslims to come to a deeper understanding of a God who lives and suffers with human beings. The death of Jesus, endured in the name of this very God, might provide meaning for suffering and failure, not only for success. Islam has been a religion of success; failure, however, is also a reality in human life.

b) How might *Christians* view *Muhammad*? Many Christians already look on him as a prophet of importance for many peoples of this earth, who was blessed with great success in his lifetime and throughout these subsequent centuries.

Certainly, for Christians, Jesus Christ and the good news he proclaimed are the decisive criteria for faith and conduct, life and death: the definitive Word of God (Heb. 1:1ff.). Thus Christ is and remains the *definitive regulating factor* for us Christians, for the sake of God and humanity.

However, insofar as Christians, following the New Testament, acknowledge the existence and value of prophets even after Christ, should they not take Muhammad and his message more seriously—especially because Muhammad understood himself to be part of the Judeo-Christian tradition?

Christians need to take Muhammad more seriously in order that the one, true, incomparable God might always occupy the center of their faith. I think my friend John Cobb would agree that Christocentrism without theocentrism is valueless, for Jesus is the Word and, as Cobb has stressed, the Wisdom of God. Christians also need to hear Muhammad's warning against the dangerous idolatry of listening to other gods, as well as his admonition that faith and life, orthodoxy and orthopraxis, belong together, even in politics. Thus, Muhammad could provide for us Christians, not the decisive, guiding norm that Jesus gives us, but a *prophetic corrective* in the name of the one and same God: "I am nothing but a distinctive warner" (sura 46:9).

The questions and issues we have looked at can present difficult challenges for everyone involved: Eastern Christians, Western Christians, Hellenistic Christians, Judeo-Christians, and of course for our Muslim brothers and sisters. The observation of a Pakistani friend of mine, a Muslim scholar, Riffat Hassan, is appropriate:

> Every religion has its problematic point, a crucial point that seems to be indisputable, not negotiable, and which is the main difficulty for the others. For Christians, this point is christology, that Jesus is the Son of God. For Jews, it is the promise that Israel, with its land, is the People of God. For Muslims, it is the Qur'ān as the Word of God—Son of God, People of God, Word of God.

I think, as she does, that we should discuss these issues with reverence, with great esteem for all those who hold one of them as their professed faith, knowing that this matter is very delicate.

But I come back to my beginning: we stand before the alternatives of war and peace. I am certain we can have peace among nations only if there is peace among the religions, and especially among Judaism, Christianity, and Islam. And that will happen only if we are able to speak together as brothers and sisters.

NOTES

1. Adolf Schlatter, *Die Geschichte der ersten Christenheit* (Tübingen, 1926), pp. 367f.
2. Adolf Schlatter, "Die Entwicklung des jüdischen Christentums zum Islam," *Evangelisches Missionsmagazin* (1918), 251–64.
3. This is documented in Adolf Harnack, *Lehrbuch der Dogmengeschichte* (Tübingen, 4th ed., 1909) vol. 1, p. 537.
4. Hans-Joachim Schoeps, *Theologie und Geschichte des Judenchristentums* (Tübingen, 1949), p. 342.

IV. 1.

Interreligious Dialogue and the Islamic "Original Sin"

KHALID DURAN

MUSLIM OPENNESS TO DIALOGUE

Ever since I went to Europe some nine years ago, I have hardly been pursuing theology or the study of religion—certainly not in any systematic way and not as a university discipline. After leaving the Islamic Research Institute in Islamabad and taking up assignments in Europe, I became more and more restricted to the field of political science, a development probably indicative of the state of affairs, if not the state of mind, in the Muslim world at large—and this not just because of the rise of fascism in countries such as Pakistan, Iran, and Sudan, but also because we are still fighting national wars of liberation. In Afghanistan we have been set back some thirty or forty years, in the sense that once again we have to fight against premodern European-style colonialism, with a racialist tinge, animated by a missionary zeal and the crusading spirit of once-upon-a-time—the difference being one of nomenclature. This time the crusade is undertaken in the name of Marxism-Leninism, but *la mission civilisatrice* remains the same as in former days in Algeria and elsewhere.

It might be felt that this is not exactly the topic for which we have come together, but these facts need to be mentioned, because too often complaints are heard about a lack of openness to dialogue among Muslims, or of a lack of interest, or even of a lack of sense for interfaith enterprises. The problem in the Muslim community, however, is in fact quite different. As a result of recent events in the Muslim world, Western Europe is being flooded with intellectuals from Muslim countries. If one wants to meet the true elite of Iran, Afghanistan, Pakistan, or Turkey—come to France, Germany, England, the Netherlands, Italy, or Spain. Besides many a religious leader, numerous intellectuals of the highest caliber who are deeply involved in religion are to be found there. There is no question of any resistance to or even hesitation about interreligious dialogue—not even where Israelis are involved! That is not at all an issue. But how can one expect Muslim thinkers to sit down for interfaith talks or to take part in dialogue experiments when all their energies are absorbed in a struggle against the most ruthless dictatorship at home or in an outright battle for survival against an expanding colonial empire?

Let me give just one typical example. Several weeks ago some Christian friends paid me a surprise visit while I was hosting Dr. Sa'ed, a former vice-rector of Kabul University. All the outstanding former Afghan newspaper editors, writers, and poets as well as former ministers, now refugees in Germany, had assembled to meet him. Dr. Sa'ed speaks German, English, and French fluently. Although he is a chemical engineer by training, my Christian friends discovered to their amazement that his first degree had been in theology and that he was a very profound Sufi—or "Hassidic" Muslim, if you wish. Immediately they started to complain to me: "Khalid, why do you keep these pearls hidden from us? These are exactly the Muslim partners we have always been longing for!" Of course, I had not shielded those precious gems from interreligious dialogue, but Dr. Sa'ed was on his way to Paris, where he has subsequently opened an office of Afghan resistance, while other friends have been busy finding the means to maintain that office. As said before, this is just one example illustrating the point.

Inasmuch as I am neither an Afghan, nor an Iranian, nor Pakistani, Sudanese, Turk, Palestinian, nor Lebanese, I am always being urged by groups of exiles and laborers from those countries in Europe to act on their behalf as a spokesman for religious affairs, particularly where interreligious dialogue is concerned. This has earned me an honorary chairmanship of half a dozen national associations and clubs, a burden almost impossible to cope with. It has led, inter alia, to the creation of a budding Islamic Academy in Hamburg in response to an appeal by the former Turkish prime minister, Bulent Ecevit. Among my Jewish and Christian partners in dialogue, however, the impression persists that Muslims, on the whole, are not eager for dialogue, that their reluctance is simply too strong, their resentment too deep. The contrary, in fact, is true, but the historical phase we are passing through is not propitious for such an exercise.

These complaints come most frequently from Christian theologians who used to be enthusiastic about the Iranian movement called Mujahidin-e Khalq, because at one stage that movement produced a large amount of religious literature and these Christian friends started dreaming of a universal theology of liberation. However, when the first seminar with exiled priests from Argentina was convened, there were among the Iranians present none who were competent to speak on religious matters. The trained ones had all gone back to Iran to fight the fascist regime, and had been killed in the process. Some of my friends sometimes wonder why I wear this typically Shi'ite Iranian ring on my finger. It belonged to a brilliant young scholar of religion who left German comfort to fight Khomeini in Iran—and was executed. This is the situation we find ourselves in. We are simply under duress—and even that is an understatement.

Nonetheless, as the Muslim co-chairman of the "Standing Conference of Jews, Christians, and Muslims in Europe," I manage every year in March to bring a dozen or two really competent Muslim students from various countries together to participate in the annual "Students' Week" trialogue. Despite a host of shortcomings, I still consider this to be one of the most noteworthy experiments in trialogue. From these and other experiences it is clear that we all have much to learn from each other.

I do not wish to claim that I have "grown old" in what some friends have started to call the "dialogue business," but I do concede to Hans Küng the advantage of being a newcomer to the dialogue with Islam, or the Jewish-Christian-Muslim trialogue. This enables him to enter the fray with a "naivety" that is at times disarming—just as it can also be refreshing. Much of what he calls "new findings" appear almost like ancient history to us "old-timers in the field," if I am allowed to say that—and I say it without any animus. In fact, his "new findings" sum up what we have been working at in various dialogue bodies over the last twenty years and more. This does not detract from the value of his "popularization" of those positions, however. After all, where are the Christians, outside such conference halls as this, who know that some wise men in the Christian church have at last accepted Muhammad as a kind of prophet?

When I say "a kind of prophet," I recall a radio talk I had many years ago with the Jewish thinker Pinchas Lapide, who exclaimed: "Muhammad was recognized by Jewish scholars as early as the eleventh century as a prophet on a par with the non-Jewish biblical prophets, such as Job." If Lapide's statement were a matter of common knowledge, it would seem that all the problems have been solved long ago and all that is left to do is joint celebration—one day Shabbat, another day Iftari, then Christmas, and so on. But where are the Jews, apart from such rare scholars as Lapide, who know about such a Jewish recognition of Muhammad as *a* prophet?

This, of course, is a general problem applying to most of the other "new findings" as well. Hence, although valuing the modest but important advances made in such specialized meetings as this, I also value highly, and personally am involved in, searching for the means to have them reach to the grassroots level. As a matter of fact, in Germany we have been singularly successful in this by making use of biannual Protestant mass meetings called "Church Days" (*Kirchentage*), at which we reach tens of thousands of young Christians eager for dialogue with Islam. If I am allowed a bit more "self-glorification," I should like to mention that I initiated a "Committee for Christian/Muslim Dialogue" at the Protestant "Church Days," a committee that has developed into an important institution and had a tremendous impact, especially in Hannover in 1983, and even more so in Düsseldorf in 1985.

Muslim View of Jesus

Before making my basic observation regarding some of Prof. Küng's statements, I believe a corrective comment is in order. Such a procedure is characteristic of the initial stages of dialogue where much time is consumed with an exchange of information and clarification of each other's positions. Prof. Küng states that the portrait of Jesus in the Qur'ān is very different from the portrait of Jesus in the Gospels, for Jesus not only confirms the Law, as the Qur'ān records, but also counters all legalism with radical love, which extends even to his enemies; that is why he was executed—and this the Qur'ān fails to recognize. I find it difficult to identify with this reading of his.

The image I as a Muslim have of Jesus is in fact more or less that which Küng projects here as a gospel understanding. Muslims recognize Jesus as the greatest prophet next to Muhammad, and yet they see Muhammad's mission as more akin to that of Moses. Moses and Muhammad each brought a new law— not so Jesus, who came to recall the spirit underlying the law. For this reason many of the mystic saints of Islam see their role in relation to Muhammad as similar to the role of Jesus in relation to Moses. They combat legalism by trying to imbue the law with notions of love, and they very much see themselves in the tradition of Jesus—to the extent sometimes of precipitating their own doom. Nothing could be more rewarding for them than being crucified, though few of them seem ever to have had the privilege of ending in exactly the same way as Jesus did, as recorded in the Gospels.

For Muslims, Jesus is an extreme, a heartrending as well as heartwarming example, but one who is to be imitated only under the most extraordinary circumstances—unlike Muhammad, who is for Muslims primarily the good exemplar, for all times and climes. So the real difference is that for Muslims Jesus lacks the catholicity Muhammad has. Jesus is of utmost importance, but more for special occasions—not all year round.

Perhaps we can understand this more fully by realizing that Christians, according to the quranic image of them, are extremists in that they take love, patterned on the radical love of Jesus, to the extremes of world-renunciation and extraordinary forms of penitence. Apparently the many Christian hermits who relished Arabian abodes during the time of the Prophet were seen as something like "drop-outs," good-natured cranks, loveable as friends or "sages," but mostly somewhat "off-track." In the Muslim daily prayer (*Al-Fātihah*, the "Muslim Paternoster"), Muslims ask God to lead them on the straight path—which elsewhere has been explained as the Aristotelian *via media*, the golden mean between a Jewish extreme of materialist this-worldliness and a Christian extreme of spiritualist other-worldliness. This is a traditional explanation for "those on whom there is the wrath of God" (the Jews) and "those who go astray" (the Christians). Had Hans Küng said that Muslims overgeneralize in their extreme images of Jews and Christians, I could have agreed with him. But he is on weak ground when he says that the Qur'ān fails to recognize Jesus as the apostle of radical love and the antilegalist par excellence. There is an enormous literature in Muslim tradition celebrating Jesus as precisely that. Admittedly much of those materials owe their inspiration to the Christian background of numberless converts, but the source stimulus was provided by the Qur'ān itself.

Trialogue and the Thrust toward Unity

Let this be enough of corrective statements. I should like to concentrate on one major point in Hans Küng's paper; it is an issue that has proved bedeviling to myself and many of my coreligionists. Prof. Küng implicitly states that Islam is a great faith because it means submission to God, but that it needs to be liberated from the oppressiveness of legalism—though surely not from law. I fully agree that we Muslims suffer from legalism. Our "sacred law," the *sharī'ah*, in its present stagnated form as it was handed down to us from seventh-century Arabia, has certainly become oppressive under the changed circumstances of the twentieth-century pluralist world community. It no longer suits the needs and standards of what we call the emerging universal civilization of a global society.

If our Christian friends take upholders of the *sharī'ah* as their partners on the Muslim side, then there can simply be no consensus on the question of human rights. The *sharī'ah* that is now being reinforced by atavistic Islam is a petrified law, and the oil dollars that go into its present worldwide propagation tend only to further petrify it. One might think that this position is very much in line with what Küng is saying. But there is one important difference. He tends to think of the *sharī'ah* as a nonbiblical element, the murkier Arabian side of Islam. I believe this is only partially true. I see the *sharī'ah* more like the product of Jewish traditions, as a biblical legacy—and I do not feel at all comfortable with this particular linkage. Although it no doubt endows Jews, Christians, and Muslims with common notions that allow us to become more familiar with one another, it also bogs me down as a Muslim in my religious development—and I would almost say in my spiritual edification as well.

Interreligious dialogue often proceeds on the assumption that there is a core of religious heritage to start with, a kind of family tree representing Judaism, Christianity, and Islam. It is somehow assumed that because these three traditions have so much in common, they could provide the starting point for dialogue on a universal scale. It is as if some of us believed that charity begins at home, or that it is easier first to reconcile family members before arriving at a deeper understanding with outsiders, which in this case would mean Buddhists, Hindus, and others. In fact, such notions are especially strong among Muslims. First, there are the ringing verses of the Qur'ān that speak of a common platform, calling Jews and Christians to join Muslims on the basis of a common denominator—that is, belief in the one and only God. (Incidentally, these appeals give evidence that Christian monotheism is very well recognized in the Qur'ān, despite the "uneasiness" created by such symbols as the Trinity.)

Then there is the designation "people of the book" for Jews and Christians, which affords them a special status in the Muslim worldview; they are seen as standing in the prophetic tradition on which Islam bases its self-understanding.

All this, however, is mere surface. Beneath it we discern the historical development of incipient Islam as a religious community apart. Even a cursory acquaintance with Islam renders it clear that there are two levels of understanding the word "Islam": a primary one, which refers to the prophetic tradition of Judaism, in which Jesus is included, and a secondary one, which designates a new community, the followers of Muhammad, the new prophet—so to say, an alternative to the two previous attempts (Judaism and Christianity) that seemed no longer workable. The history of that evolution need not detain us here. What deserves to be emphasized is the fact that the separation of these two meanings of the term "Islam" has never been fully resolved.

For "official" Islam, for the religious establishment associated with government and power, the emergence of Islam as a new and superior community was never in doubt. This "communal Islam" of history was sure of its mission to dominate the world. Within a broad spectrum of Islamic theology, however, especially where it merges into the mystic currents that proved at times overwhelming, the primary meaning often reasserted itself, at least in the form of a question as to what had become of it or what relevance it still held. After all, it was very much there, enshrined in the quranic revelation, and could not be brushed aside so easily. Added to this was sometimes a third meaning, when Islam was understood not only in its abstract literal meaning, but even in a futuristic sense, as an ideal toward which all of us must strive together—Jews, Christians, and Muslims (in the "communal" sense).

Thus we are confronted with at least one tradition within the Islamic heritage that is strongly motivated by a desire for religious unification, by a longing to break down communal barriers and bring humankind together through belief in one God, which goes back to the initial vision of Muhammad when he conceived of himself not as the founder of something new, but as the reaffirmer of the prophetic tradition. It would be patently wrong to relegate this tendency solely to the realm of Islamic mysticism, which derived much of its inspiration from external sources. Rather we should ask whether this openness to "foreign" elements was not prompted by the very revelation of the Qur'ān itself. This is an age-old discussion on which many learned tomes have been written. But it has rarely been related to the phenomenon of the many syncretist movements, sects, and new faiths that sprang from the soil of Islam and that always emphasize the unifying aspect. Here is a tradition that makes Islam appear as the motivator of religious unification per se—all the fervid communalism of Muslim fundamentalists notwithstanding.

For this brand of Muslim thought, interreligious dialogue is highly attractive. It is as if the followers of the other faiths had finally seen the point and had come around to a demand that is as old as the revelation of the Qur'ān in history. Obviously this poses dangers of a special kind, for in this way interreligious dialogue may quickly "degenerate" into what is precisely not the purpose

of our coming together here—the deepening of each of us in our own foundations through the stimulating process of learning from the other.

JEWISH/CHRISTIAN ORIGINS AND ISLAMIC "ORIGINAL SIN"

Much of this is due to Islam's indebtedness to the Jewish/Christian tradition, although more in the "communal" than in the "syncretist" form. For
many Muslim scholars of religion, especially those falling within the restrictive
fold of fundamentalism, Muhammad's anchorage in the world of ideas pro-
pounded by Jewish-Christianity will hardly be a matter of dispute. But it does
not do justice to another fundamental concern of Muslim thought, which is the
emancipation from a Jewish/Christian tradition that ties Muslims down to a
narrow geographico-historical confine.

The quranic view of religious history is obviously an evolutionary one that
sees prophethood as culminating with Muhammad, after whom humanity
needs no further direct intervention from on high: humanity can now stand on
its own feet. The prophetic quality has become a common property, manifest-
ing itself in saints and reformers until it is to be shared by large masses of
"friends of God," to use Sufi eschatological terminology. This presupposes,
however, outgrowing the historical molds that revelation, of necessity, had to
assume in its historical unfoldings. For this development the Jewish/Christian
childhood of Islam may certainly prove helpful—provided it is finally out-
grown. Otherwise it could be retarding as well.

This is precisely my overall reaction to Hans Küng's paper. In the final
analysis I feel obstructed by being time and again tied down to that particular
past. I accept that those bridges are important, but I am not fond of being
reminded of the crossings I have made. It was not so pleasant. In many ways I
feel freer with Buddhists and Hindus. Moreover, I notice that the interreligious
dialogue in India seems to be making more headway. When Muslims meet
Buddhists and Hindus, there is not so much past history they have to come to
terms with. The historical bitterness between Hindus and Muslims is not
reflected in their holy scriptures. Therefore they can straightaway proceed to
more essential issues with a philosophical approach.

At the meetings of the "Standing Conference of Jews, Christians, and
Muslims in Europe" we hold daily services—one day Jewish, another day
Christian, then Muslim. Everybody participates in each service. At one such
occasion I had selected a passage from the Qur'ān and asked an Egyptian
participant to read it in the Arabic original. While chanting, the man fell in love
with his own voice and read beyond that passage dealing with Abraham and the
other biblical prophets. He read and read until he came to a passage that says
Muslims should never trust Jews or take them as friends. The Yugoslav Muslim
I had chosen to read the text in German was a formalist who read not only what
I had indicated beforehand, but also up to the point where the Egyptian had
ended his recitation. There were some thirty Jews in the hall. They told me later
on that they realized very well what had happened, and they now realized that

dialogue was more difficult than they had previously thought.

Some of us Muslims, too, felt that God could have made it easier for us by dispensing with those many references to the biblical past in the Qur'ān and allowing us to start with a clean slate. To me this Jewish/Christian legacy appears sometimes almost as if it were our "original sin," and it is extremely difficult for us Muslims to free ourselves of it. In the form of the *sharī'ah*, this legacy is altogether tragic. Contrary to what both some of my Christian friends and some of my Muslim friends say, only a minor part of the *sharī'ah* derives from the Qur'ān or the example of the Prophet. A large portion of it is Hebraic, biblical, particularly where it conflicts with our present-day notions of human rights.

IV. 2.

A Step toward "Ecumenical Esperanto"

ELLEN ZUBRACK CHARRY

By nature, the task of developing an ecumenical language is both political and theological. Because of historical and theological considerations, thinkers in certain traditions will understandably feel a greater need to address some questions and problems more than others. A dialogue between Christians and Vaisnavas may be interesting but hardly pressing, whereas absence of dialogue between Muslims and Jews is at the moment distressing. In many cases, bilateral conversations are necessary for the self-understanding of historically related traditions like those between Hindus and Buddhists or among Jews and Christians and probably Muslims. It is perfectly understandable, therefore, why Prof. Küng has chosen to focus on how Christians can come to terms with the claims made by Muslims about themselves. As a non-Christian, non-Muslim, it would be inappropriate for an outsider to intrude on that conversation born out of the particular historical and theological needs of those traditions.

Prof. Küng's question can, however, be stated in more general terms: How can non-Xs take seriously the claims made by Xs about themselves? This question is, as Prof. Swidler phrased it and Prof. Küng responded to it, a theological rather than a political question. It is a theological question asked "from below." We ask and answer it for ourselves from our own time and place in history based on our experience and reasoning, and with the help of the resources of our respective traditions. It is not a question asked "from above"—that is, from God's or an eternal point of view. To ask a theological question from below may in itself exclude some persons from the conversation. They may say that the very starting point of this endeavor is illegitimate, on the grounds that the pragmatic concern for harmony and peace among adherents of religions and ideologies should not supercede the quest for and insistence on truth; practical concerns must await metaphysical consensus.

Two points can be raised in response to such objections. First, to begin by asking questions about ourselves does not preclude the need to ask metaphysical questions as well. It merely suggests that seeking commonality from below may be a more productive point of entry into this new area: the likelihood of a common metaphysics is certainly not on the horizon. There is a pragmatic concern underlying this conception of a global theology: a yearning for an end to religiously motivated violence and contempt among adherents of differing traditions. There is nothing particularly illegitimate in that. One would hope, however, that the anthropocentric starting point of this discussion will be broad enough to include those who wish to pursue metaphysical issues.

Secondly, seeking commonality from below is, in most cases, inextricably bound up with the metaphysical enterprise in any case. Each tradition and comprehensive worldview—whatever else it may claim to do—does formulate general conceptions about the nature of human beings, develop doctrines, and recommend courses of action for its adherents that are consequences of its larger metaphysical convictions. For this reason ethnic groups would not easily find a place in this particular conversation: they tend to make limited rather than general formulations about human problems. An anthropological rather than a metaphysical starting point for an ecumenical theology may be a broad but circumscribed way of beginning the task of transcending metaphysical impasses of the past.

With these methodological considerations in mind, if not settled, one possible foundation for an ecumenical theology might be developed by identifying threads of a common theological anthropology among the world's religious traditions and worldviews. The task of identifying an ecumenical theological anthropology is an awesome one: different traditions are not always sympathetic to one another's questions about, let alone answers to, the basic issues of human life and death.

For example, and at the risk of oversimplification, Hindus are concerned to escape from the ceaseless cycle of rebirth and redeath, whereas Christians have been concerned to achieve eternal life. Marxists are concerned with transformation of the material world, whereas some Buddhists are concerned with transformation within themselves in order to let go of the world. Protestants maintain that humans are unable to save themselves, being wholly dependent upon God's grace, whereas Muslims believe that one earns one's salvation by obedience to divine law. Additionally, and this is particularly evident in the U.S.A. at the moment, some religious persons see religious faith as crucial to preserving stability in the world, and productivity and morality at home, whereas nonreligious persons see religious faith as a source of division and prejudice among human beings, and await the day when religion will wither away. Finally, there are those who cling to this world and press for accommodation among opponents, and those who see the world passing away in any case, and so are not as concerned with the resolution of ancient or modern religio-political conflicts.

Nevertheless, and acknowledging the inevitability of oversimplification, what follows is a proposal for beginning to identify an ecumenical anthropology by examining how several traditions might assess the human condition. The audacity of this project is at once overwhelming and unavoidable. It is an ecumenical experiment in a field known for a paucity of such attempts. I shall attempt to draw a macrosketch of some of the world's religions and ideologies to see if there might be threads of a common anthropology. The traditions included in this macrosketch are Buddhism (primarily Mahayana), Christianity (primarily Western), existentialism (primarily the modern nontheistic West European school of thought), Hinduism (primarily the nondualism of the school of Sankara), Islam (primarily the nonmystical movements in Islamic thought), feminism and black theology, Judaism, and the thought of Karl Marx and liberation theology.

A further caveat is in order before proceeding. It has often been maintained that many of the world's traditions are exclusive, so that one cannot be, say, a Christian and a Muslim simultaneously, but this generalization is beginning to give way to a more complex picture. Today we have many Christian Marxists, and many existentialist Christians. There is also strong evidence of the blending of Christianity and Buddhism in both directions and even the development of Christian Judaism, a phenomenon thought to be a contradiction in terms since the middle of the second century C.E. All this is to say that opening one's ears to listen to other persons' questions about and assessments of the human predicament or of ultimate reality involves genuine risk, including the risk that one will be moved to redefine one's ancestral home, or leave it altogether. Without documentation of these developments, some of which are yet too embryonic to quantify, it is difficult to judge, but perhaps an ecumenical theology is evolving, created in part by scholars and theologians, and in part by individuals in their spiritual and intellectual life journeys.

At the risk of reducing complex and ancient traditions to a simplicity their own adherents would not accept, it will be helpful for my purposes to state as simply as possible how each tradition phrases one central problem in human life that it tries to enable its adherents to solve.

1. Buddhists look at the human condition and see suffering. They seek its source and a potential therapy for the problem within reach of the individual. Craving, desire, ego, are all ways of putting the source of the problem. Extinction of ego stops desire and consequently brings happiness. How to extinguish desire and bring tranquility and harmony vary greatly within the extremely diverse traditions that comprise Buddhism. Meditation, ritual, prayer, and divorce from worldly pursuits are all mechanisms for achieving salvation, whether it be perceived in this-worldly or other-worldly terms, whether with the help of a savior or on one's own.

2. Christians look at the human condition and see sinfulness, separation from the source of life that is God. A central question, how sinfulness is

overcome, is answered by the conviction that the source of salvation is God—that is to say, not from within the individual as Mahayanists claim. Because salvation is of God and not of humanity, God compassionately reached out to humanity to do for it what it cannot do on its own. Jesus Christ, "the way, the truth and the life," is the bridge between human sinfulness and God's salvation. Access to God in Christ is through faith, sacraments, and the companionship of the community that guides and nurtures one, after the recognition that without God one is lost.

3. The Western existentialist tradition looks at the human condition and sees meaninglessness. This is well exemplified in Albert Camus's "The Myth of Sisyphus." Life and death are equally random and purposeless. There is no underlying teleological or redeeming force to make things come out right so that one could say all is well, as the Christian says. Each person is ultimately alone, shorn of any self-deluded hope of salvation or bliss after a life of possible suffering. The only hope of remission of meaninglessness is to live an "authentic existence," to rise to the challenge of meaninglessness and to conquer it by force of will. The excitement of existentialism is, as Sartre has said, that "it puts every man in possession of himself as he is, and places the entire responsibility for his existence squarely upon his own shoulders. And when we say that man is responsible for himself, we do not mean that he is responsible only for his own individuality, but that he is responsible for all men" (Jean-Paul Sartre, "Existentialism is a Humanism," in *Existentialism from Dostoevsky to Sartre* [New York: New American Library, 1975], p. 34).

4. Hinduism has both theistic and nontheistic schools, the dualistic school of Ramanuja being closer to Western theism than is the nondualism of Sankara. But whether dualist or nondualist, the Hindu view of the human condition is that we are caught in a web of finitude. The nondualist solution to the problem is to find a path beyond finitude to union with eternal sureness beyond time and space, Brahman. Whether the path be devotion, action, knowledge, or a combination of them depends on one's personality and taste. Guidance in creating one's own way is with the help of a teacher but is accomplished only with diligent effort. Release from the web of illusory existence comes possibly within one's lifetime and possibly not.

5. Islam is a deeply humanistic tradition assessing that there is indeed a problem with human existence and labels the problem forgetfulness. The divine nature is dormant in every human being, waiting to be awakened to a life lived in obedience to the will of God. The Islamic solution to the problem of forgetting the will of God is spelled out in God's holy book, the Qur'ān, and made readily available to all humans there and in *sharī'ah*. Muslims have no doubt as to the availability of salvation—it is there for the taking. Just as Christians maintain that in Adam all sinned, Muslims claim that the potential for obedience to the divine law lies within each of us.

6. Feminism and black theology look at the human condition and see division on the basis of sex and color. Our ways of thinking, relating to other humans, and making judgments are irreducibly and ineradicably imbedded in

biology. The problem from the feminist and black perspectives is the illegiti-mate imposition of a myth of masculine white supremacy over half of the world population. The solution comes not through obedience, as Muslims would say, or of letting go, as Buddhists would say, or of devotion to God or yoga—but, with Marxists, they point to the legitimacy of throwing off author-ity that is deemed illegitimate and oppressive.

7. Judaism, as we can discern from its scriptures, assesses the human family as rebellious and unable to escape the political conditions of its own making—a sort of karmic justice, if you will. Judaism agrees with Christianity that God intervenes in history to rescue human beings from destruction at their own hands and that God established a covenant with the Jewish people. Yet, with Islam, Jews claim that all humans can live in obedience to the will of God (Torah, Halaka), though only a minority seems to do so.

8. Karl Marx and, more recently, Christian liberation theologians see the human condition as permeated with suffering, as do Buddhists. But Marx identified the source of that suffering outside the individual, in alienation from those aspects of economic and social structures that bring about happiness. That human beings are demeaned, degraded, and manipulated is not to be attributed to an inherent sinfulness in us. It is not our craving, or the will of God, that destroys us; suffering results from historical circumstances that enable a few to control the lives of the many. The solution to the problem lies with the individual or the community: to seize the opportunity to right the wrongs of the few on behalf of the many. It is one's own responsibility to overturn all oppressive structures and replace them with social configurations that promote just distribution of income and goods, and provide access to the means by which income and goods are produced.

It seems from these brief sketches that there is some common ground. All these traditions assess the human condition as problematic, and everyone in pain seeks relief. All these traditions provide an analysis of the problem and propose a solution that applies to every human being. Overwhelmingly the evidence of the ages is that human beings are not happy with their lot. All these traditions conclude that something is wrong that should and can be made right. At this point the question arises: If some adherents of these traditions were able to recognize themselves in a (modified) characterization other than their own, would they find common cause with questions and answers of that other tradition?

For example, is the Marxist notion of suffering totally unrecognizable to the Buddhist? Or is it possible that in identifying suffering and oppression, respec-tively, as a central problem, each has excluded an aspect of suffering upon which the other has fastened? How far is the existentialist naming of the problem as meaninglessness from the Hindu expression of the problem as entanglement in finitude? Is there any common ground between the Hindu naming of the solution as liberation from redeath and the existentialist naming of the solution as living an authentic existence? Is the Christian diagnosis of sin unrecognizable to the Muslim who speaks of forgetfulness of the divine nature (for why would we need God's gift of the Qur'ān and *sharī'ah* if we were able to save ourselves?), or to the Marxist who sees human greed as destroying the lives of those in grinding poverty? Is the Jew able to hear the Islamic claim about the universality of God despite Judaism's claim to an exclusive covenant between God and the Jewish people? Are feminist and black theologians unsympathetic to the Buddhist insight that all suffer because all crave? Can the Marxist readily ignore the existentialist claim that economic arrangements, important though they be, do not begin to diminish Sisyphus's misery? Is the Christian's concern over alienation from God unrelated to the Buddhist concern to extinguish craving for things of this world (e.g., fame, honor, and power), or to the Muslim's distress that one is tempted to ignore the will of God?

In addition to trying to stretch language to empathize with other diagnoses of the human predicament, what about identifying the source of the problems? Here we come to an interesting observation. Again, if these characterizations are at all helpful, it appears that with the exception of Marxism, the others agree that the pain we humans suffer is inherent in the very notion of what it means to be human. (It is not clear how some black and liberation and feminist theologians would answer this question. It may be significant in this regard that many of them have been influenced by Marx.) Recent theology points out a connection between the Christian analysis of sin and alienation, and the Marxist assessment of the human propensity to oppress the poor and the weak, indicating that the distance that Marx himself asserted between Christianity and his own thought is more apparent than real. In all but the Marxist analysis, pain, however it is defined, is always with us. Perhaps it is scant cause for rejoicing, and old news at that, but common ground it may be.

A look at the source of the solutions prescribed by the traditions also yields an interesting finding. It appears that with the exception of Christianity (and one might add the additional stricture, perhaps only in the most Protestant of cases) and some forms of Buddhism, these traditions generally stress the ability of the individual to contribute to one's own salvation. The Muslim, Jew, Vaisnava, Marxist, humanist, existentialist, and Theravadin surely agree that the situation is remediable by effort. As in the former case, where the Marxist was the exception to the rule, it would be helpful to the majority to hear the minority report clearly articulated. In the Christian case the Pelagian-Augustinian debate has been lively.

There are, of course, many other questions that should be asked. But it seems from this brief sketch that, with a few important exceptions, far from being deeply divided, the traditions examined here suggest that an ecumenical anthropology could be identified. The traditions by and large agree that human beings are in pain and that release from pain defined in multiple ways is available with sufficient trust or faith, attention, study, devotion, ritual, prayer, obedience, work, meditation, political action, or—if I might add a personal note—just plain luck. Adherents of all these traditions have, over the course of centuries and in many cases millennia, devised prescriptions for dealing with the problems. Perhaps this conclusion says precious little. But perhaps after millennia of isolation and alienation a little is a lot.

IV. 3.

Hans Küng's Theological Rubicon

PAUL F. KNITTER

In Hans Küng's address to this conference he has once again proven himself a pioneer of interreligious dialogue. What he has been doing throughout most of his theological career, he was doing again—exploring new territory, raising new questions in the encounter of Christianity with other religions. Although Küng has made his greatest contributions in the inner-Christian, ecclesial arena, he has always realized—and increasingly so in more recent years—that Christian theology must be done in view of, and in dialogue with, other religions. As he has said, Christians must show an increasingly "greater broad-mindedness and openness" to other faiths and learn to "reread their own history of theological thought and faith" in view of other traditions. As a long-time reader of Küng's writings, and as a participant with him in a Buddhist-Christian conference in Hawaii, January 1984, I have witnessed how much his own broad-mindedness and openness to other religions has grown. He has been changed in the dialogue.

Yet I suspect—and this is the point I want to pursue in this response—that in his exploration of other faiths Küng the pioneer has recently broken into unsuspected territory and stands before new paths. He has been led where he did not intend to go. I think Küng, in his dialogue with other religions, now finds himself before a theological Rubicon—a Rubicon he has not crossed, one that he perhaps does not feel he can cross. I am not sure. That is what I want to ask him.

In Küng's previous efforts at a Christian theology of religions, he inveighs against the Christian exclusivism that denies any value to other religions; he rejects an ecclesiocentrism that confines all contact with the Divine to the church's backyard. Yet despite this call to greater openness, it seems to some that Küng hangs on to a subtle, camouflaged narrowness. Even though he proposes that we replace ecclesiocentrism with theocentrism, he still adheres to a Christocentrism that insists on Jesus Christ as "normative" (*massgebend*)— that is, as "ultimately decisive, definitive, archetypal for humanity's relations with God."[1] Because Christ is normative for all other religions, Küng ends up by replacing Christian exclusivism with a Christian inclusivism that recognizes the value of other religions but insists that this value must be fulfilled, "critically catalyzed," and find "full realization in Christianity." "That God may not remain for them [non-Christians] the unknown God, there is needed the Christian proclamation and mission announcing Jesus."[2] Jesus and Christianity remain for all other religions the final norm, the only real fulfillment.

This is what Küng proposed in *On Being a Christian*. From recent conversations and from his conference paper, I think that he is now not so sure about these earlier christocentric, inclusivist claims that insist on Jesus as the final norm for all. I suspect that, like many Christians today, he stands before a theological Rubicon. To cross it means to recognize clearly, unambiguously, the possibility that other religions exercise a role in salvation history that is not only valuable and salvific but perhaps equal to that of Christianity; it is to affirm that there may be other saviors and revealers besides Jesus Christ and equal to Jesus Christ. It is to admit that if other religions must be fulfilled in Christianity, Christianity must, just as well, find fulfillment in them.

From my reading of his paper, I see Küng standing at this Rubicon, at river's edge, but hesitating to cross. Let me try to explain.

MUHAMMAD, MORE THAN A PROPHET?

In his efforts to urge Christians to recognize Muhammad as an authentic prophet, Küng can only be applauded. Most Christian theologians in dialogue with Muslims hesitate to dare such an admission.[3] But in recognizing Muhammad as a prophet, Küng, it seems to me, is *implicitly* affirming Muhammad as "more than a prophet"—that is, as a religious figure who carries out a role analogous to that of Jesus Christ.

Küng admits that as a prophet Muhammad is "more to those who follow him . . . than a prophet is to us." He is a "model," an archetype, for all Muslims—he through whom God "has spoken to humankind." Such an understanding of Muhammad, however, is essentially the same as that of the early Jewish christology that was lost and that Küng seeks to retrieve. This early christology, this picture of Jesus "as viewed by his first disciples"— which, as much as we can tell, most likely reflects Jesus' own view of himself— saw Jesus as a prophet, as the eschatological prophet, as he who was so close to God that he could speak for God, represent God, mediate God. But this is basically the same description of Muhammad's role. Therefore, in its origins, the Christian view of Jesus was essentially the same as the Muslim view of Muhammad: they were both unique revealers, spokespersons for God, prophets.

Küng's own christology enables Christians to go even further in affirming analogous roles for Muhammad and Jesus. Küng recognizes the truth and validity of the Chalcedon Hellenistic christology, with its stress on two natures, one person, pre-existence. Yet in his own christology as presented in *On Being a Christian,* in his own efforts to interpret what it means to call Jesus Son of God and savior, Küng uses what is much more of an early Jewish-Christian, rather than a Hellenistic, model.

To proclaim Jesus as divine, as the incarnate Son of God, means, Küng tells us, that for Christians Jesus is God's "representative," "the real revelation of the one true God," God's "advocate . . . deputy . . . delegate . . . plenipotentiary."[4] But, again, this is basically the same role that Muhammad fulfills for his followers. Therefore, from a Christian perspective, Muslims in speaking about Muhammad as "the seal of the prophets" and Christians in speaking about Jesus as "son of God" are trying to make essentially the same claim about both figures. I think, therefore, that Küng could agree with Kenneth Cragg's argument that the Islamic notion of prophethood and the Christian notion of incarnation, from very different perspectives and with very different images, are saying the same thing: that their founders were closely "associated" with God and were "sent" by God, and are utterly reliable revelations of God.[5]

So I think that Küng might go a further, logical step in what he can say about Muhammad. He points out that if Jesus is understood according to the model of early Jewish Christianity as God's messenger and revelation, Muslims would be more able to grasp and accept this Jesus. I am suggesting that if Jesus is so understood, then Christians would be more able to accept Muhammad and recognize that in God's plan of salvation, he carries out a role analogous to that of Jesus. If, following Küng's keen insights and suggestions, Muslims might be able to recognize Jesus as a genuine prophet, Christians might be able to recognize Muhammad as truly a "son of God." (And if the title "son of God" is understood, as Küng recommends, not so much as God's "ontological" son but as God's reliable representative and revelation, perhaps Muslims would be more comfortable in using this title for Muhammad.)

But for Christians, for Prof. Küng, to make this move, to recognize the parity of Jesus and Muhammad's missions, would be to step across a theological Rubicon (as it would be for Muslims as well!). I'm not sure if Küng feels willing or able to make this step. I think I can put my finger on the chief reason for his hesitation.

HOW IS JESUS UNIQUE?

The chief stumbling block in Christian dialogue with Islam is not, as Küng suggests, "the person of Jesus and his relationship with God." In his paper Küng has convinced me that Jesus' person and relationship with God can be so understood as to allow for the person of Muhammad to share in this same relationship—in Muslim terminology, both are prophets; in Christian terms, both are sons of God. The problem comes not from the way Küng understands Jesus' relationship to God, but from the exclusivist *adjectives* he feels must qualify that relationship: Jesus is not only a prophet but the *final*, normative prophet; he is not only son of God but the *only*, the unsurpassable son of God. (Muslims, with their insistence that Muhammad is the seal of the prophets, reflect this same problem. Here I am addressing my fellow Christians.)

This, I suggest, is the pivotal, the most difficult, question in the Christian-Muslim (as well as the Christian Buddhist/Hindu dialogue): Is Jesus the one and only savior? (For Muslims: Is Muhammad the final prophet?) Is Jesus God's final, normative, unsurpassable revelation, which must be the norm and fulfillment for all other revelations, religions, and religious figures?

As I suggested before, Küng, in his earlier publications, would answer all these questions with a firm yes. Although all religious figures can be said to be unique, for Küng Jesus' uniqueness is in a different category; Jesus is God's normative, ultimate criterion for judging the validity and value of all other revelations. Küng expressly warns against placing Jesus among the "archetypal persons" that Karl Jaspers has identified throughout history; Jesus is ultimately archetypal.[6] It is this insistence on Jesus' absolute, normative uniqueness that keeps Küng from going further in his recognition of the value of other religions. Muhammad may be a prophet; but he cannot be "more than a prophet," as was Jesus. If other religions are valid, Christianity possesses "absolute validity."[7] If other religions are ways of salvation, they are so "only in a relative sense, not simply as a whole and in every sense."[8]

If one presses Küng or most Christian theologians for the central, the foundational, reason why they maintain this absolute, normative uniqueness for Jesus, I think the only real reason they can give is an appeal, perhaps indirect and uncritical, to the *authority* of tradition or the Bible. This is what scripture affirms of Jesus; this is what tradition has always taught—there is "no other name" by which persons can be saved (Acts 4:12). There is "one Mediator between God and humanity, the man Christ Jesus" (1 Tim. 2:5). Jesus is the "only-begotten Son of God" (John 1:4). True, Küng, in *On Being a Christian,* attempts to give some empirical verification of this traditional assertion of the superiority of Christ's revelation. As I have attempted to show elsewhere, however, serious objections can be raised to his claims that without Christ the other religions cannot really adapt their spiritualities to "modernity," to the demands of our world-affirming technological age. I am not at all certain, as Küng suggests, that without the gospel the other religions are caught in "unhistoricity, circular thinking, fatalism, unworldliness, pessimism, passivity, caste spirit, social disinterestedness."[9] So the chief reason, it seems, for claiming the finality and normativity of Christ over all other religious figures remains the inner-Christian, traditional one: this is what the Bible and tradition have always maintained.

I believe that Küng, along with many other Christians, however, is feeling the inadequacy of these traditional claims. I think he is on the brink of suggesting that such claims for the universal finality and normativity of Christ may not be an essential element in the Christian witness to all peoples. Yet, from his conference paper, I am not sure. For instance, when he tells us that "For

Christians, Jesus Christ and the good news he proclaimed are the decisive criteria for faith and conduct, life and death: the definitive Word of God (Heb. 1:1ff)" and that Christ is "the definitive regulating factor for Christians, for the sake of God and humanity," is he using the phrase "for Christians" as a restrictive qualifier? *Only* for Christians? Would he be ready to recognize that for Muslims, Muhammad is "the definitive Word of God"? For Buddhists, Buddha is "the definitive regulating factor"? In such a view, Christians and Muslims and Buddhists would still have to witness to each other. Jesus, Muhammad, and Buddha would all have universal relevance for all peoples. But there would be no one, final, normative revelation for all other revelations. If Küng is saying this, he is saying something different from what he has said in earlier publications. He has crossed a theological Rubicon. But has he?

CROSSING THE RUBICON FROM INCLUSIVISM TO PLURALISM

I am asking Küng—as well as other theologians (e.g., John B. Cobb)—for greater clarity on this "Rubicon question" concerning the uniqueness and finality of Christ. Such clarity is needed by both fellow Christians and non-Christian partners in dialogue. Although Küng, echoing Arnold Toynbee, does well to excoriate "the scourge of exclusivism," is he perhaps unconsciously advocating a more dangerous, because more subtle, scourge of inclusivism? As Leonard Swidler has pointed out, authentic, real "dialogue can take place only between equals . . . *par cum pari*."[10] But no matter how much truth and good one recognizes in another religion, if one enters the dialogue convinced that by God's will the final, normative, unsurpassable truth for all religions resides in one's own religion, this is *not* a dialogue between equals. It is, as Henri Maurier attests from years of experience in African interreligious dialogue, a conversation between "the cat and the mouse."[11]

It seems to me that an inclusive christology, which views Christ and Christianity as having to include, fulfill, perfect other religions, is really only a shade away from the theory of "anonymous Christianity" so stoutly criticized by Küng. The theory of "inclusive Christianity" may not assert that other believers are already Christians without knowing it; but it does affirm that these believers must become Christians in order to share in the fullness of revelation and salvation. Küng has called persons of other religions "Christians *in spe*" (in hope) who must be made "Christians *in re*" (in fact).[12] It seems to me that Küng's evaluation of Radhakrishnan's Hindu tolerance might apply to his own understanding of Christian tolerance: It is "conquest as it were by embrace in so far as it seeks not to exclude but to include all other religions."[13]
Does Küng still hold to such an inclusive christology and theology of religions? Does he realize its possible harmful effects on dialogue in the way it implicitly but assuredly subordinates all other religions to Christianity?
My question takes on a sharper focus in Küng's concluding exhortation that we stop thinking "in terms of alternatives—Jesus *or* Muhammad"—and start

thinking "in terms of synthesis—Jesus *and* Muhammad, in the sense that Muhammad himself acts as a witness to Jesus." I am not sure just how Küng does or can understand that "and." Is it the "and" of equality (like "Son and Spirit") or the "and" of subordination (like "law and gospel")? Previously, Küng would have had to come down, I believe, on the side of final subordination insofar as he has insisted that Christ is God's final norm for all persons of all times. But I am not sure what he would say today.

My final question is more of a personal request. In asking for more clarity, I am really asking Hans Küng to step across the Rubicon. I believe that his own christology, as well as his own doctrine of God, implicitly allows him to do that. I suspect that the press of interreligious dialogue has also made the possibility of crossing more urgent.

Might I also point out that in making the crossing, he would be in good company. Other Christian thinkers have moved from an earlier inclusivist position of viewing Christianity as the necessary fulfillment and norm for all religions, to a more pluralist model that affirms the possibility that other religions may be just as valid and relevant as Christianity. They have admitted that other religious figures, such as Muhammad, may be carrying out, in very different ways, revelatory, salvific roles analogous to that of Jesus Christ. Among such thinkers are not only Ernst Troeltsch and Arnold Toynbee, but also a number of Christian theologians who have more recently shifted from an inclusivist Christocentrism (Christ at the center) to a pluralist theocentrism (God/the Ultimate in the center): Raimundo Panikkar, Stanley Samartha, John Hick, Rosemary Ruether, Tom Driver, Aloysius Pieris.[14]

Granted Prof. Küng's respectability and his influence, and given the caution and thoroughness with which he makes all his theological moves, I feel that if he were to cross the Rubicon to a more pluralist theology of religions that does not need to insist on Christ or Christianity as the norm and fulfillment of other religions, he would be, once again, a pioneer leading other Christians to a more open, authentic, and liberative understanding and practice of their faith.

But I ask you, Hans Küng, do you think such a new direction in Christian attitudes toward other religions, such a crossing of the Rubicon, is possible? And would it be productive of greater Christian faith and dialogue?

NOTES

1. Hans Küng, *On Being a Christian* (New York: Doubleday, 1976), pp. 123f.

2. Ibid., pp. 113, 447.

3. See David Kerr, "The Prophet Muhammad in Christian Theological Perspective," *International Bulletin of Missionary Research,* 8 (1984) 114.

4. Küng, *On Being a Christian,* pp. 390f., 440, 444, 449.

5. Kenneth Cragg, "Islam and Incarnation," in John Hick, ed., *Truth and Dialogue in World Religions: Conflicting Truth-claims* (Philadelphia: Westminster, 1974), pp. 126–39.

6. Küng, *On Being a Christian,* p. 124.

7. Ibid., p. 114.

8. Ibid., p. 104.

9. Ibid., p. 110; see also pp. 106–119; and Paul F. Knitter, "World Religions and the Finality of Christ: A Critique of Hans Küng's *On Being a Christian,*" *Horizons,* 5 (1978) 157, 159.

10. Leonard Swidler, "The Dialogue Decalogue," *Journal of Ecumenical Studies,* 20/1 (1983) 10.

11. Henri Maurier, "The Christian Theology of the Non-Christian Religions," *Lumen Vitae,* 21 (1976) 70.

12. Hans Küng, "The World Religions in God's Plan of Salvation," in Joseph Neuner, ed., *Christian Revelation and World Religions* (London: Burnes and Oates, 1967), pp. 65f.

13. Hans Küng, *Does God Exist? An Answer for Today* (New York: Doubleday, 1980), p. 608.

14. Raimundo Panikkar, *The Unknown Christ of Hinduism* (Maryknoll, N.Y.: Orbis, revised edition, 1981); Stanley J. Samartha, *Courage for Dialogue: Ecumenical Issues in Inter-religious Relationships* (Maryknoll, N.Y.: Orbis, 1982); John Hick, *God Has Many Names* (London: Macmillan, 1980); Rosemary Ruether, *To Change the World: Christology and Cultural Criticism* (New York: Crossroad, 1981); Tom Driver, *Christ in a Changing World: Toward an Ethical Christology* (New York: Crossroad, 1981); Aloysius Pieris, "The Place of Non-Christian Religions and Cultures in the Evolution of Third-World Theology," in Virginia Fabella and Sergio Torres, eds., *Irruption of the Third World: Challenge to Theology* (Maryknoll, N.Y.: Orbis, 1983). See also Paul Knitter, *No Other Name?* (Maryknoll, N.Y.: Orbis, 1984).

V.

What Is True Religion?
Toward an Ecumenical Criteriology

HANS KÜNG

No question in the history of the churches and of religions has led to so many disputes and bloody conflicts, indeed, "religious wars," as the question about the truth. Blind zeal for the truth, in all periods and in all churches and religions, has ruthlessly injured, burned, destroyed, and murdered. Conversely a weary forgetfulness of truth has had as a consequence a loss of orientation and norms, so that many no longer believed in anything.

The Christian churches, after a history of bloody conflicts, have learned to moderate the dispute concerning the truth and to come to common answers in an ecumenical spirit, which of course in the end should lead to practical results. The same lies in the future for the relationship between Christians and other religions. And yet some ask whether there can in any sense be a theologically responsible way open to Christians by which they can accept the truth of other religions without giving up the truth of their own religions, and thereby their own identity?

There are still others who ask, conversely, whether for us descendants of the Enlightenment this is still a question at all? Are we not fighting rearguard battles in intellectual history simply because we are still anxious about a diffusion of our own identity?

A PRAGMATIC SOLUTION?

Has not a solution long since been available on the pragmatic level? "Of these three religions, only one can be the true one," insisted the Sultan Saladin in Lessing's famous "Dramatic Poem," and, turning to the wise Nathan, he added: "A man like you does not remain standing there where the accident of birth has placed him; or if he remains, he remains because of insight, reasons, the choice of the better."

On what, however, does this insight rest? What are the reasons for the choice of the better? Lessing's solution is, as is known, expressed in the parable of the three rings: If—and that is the presupposition—the theoretical clarification of the truth question does not succeed, if "the correct ring is not truly discoverable," what then? The answer: Praxis alone! Let each one "freely be zealous . . . in his love, unburdened by prejudices!" Then the power of the genuine ring will disclose itself: "With gentleness, with heartfelt peaceableness, with good deeds, with the inmost submission to God." Confirmation therefore only through a God-granted humanness in life itself! For our problem this means that every religion is genuine, is true, insofar as it de facto and practically shows forth the "wondrous power" to make us pleasing before God and our fellow human beings. Is this a standpoint that is as clear as it is simple, and spares us having to face the fateful truth question?

In our century it was primarily the Americans Charles Sanders Peirce, William James, and John Dewey who pursued a pragmatic solution to the question about truth. Accordingly, in regard to the true religion, it was simply asked how a religion as a whole "works," what practical consequences it has, what its factual value for the formation of personal life and social life it had— in history and here today.

Who can dispute that such an interpretation of the function and usefulness of a religion has much to commend it? Do not theory and practice flow into one another precisely in religion? Must not the truth of a religion de facto show itself in praxis? Must not the "value" of a religion show itself in practice, in line with the scriptural citation: "By their fruits you shall know them"?

The only question is whether truth can simply be equated with practical usefulness. Can the truth of a religion be reduced to usefulness, serviceability, satisfaction of needs—indeed, if necessary, be sacrificed to tactics, to commercial or political exploitation? And could not a religion that is little practiced nevertheless be true? Could not a prescribed way of life that is continually violated nevertheless be correct? Could not a message that attracts little or no attention nevertheless be a good message?

Of course it can be asked whether there is not a deeper understanding of pragmatism than that reflected in a strictly utilitarian approach—not a mere reduction of religion to practical reality, but a search for the synthesis of religion and a truly good life in practice.

In any case the question stands: According to what criteria should such complex phenomena as the great religions be judged? Can the effects of Buddhism in Asia or Catholicism in Europe over millennia simply be designated good or bad? Does not the ledger of all contemporary religions have both credit and debit entries? And will it not always be misleading to compare the high ideals of one's own religion with the low level of implementation of the ideals of another religion—for example, to compare a real Hinduism or a real Islam with an ideal Christianity?

Thus, the question remains: What is true religion? William James, at the beginning of his classic work, *Varieties of Religious Experience* (1902), mentions as a useful criterion for judging religion not only "ethical corroboration," but also "philosophically demonstrable rationality." But what does "philosophically demonstrable rationality" mean in this connection? In any case, one does not get to the roots of the truth question by a practical orientation only.

FOUR FUNDAMENTAL POSITIONS

1. *No religion is true.* Or: *All religions are equally untrue.* The atheistic position, though it is not my theme here, should not simply be ignored. Rather, it is an ongoing challenge for all religions. Normally the lamentable condition of a religion is itself sufficient basis for the judgment that its doctrines and rites amount to nothing, that religion is nothing other than projection, illusion, false consolation—in short, that there is no truth in it, or indeed in any religion.

I cannot and will not try to prove that religion in fact is focused on a reality, indeed a most real, primordial Ultimate Reality. However, can atheistic opponents of religion provide proof that religion in the end focuses on nothing? Just as God is indemonstrable, so also this "nothing" is indemonstrable. Our purely theoretical reason is bound to this world and simply does not reach far enough to answer this question; in that Kant was correct for all time. Positively put, we are concerned here with the famous "Gretchen question" of religion, which deals with nothing more and nothing less than the great question of *trust* in our lives. Despite all the apparent contradictions in this world, we nevertheless utter a yes in a tested, illusion-free, realistic trust in an ultimate ground, ultimate content, and ultimate meaning of the world and human life. Such is presumed in all the great religions. And this is a completely reasonable yes insofar as it has good reasons at its base, even though they may not, strictly speaking, be proofs.

Whoever says no will have to answer to history. The ancient religious history of humanity—traced back at least as far as the interment rites of the Neanderthals—greatly relativizes atheism, closely bound as it is to specifically Western culture and intellectual history (Nietzsche's "God is dead" presumes twenty-five hundred years of occidental metaphysics!). Whether one views humanity diachronically in its many-thousand-year history, or synchronically in its global dispersion, no human grouping will be found in which belief in a transcendent being is lacking. Globally viewed, large-scale atheism is a typically Western "accomplishment," even if it has likewise spread to the Orient. It is, consequently, an affair of a cultural minority in our century.

2. *Only one religion is true.* Or: *All other religions are untrue.* The traditional Catholic position, anticipated in the early Christian centuries by Origen, Cyprian, and Augustine, and defined by the Fourth Lateran Council (1215) and the Council of Florence (1442), left no room for doubt: salvation demanded membership in the Catholic Church (see above, pp. 195–96). Was not the claim of the other religions to truth and salvation thereby once and for all eliminated? It was, so it appeared, at least from the fifteenth to the sixteenth century.

With the European discovery of new continents, Catholic theology attempted to understand anew the dogma, *extra ecclesiam nulla salus* (outside the church no salvation). For the most part this meant a reinterpretation, and ultimately a reversal, of the earlier teaching. It would never openly "correct" it, because it was "infallible." The Council of Trent, and theologians such as Bellarmine and Suárez, recognized an unconscious "desire" (*desiderium*) for baptism and the church as sufficient for eternal salvation. In the seventeenth century, Rome, in opposition to rigoristic French Jansenism, condemned the proposition, *extra ecclesiam nulla gratia* (outside the church no grace; Denz. 1295, 1379). In 1952 the Holy Office found itself obliged, paradoxically, to excommunicate the student chaplain at Harvard University who, along with the ancient church fathers and the Council of Florence, maintained the damnation of all human beings outside the visible Catholic Church. Again without formal correction of earlier teachings, the Second Vatican Council admitted the possibility of salvation for all human beings, and acknowledged the existence of "true and holy" elements, in non-Christian religions.

The *traditional* Catholic position is today no longer the *official* position. Because the human being is indeed bound to the historico-socially shaped forms of religion, even the non-Christian religions can be ways to salvation—perhaps not the normal, completely "ordinary" ways, but nevertheless "extraordinary" ways. In fact, in contemporary Catholic theology, on the basis of this reversal, one makes a distinction between the "ordinary" (= Christian) way to salvation, and the "extraordinary" (= non-Christian) ways to salvation (sometimes also between "the way" and the various "paths").

However one may judge this theological solution and terminology, what is important is that for the first time in its history the Catholic Church has clearly spoken *against* a narrow-minded and pretentious *absolutism,* which made its own truth "ab-solute," "dis-connected" from the truth of others. It has turned away from the standpoint of exclusivity that had condemned the non-Christian religions and their truth, and had opened the door to imperious apologetics, incorrigibility, and self-righteousness. In short, it has turned away from the dogmatism that imagined that it from the beginning had the complete truth in its own possession and faced other positions only in terms of condemnation and a demand for conversion. Disdain for other religions should now be replaced by appreciation, their neglect by understanding, their being "missionized" by study and dialogue.

With this the Catholic Church in the 1960s took a step that many Protestant theologians still hesitate to take. Still following in the tracks of the younger Barth and dialectical theology—often without a very deep knowledge or analysis of the other world religions—they can only contemn their truth claims: their "religion" is nothing other than "natural theology," a self-empowered, sinful uprising against God—unbelief, pure and simple. Some even maintain that Christianity, for its part, is no religion at all, because the gospel is the end of all religion. I suggest, however, that such a "dialectical theology" must become more dialectical!

The other world religions may be neither condemned nor ignored. A high-minded *ignoramus* ("we do not know") is more than ever irresponsible. And if Christian theology has no answer to the question of the salvation of the majority of humankind, can it wonder that commentators today, as in the time of Voltaire, heap their scorn upon its arrogant claim of monopolizing salvation, or its contentment with an enlightened indifferentism? The stand of the World Council of Churches is likewise unsatisfactory, for neither in its "Guidelines for Dialogue with Persons of Other Religions and Ideologies" (1977–79) nor at its plenary assembly in Vancouver (1983) was it able to take a stand on the question of salvation outside the Christian churches, because of contradictory positions held by member churches.

Since the European discovery of previously unknown continents, the other world religions were first of all an external, *quantitative* challenge to Christianity. Now, however, they have become—not only for a few interested persons, but for the Christian churches as such—an internal, *qualitative* challenge. Now it is no longer simply the fate of the other world religions that stands in question, as during the "Christian" colonial period. The fate of Christianity itself hangs in the balance in this period of postcolonialism and postimperialism.

A different question is posed today: What is the Christian proclamation today when it finds, not poverty in other religions, as earlier, but a wealth of meaning and truth? What does Christianity have to offer? If it now perceives light all around, how can it intend to *bring* "the light"? If all religions contain truth, how can Christianity be *the* truth? If there is salvation outside the church and Christianity, why should there be the church and Christianity at all?

3. *Every religion is true.* Or: *All religions are equally true.* Whoever really knows a number of religions will hardly maintain that they all are the same. For thus the fundamental differences between the basic types of mystical and prophetic religion would be glossed over, as would also all the contradictions among individual religions. And it is a fact that even an individual religion does not simply remain the same throughout the course of its history, as has been pointed out especially by Wilfred Cantwell Smith, but rather—often to an astonishing degree—develops and complexifies.

Moreover, must not *objective* religion (the various myths, symbols, doctrines, rites, and institutions that often are contradictory in different religions) be distinguished from *subjective* religion, from religiosity, from the fundamental religious experience of the All-One and Absolute to be found at the foundation of all religions? However, even recourse to the fundamental religious "mystical" experience, which is allegedly everywhere the same, does not resolve the truth question. Why? Because there never is a religious experience in isolation, never "in itself," never free of all interpretation. Religious experience from the beginning is interpreted experience, shaped by the religious tradition in question and its various forms of expression.

Does the position that in principle all religions are equally true specifically exclude from the religious arena the possibility of error, or from humanity the possibility of moral fallibility? Why should it not also be true for religion that *errare humanum est?* Is there a religion that does not have human forms? Or should, for example, all religious statements, all myths and symbols, all revelations and confessions, and finally all rites and customs, authorities and appearances, in Hinduism, Buddhism, Islam, Judaism, and Christianity be equally true and valid? The reality of the one experiencing it in no way guarantees the reality of that which is experienced. There is a difference between religious and pseudo-religious experiences, and one cannot place magic or belief in witches, alchemy, or the like, on the same level with belief in the existence of God (or in the reality Brahman), in salvation and liberation. There should be no talk about all "religious experiences" being equally true.

Just as not everything is simply one, so also is not everything religious equally valid, not even in one and the same religion! The slogan "anything goes" least of all can satisfy the basic questioning of human life for *truth,* ultimately binding and trustworthy. Or should perhaps everything precisely in the religious sphere be legitimate because it once happened ("the power of the factual") and possibly comes down to us picturesquely clothed (religion in the garment of folklore)? If it is the "truth" and only the truth that—to quote the Gospel of John—"makes us free," then we must search further.

Together with exclusivistic absolutism, the crippling *relativism* that makes all values and standards the same must be avoided. That incidentally was also already true for Lessing. For the arbitrary pluralism—already developing in his time and intellectually "in" today—that approved its own and other religions in an undifferentiating manner can call upon Lessing as little as the indifferentism for which all religious positions and decisions are equally unimportant, and which thereby saves itself the effort of "discerning the spirits."

4. *One religion is the true one.* Or: *All religions participate in the truth of the one religion.* If the standpoint of exclusivism, which acknowledges no truth apart from its own, is as unacceptable as a relativism that "relativizes" all truth and is indifferent toward all values and standards, affirming and approving in undifferentiated manner its own and other religions, would not then the standpoint of a generous, tolerant *inclusivism* be the real solution?

We encounter this above all in the *religions of Indian origin:* all empirical religions represent only various levels, partial aspects, of the one universal truth. The other religions are not untrue—simply preliminary. They participate in the universal truth. By calling upon mystical experience, a "higher knowledge" can thus be claimed for one's own religion. The consequence? Every other religion is de facto degraded to a lower or to a partial knowledge of truth, whereas one's own religion is raised up to a superlative system. Every other religion is designated a preliminary stage or a partial truth; a special claim is denied them. What looks like tolerance proves in practice to be a kind of conquest by embrace, assimilation by exterior validation, integration by relativization and loss of identity.

A variant form of this inclusivism is found—paradoxical though it may sound—*also in Christianity.* Karl Rahner's theory of an "anonymous Christian" is ultimately dependent upon a (Christian) *superiority standpoint,* which starts out with the assumption that one's own religion is the true one. For according to Rahner's theory, which attempts to resolve the dilemma of the *extra* dogmas, Jews, Muslims, Hindus, and Buddhists will be saved, not because they are Jews, Muslims, Hindus, and Buddhists, but because they are ultimately Christians, "anonymous Christians." No, the embrace here is no less subtle than in Hinduism. The will of these persons, who are not Christians and who do not wish to be Christians, is not respected, but rather is interpreted according to one's own interests. However, you will not find a serious Jew or Muslim, Hindu or Buddhist, who does not feel such a claim that they are "anonymous," and indeed "anonymous Christians," as arrogance. This is without taking into consideration the completely distorted use of the word "anonymous": as if these human beings did not know who they were! Such a speculative assimilation of one's conversation partner blocks off dialogue before it has even begun. We must affirm: members of other religions are to be respected as such, and are not to be subsumed in a Christian theology.

What, then, is demanded today of a basic Christian attitude toward the other world religions? Instead of an indifferentism for which everything is equally valid, let there be somewhat more *indifference* toward the alleged orthodoxy that makes itself the measure of the salvation or damnation of human beings, and wishes to make good its truth claim with instruments of power and force. Instead of a relativism for which there is no absolute, let there be more sensitivity for *relativity* in every human setting up of absolutes that hinders a productive coexistence of the various religions, and let there be more sensitivity for the *relationality* that allows every religion to be seen within its own web of relationships. Instead of a syncretism where everything possible and impossible is "mixed together," melted into one, let there be more commitment to a *synthesis* of all confessions and religious oppositions, which still take their daily toll of blood and tears, so that instead of war, hate, and dispute, peace may reign among all religions.

In face of all religiously motivated impatience, one cannot demand too much patience, too much religious freedom. There should be no betrayal of freedom for the sake of truth, but at the same time there should be no betrayal of truth for the sake of freedom. The truth question must not be trivialized and sacrificed to the utopia of a future world unity and one world religion, which— especially in the Third World, where the history of colonization and the history of the missions bound up with it are in no way to be forgotten—would be feared as a threat to one's own cultural and religious identity. On the contrary, as Christians we are challenged to think through anew in a Christian-based *freedom* the question of *truth*. For freedom, unlike arbitrariness, is not simply freedom *from* all bindings and obligations—that is, purely negative. Rather, it is at the same time a positive freedom *for* new *responsibility* toward one's fellow human beings and the Absolute. True freedom is freedom for truth.

THE CRITERIA OF TRUTH

One could proceed with long and complicated discussions of the question of what truth is and take a position on the various contemporary theories about truth (correspondence, reflection, consensus, coherence theories). However, the question about the true religion must remain very much in the foreground here. As a presupposition for everything that follows concerning the lack of truth in religion, I offer the following thesis as a starting point: the Christian possesses *no monopoly on truth,* and also of course no right to forego a *confession of truth* on the grounds of an arbitrary pluralism; dialogue and witness do not exclude each other. A confession of truth includes the courage to sift out untruth and speak about it.

It would certainly be a gross prejudice to identify ahead of time the border between truth and untruth with that of the border between one's own and other religions. If we are serious, we would have to grant that *the borders between truth and untruth* run through each of our religions. So often are we both correct and incorrect! Criticism of another position therefore is done responsibly only on the basis of a decisive self-criticism. Likewise only thus is an integration of the values of the other responsible. That means that *not everything in the world religions is equally true and good;* there are also elements in beliefs and customs, in religious rites and practices, institutions and authority structures, that are not true, not good. It goes without saying that this also applies to Christianity.

It is not without reason that there is often a strong *criticism of Christianity by the other world religions* because Christians are much too unclear:

1. Despite its love and peace ethic, Christianity comes across to the members of other religions, in its appearance and activity, as extremely exclusivistic, intolerant, and aggressive.

2. It comes across to other religions not as holistic, but rather, because of its strong orientation to the afterlife and its negative attitude toward the world and the body, as schizophrenic.

3. It exaggerates almost pathologically the consciousness of sin and guilt at the core of allegedly corrupt humanity in order all the more effectively to bring into play its need of redemption and dependence upon grace.

4. From the start it falsifies by its christology the figure of Jesus—which the other religions almost universally view in a positive light—into an exclusively divine figure (Son of God).

It is clear that the question about the truth of a religion concerns more than pure theory. The truth never shows itself only in a system of true statements about God, human nature, and the world, nor only in a series of propositional truths over against which all others would be false. It always at the same time likewise concerns *praxis,* a way of experience, enlightenment, and endurance as well as illumination, redemption, and liberation. If religion offers an ultimately comprehensive meaning of life and death, proclaims a highest, indestructible value, sets unconditionally binding standards for our behavior and suffering, and shows the way to a spiritual home, then this means that the dimensions of the *true (verum)* and the *good (bonum),* the meaningful and the valuable, merge together in religion, and the question about the (more theoretically understood) truth or meaningfulness of religion is at the same time a question about its (more practically understood) goodness or value. A "true" Christian or Buddhist is the "good" Christian or Buddhist! To this extent the question about what is true and what is false in religion is identical with the question of what is good and bad religion.

The fundamental question about true religion must thereby be posed in a differentiated manner: How can one distinguish between the true and the false, the valuable and the valueless, in the various religions? In this one may not focus only on the Hindu caste system, the Shakti form of Tantric Buddhism with its sexual practices, and the "holy wars" and cruel punishment in Islam; one must also recall such appearances in Christianity as the Crusades, the burning of witches, the Inquisition, and the persecutions of Jews. Thus one can easily see how delicate and difficult the question about the *criteria of truth* is if they are not merely to spring from subjective arbitrariness or to be used simply to refute others.

Naturally no religion can completely forego applying its own *specific* (Christian, Jewish, Islamic, Hindu, Buddhist) *criteria of truth* to the other religions (more about this later). Dialogue indeed does not mean self-repudiation. However, one must be clear about the fact that these criteria first of all can be relevant and indeed binding only for oneself, not for the others. Should all participants absolutely insist on their own criteria of truth, genuine dialogue is nipped in the bud.

Thus, for example, the Bible can fulfill its criteriologico-liberative function only in discussions among Christian churches, and to some extent in discussions between Christians and Jews. However, in conversation with Muslims, and certainly with Hindus and Buddhists, a direct appeal to the Bible as a criterion of truth would be inappropriate. What, however, then remains if in the dialogue with other religions Christians can no longer simply appeal to the Bible (or Muslims to the Qur'ān, Hindus to the Gita, or Buddhists to their canon) as an indisputable authority in order to stand vis-à-vis the other in the right, in the truth? With all due caution, another way will be *attempted* here and presented for discussion. I move inwardly, so to speak, in a spiral fashion in three thought movements—from a generally ethical to a generally religious, and only then to a specifically Christian criterion.

THE *HUMANUM* AS A GENERAL ETHICAL CRITERION

When we compare our religion with the others, and also when we reflect on the misuse of our own religion, a question arises for all religions concerning the criteria of the true and the good—that is, concerning *general criteria* analogically applicable to all religions. This is important, it seems to me, not least of all for questions concerning national and international law. The descriptive comparative study of religion (little interested in normative criteria), which, however, presumes specific (often untested) understandings of humanity, nature, history, and the divine (for example, with a covert predilection for the "mystical"), has not carried out this difficult criteriological work. Nor has Christian theology done so. To date, it has not seriously compared itself with other religions and for the most part has avoided this difficult criteriological problematic. It is precisely this defect in theory, however, that calls for a solution.

With this, the first and foundational question must be posed: Can any and all means be sanctified by a religious purpose? Is anything, everything, allowed in the service of religion—even the misuse of economic-political power, of sexuality, of aggression? May religion command what appears to be inhuman, what obviously slights, injures, perhaps even destroys the human person? Every religion offers a plethora of examples (not all anachronistic). Are human sacrifices acceptable because they are offered to a god? For reasons of faith, may children be slaughtered, widows burned, heretics tortured to death? Does prostitution become a worship service if it takes place in a temple? Are prayer *and* adultery, asceticism *and* sexual promiscuity, fasting *and* the consumption of drugs to be justified if they serve as means and ways to "mystical experience"? Is chicanery and miracle-peddling, and all kinds of lies and trickery, allowable if they are for an allegedly "holy" purpose? Is magic, which attempts to coerce the divinity, the same as religion, which petitions the divinity? Are imperialism, racism, or male chauvinism justifiable if they are religiously based? Is no objection to be raised against mass suicide as in Guyana because it was religiously motivated?

Institutionalized religion is not automatically, in any and all ways, "moral"; even some collectively developed customs are in need of reconsideration. In addition to the specific criteria that every religion has for itself, there is need today, more than ever before, for a discussion of *universal ethical criteria.* Here I cannot, of course, enter into the increasingly complex hermeneutical questions in connection with the fundamental forms of present-day ethical argumentation (empirical, analytic, or transcendental-anthropological) and the grounding of norms. An orientation on the *humanum,* on the genuinely human, does not in any case mean—and this is said in the beginning to avoid any misunderstanding—a reduction of the religious to the "merely human."

Religion has always shown itself most persuasive precisely where—long before all of the modern strivings for autonomy—it has succeeded in effectively realizing the *humanum* precisely on the horizon of the Absolute—the Decalogue, the Sermon on the Mount, the Qur'ān, the sermons of Buddha, and the Bhagavad Gītā may suffice as examples.

In general of course it is precisely Christianity—which polemicized so long against freedom of belief, conscience, and religion—that has profited from the fact that, in its area of influence, through modern processes of emancipation, a secularist humanism critical of religion secluded itself from it. The result of the whole process was that in a new way the realization of values—at bottom fundamentally Christian, such as freedom, equality, fellowship, and "human dignity" (the quintessence of the *humanum* that has been codified in law, as for example in Article 1 of the constitution of West Germany)—can be demanded of the Christian churches. For precisely because the *humanum* was emancipated from religious and ecclesiastical confines in modern autonomy, could it once again find itself at home within the borders of Christianity—more so than with other religions.

Christianity, and other religions—precisely at a time of disorientation, atrophication of the sense of obligation, and widespread permissiveness and cynicism—can establish for the conscience of the individual—beyond psychology, pedagogy, and even positive law—why morality, ethos, is more than a matter of personal taste and judgment or social convention; why morality—ethical values and standards—oblige *unconditionally* and thus *universally*. In fact, only the Unconditioned can oblige unconditionally; only the Absolute can bind absolutely. Only religion can establish an unconditioned and universal ethos, and at the same time concretize it, as it has been doing now for millennia—sometimes badly, sometimes well.

In any case it is unmistakable that in the search for the *humanum* a process of reflection has developed in other religions as well. Thus the question of *human rights,* for example, is being intensively discussed in Islam, especially after it has been shown that the *sharī'ah,* Islamic law, stands in stark contradiction to the Universal Declaration of Human Rights of the United Nations (1948), especially with regard to equal rights for women (the right to marriage, divorce, inheritance, and employment) and for non-Muslims (with regard to the choice of professions in Muslim society, etc.), which of course contains questions directed back to the Qur'ān itself.

Despite all the difficulties involved in questions of human rights and ethical *structural criteria,* there is reasonable hope that a foundational consensus on the "basic premises of human life and living together" (W. Korff) among the world religions can be built on the heights of modern, humane mentality. Key convictions on fundamental human values and demands, although they entered human consciousness only in the course of historical development, thereafter—witness the Copernican worldview—attained lasting, irreversible, unconditioned validity. Indeed, they often found their way into legal codification (as "human rights" or "fundamental rights"). Of course, from time to time they need to be given new expression.

Progress in the direction of humaneness within the various religions—despite various lags in consciousness—is in any case unmistakable. One thinks, for example, of the elimination of the abominable use of fire and torture by the Inquisition, practices that lasted within Catholicism until well into the modern age, or of the new humane interpretation of the doctrine of "holy war" and the reform of penal law in more progressive Islamic lands, or of the elimination of human sacrifice and the burning of widows (from the beginning rejected by Indian Buddhists and Christians) carried out in parts of Hindu India until the English occupation.

Numerous conversations in the Far and Near East have convinced me that in the future all the great religions will foster a vital awareness of the guarantee of human rights, the emancipation of women, the realization of social justice, and the immorality of war. The world movement of religions for peace has made especially significant progress. All these religious motivations and movements have become politico-social factors that are to be taken very seriously. Therefore, my question: Should it not be possible to formulate *fundamental ethical criteria* with an appeal to the *common humanity of all,* which rest upon the *humanum,* the *truly human*—concretely, on *human dignity* and the *fundamental values* inherent in it?

A new *reflection about the human* is in process among the religions. An especially clear example was the declaration of the World Conference of the Religions for Peace in Kyoto, Japan, in 1970 (see above, pp. 29–30).

The fundamental question in our search for criteria, therefore, is: What is *good* for human beings? The answer: What helps them to be truly human. The fundamental ethical norm is accordingly that human beings should not live inhumanly, but humanly; they should realize their humanness in all its levels and dimensions. The morally good, then, is that which allows human life in its individual and social dimensions to succeed and prosper in the long run, enables an optimal development of human beings in all their levels and dimensions. Human beings should accordingly realize their humanness in all their levels (including the level of feeling and instinct) and dimensions (including their relationships to society and nature) both as an individual and in society. That means, consequently, that at the same time humanness would be flawed in its core if the dimension of the "transhuman," the unconditioned, the encompassing, the ultimate, were denied or eliminated. Without this dimension humanness would be truncated.

Good and evil, true and false, can be distinguished according to the fundamental norm of authentic humanness; so too can what is fundamentally good and evil, true and false, *in each individual religion.* This criterion might be formulated in regard to a particular religion as follows:

1. *Positive criterion.* Insofar as a religion serves humanness, insofar as in its credal and moral doctrines, its rites and institutions, it *fosters* human beings in their human identity, meaningfulness, and value, and helps them gain a meaningful and fruitful existence, it is a *true* and *good* religion.

This means: whatever clearly protects, heals, and fulfills human beings in their physico-psychic, individual-social humanity (life, integrity, freedom, justice, peace), whatever, therefore, is human, truly human, can with reason call itself "divine."

2. *Negative criterion.* Insofar as a religion spreads inhumanness, insofar as in its credal and moral doctrines, its rites and institutions, it *hinders* human beings in their human identity, meaningfulness, and value, and thus helps them fail to gain a meaningful and fruitful existence, it is a *false* and *bad* religion.

This means: whatever clearly suppresses, injures, and destroys human beings in their physico-psychic, individual-social humanity (life, integrity, freedom, justice, peace), whatever, therefore, is inhuman, not truly human, cannot with reason call itself "divine."

There are ambivalent cases in every religion: I have merely indicated that in the history to date of neither Hinduism, Buddhism, Judaism, Christianity, nor Islam is there a lack of clear examples of good *and* evil, true *and* untrue. Wherever the dignity of human beings or of a racial grouping, class, caste, or sex is devaluated by a religion, wherever individual human beings or whole groups are physically, psychically, or spiritually acted against or indeed annihilated, we are dealing with a false and bad religion. With this it is to be reflected that precisely in the area of religions my self-realization and the realization of others are at stake; however, our common responsibility for society, nature, and cosmos are likewise at stake in an indissoluble bond.

All religions must reflect anew, therefore, on the requirements of being human. The *humanum* given to all human beings is a general ethical criterion that holds for all religions. However, the religions must also continually recall—and here our spiral turns inward—their own *primordial "essence"* ("nature," *Wesen*) as it shines forth in their origins, in their authoritative scriptures, in their authoritative figures. And they will be continually reminded of these facts by their critics and reformers, prophets and sages, whenever a religion becomes untrue to its "essence" ("un-nature," *Un-wesen*): the proper, original "essence" of every religion, its authoritative *origin,* or its normative *canon* ("measuring stick"), is a general criterion for all religions by which they can be measured.

THE AUTHENTIC OR CANONICAL AS A GENERAL RELIGIOUS CRITERION

In the face of religiously false attitudes and false developments, in the face of religious decadence and deficiency, Christian theology always brought the criterion of its origin or canon into play—but not because the older is ipso facto the better! It is no more so than is the new. Rather, it is because the *original* or *canonical* was from the beginning the normative: primordial Christianity, the primordial witness of the Bible, the origination of Christian faith. Christians measure themselves against their origin. However, they are often also so measured by non-Christians: "You appeal to the Bible, to Christ—and behave thus?" The Bible, especially the New Testament, serves Christianity as its canon, its normative measure.

And is the Torah not normative for Jews, as the Qur'ān and the figure of Muhammad (as an embodiment of the Islamic way) are for Muslims, and the teaching (dharma) and the figure of Buddha for Buddhists? What, then, does it mean to the search for criteria when, for example, Shakti Tantrism (in all its striving for salvation) contradicts in essential elements the monastic way of life, which according to Buddha is to be striven for? With its consumption of alcohol, its sexual practices? To what degree, then, is such a Tantrism still (or was it ever) Buddhist? Here indeed an inner-Buddhist critique now also comes into play: the great majority of Buddhists agree with Christians that sexuality certainly has its own place and value—but precisely for that reason it does not belong in this meditation or worship, especially not in a public act and with an exchange of partners. The religion of sexuality and the sexuality of religion are no longer distinguished, and the door is opened wide to libertine abuses.

Having a criterion for the authentic (original) or the canonical (authoritative) is not, then, an exclusively Christian prerogative. There is a *general religious criteriology:* a religion can be measured against its *authoritative teaching or practice* (Torah, New Testament, Qur'ān, Vedas, or Gita), and in some instances against an authoritative *personification* (Christ, Muhammad, Buddha). This criterion of "authenticity" or "canonicity" can therefore be applied to all the great religions—mutatis mutandis, of course: adapted to each religion, more easily to some (e.g., Islam) than to others (e.g., Hinduism).

It seems to me that, at a time of great social change and rampant secularization, this religious criteriology has an enhanced significance for the fundamental orientation of the non-Christian religions. What is "essential," what is "enduring," what is "binding," and what is not? It concerns one's religious identity. In this there is indeed unity among the religions: a primordial religious heritage should not be dissipated in the modern world; rather, it should once again be made fruitful in it. Reflection on the original (authentic) or the authoritative (canonical) has given to reform movements (which time and again spring up in all the great religions) an unusually strong impulse: religious *re-formatio,* recollection of the original form, *and* at the same time *re-novatio,* renewal for the future.

In many cases, only the application of the criterion of authenticity or canonicity has brought the *quintessence* of a religion clearly into relief. Does that not answer, and convincingly, the question of what in theory and in practice true Christianity, true Judaism, true Islam, true Buddhism, and true Hinduism is and is not? To be sure, this reconnection to origin or canon— event, person, or scripture—is of a completely other significance in the historically oriented religions. However, it is also by no means unknown in the mystical religions. Let me briefly illustrate:

1. *True Hinduism* is in principle only the religion based on the revealed writings of the Vedic seer. Thus, numerous though the religions and their gods may be in India, and though Hindu tolerance is far-reaching, nevertheless, because Buddhism (as also Jainism) rejected the Vedas, it cannot for Hindus be the true religion and therefore is rejected, as is also Indian Islam. Something similar can be said from the perspective of the canons of the monotheistic religions of India such as Vishnuism and Shivism.

2. *True Buddhism* can only be the religion that finds its foundation in the Buddha (who brought the "wheel of doctrine" into motion), in the "doctrine" (dharma), and in the "community" (sangha). As great as the differences are between Theravada and Mahayana Buddhism, and as numerous as the various Buddhist "sects" may be, religions that reject the Buddha, dharma, or sangha will not be accepted as the true way.

3. *True Islam* is only the religion that bases itself on the Qur'ān revealed to Muhammad. As far-reaching as religious and political differences may be between Shias and Sunnis, both nevertheless base themselves on the Qur'ān, which for them is the word of God; whoever deviates therefrom stands outside the true religion and falls under "excommunication." Something similar, despite all its dogmatic tolerance and different interpretations of the Law, can also be said about *Judaism.*

4. Though much less so for the mystical religions of Asia, for the historical religions the *origin* answers the question about true religion. And with that now—and there I take a second inward turn on the spiral—the general religious

criterion for truth can be concretized in a specifically Christian form, to which I now turn. (There would also be a specifically Jewish, Islamic, etc., formulation of the general religious criterion of true religion.)

THE SPECIFICALLY CHRISTIAN CRITERION

What has been attained up to this point? According to the general *ethical* criterion, a religion is true and good if, and insofar as, it is *human,* does not suppress or destroy humanness, but rather protects and fosters it.

According to the general *religious* criterion, a religion is true and good if, and insofar as, it remains true to its own *origin* or *canon:* to its authentic "essence," its authoritative scripture or personification on which it bases itself.

According to the *specifically Christian criterion,* a religion is true and good if, and insofar as, in its theory and praxis it lets the spirit of Jesus Christ be felt. I apply this criterion *directly* only to Christianity: by use of self-critical questioning as to whether and how far the Christian religion is authentically Christian. *Indirectly*—and without any presumptuousness—this same criterion of course can also be applied to other religions: for the sake of a critical clarification of the question of whether and in how far something of the Christian spirit is also found in other religions (especially in Judaism and Islam).

One can also view Christianity, as every other religion, completely *from outside* as a "neutral" observer, as a historian of religion, as a non-Christian, or a former Christian—without any special commitment to the Christian message, tradition, or community. Christianity takes its place as one of the several world religions and must satisfy the various general ethical and religious criteria of truth. From this perspective we shall find *many true* religions.

But this consideration from the outside does not exclude another *internal* perspective. And for the individual person it is perfectly honest and sincere to integrate both perspectives. This external-internal relationship is valid not only for religion. When an international lawyer, for example, compares various national constitutions with one another, or when he attempts to arrive at an understanding of a disputed point in international negotiations, he likewise views his national constitution (and his state) "from outside." However, he views the same constitution (and his state) "from within" when, as a loyal citizen, he feels himself obliged precisely to this (and no other) constitution and holds himself bound to it in conscience.

If I, as a Christian (and as a theologian), view Christianity—just as all non-Christians can view their own religion—*from within,* as an adherent of this religion, and in my case, therefore, as a Christian, then Christianity—like every other religion—is more than a system that I assimilate intellectually. Then Christianity, like every other religion (unlike philosophy), is at once a message of salvation and a way of salvation. I encounter there not simply a philosophico-theological argumentation that demands my reflection, but rather a religious provocation, and in the case of Christianity, a prophetical message that calls for a completely personal taking of a stand, a following.

Only thus does one directly understand this religion in all its depth.

When I, therefore, from this point onward express my understanding in the language of confession, it is not because I am retreating again into my religion out of anxiety over "ultimate consequences," but rather because I presume that no religion can be grasped in its deepest reality if one has not affirmed it from within, with ultimate existential seriousness. Only when *a* religion has become *my* religion does the discussion about the truth reach its deepest depths. Truth for me, therefore, means *my faith,* just as for the Jew and the Muslim, Judaism and Islam, and for the Hindu and the Buddhist, Hinduism and Buddhism, are *their* religion, *their* faith, and thereby *the* truth. My religion, and also the other religions, are concerned not about a general, but an existential truth: *tua res agitur.* In this sense there is—for me as for all other believers—only *one true religion.*

This means that in the search for true religion, searchers do not abstract from their own life and experience. There has never been a theologian or a historian of religion, a religious or a political authority, who stood over *all* religions so that she or he could "objectively" judge them all from above. Those who think they stand "neutrally" above all traditions will never have any influence in any. And those who (to take up an image used by Raimundo Panikkar), while looking out of *their own* window at the *whole* of reality along with the others who are likewise looking out of *their* window, hesitate to speak with them, who think they can float above all and judge all, they have lost the ground under their feet; they will easily—like Icarus—melt their wax wings in the sun of truth.

I profess myself then to hold to my historically conditioned standpoint: This one religion is *for me the true religion,* for whose truth I can give good reasons, which possibly may also convince others. Christianity is the way for me, the religion in which I believe I find the truth for my life and death. However, at the same time it is true that *other* religions (which for hundreds of millions of human beings are *the true religion*) are therefore *by no means untrue* religions, are by no means simply untrue. They not only have much truth in common with Christianity, they also have each their own truth, which we do not ("anonymously" or "implicitly") have. It must be left to Jewish, Muslim, Hindu, and Buddhist theologians (philosophers) to spell out why they are Jewish, Muslim, Hindu, or Buddhist. Christian theologians for their part must at least fundamentally be able to name the specifically Christian criterion and seek to answer the question about what it is that concretely distinguishes, or should distinguish, Christians from non-Christians, what makes Christians to be Christians.

Why, therefore, am *I* a Christian? It would take more than one lecture to lay out within a new context of comparative religion the reasons that I have for not being a Hindu or a Buddhist, for not being a Jew or a Muslim, but rather a Christian. Only the most decisive reason can be singled out here: I am a Christian because I—as a consequence of the Jewish, and in anticipation of the Islamic, faith in God—with confidence and in practice trust that the God of Abraham, Isaac (Ismael), and Jacob has acted not only in the history of Israel (and Ismael), and has spoken through the prophets, but has also bestowed self-revelation in an incomparable, and for me a decisive, manner in the life and work, suffering and death, of the Jew Jesus of Nazareth. The first generation of his disciples was convinced that, despite his scandalous death on the gibbet of the cross, he has not remained in death, but was taken up into God's eternal life. He stands now ("at the right hand of God") as one sent definitively by God, as the Messiah or Christ, as the word become flesh, as the image of God, or—to use an ancient royal title of Israel—son of God. In short, I am a Christian because and insofar as I believe in this Christ and attempt practically, now well, now badly, to follow him—in a different period of world history and along with millions of others each in their own way—and take him as the one who shows me my path: He is, therefore, according to the words of the Gospel of John, for us *the* way, *the* truth, and *the* life!

This means, in a self-critical address to Christians: Christians *do not believe in Christianity.* Christianity as a religion—with its dogmatics, liturgy, and discipline—is like every other religion, a highly ambivalent historical reality; Karl Barth was completely right in emphasizing that point. From this it follows that it would be untenable to maintain that Christianity is the "absolute religion," as Hegel still thought he could do; as a religion, Christianity appears in the history of the world just as relatively as do all other religions.

No, the only absolute in the history of the world is the Absolute itself. For Jews, Christians, and Muslims this Ultimate Reality of course is not ambiguous and indistinct, wordless, voiceless. The Absolute has spoken through the prophets. For believing Christians the Absolute is also not faceless, without a countenance. The Absolute has been revealed in the relativity of the human being Jesus of Nazareth. For believers—and only for them—he *is* the word and image, he is the way, and for others at least an invitation to this way. Therefore, Christians do not believe in *Christianity,* but rather in *the one God,* who after many prophets and enlightened ones has sent this human being Jesus as the *Christ,* the anointed emissary. Jesus Christ is for Christians the *decisively regulative* norm.

And insofar as concrete Christianity bears witness to this one God and the Christ can it—in a derived and limited sense—be called for believers themselves *the true religion,* which even Karl Barth acknowledged. Insofar, however, as that concrete Christianity ever and again deviated from this one God and Jesus Christ, from this decisively regulative Christ, was it also ever and again *untrue* religion, was always, even after Christ, in need ever and again of the *prophetic corrective,* of the prophets in the church, and—we see this ever more clearly today—of the prophets and enlightened ones outside the church, among whom indeed in an outstanding manner the prophet Muhammad and Buddha may well be numbered.

A decision for the one God—who is not only the "God of the philosophers and sages" (the God of the Greeks), and the "God of Abraham, Isaac, and Jacob" (the God of the Jews), but finally and ultimately the "God of Jesus Christ" (the God of the Christians)—is in the deepest possible manner a *decision of faith.* A reasonable trust, this decision of faith is in no way purely subjective and arbitrary, but is *rationally responsible.* The detailed arguments for this decision to be a Christian—rather than a Jew, Muslim, Hindu, or Buddhist—I have laid out elsewhere. If we do not wish to simply hide behind a dogmatic postulate, we cannot as Christians shirk the effort to give a substantive, empirical grounding for the significance of Jesus Christ. Reference to a dogmatically elaborated doctrine of the Trinity and of divine filiation is of little help here. It must be possible to show concretely from the person, message, life and fate of Jesus why I am a Christian, and we must do this today in a new manner, and in a critical comparison with the other great religious figures. For this the research of comparative religion is indispensable. What is demanded is not the division of theology and the history of religion (as by Karl Barth), or their identification (and thereby de facto the reduction of theology to the history of religion, or the other way around), but rather their critical cooperation.

I should like to refer to one—to be sure, extremely central—aspect of the mission of Jesus of Nazareth, which shows in a striking way that for Christian faith the specifically Christian criterion is congruent not only with the general religious criterion of origin but also ultimately with the general ethical criterion of the *humanum*—the spiral maintains its consistency. At what—as a consequence of the proclamation of the reign and will *of God*—does the Sermon on the Mount, the entire moral teaching of Jesus, aim? At nothing more nothing less than a new, *true humanity:* the Sabbath, the commandments, are for the sake of humanity, and not the other way around.

This new humanity means a *more radical humanity,* which manifests itself in *solidarity with fellow humanity,* even with one's enemy. From Jesus' perspective the authentic, true human being, this more radical humanity of the Sermon on the Mount—today set before a radically different world horizon—would be practiced as a solidarity of fellow humanity, including men and women *from other religions.* This solidarity of fellow humanity takes upon itself a very concrete program of action:

1. It not only foregoes religious wars, persecution, and Inquisition, and practices religious tolerance, but also, in its relationship to the other religions, it substitutes for its collective egoism (ecclesio-centrism) a phil-anthropy, a solidarity of love.

2. Instead of calculating the history of guilt among the religions, it practices forgiveness and dares a new beginning.

3. It does not simply eliminate religious institutions and constitutions (often humanly devisive), but nevertheless relativizes them for the welfare of humankind.

4. Instead of overt or covert power struggles among religio-political systems, it strives for reconciliation: not a uniform religion for the entire world, but peace among the religions as a prerequisite for peace among the nations.

This means that the more human Christianity is (in the spirit of the Sermon on the Mount), the more Christian it is; and the more Christian it is, the more it will also outwardly appear as true religion.

With this, then, the three criteria of truth have been sufficiently developed, and I can summarize its decisive elements in the next section.

ON THE WAY TO AN EVEN GREATER TRUTH

It should have become clear that if we wish to address the question of what is good for humanity, not only pragmatically or positivistically, but also fundamentally, not only abstractly and philosophically, but also concretely and existentially, not only psychologically and pedagogically, but with unconditioned commitment and general validity—then we cannot avoid dealing with religion, or, in its place, a quasi-religion. Nevertheless, conversely, every religion can be measured by the general ethical criterion of the *humanum,* and will therefore under modern circumstances not be able to overlook the results of psychology, pedagogy, philosophy, and jurisprudence. This is not a vicious circle, but rather, as is so often the case, a dialectical mutual relationship:

1. On the one hand, *true humanity is the presupposition of true religion.* This means that the *humanum* (respect for human dignity and fundamental values) is a minimal demand made on every religion. There must be at least humaneness (a minimal criterion) wherever one wishes to realize genuine religiousness.

2. On the other hand, *true religion is the fulfillment of true humanity.* This means that religion (as the expression of an all-encompassing significance, the highest values, unconditioned obligation) is an optimal presupposition for the realization of the *humanum:* there must be religion (a maximal criterion) wherever one wishes to realize humaneness with unconditioned and universal commitment.

What, therefore, is true religion? To this complex question I have attempted to give a differentiated response with the greatest possible conceptual clarity and theoretical precision, with the help of three different, but dialectically intertwined, criteria—namely, the general ethical, the general religious, and the specifically Christian, and with the help of two dimensions, external and internal. This response includes an answer to the question of whether there is true religion. In summary form the following can now be said:

1. Seen from *without,* viewed by the history of religion, there are *various true religions:* religions that, with all their ambivalence, at least fundamentally meet the governing criteria (ethical and religious). They are various paths of salvation toward a goal; to some extent they overlap and in any case can mutually fructify each other.

2. Seen from *within,* from the standpoint of a believing Christian oriented on the New Testament, *the true religion for me,* inasmuch as it is impossible for me to follow all ways at the same time, is the way I attempt to go: Christianity, insofar as it bears witness in Jesus to the one true God.

This for me—and for all Christians—one true religion in no way denies truth in *other religions,* but positively acknowledges their validity. The other religions are not simply untrue, but neither are they unreservedly true. They are for me, rather, *conditionally* ("with reservations"—or however it is to be said) *true religions,* which, insofar as they do not contradict decisive elements of the Christian message, can indeed supplement, correct, and enrich the Christian religion.

From this long and detailed explanation it should be clear that one need not suspend one's own religious convictions, or detour around the truth question, because of a maximal theological openness toward other religions. We should strive—in "fraternal striving" (Vatican II: *fraterna emulatio)*—for the sake of the true.

However, one last caution. There are not only the two "horizontal" dimensions (external-internal), there is a *third dimension. For me* as believer, *for us* as believing community, Christianity, insofar as it bears witness to God in Christ, is to be sure the *true* religion. However, no religion has the *whole* truth; *God alone* has the *whole* truth (in this Lessing was correct). Only *God*—however named—*is the* truth! This is the third, the "vertical" dimension.

And therefore, a final remark. Christians cannot claim to have comprehended God, the Uncomprehensible, to have grasped God, the Ineffable, the Unfathomable. In Christian faith we perceive with Paul the truth that is God only as in a mirror, in shadowy outline, piecemeal, dependent at all times on our extremely specific standpoint and context. Christianity is *in via,* on the way: *ecclesia peregrinans, homines viatores.* And we are not the only ones on the way, but we are together with hundreds of millions of other human beings from all possible confessions and religions who are going their own way. However, with them we are in a *process of communication,* and the longer it lasts, the deeper it becomes. In this process one should not dispute about what is mine and yours, my truth, your truth, but one should much more be utterly open to learning, to taking up the truth of the others, and without jealousy sharing one's truth.

But, some will ask, where will it all lead? History is open-ended; interreligious dialogue, just begun, is open-ended. What the future will bring the Christian religion, we do not know. And what the future will bring the non-Christian religions, we do not know. How Christian, Islamic, or Buddhist theology, indeed the church, the *ummah,* the sangha, of the year 2085 will look—who knows?

What is certain about the future is only one thing: at the end of human life as well as the end of the world, there will be no Buddhism or Hinduism, no Islam or Judaism, no Christianity. At the end there will be no religion whatsoever, but rather there will be the Unutterable, toward which all religions are directed, whom Christians also, when the incomplete has given way to the complete, will know in fullness as they themselves are known: *the* Truth face to face. Thus, at the end there will not any longer stand a prophet or an enlightened one, there will stand no Muhammad, no Buddha. The Christ Jesus in whom Christians believe will stand there no more, but rather he who, according to Paul, to whom all powers (even that of death) are subordinate, will "subordinate himself" to God so that God *("ho Theos")*—or whatever name is invoked—truly will be not only in all, but also *all in all* (1 Cor. 15:28).

Afterword

KANA MITRA

Prof. Swidler's paper, "Interreligious and Interideological Dialogue: The Matrix for All Systematic Reflection Today," was the backdrop of the conference, "Toward a Universal Theology of Religion." In this paper one extremely important charge is that in our dialogue with each other our primary motive needs to be learning from others. From the four major papers presented in this conference what I learned may be presented as follows: "Toward a Universal Theology of Religion" is an enterprise whose ultimate goal of universality can never be achieved, but nevertheless needs to be attempted, in seriousness and friendliness, for the sake of individual discipline as well as social cooperation and harmony.

Prof. Cobb's paper on christocentric theology makes it quite clear that theologians need to center themselves somewhere, although, as the story of the crocodile that was thought to be an island warns us, eventually theologians may realize that there is no solid, nondynamic center at all. Prof. Smith suggests that a universal theology of religion may be possible if we can make the center not any specific tradition but the history of all the traditions—emphasizing our "us-ness" as human beings. An all-inclusive center could provide universality. Prof. Panikkar suggests that any attempt at universalization, however inclusive it might be, is bound to be imperialistic. Hence, any such attempt should be aborted. Prof. Küng suggests that such an attempt is a necessity to promote understanding, peace, and harmony.

All the papers were not only scholarly but also full of insights. How can we put all these insights together? Perhaps we can find an answer in a somewhat koan-sounding statement: a universal theology cannot be formulated, and yet it must be attempted. That it cannot be definitively formulated is evident from all the papers, but most especially from Cobb's and Smith's. Cobb's christocentric theology can be the basis for a theology from the perspective of Christianity, but not for a universal theology. Smith's all-inclusive theology may sound more promising. However, in my judgment, his view of history itself is very much centered in "Westernness," if not Christianity in particular. This leads us straight to Panikkar's paper on taking pluralism seriously and not attempting to shape unity by any kind of uniformity, for that would amount to imperialism, which is neither ethically justifiable nor pragmatically feasible or desirable. Yet Küng's paper shows the need for such enterprise for the purpose of mutual understanding.

In the conference, concerns were expressed by various participants, as well as by Swidler's paper, that if such an enterprise were confined to academics—to the ivory tower—it would have little value. Küng wants to avoid precisely that. For him this universal theology of religion is not simply a matter of systematic theology, but also a matter of extreme practical importance. As a Christian, he is centered in Jesus, but that center for him is not a static center. That is why, it seems to me, Küng is opposed to any "reiteration-type" theology and is annoyed with any static view of truth. Dynamism need not imply a shifting of the center; it is movement in the center. I felt that was what Cobb also was implying when he spoke about enlarging and expanding the center. He suggested that, though starting from a nucleus, one needs to broaden the horizon, as when a stone is dropped in the water, ripples start to make wider and wider circles. Küng's paper suggests dynamism more in terms of succession, but it might also be understood in terms of simultaneity.

Here we again come back to Panikkar and his vehement opposition to any kind of universal theology. Emphasizing the Buddhist insight of the relationality of everything, he seems to indicate (and I agree, if my understanding of him is accurate) that all of us, individually and as members of a group, culture, society, or in whatever other way we want to identify ourselves, are what we are in relationship to all time, all space, all humans, all nonhumans, and we are not substantive in the sense of being independent and solely self-determined. We are all networks of relationships. Each individual or group is a specific yet dynamic network. Some of these networks may be more inclusive or less inclusive; yet each is a specific network, which is also in relationship to all the rest of the networks. Therefore, we can see, think, and talk only from that specific but dynamic center. To try to universalize from a specific, and hence particularistic, perspective would indeed be imperialistic.

Panikkar and Swidler seem to be at opposite poles. However, they really validate each other. Coming from the Western, particularly American, "fix-it" kind of mentality, the "activist" Swidler wants to solve the problem of intolerance and misunderstanding by proposing an "Esperanto" for a theology of religion. The term was bound to raise a lot of opposition—and it did. For Panikkar (whose thought reminds me of a bird in flight—so spontaneous) an artificial device was unthinkable! However, he de facto, although perhaps unconsciously, follows Swidler and confirms the spirit of his proposal when he creates terms such as "cosmotheandrism"—a term that can be shared by Christians, Hindus, and Buddhists!

The conference itself makes it very evident that a universal theology of religion cannot be done. However, it also showed that it must be attempted. The conference generated different insights via the exchanges of all. When participants prepared and presented their papers, they tried to think, write, and communicate as carefully as they could, and thus it was a discipline for them. As Prof. Smith suggested, when he first started to study the different religions he did not begin by perceiving the presence of transcendence in history. Through careful study, however, he now has gained that and other insights into reality, which he did not have before. Each participant, if we read their earlier and later works, shows growth and development. Thus the attempt at universality of thought may well be one of the many ways of individual, and communal, growth and development. It may also produce mutual understanding and thereby promote harmony. We need to become childlike in order to inherit the kingdom; we need to be playful—and we can be, if we realize that all the universe is a divine play.

Contributors

Ellen Zubrack Charry (Jewish) received a Ph.D. in relgion from Temple University in 1985, was a participant in the Georgetown Jewish-Christian Muslim Trialogue, 1979-83, was *Journal of Ecumenical Studies* Book Review Editor, and is Associate Program Director of the National Conference of Christians and Jews. Her latest book is: *Franz Rosenzweig on the Freedom of God*, 1987.

John B. Cobb, Jr. (Methodist) was born in Japan and lived there until 1939. He received a Ph.D. from the University of Chicago Divinity School in 1952. He has published and edited almost two dozen books, including *Christ in a Pluralistic Age*, 1975, and *Beyond Dialogue*, 1982. He is Professor of Theology at Claremont Graduate School and Director, Center for Process Studies.

Thomas J. Dean (Protestant) received a B.D. from Harvard Divinity School, and a Ph.D. in religion from Columbia University in 1968. His publications include *Post-Theistic Thinking: The Marxist-Christian Dialogue in Radical Perspective*, 1975. He is a professor in the Religion Department at Temple University, specializing in cross-cultural philosophy of religion.

Khalid Duran (Muslim) studied in Spain, Germany and Pakistan, was since 1968 Associate Professor in the Islamic Research Institute in Pakistan, in 1978 joined the Deutsches Orient Institute in Hamburg and is Visiting Professor at Temple University. His latest book is: *Islam und politischer Extremismus*, 1985. He is Associate Editor of the *Journal of Ecumenical Studies*.

Antony Fernando (Catholic) is a native of Sri Lanka, where he took a Ph.D. in Buddhist studies; he also has a doctorate in Catholic theology from the Gregorian University in Rome. At present he is Chairperson of the Department of Classical and Christian Cultures of Kelaniya University of Sri Lanka. His latest book, with Leonard Swidler, is *Buddhism Made Plain*, 1985.

Charles Wei-hsun Fu (Taoist/Buddhist) studied at the National Taiwan University, the universities of Hawaii, California and Illinois, where he received a

Ph.D. in philosophy, has published many books and articles on Buddhism, Marxism, Chinese philosophy and religion, and is Professor of Religion at Temple University and Associate Editor of the *Journal of Ecumenical Studies*.

Stanley S. Harakas (Greek Orthodox) has a B.D. from Holy Cross Greek Orthodox School of Theology and a Th.D. from Boston University. He is the author of many articles and several books, including: *Contemporary Moral Issues Facing the Orthodox Christian*, and *Living the Liturgy*. He is Professor at Holy Cross Greek Orthodox School of Theology, Brookline, MA.

Kenneth K. Inada (Buddhist) studied in both the United States and Japan and is the author of over forty scholarly articles and editor and author of several books covering Buddhism and comparative thought. He is Series Editor of *SUNY Series in Buddhist Studies*, and is Professor of Philosophy at the State University of New York (SUNY) at Buffalo.

Paul F. Knitter (Catholic) received a Licentiate in Sacred Theology from the Gregorian University in Rome and a Th.D. from the Protestant Faculty of the University of Marburg, Germany. His latest book is: *No Other Name? A Critical Survey of Christian Attitudes toward World Religions*, 1985. He is a professor of theology at Xavier University, Cincinnati, Ohio.

Hans Küng (Catholic) studied at the Gregorian University in Rome and at the Sorbonne and Institut Catholique in Paris, where he received his Ph.D. He was Professor of Dogmatics on the Catholic Theology Faculty of the University of Tübingen 1960-80, and of Ecumenical Theology since 1964, and is an Associate Editor of the *Journal of Ecumenical Studies*. His bibliography covers 50 pages.

Kana Mitra (Hindu) received an M.A. in philosophy from Calcutta University and a Ph.D. in religion from Temple University. Her latest book is: *Catholicism-Hinduism. Vedantic Investigation of Raimundo Panikkar's Attempt at Bridge Building*, 1987. She is on the religion faculties of Villanova and La Salle universities, and is an Associate Editor of the *Journal of Ecumenical Studies*.

Raimundo Panikkar (Catholic/Hindu/Buddhist) has three Ph.D.'s: in science, philosophy and theology. He has published 300 articles and 30 books, including: *Kultmysterium in Hinduismus*, 1964, *Religione e Religioni*, 1964, *El silencio del Dios*, 1970, *Intra-religious Dialogue*, 1979, *The Unknown Christ of Hinduism*, 1981, and is an Associate Editor of the *Journal of Ecumenical Studies*.

Zalman Schachter (Jewish), born in Poland, came to the U. S. in 1941, was ordained by the Lubavitch Hasidic Yeshivah in Brooklyn, received an M.A. in psychology of religion from Boston University and a D.H.L. from Hebrew Union College. His writings include: *Fragments of a Future Scroll*, 1975. He is Professor of Judaica and Psychology of Religion at Temple University.

Wilfred Cantwell Smith (Presbyterian) received a Ph.D. in oriental languages from Princeton University and spent ten years working and teaching in Lahore, India (now Pakistan); he also taught for many years at both McGill University and Harvard University. His writings include: *The Meaning and End of Religion*, 1963, 1978, and *Towards a World Theology*, 1981.

Leonard Swidler (Catholic) received a Ph.D. in history and philosophy from the University of Wisconsin and an S.T.L. from the Catholic Theology Faculty of the University of Tübingen. He is Professor of Catholic Thought and Interreligious Dialogue at Temple University and Editor of the *Journal of Ecumenical Studies*. His latest book is: *The Church In Anguish,* 1987.

Bibhuti S. Yadav (Hindu/Buddhist) received a Ph.D. in philosophy from Banaras Hindu University in 1970, and has been a professor of Indian religions at Temple University since 1972. His scholarly articles have appeared in a wide range of journals, such as *Journal of Dharma* and *Indian Philosophical Quarterly*. He is an Associate Editor of the *Journal of Ecumenical Studies*.